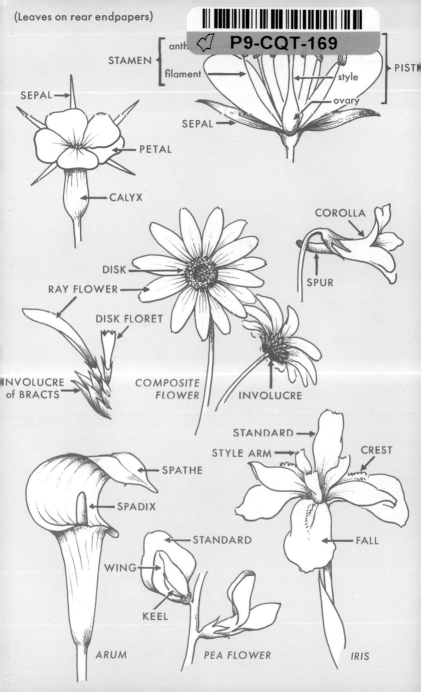

(Leaves on rear endpapers)

P9-CQT-169

STAMEN — anther / filament

PISTIL — style / ovary

SEPAL

SEPAL

PETAL

CALYX

DISK

RAY FLOWER

DISK FLORET

INVOLUCRE of BRACTS

COMPOSITE FLOWER

INVOLUCRE

COROLLA

SPUR

STANDARD

STYLE ARM

CREST

FALL

SPATHE

SPADIX

STANDARD

WING

KEEL

ARUM

PEA FLOWER

IRIS

A Field Guide to Wildflowers

of Northeastern and North-central North America

THE PETERSON FIELD GUIDE SERIES

A Field Guide to Wildflowers

of Northeastern and North-central North America

by
ROGER TORY PETERSON
and
MARGARET McKENNY

A Visual Approach
Arranged by Color, Form, and Detail

Illustrations by
ROGER TORY PETERSON

HOUGHTON MIFFLIN COMPANY BOSTON

V   16   15   14   13   12   11   10

ISBN 0–395–08086–X hardbound
ISBN 0–395–183251 paperbound
Library of Congress Catalog Card Number: 67–13042

Printed in the United States of America

Contents

> *Note:* This includes purple or purplish, that difficult to define color bracket ranging between the lavender–red category and the violet–blue category (next group). Some flowers are repeated, but if there is doubt about the color and the flower is not found in one section, look for it in the other.

> *See note above.*

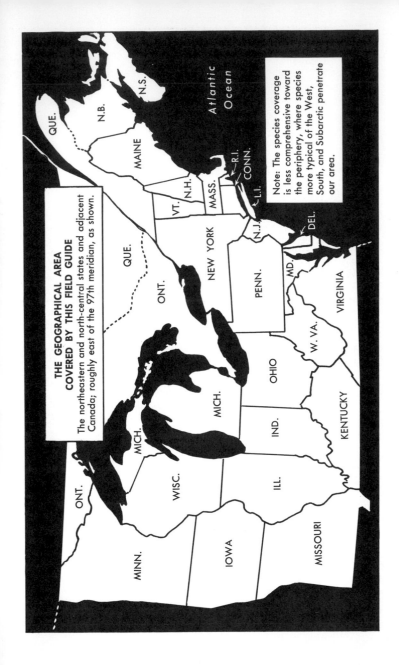

THE GEOGRAPHICAL AREA
COVERED BY THIS FIELD GUIDE
The northeastern and north-central states and adjacent
Canada; roughly east of the 97th meridian, as shown.

Note: The species coverage
is less comprehensive toward
the periphery, where species
more typical of the West,
South, and Subarctic penetrate
our area.

QUE.

N.S.

N.B.

MAINE

Atlantic
Ocean

QUE.

VT. N.H.

ONT.

NEW YORK

MASS.

R.I.

CONN.

L.I.

PENN.

N.J.

DEL.

MD.

MICH.

OHIO

W. VA.

VIRGINIA

ONT.

MICH.

IND.

KENTUCKY

WISC.

ILL.

MINN.

IOWA

MISSOURI

Introduction

BY ROGER TORY PETERSON

TWENTY years ago Margaret McKenny and I first discussed this book. At that time I was merely to act as editor, as I have for so many other titles in the Field Guide Series. However, we ran into a snag on the illustrations. The artist we had chosen begged off; her publisher would not release her from another project. So, in an unguarded moment, I said, "Well, then I will do the drawings."

Such a simple thing to say, but such a staggering commitment! Since then I have made well over 1500 drawings of flowers — 1344 of which appear in this book. I covered thousands of miles by car in the eastern and midland states, trying to catch the brief period of bloom of various species. My station wagon crawled at its slowest speed along back country roads while I kept one eye on the road and the other on the flowers; indeed, I became slightly walleyed. My battered vasculum was crammed with my finds, which I usually drew in the evening in some tourist cabin or motel. In the case of rare orchids, gentians, or other species, where prudence forbade my picking them, I often drew them while lying flat on the ground. But most of the flowers were drawn in motels. In my suitcase I carried a 200-watt daylight bulb that I often substituted for the weak 40- or 60-watt bulb in my quarters. To this day I am able to look at each drawing and bring back by association the place where I found the flower, the circumstances in which I drew it, and incidents — some pleasant, others trying. This odyssey was very educational, and I want to record here some of my impressions about flowers in general.

Birds have wings; they can travel, mix, and standardize their populations. They usually look precisely the way they are supposed to look (unless they are in molt). On the other hand, flowers are rooted to the earth. They are often separated by broad barriers of unsuitable environment from other "stations" of their own species. Therefore, over the centuries, subtle differences have often developed, strains, as it were. Some of these are so marked that botanists have given them varietal names. Others are ignored, because they would overburden an already complex taxonomy. Or a flower, from the same seed, may be "depauperate" in a sterile soil and oversized in a rich soil or where lack of competition has favored it in some way. So then, I found, as I zigzagged from Minnesota to Maine and from Ontario to Virginia, that a flower I knew well could, at times, look strangely unfamiliar. Sometimes it did not seem to key down properly even in the two standard technical works, *Gray's Manual of Botany* and *The New Britton and Brown Illustrated Flora*. I became worried at first about my ineptitude, but later was reassured when I discovered that trained botanists to whom I showed such plants seemed frankly puzzled. Flowers are plastic; at least many of them are, particularly the flowers of late summer and fall. Furthermore, many of them hybridize; so we should not expect to score 100 percent on our identifications.

Some people, those with orderly minds, are able to use keys in running down their flowers, but many throw up their hands in despair because of the bewildering terminology (Fernald in the Eighth Edition of *Gray's Manual of Botany* defines 1141 technical terms in his glossary). There are at least 60 ways to say that a plant is not smooth, that it has fuzz, hair, prickles, or roughness of some sort: aculeate, aculeolate, asperous, bristly, bullate, canescent, chaffy, ciliate, ciliolate, coriaceous, corrugated, downy, echinate, floccose, flocculent, glandular, glanduliferous, glumaceous, glutinous, hairy, hispid, hispidulous, hirsute, hirsutulous, hirtellous, hoary, lanate, lepidote, nodose, paleaceous, pannose, papillose, penicillate, pilose, pilosulous, prickly, puberulent, puberulous, pubescent, rugose, scabridulous, scabrous, sericeous, setiferous, setose, setulose, spinous, spinulose, strigose, strigulose, tomentose, tomentulose, velutinous, velvety, verrucose, verruculose, villose, villosulous, villous, viscid, and woolly! Of course, most of these mean different or slightly different things, but in using a key one must know exactly what the author had in mind when he employed a certain term. That is why the best of keys often fail. The reader's concept of a term and the author's might not coincide. But why use aculeate or echinate when prickly means the same thing?

However, if one can master them, keys are the proper formal approach to flower identification. But, I am afraid, most of us belong to the picture-matching school, and it is for this audience that our *Field Guide* has been planned. Our system is based on visual impressions: (1) color, (2) general shape or structure, and (3) distinctions between similar species — the field marks.

The breakdown by color is not new; it has been employed in other flower books. In sorting flowers by color we encounter problems. Some species may have more than one color phase, if we may call it that; they must be repeated. Chicory, usually blue, may also be white or, rarely, pink. There are also a few flowers in which two colors are equally prominent on the same blossom — the Showy Orchis is an example. Most troubling are those borderline species between the violet–blue category and the lavender–red category, those difficult to define purplish flowers that are midway between the blues and the reds. These must also be repeated.

However, in other books arranged by color the visual approach usually ends there and phylogenetic, or technical, order takes over.

In our book we extend our analysis to shape and then to other visual aids. We use arrows where we can, pointing to principal details. This plan, in a sense a pictorial key, is consistent with the fundamental philosophy of the other *Field Guides*, which is based on readily noticed visual impressions rather than on technical features.

The region where this *Field Guide* is useful is roughly the area covered by Gray and Britton and Brown (see map, p. vi): northeastern and north-central North America, east of the 97th meridian and the shortgrass plains; north of the southern boundaries of Virginia, Kentucky, and Missouri; south of the Gulf of St. Lawrence and the 47th parallel of latitude in Canada. It extends into the coniferous forest in the North and through Minnesota, Iowa, and Missouri in the West. The species coverage is most adequate for the northeastern and Great Lakes area, less complete toward the periphery, where species more typical of the South, the West, and the Subarctic penetrate our area. If in outlining a plant's range we do not list the states or the southern edge but merely state "south," we mean that the plant ranges through and south of the area as indicated on our area map (p. vi).

There are 1293 species in 84 families discussed. Nearly all are herbaceous plants, but a few showy flowering shrubs, such as azaleas and laurels, and a few woody vines have been included. For flowering trees, shrubs, and woody vines see *A Field Guide to Trees and Shrubs* by George A. Petrides (Field Guide No. 11).

"Alien" is employed to point out those plants originally not native to our area but now established by introduction or as escapes. Unless otherwise specified, "preceding species" means the single preceding boldface entry.

The scientific names used are those in *Gray's Manual of Botany*, Eighth Edition, by Merritt Lyndon Fernald (New York: American Book Company, 1950). The vernacular names are those we believe to be in most frequent use; they do not adhere strictly to any one authority.

Some botanists may raise their eyebrows because the plants in our guide are not arranged in the traditional order of their relationships. There are many formal botanies so arranged, and therefore we decided to take a different tack. Our system is admittedly an artificial one, a visual one, but we believe this offers a shortcut to identification that will make it easier for the beginner to recognize most of the flowers he sees. Actually, as I have indicated earlier, the proper way to acquire a competence in systematic botany is to learn to use the keys and to master the technical descriptions in either *Gray's Manual of Botany* or *The New Britton and Brown Illustrated Flora*. Also, there are a number of popular guides arranged according to the approved systematics. We especially recommend Harold William Rickett's *New Field Book of American Wild Flowers* (New York: Putnam, 1963) and its predecessor, F. Schuyler Matthews and Norman Taylor's *Field Book of American Wild Flowers* (Putnam, 1955). For the library,

Rickett's lavishly illustrated *Wild Flowers of the United States* (New York: McGraw-Hill, 1966), Vol. I, is recommended.

The professional systematist often moves about in a rarefied atmosphere. He might dispute with his colleagues as to whether there are 4660 species of flowering plants and ferns (as in Britton and Brown) in the northeastern quarter of the continent, or 5520 (as in Gray), or even more, depending on his views on taxonomy and whether he recognizes certain plants as "good" species or merely forms or variants — in other words, whether he is a "lumper" or a "splitter." In some instances the differences of opinion are extraordinary. For example, Fernald recognizes 32 species of *Antennaria* (Pussytoes), whereas Gleason allows only 6, regarding them as very plastic species with a number of varietal forms.

It would plainly be impossible to describe and illustrate all of the several thousand species in a single volume smaller than a good-sized telephone directory. Even if this could be done the average layman would be unwilling to face such a formidable galaxy. This *Field Guide*, then, is selective, and the almost 1300 species covered here include the most representative herbaceous species; they are also those that he is most likely to encounter. We do not include trees, shrubs (with a few exceptions), ferns, grasses, sedges, rushes, etc. We also have ignored many of the more obscure herbaceous species, most of the "disputed" forms that may or may not be valid species, hybrids, most of the extremely local rarities, most of the peripheral invaders, and most of those aliens that have not become widely established. In spite of these many deletions, we believe that this book, within its sphere, will give a ready answer at least 95 percent of the time.

Actually, the student will also learn relationships and the families (even though indirectly) through the family symbols in the margins of the text pages. In addition, a nontechnical capsule analysis of each family can be consulted in "The Families of Flowers" section of the book (pp. xv–xxviii).

Margaret McKenny prepared the first text draft, originally covering about 650 species. This was to have been the main running text; my own assignment, in addition to the illustrations, was to be the legend pages opposite the pictures. After this ample and graceful text was written we realized that the species coverage was not great enough. I eventually drew 1300 species, and space would not permit the full cross-referenced treatment between text and legend pages. The only answer was to settle for a more telegraphic text, self-contained on the legend pages opposite the illustrations. This adaptation and the preparation of the additional 650 entries became my responsibility because of the necessity of close integration with the pictures.

Although a majority of the illustrations were drawn from fresh specimens, a few were made from photographic transparencies and a number from herbarium specimens. All of the illustrations were drawn by myself, but approximately 360 of my line drawings, sketched in pencil in the field, were later inked in skillfully by Michael Bevans.

To the National Herbarium in Washington, D.C., and the Yale Herbarium in New Haven, Connecticut, I am indebted for the extensive use of specimen material. The latter herbarium also houses the collection of the Connecticut Botanical Society, which was put at my disposal by Dr. and Mrs. John Reeder of the Yale Botanical Library.

In addition to our own transparencies we availed ourselves (for study and illustration) of some of the slides made by Perry Reynolds of Detroit, who donated the use of his own extensive collection of Kodachromes (a memorial to Mrs. Reynolds). Tudor Richards of Dublin, New Hampshire, also loaned several slides.

We cannot begin to acknowledge all the people who have shown us a flower here or directed us to one there, but we must single out several who have spent many hours of their time, indeed days, in the field helping me find my flowers, and helping me to key them out: Farida Wiley at the Audubon Camp at Medomak, Maine; Leonard Bradley at the Audubon Nature Center at Greenwich, Connecticut; Dr. Jeff Swinbroad and Dr. Jacque Vallier at the Audubon Camp of Wisconsin; Dr. Neil Hotchkiss at the Patuxent Research Refuge, Laurel, Maryland; and Dr. Elzada Clover, at the Biological Station of the University of Michigan. In addition to many days of driving on some of the field excursions, the long job of typing and retyping fell to my wife Barbara. In the latter chore she was ably assisted by Mrs. Dorothy Umberger.

Paul Brooks, Editor-in-Chief of Houghton Mifflin Company, has not only given us constant encouragement and counsel since the book's inception but has acted as a gadfly to R.T.P. for his unpardonable delay in finishing the illustrations and the revised text. Helen Phillips, who has worked on many of the *Field Guides*, was the fine-toothed comb for the final draft of the manuscript. Morton H. Baker, Benjamin Tilghman, Arnold Paine, and Katharine Bernard of the production staff of Houghton Mifflin, as well as Lovell Thompson and David Harris, have also lavished their skills on this long overdue book.

Finally, with humility we acknowledge our fundamental debt to the many botanists, past and present, who have slowly and steadily built the background of literature and scientific information upon which all books such as this must depend for their substance and accuracy.

Survival

THE MAJORITY of flowers that grow in vacant lots and along roads are aliens. Hundreds of wayside plants came from Europe. The list is long: Black Mustard, Bouncing Bet, Red Clover, White Clover, Wild Carrot, Spearmint, Peppermint, Mullein, Butter-and-eggs, Teasel, Chicory, Dandelion, Ox-eye Daisy, and many, many others. Some, like the Day-lily of Asia, escaped from gardens, but most came unseen, as seeds mixed in with shipments from across the sea. The first known station for a foreign plant is often at a seaport or along a railroad track.

A city or a farm is much the same the world over. A house mouse, a rat, or a starling finds little difference between London and New York; similarly the many weeds that have followed man across the Atlantic. These immigrants almost invariably grow in disturbed soils, few of them venture far from the roadside, where they apparently cannot compete with our preadapted native flowers. One exception that comes to mind, however, is a lovely European orchid, the Helleborine (*Epipactis*), which now blooms profusely in wild woodlands of the Berkshires and upstate New York. Conversely, most native flowers cannot compete along the roadside.

Whereas European immigrants come by boat, it is quite likely that certain prairie flowers have recently reached our seaboard by way of the airfields. And, speaking of prairies, we have very few remnants of the original prairie left. Perhaps the best place to find remnants of the prairie flora is along the railroad right-of-way, where fences exclude cattle. Roadsides are relatively poor for them now because of mowing and plant-spraying operations. Our coastal marshes, ditched and drained, have lost most of their flowers, too. The best remaining natural flower gardens I have seen along the East Coast are in Delaware.

What of the future of rare native wildflowers? Because of the attrition of habitat, some are in a very precarious position. Bogs along the southern margins of glaciated country are becoming fewer and orchids requiring bog conditions are harder to find. When a forest has been cut, its shade-loving orchids may also disappear, and half a century or more may pass before succession makes the forest suitable again for them. How can they return? Birds are mobile; they can return easily to their niche. And some seeds have parachutes or are carried by birds. But what about the others? Can seeds remain viable in the soil for half a century or more, until succession renders their habitat suitable again? We know little about this.

Glossary

WE HAVE avoided a complex terminology in this *Field Guide*. Most words used in the descriptions are familiar and need no explanation. However, a few terms, mainly applying to plant parts, require definition. See the endpapers for illustrations (front endpaper, flowers; rear endpaper, leaves).

Achene: A small, dry, hard, nonsplitting fruit with 1 seed.
Alien: Foreign, but successfully established in our area by man, or as an escape.
Alternate (leaves, etc.): Not opposite each other.
Anther: The enlarged part of the stamen holding the pollen.
Axil: The angle (upper) where the leaf joins the stem.

Bloom: A waxy or whitish coating on stem, leaf, or fruit.
Bracts: Modified leaves (green or colored) associated with the flower.

Calyx: The outer circle of floral leaves (sepals); usually green, sometimes like petals; may be separate or joined.
Compound (leaf): Divided into separate smaller leaflets.
Corolla: The showy inner floral envelope. The segments (called petals) may be separate or joined.

Disk (in composites): The round or buttonlike center (as in a daisy), composed of numerous tiny tubular *disk flowers*, usually surrounded by a circle of ray flowers.
Drupe: A fleshy fruit with a hard nut or stone (as a cherry).

Entire (leaf): Without lobes or teeth.

Glabrous: Smooth; without hairs.
Glands: Minute globules, secreting sticky or oily substances.
Glaucous (stems, leaves): With a waxy, whitish bloom (coating).

Head: A crowded cluster of stalkless (or nearly stalkless) flowers.
Herbs, herbaceous: Fleshy, nonwoody plants. Does not include trees and shrubs, which are woody. With few exceptions the plants in this book are herbs.

Inflorescence: The flower cluster.
Involucre: A circle of bracts (modified leaves) supporting a flower or flower cluster (as in a daisy).
Irregular (flower): Not symmetrical; may be lopsided, lipped, etc.

Linear (leaf): Long, narrow; veins parallel.
Lip: See front endpaper.
Lobed (leaf): Indented, with outer projections rounded.

Nerve: A leaf vein that is linear and not branched.

Ovary: The swollen base of the pistil where seeds develop.

Palmate (leaf): Divided or lobed so as to radiate from one point (as fingers from a palm).
Panicle: An elongated, compound (branched) flower cluster.
Pappus: In Composite Family — the hairs, bristles, or scales at the tip of the achene ("seed"); such as the silk or down on thistles.
Petal: One of the segments of the corolla; usually colored; may be joined basally or separate.
Petiole: The leafstalk.
Pinnate (leaf): Compound, with several or many leaflets arranged (in pairs or alternately) along a midrib.
Pistil: The central female organ of a flower which comprises (1) a swollen *ovary* at the base, (2) a slender stalk, the *style;* and (3) a divided or knobbed tip, the *stigma.*
Pubescent: With soft, downy hairs.

Raceme: A longish cluster of flowers arranged singly along a stalk, each flower with its own small stalk.
Rays, ray flowers (composites): The flat straplike blades that encircle the disk flowers (as in a daisy).

Sepal: An individual segment of the calyx (usually green); a small modified leaf near the rim of the flower.
Sessile: Without stalk.
Spadix (arums): A club-shaped stalk on which are crowded tiny blossoms (the yellow center stalk in a Calla Lily).
Spathe (arums): The hooded or leaflike sheath partly enfolding the spadix (the white "petal" of a Calla Lily). Onions, dayflowers, and certain other plants may also have a spathe at the base of their flower cluster.
Spike: A longish flower cluster, the stalkless or near-stalkless flowers arranged along the stem.
Spur: A hollow, tubular extension on a flower.
Stamen: The male flower organ (usually several) composed of a slender stalk with a knoblike *anther*, bearing pollen.
Stigma: The tip of the pistil (often knobbed or divided; sticky).
Stipule: A small leaflike appendage at the base of a petiole (leafstalk).
Style: The slender stalk of the pistil.

Umbel: An umbrellalike flower cluster with all flower stalks radiating from the same point.

Whorl: Three or more leaves, etc., radiating from a single point.
Wing: A thin membranous flap extending along a stem, stalk or other part of a plant.

The Families of Flowers

WE OFFER the following nontechnical, capsule descriptions of the families treated in this *Field Guide*. We also introduce the family symbols employed in the margins throughout the book. As a point of further interest, when taxonomies differ we compare the number of species in our area as recognized by *Gray's Manual of Botany* (Eighth Edition by Fernald) and Britton and Brown's *Illustrated Flora* (Gleason edition). Finally, we list the pages where the representatives of each family are to be found in this *Field Guide* and indicate the color sections.

 CATTAIL FAMILY (Typhaceae). Tall marsh plants growing in dense stands. Leaves long, erect, bladelike; stem stiff, with a cylindrical sausagelike brown head of minute, tightly packed, pistillate female flowers. Above this is a more slender "tail" of paler, staminate, male flowers. Species in our area, 4 (Gray); 3 (B. & B.). See p. 388 (green–brown).

 BUR-REED FAMILY (Sparganiaceae). Mostly erect, reedlike marsh plants with globular, petal-less flower heads at intervals along stem. Species in our area 10. See p. 384 (green–brown).

 ARROWHEAD FAMILY (Alismataceae). Plants of freshwater swamps, slow streams, and wet mud. Leaves smooth, firm (arrow-shaped, lance-shaped, or oval). Flowers usually in whorls of 3 with 3 roundish petals (usually white), 3 sepals. Species in our area, 24 (Gray); 16 (B. & B.). See p. 8 (white).

 ARUM or CALLA FAMILY (Araceae). In many species, a large floral leaf, called a spathe, surrounds or partly enfolds a spikelike stem called the spadix, on which many minute florets are crowded. The Calla Lily is a familiar example (the white "petal" is the spathe, the yellow club the spadix). Golden Club lacks spathe (very small, soon falling). Leaves of arums are usually large, smooth, glossy. Species in our area, 10 (Gray); 8 (B. & B.). See pp. 6 (white); 116 (yellow); 368, 388 (green–brown).

 YELLOW-EYED GRASS FAMILY (Xyridaceae). Rushlike plants with linear, grasslike, basal leaves and a stiff stalk topped by a knob or head of brownish bracts. The small yellow flowers have 3 roundish petals, 3 unequal sepals. Species in our area, 12 (Gray); 9 (B. & B.). See p. 116 (yellow).

SPIDERWORT FAMILY (Commelinaceae). Plants with leafy stems (leaves linear, parallel-veined) and terminal clusters of flowers that open one or two at a time. Three roundish petals (equal in spiderworts, lower one smaller in dayflowers), usually blue; subtended by a leafy spathe in dayflowers. Species in our area, 15 (Gray); 17 (B. & B.). See p. 314 (violet–blue).

PICKERELWEED FAMILY (Pontederiaceae). Plants of mud and shallow water with glossy dark leaves (emergent in Pickerel-weed, often floating in mud-plantains). Flowers of Pickerelweed are clustered in a hyacinthlike spike; those of mud-plantains are smaller, blue or white, 6-pointed. Species in our area, 6 (Gray); 7 (B. & B.). See pp. 6 (white); 116 (yellow); 316, 326 (violet–blue).

LILY FAMILY (Liliaceae). Includes lilies, trilliums, onions, tulips, hyacinths, etc. Bulbed perennials with parallel-veined leaves. Flowers usually bell-like or triangular, with plan of 6 or 3. Typical lilies have 6-parted flowers with 6 stamens and a long pistil ending in a 3-lobed stigma. Trilliums are triangular, with 3 leaves, 3 petals, 3 sepals. Species in our area, 104 (Gray); 106 (B. & B.). See pp. 4, 10, 64, 66 (white); 102 (yellow); 206 (orange); 212, 240, 254, 284, 292, 296 (pink–red); 316 (violet–blue); 366, 370 (green–brown).

DAFFODIL or **AMARYLLIS FAMILY** (Amaryllidaceae). Bulbed plants with narrow, grasslike leaves and showy, 6-parted, often lily-like flowers (differ from lilies by having "petals" attached to, or part of, seed receptacle). Species in our area, 14 (Gray); 12 (B. & B.). See pp. 10 (white); 116 (yellow); 254 (pink–red).

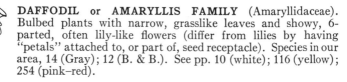

IRIS FAMILY (Iridaceae). Plants with flat swordlike or grass-like leaves ranked edge to edge basally. Showy flowers in plan of 3 (3 sepals, 3 petals, 3 stamens, 3 styles); irregular in true *Iris* with 3 broad, petal-like sepals ("falls") heavily veined and arching down, 3 erect petals ("standards"), and 3 prominent styles (which look like shorter petals) over the sepals. Blue-eyed Grass (*Sisyrinchium*) and Blackberry-lily (*Belamcanda*) have sepals and petals alike, seeming 6-petaled. Species in our area, 21 (Gray); 25 (B. & B.). See pp. 100 (yellow); 208 (orange); 230 (pink–red); 314, 326 (violet–blue).

ORCHID FAMILY (Orchidaceae). Many tropical orchids are epiphytic (perched on trees); ours are terrestrial. Flowers 6-parted, irregular, with 3 sepals, 2 lateral petals, and a 3rd petal, usually larger, sometimes saclike or liplike, and often with a spur. Flowers single, in clusters or spikes. Leaves entire, parallel-veined (sometimes scale like). Species in our area, 76 (Gray); 67 (B. & B.). See pp. 14–20 (white); 104, 118, 120 (yellow); 208 (orange); 212, 214, 224, 242 (pink–red); 372, 392 (green–brown).

 LIZARD'S-TAIL FAMILY (Saururaceae). Succulent plants with jointed stems, coarse toothless leaves and long fuzzy "tails" of tiny flowers lacking petals and sepals. Species in our area, 1. See p. 60 (white).

 FOUR-O'CLOCK FAMILY (Nyctaginaceae). In our area this mainly tropical family is represented by a small genus (*Mirabilis*) of weedy plants that have their flowers in small clusters seated in green cuplike circles of joined bracts. Species in our area, 5. See p. 292 (pink–red).

 SANDALWOOD FAMILY (Santalaceae). Parasitic plants, mainly tropical. Our most familiar genus, *Comandra*, has small, alternate oval leaves and clusters of 3 to 5 petal-less flowers in simple cymes (1 terminal flower with 2 lateral flowers from its stalk). The flowers are small cups, each with 5 short sepals and 5 short stamens on its rim. Species in our area, 7. See p. 70 (white).

 BIRTHWORT FAMILY (Aristolochiaceae). Mainly tropical. Our genera have large heart-shaped leaves and reddish-brown flowers with 3 triangular petal-like sepals (no petals) that flare out from a swollen cuplike ovary. Species in our area, 11 (Gray); 9 (B. & B.). See pp. 240 (pink–red); 388 (green–brown).

 BUCKWHEAT FAMILY (Polygonaceae). These plants, which include smartweeds, knotweeds, and buckwheat, have swollen sheaths or joints ("knots") where each leaf is attached. Stem often zigzag. The insignificant flowers are without petals, made up of sepals (often colored like petals in *Polygonum*); usually in a slender cluster or head. Species in our area, 76 (Gray); 67 (B. & B.). See pp. 60, 70 (white); 274, 276, 310 (pink–red); 380, 386 (green–brown).

 GOOSEFOOT FAMILY (Chenopodiaceae). Weedy plants with inconspicuous flowers (no corolla), often in clusters, mostly greenish, succulent. Leaves usually alternate. Species in our area, 51 (Gray); 48 (B. & B.). See pp. 310 (pink–red); 378, 386 (green–brown).

 AMARANTH FAMILY (Amaranthaceae). Weedy plants, often with clusters or spikes of inconspicuous flowers subtended by greenish bracts or bractlets that may obscure them. Species in our area, 24 (Gray); 25 (B. & B.). See pp. 378, 386 (green–brown).

 NETTLE FAMILY (Urticaceae). Plants of this family may or may not have stinging hairs. Most of our species have toothed opposite leaves and racemes of inconspicuous flowers in the leaf axils. Species in our area, 13 (Gray); 8 (B. & B.). See p. 382 (green–brown).

 POKEWEED FAMILY (Phytolaccaceae). Our species is a rank, branchy plant with large toothless leaves. Slender racemes of flowers are paired opposite the leaves. The 5 petal-like sepals later support flat purple-black berries with red stems. Species in our area, 1. See p. 60 (white).

 CARPETWEED FAMILY (Aizoaceae). A varied group, mainly fleshy, succulent. Sepals 4 or 5, stamens usually 8 or 10, no corolla. Leaves mostly opposite. Species in our area, 5. See p. 310 (pink–red).

 PURSLANE FAMILY (Portulacaceae). Small plants; 2 sepals, usually 5 petals; leaves usually opposite, toothless, thickish. Species in our area, 13. See pp. 32 (white); 164 (yellow); 238, 264 (pink–red).

 PLANTAIN FAMILY (Plantaginaceae). Leaves in a basal rosette; flowers minute, crowded in a slender cluster on a separate stalk. Species in our area, 20 (Gray); 17 (B. & B.). See p. 62 (white).

 PINK FAMILY (Caryophyllaceae). The hothouse Carnation is the best-known example. Pinks, in general, are known by swollen joints, opposite (or whorled) leaves, and flowers with 5 (sometimes 4) petals, which are usually notched, 5 sepals, and 8 to 10 stamens. Species in our area, 98 (Gray); 88 (B. & B.). See pp. 34, 36 (white); 222, 264, 266, 310 (pink–red); 386 (green–brown).

 WATER-LILY FAMILY (Nymphaeaceae). Aquatic plants with long stalks rooted in mud and floating or emergent platterlike leaves. Flowers showy, on separate stalks. Species in our area, 16 (Gray); 13 (B. & B.). See pp. 6 (white); 100 (yellow); 230 (pink–red).

BUTTERCUP or CROWFOOT FAMILY (Ranunculaceae). A large North Temperate family, best characterized by the numerous stamens and pistils that form a button or bushy cluster in the center of the flower. In many species, such as the hepaticas, the petals are absent and the sepals are showy, re-sembling petals. Species in our area, 101 (Gray); 104 (B. & B.). See pp. 6, 22, 30, 54, 60, 72, 76 (white); 130, 132 (yellow); 216, 230, 238 (pink–red); 318, 326, 338 (violet–blue); 376, 390 (green–brown).

 BARBERRY FAMILY (Berberidaceae). A family of dissimilar genera lumped on technical grounds. *Podophyllum* (May-apple) bears a showy white flower attached between 2 large palmate leaves. *Jeffersonia* (Twinleaf) has a 2-bladed leaf and a single flower on a separate stalk. *Caulophyllum* (Blue Cohosh) has a terminal cluster above its triparted, deeply cut leaves. Species in our area, 7. See pp. 4, 22 (white); 366, 390 (green–brown).

 MOONSEED FAMILY (Menispermaceae). Twining vines with broad alternate leaves and slender panicles of insignificant flowers, often in leaf axils. Fruit a round, 1-seeded berry. Species in our area, 3. See p. 76 (white).

 POPPY FAMILY (Papaveraceae): (1) **POPPY SUBFAMILY** (Papaveroideae). These plants have a milky, acrid juice (white, yellow, or red). The showy flowers have 4 petals (or multiples of 4), and 2 sepals. Stamens numerous. Leaves lobed or cut, suggesting Buttercup Family. Species in our area, 9 (Gray); 11 (B. & B.). See pp. 22 (white); 130, 178 (yellow). (2) **BLEED-ING HEART SUBFAMILY** (Fumarioideae). Delicate wood-land plants. Flowers in racemes, bilaterally symmetrical but irregular, with the 4 petals somewhat joined (1 or 2 forming a swollen spur). Leaves finely cut and dissected. Species in our area, 12 (Gray); 11 (B. & B.). See pp. 72 (white); 126 (yellow); 290 (pink–red).

 CAPER FAMILY (Capparidaceae). In tropics, often shrubs or trees; ours are herbs. One tropical species furnishes capers, the pickled buds of *Capparis spinosa*. Usually 4 petals, all grouped on upper half of blossom. Each petal has a narrowly stalked base; stamens usually much longer than petals. Species in our area, 5. See p. 230 (pink–red).

 MUSTARD FAMILY (Cruciferae). Cabbage, turnip, radish be-long to this family. The *Cruciferae* are so named because their 4 petals form a cross. There are 6 stamens (2 usually shorter). The single pistil develops into a characteristic seedpod; which in many species is slender and angles upward. Species in our area, 138 (Gray); 133 (B. & B.). See pp. 82–86 (white); 158, 160 (yellow); 226, 272 (pink–red); 376 (green–brown).

PITCHER-PLANT FAMILY (Sarraceniaceae). Bog plants with tubular leaves containing water, in which insects often succumb. Flowers single, on separate stalks; nodding, with 5 broad petals, 5 broad sepals. Note the large, 5-rayed, umbrellalike cap to the style. Species in our area, 2. See pp. 100 (yellow); 230 (pink–red)

 SUNDEW FAMILY (Droseraceae). Low bog plants that supplement their diet by capturing insects, thereby absorbing nitrogen lacking in their habitat. Leaves stringy or spatulate, covered with sticky glands or hairs. Flowers 5-petaled, in slender cluster on separate stalk. Species in our area, 7. See pp. 20 (white); 232 (pink–red).

SEDUM FAMILY (Crassulaceae). Low succulent herbs, often hugging rocks, cliffs. Frequently cultivated in rock gardens. Flowers small, in clusters; petals 4 to 5, stamens 4 to 5 or 8 to 10. Leaves stalkless, very fleshy. Species in our area, 18 (Gray); 17 (B. & B.). See pp. 56 (white); 164 (yellow); 296 (pink–red).

SAXIFRAGE FAMILY (Saxifragaceae). Closely related to the Rose Family but differing in seed characteristics. Some are widely cultivated in rock gardens. Leaves mostly basal, often forming a rosette. Small flowers in a loose cluster on a slender, erect stem. Flower plan in 4's or 5's (stamens may be 8 or 10). Species in our area, 66 (Gray); 64 (B. & B.). See pp. 32, 68 (white); 376 (green–brown).

ROSE FAMILY (Rosaceae). Among cultivated flowers the rose is paramount. Wild roses have 5 roundish petals, 5 sepals, and numerous stamens encircling the center. So do the other genera of this large family, which includes strawberries, blackberries, apples, etc. Leaves alternate, usually with stipules (small modified leaflets where leafstalk joins stem). Species in our area, 469 (Gray). See pp. 2, 28, 32, 44, 60 (white); 134, 136, 148 (yellow); 218, 224, 256, 262, 284 (pink–red).

PEA FAMILY (Leguminosae). Beans, peas, clovers belong to this family. Note the shape of the flowers (typical is the Sweet Pea of the garden). Most genera have irregular flowers with 5 petals (2 lower ones join to form a keel, 2 side ones form wings, upper one a banner); often clustered in heads as in clovers. Leaves usually alternate, compound, with stipules (or tendrils or thorns). Species in our area, 230 (Gray); 204 (B. & B.). See pp. 80 (white); 106, 150–54 (yellow); 224, 246–52 (pink–red); 316, 352 (violet–blue); 390 (green–brown).

FLAX FAMILY (Linaceae). Slender, frail plants with small narrow leaves and delicate, round-petaled blue or yellow flowers borne on tips of branchlets. Flower parts in 5's. Species in our area, 11 (Gray); 12 (B. & B.). See pp. 164 (yellow); 326 (violet–blue).

WOOD-SORREL FAMILY (Oxalidaceae). Our one genus, *Oxalis*, has somewhat cloverlike leaves on slender stalks. These leaves, divided into 3 inversely heart-shaped leaflets, may be folded down the center at times. Flowers 5-parted (5 petals, 5 sepals, 5–15 stamens). Species in our area, 9 (Gray); 7 (B. & B.). See pp. 30 (white); 148 (yellow); 238 (pink–red); 326 (violet–blue).

GERANIUM FAMILY (Geraniaceae). Pink or lavender, 5-parted flowers (5 petals, 5 sepals, 5–15 stamens). After the petals fall there remains an erect, beaklike pistil ("cranesbill"), which, when seeds mature, splits from the base into 5 curled strips. Leaves deeply cleft, suggesting buttercup leaves. Species in our area, 15. See pp. 218, 260 (pink–red).

MILKWORT FAMILY (Polygalaceae). Our one genus, *Polygala*, is composed of low plants with irregular flowers. Only one is showy (Fringed Polygala). Most have tiny flowers crowded into cloverlike heads. There are 5 sepals (2 lateral ones colored and called "wings"), 3 petals (sometimes 5), connected into a tube, the lower petal often crested. Leaves in most species alternate, small, linear. Species in our area, 16. See pp. 62 (white); 208 (orange); 214, 244 (pink–red); 366 (green–brown).

SPURGE FAMILY (Euphorbiaceae). The well-known Poinsettia belongs to this large, mainly tropical family of herbs, shrubs and trees that have acrid, milky juices. Our principal genus, *Euphorbia*, includes low plants with curious small flowers lacking sepals and petals. Either stamens or pistils rise on short stalks from supporting cups. What often look like petals are bracts or appendages. Species in our area, 57 (Gray); 55 (B. & B.). See pp. 42, 44 (white); 162 (yellow); 374, 384 (green–brown).

CROWBERRY FAMILY (Empetraceae). Creeping shrubs with short, evergreen leaves hugging stems. Flowers inconspicuous; parts in 3's. Fruit a round berry. Species in our area, 5 (Gray); 3 (B. & B.). See p. 236 (pink–red).

TOUCH-ME-NOT FAMILY (Balsaminaceae). Thin-leaved plants with watery juices and pendent, bright flowers of irregular shape. Mostly tropical. Our genus, *Impatiens*, has 1 large, colored, bell-shaped sepal from which 3 petals emerge. There are 2 smaller green sepals. The slender seedpod, when ripe, pops at a touch into 5 coiled valves and ejects the seeds. Species in our area, 5. See pp. 104 (yellow); 208 (orange).

MALLOW FAMILY (Malvaceae). The garden Hollyhock is familiar. Showy flowers with 5 broad petals, 5 sepals. The characteristic feature is a column formed by the stamens that join around the style. The tip or tips of the style project through the round cluster of anthers. Species in our area, 34 (Gray); 33 (B. & B.). See pp. 4, 32 (white); 142, 164 (yellow); 218, 258 (pink–red); 326 (violet–blue).

 ST. JOHNSWORT FAMILY (Guttiferae). Leaves paired, untoothed, and with dark or translucent dots or glands. Our principal genus, *Hypericum*, has clusters of 5-petaled flowers (usually yellow) with a bushy ring of numerous stamens surrounding a small pointed capsule. Genus *Ascyrum* has 4 petals and paired sepals. Species in our area, 27 (Gray); 30 (B. & B.). See pp. 106, 138, 156 (yellow); 264 (pink–red).

ROCKROSE FAMILY (Cistaceae). Low plants, usually with small alternate or crowded and scale-like leaves. The flowers have 5 petals, soon falling, 5 sepals (2 small), and numerous stamens. Species in our area, 14 (Gray); 13 (B. & B.). See pp. 142, 164 (yellow); 310 (pink–red).

 VIOLET FAMILY (Violaceae). The garden Pansy belongs to this family. Low plants; flowers with 5 petals, the lowest often wider, heavily veined, and extending back into a spur; the lateral petals usually bearded. Violets have a distinctive pistil with a thickened head and a short beak. The Green Violet (p. 366) does not look like a violet but can be recognized as one by its pistil. Species in our area, 52. See pp. 24 (white); 146 (yellow); 318, 328–32 (violet–blue); 366 (green–brown).

 CACTUS FAMILY (Cactaceae). Thick fleshy plants; leafless and very spiny. The swollen fleshy green joints do the chlorophyll work of leaves. The large cuplike blossoms have many petals with numerous stamens and several stigmas crowded in the center. Species in our area, 5 (Gray); 8 (B. & B.). See p. 100 (yellow).

LOOSESTRIFE FAMILY (Lythraceae). Mostly slender leafy herbs with flowers (usually purplish with 3–6 petals) in the leaf axils or in terminal clusters. Leaves simple, untoothed. The yellow flowers called loosestrifes belong to the Primrose Family. Species in our area, 13 (Gray); 12 (B. & B.). See pp. 224, 288, 310 (pink–red).

 MEADOW-BEAUTY FAMILY (Melastomataceae). Mainly tropical. Our genus, *Rhexia*, has 4 asymmetrical petals, 4 sepals, 8 stamens. The petal shape and the thin, curved, pollen-bearing anthers are characteristic. Leaves opposite; linear-veined. Species in our area, 6 (Gray); 5 (B. & B.). See p. 220 (pink–red).

 EVENING-PRIMROSE FAMILY (Onagraceae). Largely showy flowers which close after midday. Most genera have flower parts in 4's (4 petals, 4 sepals, 4 or 8 stamens). The 4-branched stigma forms a characteristic cross. Genus *Circaea* (enchanter's nightshades) has the parts in 2's (2 deeply lobed petals, 2 stamens, 2-branched stigma). Species in our area, 65 (Gray); 55 (B. & B.). See pp. 68, 70 (white); 106, 142, 156 (yellow); 224, 270, 310 (pink–red); 386 (green–brown).

 GINSENG FAMILY (Araliaceae). Mostly herbs that resemble the Parsley or Carrot Family, with compound leaves (alternate or in 3's) and small 5-petaled, 5-stamened flowers in close-set clusters. Species in our area, 8. See pp. 50, 52 (white); 366 (green–brown).

 PARSLEY or CARROT FAMILY (Umbelliferae). Plants with umbrella-shaped clusters (umbels) of numerous small 5-petaled flowers. Umbels usually compound. Leaves usually finely cut. Species in our area, 88 (Gray); 99 (B. & B.). See pp. 42, 44, 48–52 (white); 162 (yellow); 296 (pink–red); 324 (violet–blue).

DOGWOOD FAMILY (Cornaceae). Small herbs (Bunchberry) to small trees (Flowering Dogwood). All Cornaceae have clusters of small flowers with 4 or 5 petals, but in the Bunchberry and Flowering Dogwood, showy white bracts outshine the inconspicuous flowers. Species in our area, 12 (Gray); 14 (B. & B.). See p. 4 (white).

 WHITE ALDER FAMILY (Clethraceae). Shrubs or trees with small 5-petaled flowers in showy racemes. Species in our area, 2. See p. 2 (white).

WINTERGREEN or PYROLA FAMILY (Pyrolaceae). Small woodland plants, often under conifers. Leaves usually evergreen; flowers hang down, parts mostly in 5's (5 petals, 5 sepals, 10 stamens). In genus *Pyrola* flowers are arranged along a leafless stalk with leaves near base. In genus *Chimaphila*, leaves are in whorls around stem. Genus *Monotropa* has no green pigment. Genus *Moneses* has a single nodding flower. Species in our area, 15. See pp. 20, 26 (white); 122 (yellow); 232, 234 (pink red); 392 (green–brown).

HEATH FAMILY (Ericaceae). Includes rhododendrons, azaleas, blueberries. Chiefly woody, shrubby. Our species favor acid bogs, mountains. Flowers usually 5- or 10-parted, with a single pistil. Petals and sepals 4 or 5, united; stamens 8 or 10. Species in our area, 76 (Gray); 75 (B. & B.). **Note:** This does not include Pyrolaceae, regarded by B. & B. as a subfamily of Ericaceae. See pp. 2, 38 (white); 208 (orange); 228, 236 (pink–red).

 DIAPENSIA FAMILY (Diapensiaceae). Low or creeping evergreen shrubs or herbs, similar to Heath Family. Flowers have all parts in 5's, except a 3-celled pod. Species in our area, 3. See pp. 38, 62 (white).

 PRIMROSE FAMILY (Primulaceae). Most have 5 petals, with each stamen at the center of a petal instead of between petals as in most other 5-petaled flowers. Typical primroses have rather flat flowers; the shooting-stars (*Dodecatheon*) have swept-back petals and stamens united to form a beak. Leaves simple, undivided. Species in our area, 28 (Gray); 26 (B. & B.). See pp. 22, 42 (white); 106, 140 (yellow); 220, 264 (pink–red).

 SEA-LAVENDER or LEADWORT FAMILY (Plumbaginaceae). Widespread in tropics and deserts; see Sea-lavender, p. 264. Flower parts in 5's; calyx persistent, drying on the plant. Species in our area, 3. See pp. 264, 310 (pink–red).

 GENTIAN FAMILY (Gentianaceae). Flowers with 4 to 12 joined petals and an equal number of stamens joined to them. Leaves usually opposite, stalkless, undivided. Marsh-pinks, *Sabatia*, have star-shaped pink or white flowers. Gentians, *Gentiana*, are usually blue, tubular, petals united for most of length. Species in our area, 48 (Gray); 43 (B. & B.). See pp. 6, 44, 58 (white); 164 (yellow); 220, 264 (pink–red); 320 (violet–blue).

 DOGBANE FAMILY (Apocynaceae). Related to milkweeds, these plants have a milky juice and often bear slender pods with tufted seeds. Typical dogbanes, *Apocynum*, have paired, untoothed leaves and clusters of small, nodding, 5-lobed, bell-shaped flowers. The Periwinkle, or Myrtle (*Vinca*), of the garden also belongs to this family. Species in our area, 11 (Gray); 9 (B. & B.). See pp. 70 (white); 292 (pink–red); 322, 324 (violet–blue).

 MILKWEED FAMILY (Asclepiadaceae). Plants with thick, milky juice; most have leaves paired or in whorls of 4. Flower structure unique, with 5 swept-back petals and a 5-parted cup that supports 5 little horns curving onto the central structure of united stamens and stigma. Flowers borne in umbel-like clusters; fruit a long pod, with seeds attached to tufts of floss. Species in our area, 37 (Gray); 30 (B. & B.). See pp. 54, 72 (white); 208 (orange); 294 (pink–red); 390 (green–brown).

MORNING-GLORY FAMILY (Convolvulaceae). Mostly vines with bell-shaped blossoms, often showy. The 5 united petals flare out to form a bell-like corolla with very shallow lobes. The dodders (*Cuscuta*) are leafless vines with minute flowers. Species in our area, 33 (Gray); 30 (B. & B.). See pp. 12, 42 (white); 222, 254 (pink–red); 338 (violet–blue).

PHLOX FAMILY (Polemoniaceae). The garden varieties are familiar. In genus *Phlox* the 5 flat petals are joined at the narrow corolla tube, which conceals the 5 stamens and 3-pronged style; leaves simple, undivided. In genus *Polemonium* the flowers are bell-like, with drooping stamens projecting beyond the 5 joined petals; leaves pinnately divided. Species in our area, 22 (Gray); 21 (B. & B.). See pp. 34 (white); 222, 226 (pink–red); 322 (violet–blue).

WATERLEAF FAMILY (Hydrophyllaceae). Mostly hairy plants, leaves cut and divided; often marked as if stained with water. Flower parts (petals, sepals, stamens) in 5's. In genus *Phacelia* the flat flowers in a curved terminal spray may suggest the Forget-me-not Family. In genus *Hydrophyllum* the loose terminal cluster of bell-like flowers suggests *Polemonium*. Species in our area, 17 (Gray); 16 (B. & B.). See pp. 54, 56 (white); 322, 334 (violet–blue).

FORGET-ME-NOT FAMILY (Boraginaceae). Note the characteristic flower arrangement — a 1-sided, rolled-up coil that gradually unfolds with growth. Flower parts mostly in 5's (calyx lobes, corolla lobes, stamens); 1 style. Leaves alternate, undivided. Species in our area, 55 (Gray); 45 (B. & B.). See pp. 42, 56 (white); 144 (yellow); 292 (pink–red); 316, 322, 334 (violet–blue).

VERVAIN FAMILY (Verbenaceae). Plants with paired, toothed leaves and small flowers in slender spikes or flat clusters. In most of our species there are 5 flat petals, united to a corolla tube, 5 unequal sepals, 4 stamens (2 shorter). Species in our area, 16 (Gray); 25 (B. & B.). See pp. 62 (white); 286 (pink–red); 316 (violet–blue).

MINT FAMILY (Labiatae). Herbs with tiny glands that may give an aromatic odor. Most have square stems and opposite leaves. Flowers small, usually in spikes or in clusters in axils of leaves. The corolla is a tube usually with 2 flaring lips (labia, hence "Labiatae"); the upper lip notched or 2-lobed, the lower 3-lobed. Although most mints have these characters, there are exceptions. Stamens 2 to 4; style 1, forked at tip; sepals joined. Species in our area, 136 (Gray); 137 (B. & B.). See pp. 78 (white); 126 (yellow); 216, 226, 278, 280 (pink–red); 346–50 (violet–blue).

TOMATO or NIGHTSHADE FAMILY (Solanaceae). Tomatoes, potatoes, peppers belong to this family. Some species poisonous. Flower parts mostly in 5's; fruit a pod or berry with many seeds. Ground-cherries (*Physalis*) have sepals that form a papery bag about the berry. Jimsonweed (*Datura*) is spiny with a morning-glory-like flower. Nightshades (*Solanum*) have stamens and pistil united to form a beak. Species in our area, 47 (Gray); 42 (B. & B.). See pp. 12, 72 (white); 144 (yellow); 324, 338 (violet–blue).

SNAPDRAGON FAMILY (Scrophulariaceae). Flowers of this family may have swollen corolla-tubes that flare into 2 "lips" (2 lobes above, 3 below). Or, the 5 "petals" (sometimes 4) may be more regular. Thus, not all look like the snapdragons of the garden. Stamens 2 to 5 (1 or 2 may lack anthers). The style may or may not be forked. Species in our area, 152 (Gray); 132 (B. & B.). See pp. 42, 58, 60 (white); 104, 106, 124, 142 (yellow); 220, 226, 230, 268 (pink–red); 336, 344 (violet–blue); 376 (green–brown).

BIGNONIA FAMILY (Bignoniaceae). Woody plants with showy tubular flowers, beanlike pods; represented by 3 genera in our area. *Campsis* and *Bignonia* are vines with swollen, orange, trumpetlike flowers; *Catalpa* is a genus of trees with large heart-shaped leaves. Species in our area, 5 (Gray); 4 (B. & B.). See p. 216 (pink–red).

BROOMRAPE FAMILY (Orobanchaceae). Low, fleshy, leafless herbs; scales taking place of leaves. Root parasites, without chlorophyll (green coloring matter). Flowers have 2-lipped or 5-lobed corollas (united petals) suggesting those of Snapdragon Family. Species in our area, 9 (Gray); 7 (B. & B.). See pp. 122 (yellow); 232 (pink–red); 324, 326 (violet–blue); 392 (green–brown).

BLADDERWORT FAMILY (Lentibulariaceae). Low plants of wet places and water. Their 2-lipped flowers with hollow spurs suggest the Snapdragon Family (especially *Linaria*). Bladderworts (*Utricularia*) have short, naked, emergent flower stalks and feathery, threadlike, underwater leaves equipped with bladders. Butterworts (*Pinguicula*) have solitary blossoms and a rosette of fleshy basal leaves with curled edges. Species in our area, 15. See pp. 122 (yellow); 230 (pink–red); 318 (violet–blue).

ACANTHUS FAMILY (Acanthaceae). Similar to plants of Snapdragon Family but in most genera seeds attached by hooked projections to 2-cavitied capsule. Species in our area, 10 (Gray); 8 (B. & B.). See pp. 324, 338 (violet–blue).

LOPSEED FAMILY (Phrymaceae). A single species. A small plant with broad, coarsely toothed, opposite leaves, topped by a slender spike of small flowers. These flowers, in pairs, have lobed lips and when going to seed "lop" down against the stem. Species in our area, 1. See p. 286 (pink–red).

 BEDSTRAW or MADDER FAMILY (Rubiaceae). Our species are mostly low, with small or tiny 4-parted flowers (sometimes 3-parted). The leaves, usually small and slender, are in pairs or in whorls. The bedstraws (*Galium*) have square stems, leaves in whorls; tiny flowers in clusters; often bristly. Species in our area, 52 (Gray); 49 (B. & B.). See pp. 40 (white); 164 (yellow); 236 (pink–red); 336 (violet–blue).

 HONEYSUCKLE FAMILY (Caprifoliaceae). Mostly woody shrubs and vines, rarely herbs. Leaves opposite. Flowers usually bell-shaped, funnel-like or tubular; the corolla usually flaring into 5 regular or irregular lobes or points. Generally 5 stamens. Species in our area, 46 (Gray); 41 (B. & B.). See pp. 128 (yellow); 216, 236 (pink–red); 384, 390 (green–brown).

 VALERIAN FAMILY (Valerianaceae). Plants with opposite leaves and tiny flowers crowded in clusters at tips of stems and branchlets. Corolla tubelike, with 5 spreading lobes; stamens and style protruding. Species in our area, 15 (Gray); 11 (B. & B.). See pp. 296 (pink–red); 324 (violet–blue).

 TEASEL FAMILY (Dipsacaceae). Natives of Europe and Asia, escaped from cultivation in N. America. Flowers small, 4- or 5-parted, crowded in dense, bristly heads. Leaves usually opposite. Species in our area, 5 (Gray); 8 (B. & B.). See pp. 300, 308 (pink–red).

CUCUMBER or GOURD FAMILY (Cucurbitaceae). Water-melons, cantaloupes, pumpkins belong to this family. Stems creep or climb. Our species mostly have lobed, maple-like leaves, attached singly, with tendrils or flowering stalks paired with them. Species in our area, 12 (Gray); 5 (B. & B.). See p. 76 (white).

BLUEBELL FAMILY (Campanulaceae): (1) **BLUEBELL SUB-FAMILY** (Campanuloideae). Widely distributed; some tropical species are shrubs and trees. Canterbury Bells of the garden belong to this family (English Bluebells belong to the Lily Family; "Virginia Bluebells," *Mertensia*, to the Forget-me-not Family). The corolla is usually bell-shaped, with 5 flaring lobes, 5 stamens, a single style with a 2- to 5-lobed stigma. Leaves undivided, alternate. Species in our area, 16 (Gray); 13 (B. & B.). See pp. 316, 340 (violet–blue). (2) **LOBELIA SUB-FAMILY** (Lobelioideae). Our genus, *Lobelia*, is especially distinctive. Corolla tube opens along upper side; 2 lobes on upper lip and 3 lobes on drooping lower lip. Stamens joined together in tube. Leaves alternate; plant has milky juice. Species in our area, 15. See pp. 216 (pink–red); 316, 342 (violet–blue).

COMPOSITE or DAISY FAMILY (Compositae). The largest family of flowering plants, perhaps the most recent family to appear on earth. The flower heads are clusters of many small flowers growing together (hence, composite). These produce many seeds, which may be provided with bristles, prickles, or soft hairs, aiding in their distribution. Typical composites have flat strap-shaped flowers (rays) as well as small tubelike flowers (disk flowers). The rays are arranged in a circle around the center disk as in a daisy. Supporting each flower cluster is a compact involucre of small leaflets, or bracts. Some composites lack rays. Species in our area, 690 (Gray); 537 (B. & B.). See pp. 44, 46, 58, 74, 76, 88–96 (white); 108–14, 166–202 (yellow); 208 (orange); 224, 282, 284, 292, 298–308 (pink–red); 324, 354–62 (violet–blue); 366, 374, 376, 384 (green–brown).

White or Whitish Flowers

This is the largest category, but not always a clear-cut one. Some white or whitish flowers may be tinged with the faintest suggestion of yellow, pink, or greenish which may be ignored. Others may have such a strong tinge that they must be repeated under one or more of those colors.

MISCELLANEOUS FLOWERING SHRUBS

Note: This book excludes most woody plants, many of which have attractive flowers. We make a few arbitrary exceptions here. For identification of flowering shrubs, as well as trees and woody vines, see *A Field Guide to Trees and Shrubs* by George A. Petrides (Field Guide No. 11).

 ROSES *Rosa*
ROSE FAMILY (Rosaceae)
Gray lists 24 species of roses in our area. Most are pink. Here we show 2 white escapes. (1) *R. multiflora.* Note the much-toothed stipules and clusters of small blossoms. Roadsides. S. New England south. MAY–JUNE. (2) *R. rugosa* (Wrinkled Rose). Deep rose or white, stems *very bristly;* leaves *deeply wrinkled.* Sand dunes, coastal thickets, roads. Great Lakes and ne. coast south to New Jersey. JUNE–SEPT.

 SWAMP-HONEYSUCKLE *Rhododendron viscosum*
HEATH FAMILY (Ericaceae)
A hairy white azalea. Note the *long curved stamens* and reddish, sticky hairs on the flower tube. Fragrant. 3–7 ft. Swamps, thickets. Ne. Ohio, s. Maine south. JUNE–JULY

 LABRADOR-TEA *Ledum groenlandicum*
HEATH FAMILY (Ericaceae)
Note the white or rusty *wool on underside* of untoothed leaves. Leaves leathery, with *rolled edges;* fragrant. A low shrub (to 3 ft.). Cold bogs. Canada, n. U.S. MAY–JUNE

 **MEADOWSWEET** *Spiraea latifolia*
ROSE FAMILY (Rosaceae)
Note the elliptic, coarse-toothed leaves and hairless reddish twigs. Fuzzy flowers, white or pale pink. 2–5 ft. NARROW-LEAF MEADOWSWEET, *S. alba* (not shown), differs in having *narrow, fine-toothed leaves* and may have hairy, yellowish twigs. Damp meadows. Canada to n. U.S.; in mts. to N. Carolina. JUNE–SEPT.

SHADBUSHES, JUNEBERRIES *Amelanchier*
ROSE FAMILY (Rosaceae)
Shrubs or small trees with oval, toothed leaves, slender reddish buds, huckleberrylike fruits. The drooping flower clusters appear in early spring, often before leaves. A complex genus. For analysis see *A Field Guide to Trees and Shrubs.* Thickets, woods. Nearly throughout. APRIL–JUNE

 SWEET PEPPERBUSH *Clethra alnifolia*
WHITE ALDER FAMILY (Clethraceae)
Note the dense, slender spikes of flowers and narrow-based leaves. To 10 ft. Swamps, sandy soils. S. Maine south, near coast. MOUNTAIN PEPPERBUSH, *C. acuminata* (not shown), has more pointed leaves. Mt. Woods. W. Virginia south. JULY–SEPT.

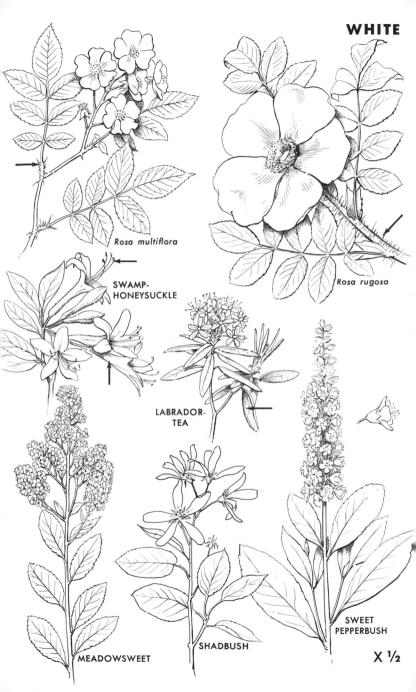

WHITE

Rosa multiflora

Rosa rugosa

SWAMP-
HONEYSUCKLE

LABRADOR-
TEA

MEADOWSWEET

SHADBUSH

SWEET
PEPPERBUSH

X ½

AQUATIC FLOWERS: MISCELLANEOUS

FRAGRANT WATER-LILY   *Nymphaea odorata*
WATER-LILY FAMILY   (Nymphaeaceae)
Note the platterlike floating leaves (purplish beneath) and the numerous tapering petals, diminishing in size toward the center. Flowers 3 to 5 in. across; very fragrant. Ponds, quiet waters. Manitoba, Newfoundland south.   JUNE–SEPT.

TUBEROUS WATER-LILY (not shown)   *Nymphaea tuberosa*
WATER-LILY FAMILY   (Nymphaeaceae)
Similar, but *not fragrant.* Leaves usually *green* below. Petals *broadly rounded.* Ponds. Mainly west of mts.   JUNE–SEPT.

BUCKBEAN   *Menyanthes trifoliata*
GENTIAN FAMILY   (Gentianaceae)
Note the *fuzzy beards* on the petals. The raceme of frosty flowers and the 3 oval leaflets emerge from the shallow water of ponds, bogs. N. Canada south to Illinois, Indiana, Ohio, W. Virginia, Maryland.   APRIL–JULY

FLOATING-HEARTS   *Nymphoides*
GENTIAN FAMILY   (Gentianaceae)
Note the combination of floating water-lily-like leaves and the umbel of small 5-petaled flowers. Ponds. The species shown is the LARGER FLOATING-HEART, *N. aquatica*, found near the coast from New Jersey south. A smaller species, *N. cordata*, is found north to Newfoundland.   JUNE–SEPT.

WHITE WATER-BUTTERCUP   *Ranunculus longirostris*
BUTTERCUP FAMILY   (Ranunculaceae)
Note the small, 5-petaled white blossom on the surface of the water and the *submerged tufts of feathery leaves.* There are 3 similar species, separated by technical characters. The leaves of this species are fairly stiff; those of *R. trichophyllus* (not shown) are flaccid. Ponds, slow water. S. Canada to Kansas, Tennessee, Pennsylvania, Delaware.   MAY–SEPT.

MUD-PLANTAIN   *Heteranthera reniformis*
PICKERELWEED FAMILY   (Pontederiaceae)
Note the wide, dark green, floating leaves and the emergent spike of 5-petaled white or pale blue flowers (3–8 flowers). Ponds or wet mud. Missouri, s. Illinois, e. New York, Connecticut south.   JULY–OCT.

WILD CALLA, WATER-ARUM   *Calla palustris*
ARUM FAMILY   (Araceae)
Note the *broad white spathe* ("petal") partially clasping the short golden spadix (crowded with tiny flowers). Leaves heart-shaped. Fruit a cluster of red berries. Bogs, pond edges. C. Canada to Minnesota, Wisconsin, Indiana, Pennsylvania, New Jersey.   MAY–AUG.

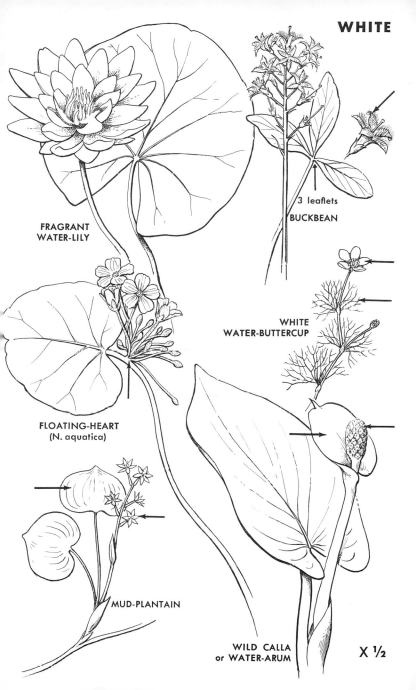

WHITE

FRAGRANT
WATER-LILY

3 leaflets
BUCKBEAN

FLOATING-HEART
(N. aquatica)

WHITE
WATER-BUTTERCUP

MUD-PLANTAIN

WILD CALLA
or WATER-ARUM

X 1/2

AQUATIC FLOWERS: 3 PETALS
ARROWHEAD FAMILY (Alismataceae)

ARROWHEADS   *Sagittaria*
The *3 roundish petals* and the arrangement of the flowers in
whorls of 3 are characteristic of the genus *Sagittaria*. There is
much variation in leaf form from broadly arrowhead-shaped
to lance-like or grasslike (sometimes within the same species).
On the basis of technical characters Gray recognizes 16 species
in our area; we mention but 5 here and refer the reader to more
technical works for critical identification. Pond edges, shallow
water. Throughout our area.   JULY–OCT.
BROAD-LEAVED ARROWHEAD, *S. latifolia*. This is the
commonest species, its arrow-shaped leaves varying greatly
in width. Throughout our area.
GRASS-LEAVED ARROWHEAD, *S. graminea*. Lance-like
or grasslike leaves only. Most of our area.
ENGELMANN'S ARROWHEAD, *S. engelmanniana*. Similar
to narrower-leaved forms of *S. latifolia* but fewer stamens
(15–25). Near coast from Massachusetts south.
SLENDER ARROWHEAD, *S. teres* (not shown). Leaves
stringlike, or cylindrical and pointed, usually without blades.
Near coast. Massachusetts to Maryland.
SESSILE-FRUITED ARROWHEAD, *S. rigida*. Note the
sessile (*stalkless*) pistillate flowers and fruits. Leaves oval-
pointed, sometimes with narrow appendages. Minnesota,
Quebec, Maine south to Missouri, Virginia.

WATER-PLANTAIN   *Alisma triviale*
The flowers resemble tiny miniatures (¼ in.) of arrowhead
but are borne in whorls of 4 or more on a much-branched
stalk. Leaves ovate. A similar species, *A. subcordatum* (not
shown), has smaller flowers (¹⁄₁₂ in.). Shallow waters or mud.
Quebec south to Nebraska, Iowa, Michigan, W. Virginia,
Maryland.   JUNE–SEPT.

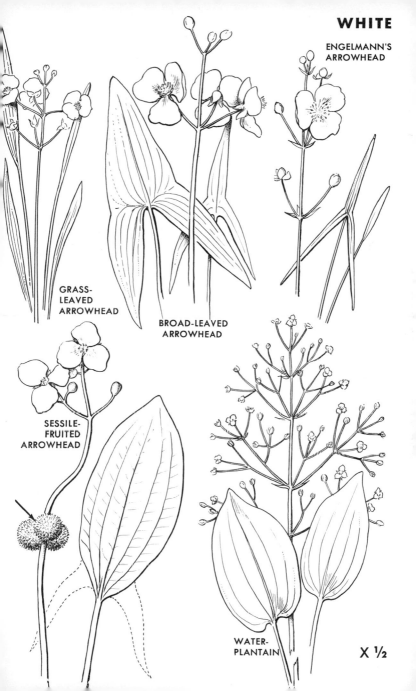

WHITE

ENGELMANN'S
ARROWHEAD

GRASS-
LEAVED
ARROWHEAD

BROAD-LEAVED
ARROWHEAD

SESSILE-
FRUITED
ARROWHEAD

WATER-
PLANTAIN

X ½

SINGLE, LARGE 3- AND 6-PART FLOWERS

ATAMASCO-LILY   *Zephyranthes atamasco*
DAFFODIL FAMILY   *(Amaryllidaceae)*
Note the large, waxy, erect, lily-like flower; white or pinkish.
Leaves linear, channeled. 6–15 in. Wet woods, clearings. Se.
U.S. north to Virginia.   APRIL–JUNE

WHITE TROUT-LILY   *Erythronium albidum*
LILY FAMILY   (Liliaceae)
Similar to the familiar yellow Trout-lily (p. 102), but white; may
be tinged with yellow in center and with violet on back of
petals. Leaves 2, basal, paired; seldom mottled. 6–9 in. Woods,
moist ground. Minnesota, s. Ontario south to Missouri, Kentucky; mainly west of mts.   APRIL–JUNE

LARGE-FLOWERED or WHITE TRILLIUM
LILY FAMILY (Liliaceae)   *Trillium grandiflorum*
Three broad leaves and 3 showy petals mark the trilliums. This
is our largest and most variable species; white flowers (2–4 in.)
turn pink with age. 12–18 in. Rich woods. Minnesota, Wisconsin, Michigan, s. Ontario, w. New England south.
                                             APRIL–JUNE

SNOW or DWARF WHITE TRILLIUM   *Trillium nivale*
LILY FAMILY   (Liliaceae)
Our smallest and earliest species with petals *less than 1 in. long*
and *narrow* 1- to 2-in. leaves. 2–6 in. Rich woods. West of
Appalachians, Minnesota, Ohio, w. Pennsylvania south to
Missouri, Kentucky.   MARCH–MAY

NODDING TRILLIUM   *Trillium cernuum*
LILY FAMILY   (Liliaceae)
Note the way the flower *dangles* below the leaves. May be
white or, rarely, pink; *anthers pink*. 10–18 in. Acid or peaty
woods. Manitoba, Quebec, Newfoundland south to northern
states and in mts. to Georgia.   APRIL–JUNE

DROOPING TRILLIUM (not shown)   *Trillium flexipes*
LILY FAMILY   (Liliaceae)
Another drooping species, similar to *T. cernuum*, but leaves
coarser, broader; *petals not recurved*, white or purple; *anthers
creamy white*. To 15 in. Woods. Minnesota, Michigan, Ohio to
Missouri.   APRIL–JUNE

PAINTED TRILLIUM   *Trillium undulatum*
LILY FAMILY   (Liliaceae)
Note the *red blaze* in the center (see color plate, p. 212). Acid
woods, bogs. 8–20 in. S. Canada, northern tier of states, and
south in mts. to Georgia.   APRIL–JUNE

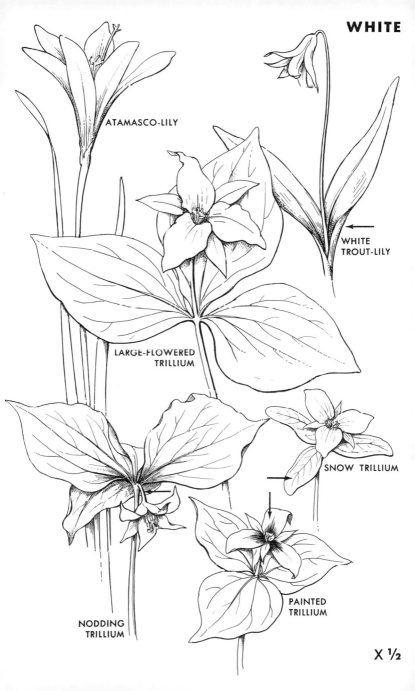

WHITE

ATAMASCO-LILY

WHITE TROUT-LILY

LARGE-FLOWERED TRILLIUM

SNOW TRILLIUM

PAINTED TRILLIUM

NODDING TRILLIUM

X ½

SHOWY BELL-LIKE OR TRUMPETLIKE FLOWERS

WILD POTATO-VINE   *Ipomoea pandurata*
Morning-glory Family   (Convolvulaceae)
Morning-glories, with their big bell-like flowers, are mostly
trailing vines with leaves attached singly. In this species note
the *heart-shaped leaves* and large white flowers (2–3 in.) with
pink stripes radiating from the center. Dry soil, fields, roadsides. Illinois, Michigan, s. Ontario, New York, Connecticut
south.   June–Sept.

HEDGE BINDWEED   *Convolvulus sepium*
Morning-glory Family   (Convolvulaceae)
Note the *arrowhead-shaped* leaves (2–5 in.) and the *blunt* basal
lobes. Flowers (2 in.) white or pink. Thickets, roadsides. Most
of our area.   May–Sept.

UPRIGHT or LOW BINDWEED   *Convolvulus spithamaeus*
Morning-glory Family   (Convolvulaceae)
A short (6–12 in.), *erect* species. Note the *oval* leaves. Dry,
sandy or rocky soil. Minnesota, Ontario, s. Maine south.
                                              May–July

IVY-LEAVED MORNING-GLORY   *Ipomoea hederacea*
Morning-glory Family   (Convolvulaceae)
Note the *3-lobed* leaves and hairy, long-pointed sepals. Flowers
white, pink, or blue. Fields, roadsides. Minnesota, Illinois,
Ohio, New York, New England south.   June–Oct.

SMALL WHITE MORNING-GLORY   *Ipomoea lacunosa*
Morning-glory Family   (Convolvulaceae)
Note the *very small* flowers (½–1 in.) and heart-shaped (or 3-
lobed) leaves. Thickets, fields, roadsides. Missouri, Illinois,
Ohio, Pennsylvania south.   Aug.–Oct.

FIELD BINDWEED Alien   *Convolvulus arvensis*
Morning-glory Family   (Convolvulaceae)
Similar to Hedge Bindweed but *leaves smaller* (1–2 in.), less
tapering. Flowers less than 1 in.; white or pink. Fields, waste
places. Most of our area.   June–Sept.

JIMSONWEED Alien   *Datura stramonium*
Tomato Family   (Solanaceae)
A coarse, erect, poisonous weed with trumpet-shaped white or
pale violet flowers 3 to 5 in. long. Note the coarse-toothed
leaves, spiny seedpods. 2–5 ft. Waste places. Most of our area.
                                              June–Sept.

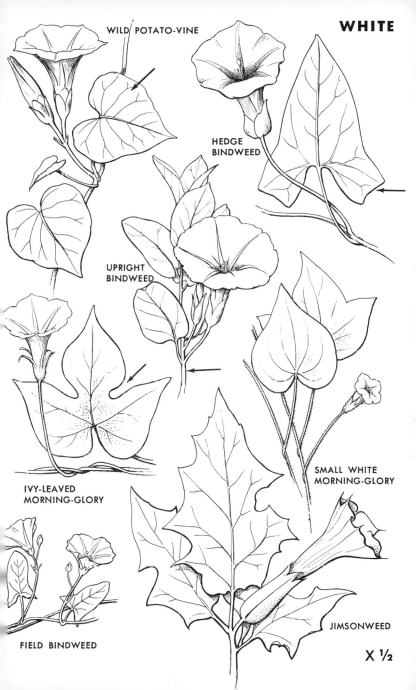

WILD POTATO-VINE

WHITE

HEDGE
BINDWEED

UPRIGHT
BINDWEED

IVY-LEAVED
MORNING-GLORY

SMALL WHITE
MORNING-GLORY

FIELD BINDWEED

JIMSONWEED

X ½

LADY'S-SLIPPERS AND OTHER
WIDE-LEAVED ORCHIDS
ORCHID FAMILY (Orchidaceae)
See also wide-leaved orchids, p. 16.

SMALL WHITE LADY'S-SLIPPER *Cypripedium candidum*
Note the waxy white "slipper," veined with purple inside; side
petals and sepals greenish, spotted with purple. Leaves ascend
stem. In albino Moccasin-flower (below), slipper is wrinkled,
leaves are basal. 6–12 in. Limestone areas, boggy meadows,
prairies. E. N. Dakota, s. Minnesota, s. Ontario, w. New York
south to Missouri, Kentucky.   MAY–JULY

SPARROW'S-EGG LADY'S-SLIPPER
Cypripedium passerinum
A small, far-northern species, differing from the above by the
violet-purple spots inside and outside the blunt white slipper.
Side petals and sepals *much shorter*. Conifer forests, edges of
streams. Mostly north of our area in Canada; Manitoba, n.
Ontario, Quebec.   JUNE–JULY

SHOWY LADY'S-SLIPPER   *Cypripedium reginae*
See text and color plate, p. 212. Slipper rose, petals white.

SHOWY ORCHIS   *Orchis spectabilis*
See text and color plate, p. 212. Bicolored.

MOCCASIN-FLOWER (white form)   *Cypripedium acaule*
Usually pink (see text and color plate, p. 212). The white form
is rare and local. Note the 2 basal leaves and the veiny slipper
with its crease or fissure along the front.

SMALL ROUND-LEAVED ORCHIS   *Orchis rotundifolia*
Note the spotted and lobed lip and the single broad basal leaf.
Petals white to mauve, lip white, spotted with magenta. 8–10 in.
Conifer swamps, bogs, spruce forests, peaty soil. N. Canada
south, sparingly, to cold woods of northern parts of Minnesota,
Wisconsin, Michigan, New York, Vermont, Maine. JUNE–JULY

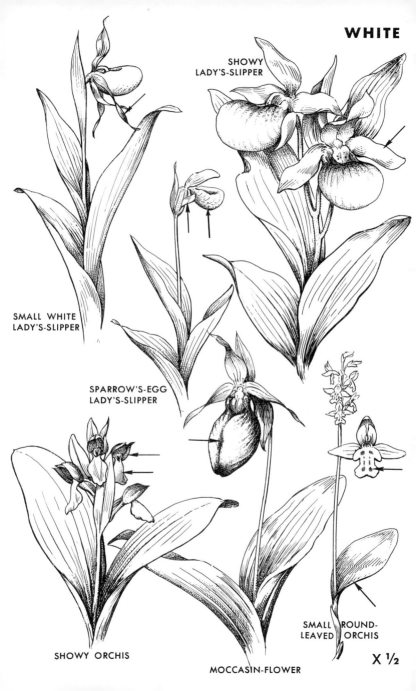

WHITE

SHOWY
LADY'S-SLIPPER

SMALL WHITE
LADY'S-SLIPPER

SPARROW'S-EGG
LADY'S-SLIPPER

SHOWY ORCHIS

MOCCASIN-FLOWER

SMALL ROUND-
LEAVED ORCHIS

X ½

SPURRED ORCHIDS IN SHOWY SPIKES
ORCHID FAMILY (Orchidaceae)
Genus *Habenaria*. Note the long spurs (insets).

WHITE FRINGED ORCHIS　　　　　*Habenaria blephariglottis*
Note the *long, deeply fringed lip* (½–1 in.). Southern plants
have larger flowers, longer spurs. A fringeless variety (*integrilabia*) is dominant in Kentucky, Tennessee. 12–30 in.
Meadows, bogs. Michigan, s. Quebec, Gulf of St. Lawrence
south.　　　　　　　　　　　　　　　　　　　JUNE–SEPT.

PRAIRIE WHITE FRINGED ORCHIS *Habenaria leucophaea*
Differs from the preceding by having the *fringed lip in 3 parts*
and in other details of flower structure (see inset). 1–3 ft. See
also Ragged Fringed Orchis, *H. lacera* (p. 120), which may be
whitish. Wet prairies, sphagnum bogs. Mainly Great Lakes
region and Mississippi Valley.　　　　　　　　　JUNE–JULY

SNOWY ORCHIS　　　　　　　　　　　*Habenaria nivea*
Note that the slender lip of this snowy-white orchis is *on top;*
our only *Habenaria* so arranged. The long spurs are horizontal,
not drooping. 12–30 in. Acid bogs, s. U.S.; local, s. New Jersey,
Delaware.　　　　　　　　　　　　　　　　　AUG.–SEPT.

LEAFY WHITE ORCHIS　　　　　　　*Habenaria dilatata*
Note the long leaves and the slender, *tapering unfringed lip*
that projects outward. The lip is as long as the spur. Flowers
may also be yellowish or greenish. 1–3 ft. Bogs, peaty meadows,
cool woods. Across Canada, south to Minnesota, Wisconsin,
Michigan, Pennsylvania, New Jersey.　　　　　　MAY–SEPT.

SMALL WOODLAND ORCHIS　　　　*Habenaria clavellata*
Note the *short blunt lip* and relatively naked stem, usually with
only 1 well-developed leaf. Flowers oblique, or askew; greenish
or yellowish white; spur with swollen tip. 6–18 in. Bogs, wet
woods, shores. Most of our area.　　　　　　　　JULY–AUG.

ONE-LEAF REIN-ORCHIS　　　　　　*Habenaria obtusata*
Note the *single, broad, blunt, basal leaf* and *long, tapering lip*
(slightly *longer* than spur). Flowers few, greenish white. 4–14
in. Shady woods, mossy bogs. Canada to n. Minnesota, n.
Wisconsin, n. New York, n. New England.　　　　JUNE–SEPT.

ROUND-LEAVED ORCHIS　　　　　*Habenaria orbiculata*
Note the *2 flat roundish leaves* and the long tapering lip (*shorter*
than spur). Flowers many; greenish white. Woods. Canada
and northern edge of U.S.; south in mts. A larger form, *H.
macrophylla* (not shown), has much larger leaves; the flowers
are twice as large and are white, with a longer spur. See also
Hooker's Orchis, *H. hookeri*, p. 372.　　　　　　JULY–AUG.

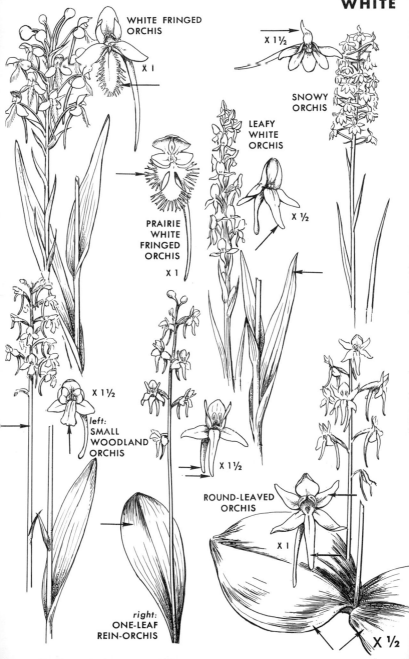

WHITE

WHITE FRINGED
ORCHIS
X 1

X 1½

SNOWY
ORCHIS

LEAFY
WHITE
ORCHIS

X ½

PRAIRIE
WHITE
FRINGED
ORCHIS
X 1

X 1½

left:
SMALL
WOODLAND
ORCHIS

X 1½

ROUND-LEAVED
ORCHIS

X 1

right:
ONE-LEAF
REIN-ORCHIS

X ½

SMALL ORCHIDS IN SPIKES OR RACEMES
ORCHID FAMILY (Orchidaceae)

LADIES'-TRESSES   *Spiranthes*
Inconspicuous spikes (6–18 in.) of small white flowers, in single
or double spirals. Leaves usually grasslike. Gray lists 11 species.
Most species bloom in late summer, autumn.
NODDING LADIES'-TRESSES, *Spiranthes cernua.* Flowers
arch downward; arranged in double spiral. Leaves basal, slender;
narrower toward base. Bogs, meadows. Most of our area.
HOODED LADIES'-TRESSES, *Spiranthes romanzoffiana.* Similar to *S. cernua;* double-spiraled, but denser; flowers *do not nod.*
Lip *narrowed toward middle.* Meadows. Canada, n. U.S.
SLENDER LADIES'-TRESSES, *Spiranthes gracilis.* Very
slender; single spiral. Bright *green spot* on lip. Short basal leaves
wither before bloom. Fields. Most of our area.
WIDE-LEAVED LADIES'-TRESSES, *Spiranthes lucida.* An
early species (May–July) with *short, wide leaves.* Lip with yellow
center and fine green lines. Most of our area.
SPRING or EARLY LADIES'-TRESSES, *Spiranthes vernalis.*
Another early species (May–Sept.). Note the *red down* on
flowers. Leaves very slender. Near coast. S. New England
south.

RATTLESNAKE-PLANTAINS   *Goodyera*
Small orchids with a *checkered leaf pattern* created by whitish
veins and cross-veins on a dark background. Leaves, broad,
in a basal rosette. Flowers in spikelike raceme.   JULY–AUG.
DOWNY RATTLESNAKE-PLANTAIN, *Goodyera pubescens.*
Note the thick cylindrical arrangement of the flowers. Stem
woolly. 6–16 in. Woods. Minnesota, Ontario, Maine south.
DWARF RATTLESNAKE-PLANTAIN, *Goodyera repens.* Note
the 1-sided arrangement of the flowers. 5–10 in. Damp woods.
Canada and northern tier of states; south in mts.
CHECKERED RATTLESNAKE-PLANTAIN, *Goodyera tes-
selata.* Flowers in a loose spiral. Note flower structure. 6–16
in. Woodlands (usually dry). Canada, northern tier of states.
GREEN-LEAVED RATTLESNAKE-PLANTAIN, *Goodyera oblongifolia* (not shown). Dark leaves often have white midvein
but lack checkered pattern. 8–16 in. Forests. Canada, northern edge of U.S.

WHITE ADDER'S-MOUTH   *Malaxis brachypoda*
Note the *single, wide,* embracing basal leaf and the *wide, heart-
shaped, pointed lip.* Flower greenish white; no spur. 4–6 in.
See also Green Adder's-mouth, *M. unifolia,* p. 372. Bogs, woods,
swales. Manitoba, Quebec south to northern edge of U.S.; in
mts. to Tennessee.   JUNE–AUG.

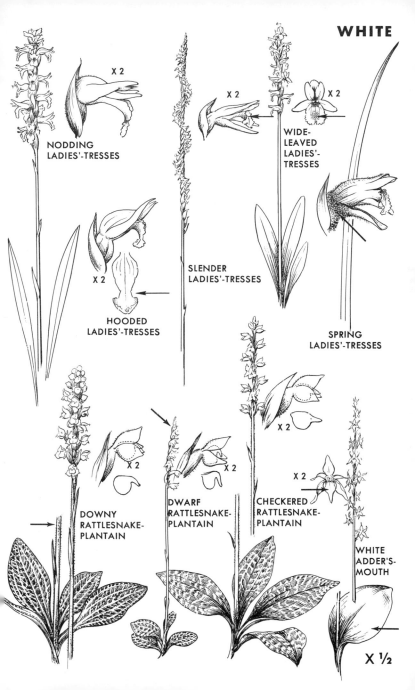

WHITE

NODDING
LADIES'-TRESSES

X 2

WIDE-
LEAVED
LADIES'-
TRESSES

X 2

X 2

SLENDER
LADIES'-TRESSES

X 2

HOODED
LADIES'-TRESSES

SPRING
LADIES'-TRESSES

DOWNY
RATTLESNAKE-
PLANTAIN

X 2

DWARF
RATTLESNAKE-
PLANTAIN

X 2

CHECKERED
RATTLESNAKE-
PLANTAIN

X 2

X 2

WHITE
ADDER'S-
MOUTH

X ½

SMALL FLESHY PLANTS; SPECIALIZED HABITS

1. INSECT-EATING PLANTS (sundews)

ROUND-LEAVED SUNDEW   *Drosera rotundifolia*
SUNDEW FAMILY   (Droseraceae)
Note the rosette of small *round* leaves (¾ in.), each on a slender
stalk and covered with *reddish glandular hairs* that exude a
sticky juice, like tiny dewdrops. Flowers, white or pink, in a
1-sided cluster, open 1 at a time. 4–9 in. Acid or peaty bogs.
Most of our area.   JUNE–AUG.

SPATULATE-LEAVED SUNDEW   *Drosera intermedia*
SUNDEW FAMILY   (Droseraceae)
This species has a longer, more *oval* leaf blade. Leafstalks *lack*
hairs, are smooth, more erect. 2–8 in. Acid bogs. Mainly near
coast and around Great Lakes.   JUNE–AUG.

SLENDER-LEAVED SUNDEW   *Drosera linearis*
SUNDEW FAMILY   (Droseraceae)
In this species the leaf blade is *very narrow* and, with its naked
stalk, usually exceeds the flower stalk. Flowers 1 to 4, often
solitary. 2–5 in. See also Thread-leaved Sundew, *D. filiformis*
(purplish), p. 232. Bogs, wet sand. Mainly along coast, Great
Lakes area, etc.   JUNE–AUG.

2. PARASITIC AND SAPROPHYTIC PLANTS; NO GREEN COLOR

These feed on roots or on decaying material in soil.

INDIAN-PIPE   *Monotropa uniflora*
WINTERGREEN FAMILY   (Pyrolaceae)
The *translucent, waxy pipes* are unique. The nodding flower is
white or pink, turns blackish later. Leaves scale-like. 4–10 in.
Shady woods. Most of our area.   JUNE–SEPT.

WISTER'S CORALROOT   *Corallorhiza wisteriana*
ORCHID FAMILY   (Orchidaceae)
Coralroots are leafless, tawny- or purple-stemmed orchids.
This species has a broad white lip spotted with red. 8–16 in.
See others on p. 242. Woods. Missouri, s. Indiana, Ohio,
Pennsylvania, New Jersey south.   APRIL–MAY

GIANT BIRD'S-NEST   *Pterospora andromedea*
WINTERGREEN FAMILY   (Pyrolaceae)
Note the tall, brown, leafless stalk, *scaled at base;* grooved and
covered with sticky hairs. Flowers small, bell-like, drooping.
1–4 ft. Pine woods. Local, Canada to Wisconsin, Michigan,
New York, Vermont.   JUNE–AUG.

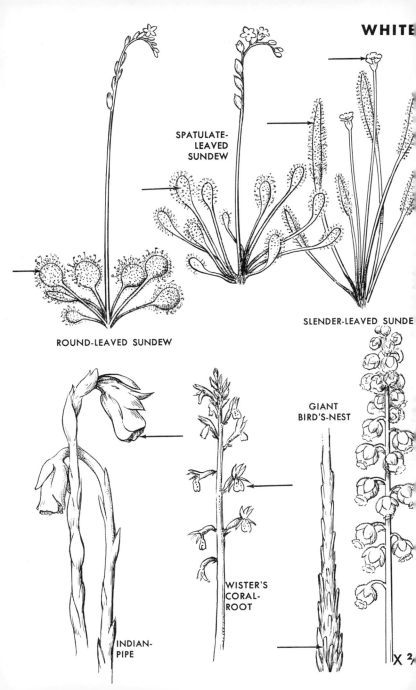

WHITE

SPATULATE-
LEAVED
SUNDEW

ROUND-LEAVED SUNDEW

SLENDER-LEAVED SUNDE

GIANT
BIRD'S-NEST

INDIAN-
PIPE

WISTER'S
CORAL-
ROOT

X 2

6 to 10 PETALS: LOW FLOWERS OF SPRING
In some cases the "petals" are really sepals.

ROUND-LOBED HEPATICA *Hepatica americana*
BUTTERCUP FAMILY (Ranunculaceae)
Rounded 3-lobed leaves, hairy stalks. Flowers white, pink, lavender, or blue. The 6 to 10 "petals" are really sepals. Note the 3 bracts below flower. 4–6 in. Leafy woods. S. Canada south.
MARCH–MAY

SHARP-LOBED HEPATICA *Hepatica acutiloba*
BUTTERCUP FAMILY (Ranunculaceae)
Similar to preceding, but lobes of leaves *pointed;* occasionally 5 to 7 lobes. Hybridizes. 4–9 in. Upland woods. Appalachians from Maine south; west to Minnesota, Missouri. MARCH–APRIL

RUE-ANEMONE *Anemonella thalictroides*
BUTTERCUP FAMILY (Ranunculaceae)
A delicate plant with 2 or 3 flowers on slender stalks above a whorl of small 3-lobed leaves. The 6 "petals" (sometimes 8 or 10) are really sepals. 4–8 in. Woods. Minnesota, Ontario, s. Maine south. MARCH–MAY

STARFLOWER *Trientalis borealis*
PRIMROSE FAMILY (Primulaceae)
Two fragile 6- to 7-pointed stars on threadlike stalks surmount a whorl of 5 to 9 shiny, tapering leaves. 4–9 in. Cool woods, high slopes. Canada, n. U.S.; in mts. to Virginia. MAY–JUNE

BLOODROOT *Sanguinaria canadensis*
POPPY FAMILY (Papaveraceae)
POPPY SUBFAMILY (Papaveroideae)
Note the *orange juice* of the broken stem. The pale, lobed leaf embraces the stalk bearing the showy 8- to 10-petaled flower. 6–12 in. Rich woods. Most of area. MARCH–MAY

PASQUEFLOWER *Anemone patens*
BUTTERCUP FAMILY (Ranunculaceae)
The 5 to 7 large petal-like sepals may be white or blue-violet. Plant covered with *silky hair;* leaves deeply cut (as in buttercup). Flowers appear before leaves. 6–16 in. Dry prairies. Wisconsin, Illinois, Missouri west. MARCH–APRIL

TWINLEAF *Jeffersonia diphylla*
BARBERRY FAMILY (Berberidaceae)
The 8-petaled blossom suggests Bloodroot, but note the *almost completely divided leaf* on a long stalk. 8 in. when in flower, twice as tall later. Woods. Wisconsin, s. Ontario, w. New York south. APRIL–MAY

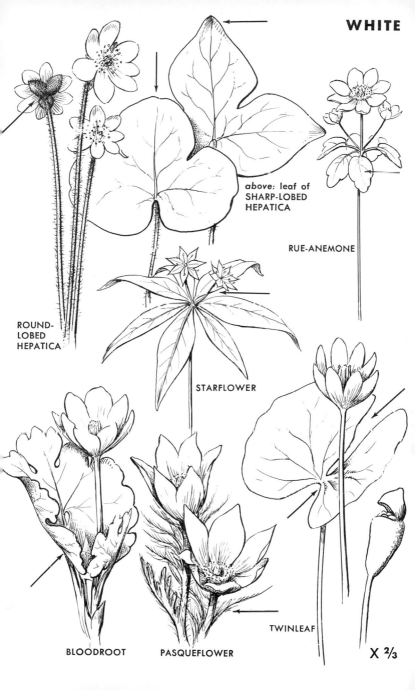

WHITE

above: leaf of
SHARP-LOBED
HEPATICA

RUE-ANEMONE

ROUND-
LOBED
HEPATICA

STARFLOWER

BLOODROOT

PASQUEFLOWER

TWINLEAF

X 2/3

5 PETALS AND A SPUR: VIOLETS

VIOLET FAMILY (Violaceae)

Lower petals veined, side petals often bearded; bottom petal with spur or sac. Note the 2 basic types below. See also Dwarf Larkspur (often white), p. 318.

1. LEAVES AND FLOWERS ON SAME STALK

CANADA VIOLET *Viola canadensis*
Note yellow base of petals and *purplish tinge* on back of petals. Stems purplish with scattered hairs. Relatively short flower stalks, small stipules. 8–16 in. S. Canada, northern edge of U.S.; south in mts. APRIL–JULY

PALE or CREAM VIOLET *Viola striata*
Differs from Canada Violet by absence of yellow at base of petals and absence of purplish on the back. Note *large deeply cut stipules* and much longer flower stalks. Stems green, smooth. 6–12 in. Low woods, streambanks. Minnesota, Wisconsin, s. Ontario, New York south. APRIL–JUNE

FIELD PANSY Alien *Viola kitaibelliana*
Note the small *spoon-shaped* leaves with their *very large*, lobed, blunt-tipped stipules. Flowers whitish or pale blue. 3–8 in. Fields, roadsides, streambanks. Michigan, Ohio, New York south. APRIL–MAY

2. LEAVES BASAL, FLOWERS ON SEPARATE STALKS

NORTHERN WHITE VIOLET *Viola pallens*
Very small, leaves nearly round or bluntly heart-shaped, seed capsule *green*. 1–5 in. Wet woods, clearings. Across Canada, n. U.S.; south in mts. APRIL–JULY

SWEET WHITE VIOLET *Viola blanda*
Similar, but more fragrant; deeper lobes at base of leaves; stems reddish; upper petals *twisted;* seed capsule *purple*. Woods. Across Canada, n. U.S.; south in mts. APRIL–MAY

LARGE-LEAVED VIOLET *Viola incognita*
Similar to *V. blanda* but leaves with *broader notch* (sinus) between lobes; lateral petals bearded, stems pubescent. Moist woods. Canada and south in mts. to Tennessee. APRIL–MAY

KIDNEY-LEAVED VIOLET *Viola renifolia*
Note leaf shape, *broader* than long. Only white violet of this group with no runners. 1–4 in. Cool woods. Canada, northern edge of U.S.; mts. to Pennsylvania. MAY–JUNE

PRIMROSE-LEAVED VIOLET *Viola primulifolia*
Note the *oblong to ovate* leaves; petioles (leafstalks) winged at top. Flower stems reddish. 2–10 in. Bogs, swamps. Minnesota, s. Ontario, Nova Scotia south. APRIL–JUNE

LANCE-LEAVED VIOLET *Viola lanceolata*
Note the *lance-shaped* leaf with the long, tapering base. 2–6 in. Bogs, swamps, wet spots. Minnesota, Michigan, s. Ontario, New Brunswick south. APRIL–JUNE

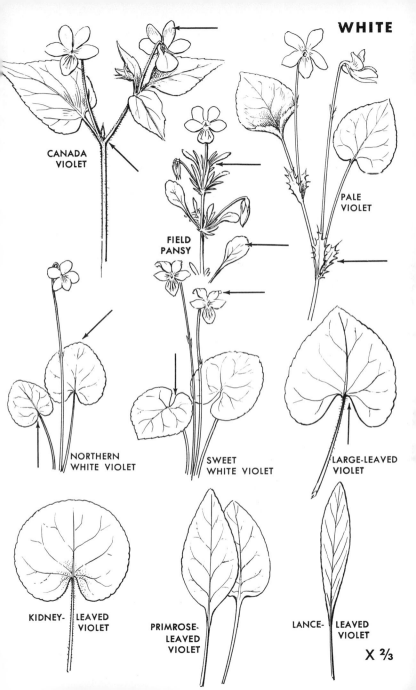

WHITE

CANADA VIOLET

FIELD PANSY

PALE VIOLET

NORTHERN WHITE VIOLET

SWEET WHITE VIOLET

LARGE-LEAVED VIOLET

KIDNEY- LEAVED VIOLET

PRIMROSE- LEAVED VIOLET

LANCE- LEAVED VIOLET

X 2/3

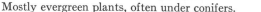

5 PETALS; SMALL, NODDING, WAXY FLOWERS

WINTERGREEN FAMILY *Pyrolaceae*

Mostly evergreen plants, often under conifers.
Leaves in basal rosettes (*Pyrola*) or in whorls of 3 to 6
toothed leaves on stem (*Chimaphila*).

PIPSISSEWA *Chimaphila umbellata*
Note the terminal cluster of waxy white or pinkish flowers, each
with its ring of reddish anthers. The dark, shiny, toothed leaves
radiate in whorls from the stem. 6–12 in. Dry woods. Ontario,
Quebec south to n. U.S.; in mts. to Georgia. JULY–AUG.

ONE-FLOWERED WINTERGREEN *Moneses uniflora*
Note the *single,* nodding waxy white or pink flower and basal
rosette of small roundish leaves. 2–5 in. Cool woods, bogs.
N. Canada to Minnesota, Michigan, Pennsylvania, Connecticut.
JUNE–AUG.

SPOTTED WINTERGREEN *Chimaphila maculata*
Note the *pale pattern* on the midribs of the tapering leaves. The
leaves are all arranged in whorls on the stem, much as in
Pipsissewa. The nodding waxy flowers may be white or pink.
4–10 in. Woods. Michigan, Ontario, Maine south, especially
in uplands. JUNE–AUG.

ONE-SIDED PYROLA *Pyrola secunda*
Note the way the white or greenish flowers are arranged *along 1
side* of the stem (which may bend). In other pyrolas, flowers
are arranged spirally. 4–8 in. Woods. N. Canada to n. U.S.;
in uplands to Virginia. JUNE–AUG.

GREENISH-FLOWERED PYROLA *Pyrola virens*
Note the small leaves with petioles often longer than blades.
The relatively large green-veined flowers separate it from next
species. 4–12 in. Conifer woods. Across Canada and northern
edge of U.S.; south in mts. to Pennsylvania. JUNE–JULY

LESSER PYROLA *Pyrola minor*
Leaves similar to those of *P. virens* but flowers much smaller;
white or pinkish. 4–8 in. Cold woods. Across Canada, south
to Minnesota, Michigan, n. New England. JUNE–AUG.

SHINLEAF *Pyrola elliptica*
The commonest *Pyrola;* leaves relatively large (up to 3 in.)
elliptical and rounded at end; blade longer than petiole. Note
the long curving pistils and red stemlets of the green-veined
flowers. 5–10 in. Woods. Across Canada and northern parts
of U.S.; south in mts. to W. Virginia. JUNE–AUG.

ROUND-LEAVED PYROLA *Pyrola rotundifolia*
Similar to Shinleaf but usually larger; leaves more leathery,
shinier, rounder, petioles often as long as leaf blades, petals
whiter. 6–15 in. Woods, bogs. Across Canada and northern
edge of U.S.; south in mts. JUNE–AUG.

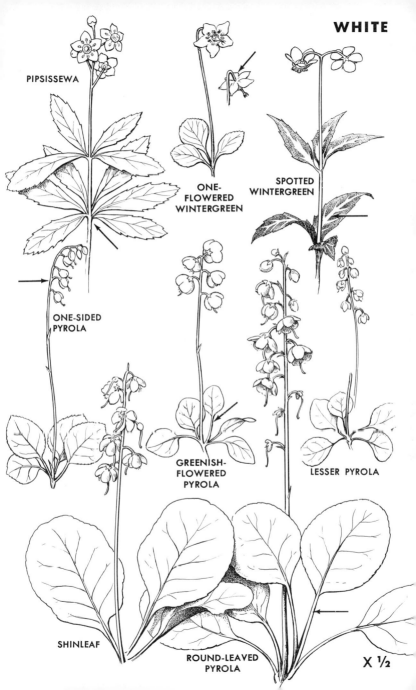

WHITE

PIPSISSEWA

ONE-FLOWERED WINTERGREEN

SPOTTED WINTERGREEN

ONE-SIDED PYROLA

GREENISH-FLOWERED PYROLA

LESSER PYROLA

SHINLEAF

ROUND-LEAVED PYROLA

X ½

5 PETALS; MOSTLY 3 LEAFLETS

ROSE FAMILY (Rosaceae)

BRAMBLES (BLACKBERRIES, ETC.) *Rubus*
Most plants of the genus *Rubus* are woody, prickly, or bristly shrubs, outside the scope of this book; most are problems for the specialist. Gray recognizes 205 species in our area. See *A Field Guide to Trees and Shrubs* for a small selection.

COMMON STRAWBERRY *Fragaria virginiana*
Similar to domestic strawberry. Hairy, with 3 coarsely toothed leaflets on a slender stalk; the round-petaled flowers in a flat cluster on a separate stalk not exceeding leaves. Variable. Small seeds *embedded in pits* in ovoid red fruit. 3–6 in. Fields, open places. Most of our area. APRIL–JUNE

WOOD STRAWBERRY Alien *Fragaria vesca*
Similar to preceding but flowers and fruits smaller, usually held *above* the leaves. Leaves more pointed, less blunt. Fruit more conical; seeds *on surface*, not in pits. 3–6 in. Rocky woods; pastures. Canada, n. U.S. south to Missouri, Virginia.
MAY–AUG.

THREE-TOOTHED CINQUEFOIL *Potentilla tridentata*
Note the *3 rounded teeth* at the tip of each shiny leaflet. Leaves turn deep red in fall. 1–10 in. Open acid soil, rocks. N. Canada to n. U.S.; south on open mts. JUNE–AUG.

WHITE AVENS *Geum canadense*
Slender, angular. Leaves usually divided into 3's (sometimes 5's or 7's), except for simple upper leaves. Variable. Flowers replaced by bristly seed receptacles. 18–30 in. Wood edges, thickets. Minnesota, Quebec, Nova Scotia south. JUNE–AUG.

ROUGH AVENS *Geum virginianum*
Similar to preceding, but hairier, leaves larger, especially upper ones. Basal leaves often rounded. Petals creamy white or pale yellow, *shorter* than sepals (in *G. canadense* petals are whiter, about as long as sepals). 12–30 in. Woods, thickets. Indiana to c. Massachusetts and south. JUNE–AUG.

BOWMAN'S-ROOT *Gillenia trifoliata*
Note the narrow scraggly petals and the almost stalkless leaves, divided into 3's. 2–3 ft. Rich woods. Michigan, s. Ontario, New York south. MAY–JULY

AMERICAN IPECAC *Gillenia stipulata*
Similar to the preceding, but with *very large stipules* that make the leaves look *5-part*. Woods, thickets. Kansas, Illinois, Ohio, sw. New York south. MAY–JULY

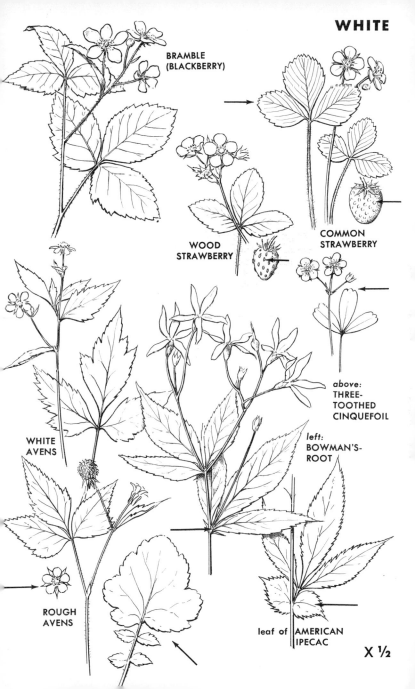

WHITE

BRAMBLE
(BLACKBERRY)

WOOD
STRAWBERRY

COMMON
STRAWBERRY

above:
THREE-
TOOTHED
CINQUEFOIL

left:
BOWMAN'S-
ROOT

WHITE
AVENS

ROUGH
AVENS

leaf of AMERICAN
IPECAC

X ½

5 "PETALS"; 3 LEAFLETS OR 3-PART LEAVES

In all except Common Wood-sorrel "petals" are really sepals.

ANEMONES *Anemone*
BUTTERCUP FAMILY (Ranunculaceae)
Anemones have no petals; but the white sepals, usually 5, look like petals. Numerous stamens and pistils cover a central knob. Midway on the stem is a whorl of 2, 3, or more deeply toothed 3- (or 5-) part leaves.

WOOD ANEMONE, *Anemone quinquefolia.* A low delicate woodland plant, usually with 5 (4–9) petal-like sepals. The deeply cut leaves appear to be divided into 3 or, more frequently, 5 leaflets. 4–8 in. Woods. Canada, n. U.S.; south in Appalachians. APRIL–JUNE

MOUNTAIN ANEMONE, *Anemone lancifolia* (not shown). Similar to preceding but larger (up to 16 in.); leaves usually 3-part. Mts. S. Pennsylvania south. APRIL–JUNE

THIMBLEWEED, *Anemone virginiana.* Tall; "petals" (sepals) often greenish white, not showy. Leaves heavily veined. Fruit head suggests a thimble. 2–3 ft. Dry open woods. Minnesota, s. Maine south. JULY–AUG.

THIMBLEWEED, *Anemone riparia.* Similar, but leaves *wedge-shaped* at base (rounded in *A. virginiana*). More northern. Canada, northern edge of U.S. JUNE–JULY

LONG-HEADED THIMBLEWEED, *Anemone cylindrica.* Similar to preceding two, but more leafy (3–10 leaves on stem); points blunter; "thimble" longer (up to 1½ in.). Dry soil, open slopes. N. U.S. MAY–JUNE

CANADA ANEMONE, *Anemone canadensis.* Note the sessile (stalkless) leaves that surround the stem. "Petals" (sepals) 1 to 1½ in. 1–2 ft. Meadows, low thickets. Canada to Missouri, Illinois, w. Virginia, n. New Jersey. MAY–JULY

GOLDTHREAD *Coptis groenlandica*
BUTTERCUP FAMILY (Ranunculaceae)
Note the bright yellow "roots" and the shiny, dark, evergreen leaves. In addition to the 5 showy sepals there are 5 small club-like petals. 3–6 in. Cool woods, bogs. Canada, n. U.S. and south in mts. MAY–JULY

COMMON WOOD-SORREL *Oxalis montana*
WOOD-SORREL FAMILY (Oxalidaceae)
Note the inversely heart-shaped, cloverlike leaflets. The 5 white or pink petals are veined with pink. 3–4 in. Woods. Canada, northern edge of U.S.; south in mts. MAY–JULY

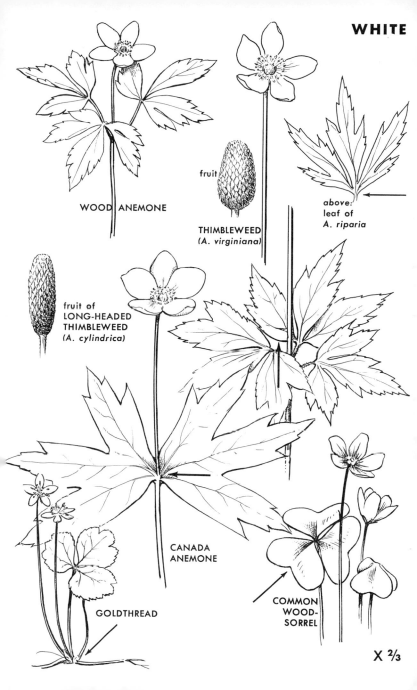

WHITE

WOOD ANEMONE

fruit

THIMBLEWEED
(A. virginiana)

above:
leaf of
A. riparia

fruit of
LONG-HEADED
THIMBLEWEED
(A. cylindrica)

CANADA
ANEMONE

GOLDTHREAD

COMMON
WOOD-
SORREL

X ⅔

5 PETALS; VARIOUS LEAVES

DEWDROP, DALIBARDA   *Dalibarda repens*
ROSE FAMILY   (Rosaceae)
Note the *round, finely scalloped leaves* and the solitary bushy-stamened flower on a separate reddish stalk. 2–5 in. Woods. S. Canada south to Michigan, n. Ohio, New England; in Appalachians to N. Carolina.   JUNE–AUG.

CHEESES, COMMON MALLOW Alien   *Malva neglecta*
MALLOW FAMILY   (Malvaceae)
A small creeping weed. *Small* white or lavender flowers in axils; petals heart-shaped (notched). Leaves with 5 to 7 shallow lobes. The name Cheeses refers to the *flat, round fruits*. See also Musk Mallow, *M. moschata*, p. 218. Waste places, gardens. Throughout.   APRIL–OCT.

CLOUDBERRY, BAKE-APPLE   *Rubus chamaemorus*
ROSE FAMILY   (Rosaceae)
A dwarf herbaceous "blackberry" of the North. Stem creeping, with erect shoots 3 to 8 in. high. Flowers similar to those of other blackberries, but *solitary*. Leaf broad, 5-lobed. Berry peach color to yellow. Bogs, peat. N. Canada south to n. New Hampshire, Maine, Cape Sable I.   JUNE–JULY

SPRING-BEAUTY   *Claytonia virginica*
PURSLANE FAMILY   (Portulacaceae)
Note the pair of smooth *linear leaves* midway up the stem. Petals white or pink with darker pink veins. 6–12 in. Moist woods. Minnesota, s. Ontario, s. Quebec, s. New England south.   MARCH–MAY

CAROLINA SPRING-BEAUTY   *Claytonia caroliniana*
PURSLANE FAMILY   (Portulacaceae)
Similar to *C. virginica*, but leaves *much wider, with slender petioles*. Woods, uplands. S. Canada south through Appalachians and westward.   MARCH–MAY

GRASS-OF-PARNASSUS   *Parnassia glauca*
SAXIFRAGE FAMILY   (Saxifragaceae)
Note the spadelike basal leaves and the single small leaf embracing the flowering stem. *Green veins* line the petals and 5 yellow anthers lie between the petals. 8–24 in. Wet meadows. Canada south to Iowa, n. Illinois, Indiana, Ohio, Pennsylvania.   JULY–OCT.

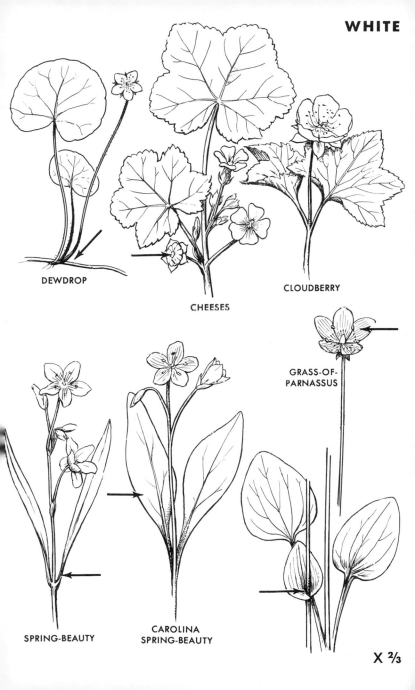

WHITE

DEWDROP

CHEESES

CLOUDBERRY

GRASS-OF-
PARNASSUS

SPRING-BEAUTY

CAROLINA
SPRING-BEAUTY

X ⅔

5 SHOWY, NOTCHED PETALS; TUBULAR CALYX

PINK FAMILY (Caryophyllaceae), except Moss Phlox
Leaves entire, stalkless; opposite or in whorls.

STARRY CAMPION   *Silene stellata*
Note the *fringed petals*. Leaves often in whorls of 4. 2–3 ft.
Woods. Minnesota to Massachusetts and south.   JULY–SEPT.

SNOWY CAMPION   *Silene nivea*
This native species lacks the fringe, has petals merely notched,
calyx sac smooth, scarcely veined; leaves in pairs. 1–3 ft.
Woods. Minnesota to Pennsylvania and south.   JUNE–AUG.

BLADDER CAMPION Alien   *Silene cucubalus*
This weed differs from *S. nivea* by its much more inflated and
veined calyx sac, suggesting a tiny melon. Note also the much
more deeply cleft petals. 8–18 in. Roadsides, fields. Most of
our area.   APRIL–AUG.

FORKING CATCHFLY Alien   *Silene dichotoma*
A *slender-leaved*, hairy, much branched species with deeply cleft,
sessile (stalkless) flowers. The 10-ribbed calyx sac is hairy,
tubular, not inflated. Waste places. Much of our area.
                                            JUNE–SEPT.

NIGHT-FLOWERING CATCHFLY Alien   *Silene noctiflora*
Another hairy species, with broader leaves than in preceding,
and *sticky* all over. The swollen calyx sac is beautifully veined.
1–3 ft. Waste places. Most of our area.   JULY–SEPT.

EVENING LYCHNIS Alien   *Lychnis alba*
Another sticky species, often confused with the preceding; but
note the larger flowers with *5 curved styles* that protrude in the
center (flowers of genus *Silene* have 3 styles); see inset. The
calyx sac is often much inflated. 1–2 ft. Waste places. Much
of our area.   JUNE–SEPT.

BOUNCING BET Alien   *Saponaria officinalis*
Pink or whitish. See p. 266.

MULLEIN PINK Alien   *Lychnis coronaria*
Rose or white. See p. 266.

MOSS PHLOX, MOSS-PINK   *Phlox subulata*
PHLOX FAMILY   (Polemoniaceae)
Pink, violet, or white. See text and color plate, p. 322.

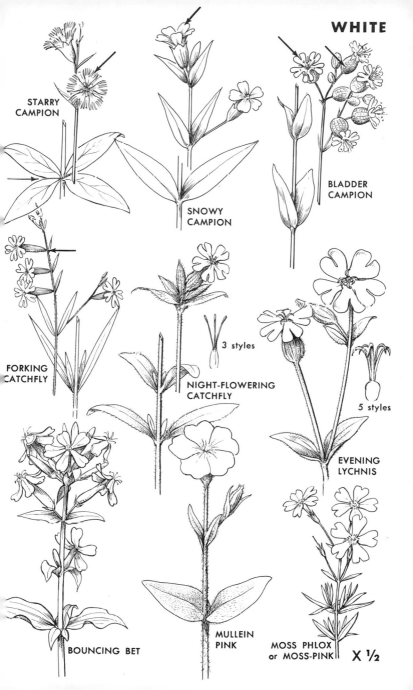

WHITE

STARRY CAMPION

SNOWY CAMPION

BLADDER CAMPION

FORKING CATCHFLY

NIGHT-FLOWERING CATCHFLY

3 styles

5 styles

EVENING LYCHNIS

BOUNCING BET

MULLEIN PINK

MOSS PHLOX or MOSS-PINK

X ½

5 PETALS, SMALL FLOWERS; LEAVES IN PAIRS
PINK FAMILY (Caryophyllaceae)

1. PETALS DEEPLY CLEFT (chickweeds)
Petals so deeply cleft that flowers often seem to have 10 petals.

COMMON CHICKWEED Alien *Stellaria media*
Note the *long petioles* (*stalks*) on the short, ovate leaves. Petals 2-parted, *shorter* than sepals. 4–16 in. Waste places, roadsides, gardens. Throughout. MOST OF YEAR

STAR CHICKWEED *Stellaria pubera*
Most leaves not stalked, fairly broad, elliptic, up to 3 in. long. Petals longer than sepals, cleft ½ or more. 6–16 in. Woodlands. Illinois, New Jersey south. MARCH–MAY

LESSER STITCHWORT Alien *Stellaria graminea*
Note the small *narrow* leaves and the flowering stalks at the summit of the stem. Petals 2-cleft. 12–20 in. Grassy places, roadsides. Much of our area. MAY–OCT.

LONG-LEAVED CHICKWEED (not shown) *Stellaria longifolia*
Similar to preceding but flowers fewer and often springing from leaf axils. Meadows, swamps. Nearly throughout. MAY–JULY

FIELD CHICKWEED *Cerastium arvense*
Narrow leaves suggest preceding two, but note broad petals notched *less than half length* and *very short sepals*. 6–10 in. Grassy or rocky places. Most of area. APRIL–JULY

MOUSE-EAR CHICKWEED Alien *Cerastium vulgatum*
Note the hairy, *sessile* (*stalkless*) *oval leaves* (¾ in.) and sticky-hairy stems. Deeply cleft petals about as long as sepals. 6–18 in. Waste places, edges. Throughout. MAY–SEPT.

2. PETALS ROUNDED OR SLIGHTLY NOTCHED (sandworts)

MOUNTAIN SANDWORT *Arenaria groenlandica*
Suggests a narrow-leaved chickweed but petals only slightly notched. Basal leaves often form tufts or mats. 2–5 in. Rocks. N. Canada south to higher peaks of New York, New England; on coast to Maine. MAY–SEPT.

PINE-BARREN SANDWORT (not shown) *A. caroliniana*
Similar to preceding; petals narrower, without notch. Coastal pine barrens. Local, Long Island south. MAY–JUNE

ROCK SANDWORT *Arenaria stricta*
Note the needlelike leaves with tufts of shorter leaves in axils; often matted. Rocky soil. Widespread. JUNE–JULY

THYME-LEAVED SANDWORT Alien *Arenaria serpyllifolia*
Note tiny ovate leaves (¼ in.), tiny rounded petals, longer sepals. 2–8 in. Sandy soil, fields. Widespread. APRIL–AUG.

GROVE SANDWORT *Arenaria lateriflora*
Round petals, oval leaves (½–1 in.) with hairy margins. Wet spots. Canada south to Missouri, New Jersey. MAY–JULY

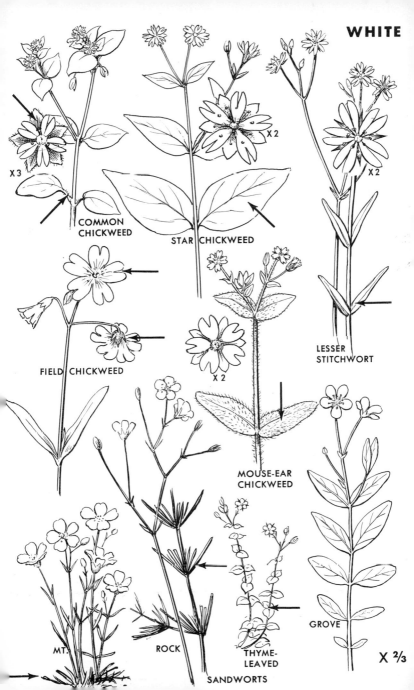

WHITE

X3

COMMON
CHICKWEED

STAR CHICKWEED

X2

X2

LESSER
STITCHWORT

FIELD CHICKWEED

X2

MOUSE-EAR
CHICKWEED

GROVE

MT.

ROCK

THYME-
LEAVED
SANDWORTS

X ⅔

LOW CREEPING OR MATTED PLANTS

Leaves in tufts, mats, or whorls.
See also sandworts, p. 36, and bedstraws, p. 40.

1. 5 SPREADING "PETALS" OR LOBES

DIAPENSIA *Diapensia lapponica*
DIAPENSIA FAMILY (Diapensiaceae)
Note the cushionlike tufts of leaves from which flowers rise *on short stalks*. The 5 stamens are fastened between 5 lobes of the flower. 1–3 in. High mountaintops from Canada to n. New York, n. New England JUNE–JULY

PYXIE *Pyxidanthera barbulata*
DIAPENSIA FAMILY (Diapensiaceae)
Note the numerous *stemless* white or pale pink flowers nestled among the sharp needlelike leaves. A trailing mosslike plant. Sandy pine barrens. New Jersey, se. Virginia south.

MARCH–MAY

TRAILING ARBUTUS *Epigaea repens*
HEATH FAMILY (Ericaceae)
Note the *oval, leathery leaves* that remain green over winter, the trailing, hairy stems, and the clusters of pink or white flowers which expand from a short tube into 5 flaring lobes. Woods. Newfoundland, Labrador to Saskatchewan and south.

MARCH–MAY

2. SMALL, DROOPING, EGG- OR BELL-SHAPED FLOWERS

WINTERGREEN, CHECKERBERRY *Gaultheria procumbens*
HEATH FAMILY (Ericaceae)
Note the thick, shiny, oval leaves (1–2 in.); evergreen, slightly toothed, fragrant. Stem creeping, with short erect branches (2–5 in.). The small, waxy, egg-shaped flowers dangle beneath the leaves. Fruit a fragrant, dry red berry. Woods, clearings. Canada, n. U.S.; south in mts. JULY–AUG.

CREEPING SNOWBERRY *Gaultheria hispidula*
HEATH FAMILY (Ericaceae)
Note the very small (½ in.), alternate, oval leaves along the creeping stems. Flowers tiny, bell-shaped, 4-lobed; in leaf axils. Fruit a white berry tasting of wintergreen. See also Partridge-berry, p. 236. Woods, bogs, logs. Canada, northern parts of U.S.; south in mts. MAY–JUNE

BEARBERRY *Arctostaphylos uva-ursi*
HEATH FAMILY (Ericaceae)
A trailing shrub with papery reddish bark and small, *paddle-shaped*, evergreen leaves. Flowers in terminal clusters; egg-shaped, with small, lobed mouth; pink or white. Fruit a red berry. Sand or rocks. Canada south locally to n. U.S.

MAY–JULY

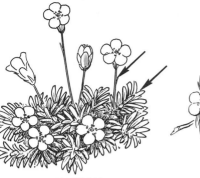

DIAPENSIA

PYXIE

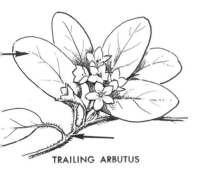

TRAILING ARBUTUS

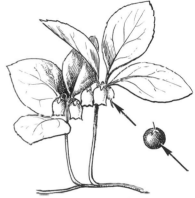

WINTERGREEN

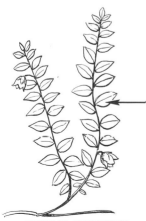

CREEPING SNOWBERRY

BEARBERRY

X ⅔

4 PETALS OR LOBES; SMALL FLOWERS

Bedstraw Family (Rubiaceae)
See also mustards, pp. 82–86.

1. LEAVES IN WHORLS, FLOWERS IN CLUSTERS (bed-straws)

Weak, reclining square stems and whorls of small leaves mark the bedstraws. The tiny flowers in open clusters usually have 4 lobes but *Galium trifidum* (leaves in whorls of 4) and *G. tinctorium* (whorls of 6) have *3 lobes*. About 30 species in our area. See also yellow bedstraws (*Galium*), p. 164.

1a. Leaves in whorls of 4
NORTHERN BEDSTRAW   *Galium boreale*
Stem smooth; leaves narrow, 3-nerved, whorls of 4. Flowers many, in tight, compound clusters. 12–30 in. Shores, rocky soil. Canada to Missouri, Ohio, Delaware.   May–Aug.
WHITE WILD LICORICE   *Galium circaezans*
Smoothish. Leaves very broad, 3-nerved, oval; whorls of 4; licorice flavor. Flowers sparse, greenish white. 1–2 ft. Woods. Michigan, New York, s. New England south.   June–July

1b. Leaves mostly in whorls of 6
FRAGRANT BEDSTRAW   *Galium triflorum*
A smooth-stemmed, prostrate species. Leaves fragrant when dried. Flowers greenish white; in groups of 3. Woods. Widespread in our area.   June–Aug.
ROUGH BEDSTRAW   *Galium asprellum*
A rough, reclining species with rasping, recurved prickles. Most leaves in 6's (some 4, 5). Thickets. Ontario to Missouri, Indiana, Ohio, New York.   July–Sept.

1c. Leaves mostly in whorls of 8
CLEAVERS   *Galium aparine*
Note the very scratchy, recurved prickles on stems. Leaves mostly in 8's. Flowers on stalks from leaf axils. Reclines on bushes in thickets. Throughout.   July–Sept.
WILD MADDER Alien   *Galium mollugo*
A smoothish species, erect or in mats; most leaves in 8's. Flowers in close clusters, very numerous. Fields, roadsides. Ontario south to Ohio, Virginia.   June–Aug.

2. LEAVES IN PAIRS

PARTRIDGEBERRY   *Mitchella repens*
Pink or white. See p. 236.
BLUETS   *Houstonia caerulea*
Blue or white. See p. 336.
LONG-LEAVED BLUETS   *Houstonia longifolia*
White or lavender. A small plant; slender paired leaves. Flowers in 2's and 3's in terminal clusters; tubed, 4-lobed. 5–10 in. Dry soil. Ontario, Maine south.   June–Sept.

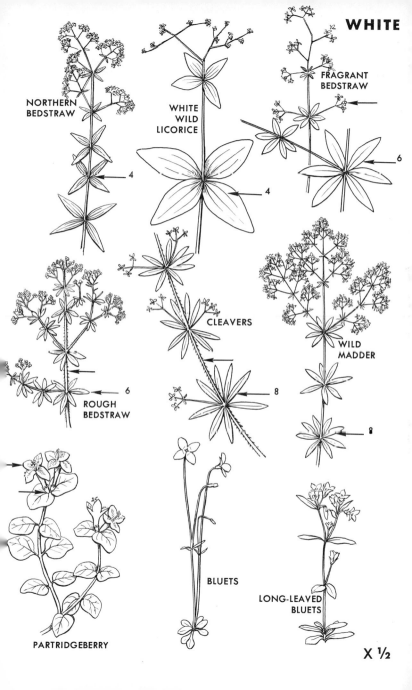

WHITE

NORTHERN BEDSTRAW

WHITE WILD LICORICE

FRAGRANT BEDSTRAW

4

4

6

ROUGH BEDSTRAW

6

CLEAVERS

8

WILD MADDER

8

PARTRIDGEBERRY

BLUETS

LONG-LEAVED BLUETS

X ½

TINY FLOWERS, MOSTLY IN LEAF AXILS

 DODDER *Cuscuta gronovii*
MORNING-GLORY FAMILY (Convolvulaceae)
Dodders are parasitic plants lacking leaves and green color.
The yellow or orange stems twine *like long tangled strings* over
and around their host plants. We have 12 species, separated
by technical characters. This common species has many clusters
of small, waxy, 5-lobed flowers. Low ground, thickets. Most
of our area. JULY–OCT.

WATER-PENNYWORT *Hydrocotyle americana*
PARSLEY FAMILY (Umbelliferae)
Note the *roundish* leaves, shallowly lobed and scalloped; deeply
notched at base. Tiny flowers (1–5) and also *runners* in leaf
axils; creeping. Wet places. S. Canada, northern edge of
U.S., and south in mts. JUNE–SEPT.

 SEA-MILKWORT *Glaux maritima*
PRIMROSE FAMILY (Primulaceae)
A pale fleshy plant. Note the pairs of short, stalkless oval
leaves. A single dull white or pink, 5-lobed flower is tucked in
each leaf axil. 2–12 in. Salt or brackish marshes, shores.
Gaspé to Virginia. JUNE–JULY

PURSLANE SPEEDWELL *Veronica peregrina*
SNAPDRAGON FAMILY (Scrophulariaceae)
A white veronica. Note the 4 petals (lowest petal smaller).
Tiny flowers tucked singly in axils of small, alternate, upper
leaves; lower leaves opposite. 3–12 in. See blue veronicas, p.
336. Roadsides. Throughout. MARCH–AUG.

 CORN GROMWELL Alien *Lithospermum arvense*
FORGET-ME-NOT FAMILY (Boraginaceae)
A rough-hairy plant with the aspect of a forget-me-not but with
insignificant, stemless, 5-petaled whitish flowers tucked among
leafy bracts in the upper leaf axils. Leaves mostly alternate;
lanceolate or long-oval. 6–18 in. Waste places, roadsides.
Most of our area. APRIL–JUNE

MILK-PURSLANE *Euphorbia supina*
SPURGE FAMILY (Euphorbiaceae)
Note the small purple-blotched leaves on this matted prostrate
weed; hairy, stem often dark red. Note also the flower structure (inset). Several similar small spurges in our area. Dry
soil, roadsides. Most of our area. JUNE–SEPT.

 EYEBRIGHT *Euphrasia americana*
SNAPDRAGON FAMILY (Scrophulariaceae)
This little plant has tiny, bristle-toothed leaves and a distinctive flower shape (3 lower lobes notched). The lower lobes are
marked with purple or violet lines. Variable. Several similar
species are recognized. Fields, roadsides. Newfoundland to
New Hampshire, Maine. JUNE–SEPT.

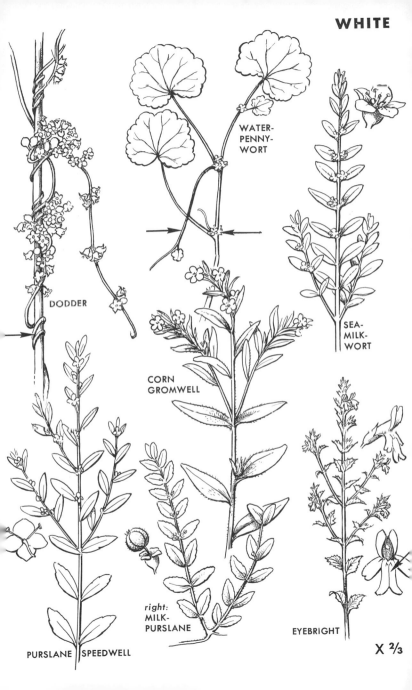

WHITE

WATER-
PENNY-
WORT

DODDER

SEA-
MILK-
WORT

CORN
GROMWELL

PURSLANE SPEEDWELL

right:
MILK-
PURSLANE

EYEBRIGHT

X ⅔

FLAT-TOPPED CLUSTERS; 5 "PETALS"

See also other flat-topped clusters, p. 46.

 YARROW Alien *Achillea millefolium*
COMPOSITE FAMILY (Compositae)
Note the soft, aromatic, much-dissected, *fernlike* leaves and flat, tight flower clusters. Although composite (inset), the 5 rays give each head the aspect of a 5-petaled flower. White, sometimes pink. 1–3 ft. *A. lanulosa* (not shown), native to western part of our area, is more densely woolly, has more narrowly dissected leaves. See also Sneezeweed Yarrow, *A. ptarmica*, p. 92. Roadsides, fields. Throughout.   JUNE–AUG.

FLOWERING SPURGE *Euphorbia corollata*
SPURGE FAMILY (Euphorbiaceae)
Note the milky juice in the broken stem. The 5 round white "petals" are really bracts that surround minute flower clusters. Leaves bright green, long-oval, smooth, alternate (except at base of inflorescence). The flat inflorescence is usually made up of 5 or 6 branches rising from a whorl of small leaves. 1–3 ft. Fields, roadsides, open woods. Minnesota, Wisconsin, Michigan, s. Ontario, New York south.   JUNE–OCT.

SNOW-ON-THE-MOUNTAIN *Euphorbia marginata*
SPURGE FAMILY (Euphorbiaceae)
Note the *broad white margins* on the leafy bracts. The tiny flowers, clustered at the center of the flat platform of bracts, have the typical spurge structure (inset). Juice milky. 1–3 ft. Prairies. Minnesota, Missouri west. Escaped from cultivation east to Atlantic.   JUNE–OCT.

 TALL CINQUEFOIL *Potentilla arguta*
ROSE FAMILY (Rosaceae)
The clammy brownish hairs and white or creamy flowers separate this from most of the other cinquefoils, which are yellow (p. 134). The flower structure and leaves, however, are typical of that genus (*Potentilla*), which belongs to the Rose Family. Leaflets 7 to 11, downy beneath. 1–3 ft. Rocky soil, dry woods, prairies. Across s. Canada and south to Missouri, Indiana, Ohio, and D.C.   JUNE–AUG.

RATTLESNAKE-MASTERS *Eryngium*
PARSLEY FAMILY (Umbelliferae)
The *spiny-edged, yucca-like leaves* and round heads of tiny 5-parted florets, often concealed by green bracts, identify these plants. Flower heads may have a bluish cast. 1½–4 ft. *E. aquaticum* is found in marshes, bogs; s. New Jersey south. *E. yuccifolium* is found in thickets, prairies; Minnesota, Wisconsin, Michigan, Ohio, New Jersey south.   SEPT.–NOV.

ROSE-PINK *Sabatia angularis*
GENTIAN FAMILY (Gentianaceae)
Usually rose; see color plate, p. 220. White in forma *albiflora*.

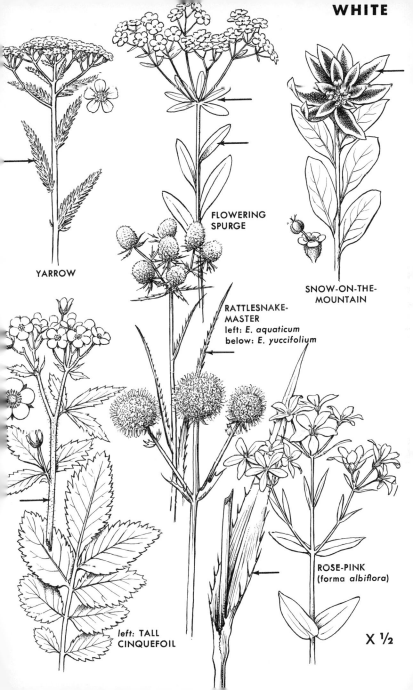

WHITE

YARROW

FLOWERING SPURGE

SNOW-ON-THE-MOUNTAIN

RATTLESNAKE-MASTER
left: *E. aquaticum*
below: *E. yuccifolium*

left: TALL CINQUEFOIL

ROSE-PINK
(forma *albiflora*)

X ½

FLAT-TOPPED CLUSTERS: THOROUGHWORTS

COMPOSITE OR DAISY FAMILY (Compositae)

The thoroughworts (*Eupatorium*), which include bonesets, Joe-Pye-weeds, etc., are composites of late summer and fall with numerous small fuzzy heads in rounded or flat-topped clusters. Leaves usually paired, sometimes in whorls. Of the 26 species in our area, about 20 are white and are best distinguished by their leaves. They are often confusing, subject to varietal forms and hybrids. We show 8 species here. See p. 298 (pink–red), p. 324 (violet–blue). See also False Boneset (*Kuhnia*), p. 88.

BONESET *Eupatorium perfoliatum*
Note the way the veiny, wrinkled leaves *unite basally* around the stem (perfoliate). A hairy plant. Low ground, thickets, swamps. Manitoba, Quebec, Nova Scotia south. JULY–OCT.

WHITE SNAKEROOT *Eupatorium rugosum*
Note the rather heart-shaped leaves on slender petioles (stalks) and the woodland habitat. Mostly smooth. Variable. Rich woods, thickets. Saskatchewan, Quebec south. JULY–OCT.

UPLAND BONESET *Eupatorium sessilifolium*
Note the slender-pointed, *sessile* (stalkless) leaves, *rounded* at base; 1 main vein. *E. altissimum* (not shown) has sessile leaves tapering at base, usually 3 main veins. Woodlands, uplands. Se. Minnesota, s. Vermont south, mainly uplands. JULY–SEPT.

LATE-FLOWERING THOROUGHWORT
Eupatorium serotinum
Note the *long-stalked* leaves, longer in general shape than the wide leaves of White Snakeroot; usually 3-veined. Low thickets, clearings, moist woods. Wisconsin, Indiana, Ohio, New Jersey south. SEPT.–OCT.

HYSSOP-LEAVED THOROUGHWORT
Eupatorium hyssopifolium
Note linear, *grasslike leaves in whorls of 4's* and smaller leaves in axils. Variable. Sandy soil, clearings, fields. Se. Ohio, Pennsylvania, s. New England south, mainly coast. AUG.–NOV.

HAIRY THOROUGHWORT *Eupatorium pilosum*
Note sessile leaves with relatively few blunt teeth (3–12 on each margin). Bogs, wet sandy soil. Coast from s. New England south and uplands from Virginia south. AUG.–SEPT.

WHITE-BRACTED THOROUGHWORT
Eupatorium leucolepis
Note the narrow, toothed leaves; often smaller leaves in axils. Bracts supporting flower heads white. Wet sandy soil. Coastal plain from Long Island south. AUG.–OCT.

ROUND-LEAVED THOROUGHWORT
Eupatorium rotundifolium
Note the *short sessile leaves*, almost as broad as long, with semi-clasping bases. Dry soil, open woods. Mainly near coast from Long Island and New Jersey south. JULY–SEPT.

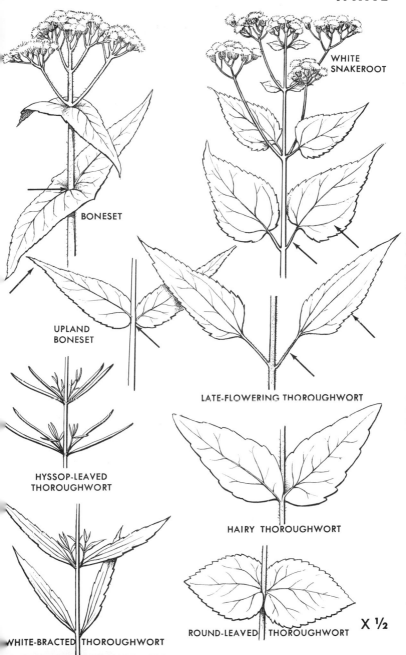

WHITE

WHITE SNAKEROOT

BONESET

UPLAND BONESET

LATE-FLOWERING THOROUGHWORT

HYSSOP-LEAVED THOROUGHWORT

HAIRY THOROUGHWORT

WHITE-BRACTED THOROUGHWORT

ROUND-LEAVED THOROUGHWORT

X ½

UMBRELLALIKE CLUSTERS (UMBELS); FINELY CUT LEAVES

PARSLEY FAMILY (Umbelliferae)
We present only a small selection of the 88 species of this family in our area. See also yellow species, p. 162.

WILD CARROT Alien   *Daucus carota*
The extremely flat clusters form a lace-like pattern (called Queen Anne's Lace); often a single tiny *deep purple* floret in center. Old flower clusters curl to form a *cuplike "bird's-nest,"* accounting for another popular name. Note the *stiff 3-forked bracts* below the main flower cluster. Leaves finely divided and subdivided. 2–3 ft. Roadsides, fields, dry waste ground. Throughout.   MAY–OCT.

FOOL'S-PARSLEY Alien   *Aethusa cynapium*
Note the way the long bracts hang, beardlike, below each secondary flower cluster. A poisonous, ill-smelling plant. 1–2½ ft. Fields, waste places. Local, s. Canada, n. U.S. JUNE–AUG.

POISON HEMLOCK Alien   *Conium maculatum*
A large, much-branched plant with finely divided, fernlike, dark green foliage. The hollow, grooved stems are *spotted with purple*. Unpleasant smell when bruised. Juices very poisonous. 2–6 ft. Waste ground. Nearly throughout.   JUNE–AUG.

HEMLOCK-PARSLEY   *Conioselinum chinense*
Similar to Wild Carrot (but with slender-branched, less showy flowers, more fernlike leaves). Similar also to Poison Hemlock (but lacks spotted stem and fatal qualities). 2–5 ft. Cold swamps, wet woods. W. Ontario and Labrador to n. U.S.; uplands to N. Carolina.   JULY–SEPT.

CARAWAY Alien   *Carum carvi*
Best known by its slightly curved, ribbed, aromatic seeds. Flower clusters usually lack bracts (Wild Carrot has 3-pronged bracts, larger flowers). Hairless; stems hollow, leaves narrowly cut. 1–2 ft. Waste places. E. Canada, ne. U.S.   MAY–JULY

MOCK BISHOP'S-WEED   *Ptilimnium capillaceum*
Note the *forked, threadlike leaves* and the forked threadlike bracts below the flower heads. 1–2 ft. Fresh or brackish marshes. S. Illinois, se. New York, s. New England south.
                                                            JULY–OCT.

BULB-BEARING WATER-HEMLOCK   *Cicuta bulbifera*
Note the very slender, simply-forked, sparsely toothed leaves and the *small bulblets* in the axils of the upper leaves. 1–3 ft. Swamps, wet places. Canada and south to Minnesota, Illinois, Indiana, Ohio, Virginia (uplands).   JULY–SEPT.

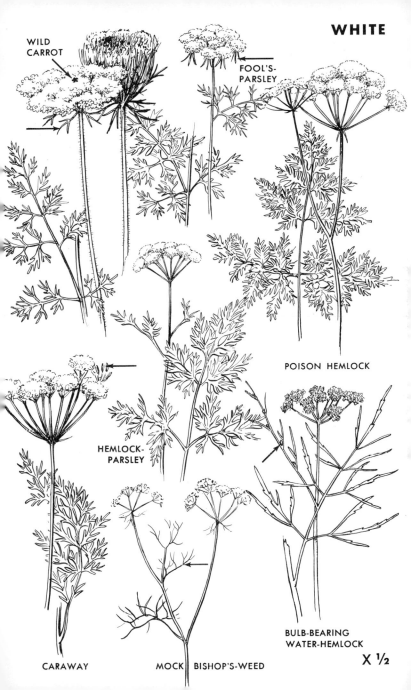

WHITE

WILD CARROT

FOOL'S-PARSLEY

POISON HEMLOCK

HEMLOCK-PARSLEY

CARAWAY

MOCK BISHOP'S-WEED

BULB-BEARING WATER-HEMLOCK

X ½

UMBRELLALIKE CLUSTERS (UMBELS); BROAD 3- OR 5-PART LEAVES

 COW-PARSNIP *Heracleum maximum*
PARSLEY FAMILY (Umbelliferae)
Huge; woolly, rank-smelling; the ridged, hollow stem may be 2 in. thick at base. Umbel up to 8 in.; petals notched, often tinged purple. Leaves often over 1 ft., divided into *3 maple-like segments; inflated sheath* at base of leafstalk. 4–10 ft. Moist ground. Canada, n. U.S.; mts. to Georgia. JUNE–AUG.

ANGELICA, ALEXANDERS *Angelica atropurpurea*
PARSLEY FAMILY (Umbelliferae)
Note the smooth, *dark purple* stem. Stalks of upper leaves with swollen basal sheath as in Cow-parsnip, but 3 leaflets may be *further divided into 3's or 5's.* 4–9 ft. Streambanks, swamps. E. Canada to Illinois, Indiana, Ohio, W. Virginia, Maryland, Delaware. JULY–OCT.

BRISTLY SARSAPARILLA *Aralia hispida*
GINSENG FAMILY (Araliaceae)
The umbels of the Ginseng Family are rounder than those of parsleys (Umbelliferae); fruits are berries. This species differs from Spikenard in being *bristly-stemmed*, fewer-umbeled; leaflets ovate, not heart-shaped. 1–3 ft. WILD SARSAPARILLA, *A. nudicaulis* (not shown), is smaller, *smooth;* flowers on separate stalk, lower than leaves. Dry open woods. Ne. Canada, n. U.S.; in mts. to N. Carolina. JUNE–AUG.

SPIKENARD *Aralia racemosa*
GINSENG FAMILY (Araliaceae)
A branching plant with a smooth blackish stem. Leaves divided and subdivided into *6 to 21 heart-shaped leaflets.* The round umbels of small flowers are arranged in a tall panicle. Roots aromatic. Fruit a dark purple berry. 3–5 ft. Rich woods. S. Canada, ne. U.S.; in mts. to Georgia. JUNE–AUG.

BLACK SNAKEROOT *Sanicula marilandica*
PARSLEY FAMILY (Umbelliferae)
The several species of *Sanicula* are recognized by long-stalked, *palmate* leaves (3 to 5 leaflets attached to same point as in Horse-chestnut.) Note *leafy bracts* at base of uneven umbels; also *round bristly fruits*. This species has 5 leaflets, lower 2 cleft so as to appear 7. *S. trifoliata* (leaf shown) has leaves divided into 3's (lateral segments cleft so as to appear 5). 1–4 ft. Thickets, open woods. Most of area. MAY–JULY

HONEWORT *Cryptotaenia canadensis*
PARSLEY FAMILY (Umbelliferae)
Leaves resemble those of Black Snakeroot, but note the slender, ribbed fruit and lack of sepals on florets. 1–3 ft. Woods. S. Canada south. JUNE–SEPT.

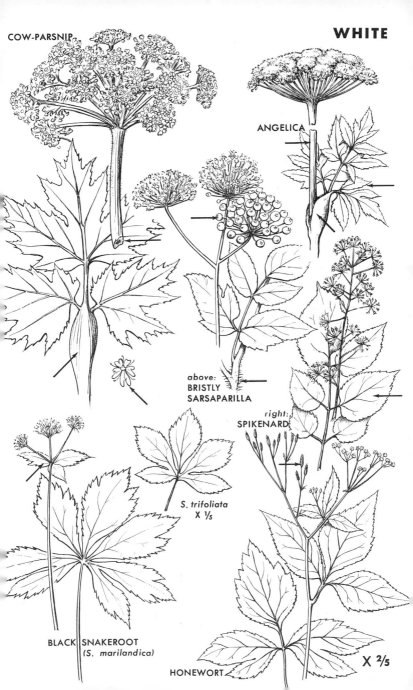

COW-PARSNIP

WHITE

ANGELICA

above:
BRISTLY
SARSAPARILLA

right:
SPIKENARD

S. trifoliata
X 1/5

BLACK SNAKEROOT
(S. marilandica)

HONEWORT

X 2/5

UMBRELLALIKE CLUSTERS (UMBELS); TOOTHED LEAFLETS

PARSLEY FAMILY (Umbelliferae), except Dwarf Ginseng

WATER-HEMLOCK, SPOTTED COWBANE *Cicuta maculata*
Note the smooth stout stem *streaked with purple*. The leaves
are twice- or thrice-compound, coarsely toothed, and often
tinged with reddish. Flowers in a looser umbel than that of
Wild Carrot (p. 48). Very poisonous to taste, as are several
other Umbelliferae. 3–6 ft. Wet meadows, swamps. S. Canada
south to Missouri, Maryland, N. Carolina (mts.). JUNE–SEPT.

WATER-PARSNIP *Sium suave*
Leaves divided into *3 to 7 pairs* of sharply toothed, *lance-shaped*
leaflets, as shown Basal leaves very finely dissected, often submerged. Stems strongly ridged. 2–6 ft. Swamps, wet meadows,
muddy water. Throughout. JULY–SEPT.

WATER-PARSNIP (not shown) *Berula pusilla*
Differs from preceding in coarser, more irregularly toothed or
incised leaves. Bracts below umbels leafier, often toothed.
Swamps, muddy water. Ontario south to Minnesota, Illinois,
Michigan. JULY–SEPT.

SWEET CICELY *Osmorhiza claytoni*
A soft, hairy plant with a round stem and wide *fernlike* leaves,
3 times compoundly divided; bluntly toothed. Lower leaves
large (often 1 ft. or more). Flowers very small; aggregate cluster
sparse. Roots with sweet odor of anise or licorice. 1½–3 ft.
A similar species, *O. longistylis* (not shown), is nearly smooth.
Moist woods. S. Canada south to Missouri and N. Carolina.
MAY–JUNE

HARBINGER-OF-SPRING *Erigenia bulbosa*
A tiny member of the family, growing from a round tuber.
Leaves 1 or 2, divided into narrow-oval or lobed segments.
Note *leafy bracts* at base of small, few-rayed umbels. 4–9 in.
Woods. Wisconsin, s. Ontario, w. New York south. FEB.–MAY

COWBANE *Oxypolis rigidior*
A tall, smooth, poisonous species. The deep green leaves are
very variable, as shown. The flat fruit has conspicuous marginal "wings." 2–6 ft. Swamps, wet places. Minnesota, Wisconsin, Michigan, Ohio, New York south. AUG.–SEPT.

DWARF GINSENG *Panax trifolius*
GINSENG FAMILY (Araliaceae))
A delicate plant with a whorl of 3 stalked leaves, each divided
into 3 (sometimes 5) stalkless leaflets. The small flowers (white
or pink) in the rounded umbel have narrower petals than those
of the Parsley Family. Root a round tuber. Fruit a yellow
berry. 4–8 in. Rich woods. S. Canada, n. U.S.; in mts. to
Georgia. APRIL–JUNE

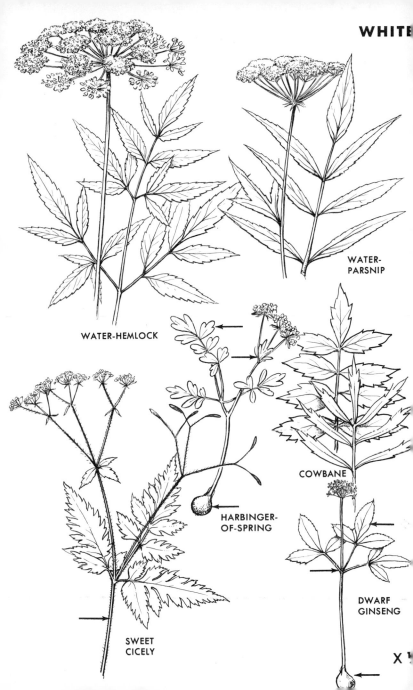

WHITE

WATER-PARSNIP

WATER-HEMLOCK

SWEET CICELY

HARBINGER-OF-SPRING

COWBANE

DWARF GINSENG

X ½

RADIATING CLUSTERS

 VIRGINIA WATERLEAF *Hydrophyllum virginianum*
WATERLEAF FAMILY (Hydrophyllaceae)
Note the long *protruding stamens* and irregularly cut *5- to 7-lobed leaves* (often marked as if stained with water). Flowers white or pale violet. 1–3 ft. See also color plate, p. 322. Woods. Manitoba, Quebec, w. New England south. MAY–AUG.

 LARGE-LEAVED WATERLEAF *Hydrophyllum macrophyllum*
(not shown)
WATERLEAF FAMILY (Hydrophyllaceae)
Similar to preceding but *rough-hairy*. Leaves more coarsely toothed; pinnately divided into *7 or more lobes*. Flowers white or pinkish. Rich woods. Illinois to Ohio, W. Virginia, and south. MAY–JUNE

 BROAD-LEAVED WATERLEAF *Hydrophyllum canadense*
WATERLEAF FAMILY (Hydrophyllaceae)
Flowers similar to above two, but note broader, *maple-like* leaves. Flower stalks below leaves. White to pale purple. 6–20 in. See also Appendaged Waterleaf, p. 322. Woods. S. Ontario, w. New England to Missouri, n. Alabama. JUNE–JULY

 WHITE MILKWEED *Asclepias variegata*
MILKWEED FAMILY (Asclepiadaceae)
Milkweeds may be known by their flower structure with 5 turned-back petals supporting a crown with 5 incurved horns (inset). This species is identified by combination of white flowers (purplish centers) and broadly ovate leaves. 2–3 ft. See also Poke Milkweed, p. 72. Upland woods. Se. Missouri, Illinois, Ohio, Pennsylvania, s. Connecticut south. MAY–JULY

WHORLED MILKWEED *Asclepias verticillata*
MILKWEED FAMILY (Asclepiadaceae)
Note the *linear leaves* in whorls of 3 to 6. Flower clusters often in leaf axils. 1–2 ft. Dry slopes, open woods. S. Manitoba, Wisconsin, Michigan, s. Ontario, New York, Massachusetts south. JUNE–SEPT.

WHITE BANEBERRY *Actaea pachypoda*
BUTTERCUP FAMILY (Ranunculaceae)
Flowers in a tight oblong cluster; very narrow petals (4–10) and long bushy stamens. Leaves divided and subdivided into sharply toothed leaflets, as shown. Fruit (inset) a cluster of white berries, each with a *thick red stalk* and a *black eye* ("doll's-eyes"). 1–2 ft. Woods. Manitoba, Ontario, e. Quebec to Oklahoma, Georgia (mts.). RED BANEBERRY, *A. rubra* (not shown), has a rounder flower cluster; berries red, on thinner stalks. MAY–JUNE

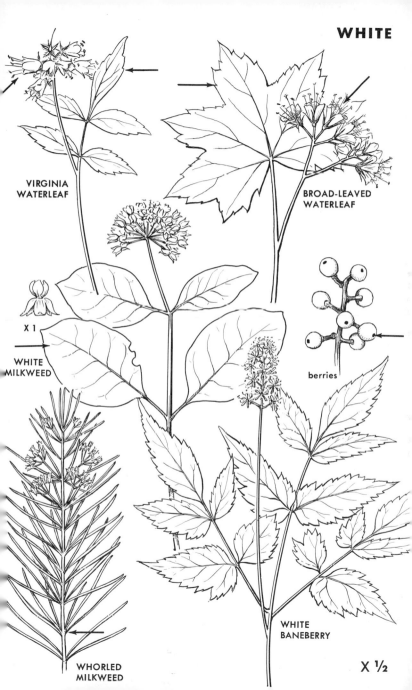

WHITE

VIRGINIA
WATERLEAF

BROAD-LEAVED
WATERLEAF

X 1

WHITE
MILKWEED

berries

WHORLED
MILKWEED

WHITE
BANEBERRY

X ½

Y-SHAPED OR DIVERGENT SPRAYS, TIPS OFTEN CURLED

 SPRING FORGET-ME-NOT   *Myosotis verna*
FORGET-ME-NOT FAMILY   (Boraginaceae)
Similar to the familiar blue forget-me-not (p. 334) but branches straighter, less curled; flowers a bit smaller, white. The 5 lobes of the calyx are unequal, bristly. 4–16 in. Dry woods, openings, banks. Minnesota to New England and south.   APRIL–JUNE

 SEASIDE HELIOTROPE   *Heliotropium curassavicum*
FORGET-ME-NOT FAMILY   (Boraginaceae)
Unlike the similar forget-me-nots, which are downy, this shore species is *smooth and fleshy*. Open, forms carpets. The sprays of white or bluish flowers are strongly curled. 6–18 in. Sandy shores, beaches, marsh edges. Mostly coastal, from Delaware south.   JUNE–OCT.

 EUROPEAN HELIOTROPE Alien   *Heliotropium europaeum*
FORGET-ME-NOT FAMILY   (Boraginaceae)
Similar to the preceding but covered with a *hoary whitish down*. Leaves oval, long-stalked. Flowers white or bluish. 6–30 in. Roadsides, waste places. Mainly from New Jersey south.
JUNE–SEPT.

 FALSE GROMWELL   *Onosmodium virginianum*
FORGET-ME-NOT FAMILY   (Boraginaceae)
Differs from the several preceding species in the flower shape; the sharp-pointed petals form a tube from which projects a long threadlike style. Tall; plant covered with harsh bristles. Flowers creamy white or yellow. 3–4 ft. Sandy soil, dry open woods. S. New England south in seaboard states. *O. occidentale* and *O. hispidissimum* (not shown) are similar whitish species of the Midwest.   JUNE–JULY

 WILD STONECROP   *Sedum ternatum*
SEDUM FAMILY   (Crassulaceae)
Flower spray usually has 3 curved or horizontal branches; petals sharply 5-pointed. Leaves very fleshy, toothless, usually in *whorls of 3*. Stems lie along ground, sending up erect stalks. 4–8 in. Damp rocks, banks. Illinois, Michigan, New York south, mostly in hills.   APRIL–JUNE

PHACELIAS (not shown)   *Phacelia*
WATERLEAF FAMILY   (Hydrophyllaceae)
The phacelias have coiled flower sprays but are usually blue (rarely white). See p. 334.

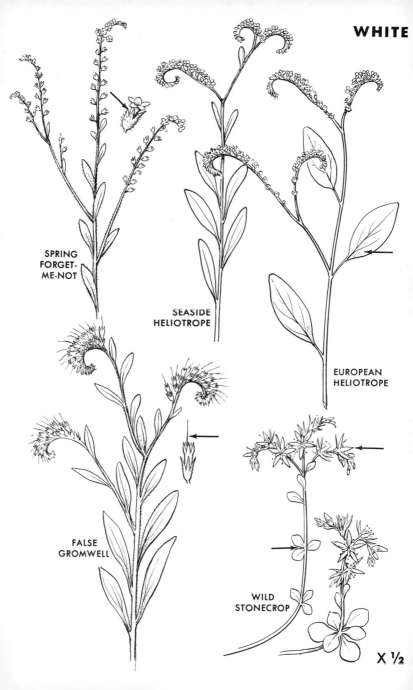

WHITE

SPRING
FORGET-
ME-NOT

SEASIDE
HELIOTROPE

EUROPEAN
HELIOTROPE

FALSE
GROMWELL

WILD
STONECROP

X ½

SHOWY SPIKES AND PANICLES

TURTLEHEAD   *Chelone glabra*
SNAPDRAGON FAMILY   (Scrophulariaceae)
The swollen, 2-lipped flowers, set in a tight cluster at the tip
of the stem, suggest the name. Upper lip arches over lower;
sometimes tinged with pink; leaves narrow, toothed, paired.
1–3 ft. Wet ground, streambanks. Minnesota, Ontario, Newfoundland south.   JULY–SEPT.

SILVER-ROD   *Solidago bicolor*
COMPOSITE FAMILY   (Compositae)
The aspect of the small, crowded, composite flowers indicates a
goldenrod. This is the only *white* species; wandlike. 1–3 ft.
Dry open woods. Across s. Canada to Maine and south.
                               JULY–OCT.

BEARDTONGUES   *Penstemon*
SNAPDRAGON FAMILY   (Scrophulariaceae)
The tubular, unevenly 5-lobed flowers derive their name from
the tuft of hairs on one of the stamens. Flower clusters stalked,
stalks rising in pairs from upper leaf axils. Leaves in pairs,
toothed, stalkless. There are at least 8 white or whitish species
in our area, mostly westward. A difficult genus, separated by
technical characters. The one shown here, FOXGLOVE BEARD-
TONGUE, *P. digitalis*, is the most widespread. 2–4 ft. See also
pp. 268, 344. Fields, prairies, open woods. S. Dakota, s.
Quebec, Maine south; adventive in East.   MAY–JULY

STRIPED GENTIAN   *Gentiana villosa*
GENTIAN FAMILY   (Gentianaceae)
The clustered tubular blossoms are of the bottle gentian type
(see blue species, p. 320). The "petals" are *joined by pleats* and
open only slightly; greenish white or purplish, striped within.
The broad, toothless leaves are narrow at the base. 6 in.–2 ft.
Open woods, pine barrens. S. Indiana, s. Ohio, New Jersey
south.   SEPT.–OCT.

WHITE MULLEIN Alien   *Verbascum lychnitis*
SNAPDRAGON FAMILY   (Scrophulariaceae)
A pyramidal cluster with short ascending branchlets. Flowers
white or yellow, smaller than other mulleins (½ in.); corolla
flat, 5-lobed, a little uneven. Plant covered with a *white woolliness;* stems branching, angled. Roadsides, sandy fields. Local,
Ontario, Massachusetts south to Virginia.   JUNE–SEPT.

MOTH MULLEIN Alien   *Verbascum blattaria*
SNAPDRAGON FAMILY   (Scrophulariaceae)
Flowers white with purplish base, or yellow (see color plate,
p. 106). Plant slender; note the scant leafage, *buttonlike buds,
orange anthers,* and *purplish beards* on stamens. 1–3 ft. Roadsides, vacant lots, waste places. Throughout (north to Quebec).
                               JUNE–OCT.

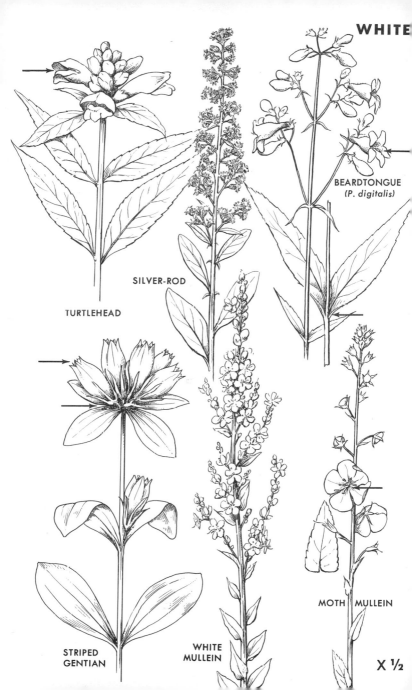

WHITE

BEARDTONGUE
(P. digitalis)

SILVER-ROD

TURTLEHEAD

STRIPED
GENTIAN

WHITE
MULLEIN

MOTH MULLEIN

X ½

SLENDER, TAPERING, DENSE CLUSTERS

LIZARD'S-TAIL, WATER-DRAGON   *Saururus cernuus*
LIZARD'S-TAIL FAMILY   (Saururaceae)
Note the *nodding tip* of the "tail" of minute blossoms and the
large, dark, *heart-shaped* leaves. 2–5 ft. Swamps, shallow water.
Minnesota, s. Michigan, s. Ontario, Rhode Island south.
JUNE–SEPT.

VIRGINIA KNOTWEED   *Tovara virginiana*
BUCKWHEAT FAMILY   (Polygonaceae)
Note the *tubed sheath* at base of each alternate leaf, the hallmark
of the smartweeds, or knotweeds (see also pp. 274, 276). This
whitish species has broad hairy leaves and sparse flowers hugging
the stem. Woods, thickets. Minnesota, s. Ontario, w. New
Hampshire south.   JULY–OCT.

CANADIAN BURNET   *Sanguisorba canadensis*
ROSE FAMILY   (Rosaceae)
Note the stalked, compound leaf with *7 to 15 toothed leaflets.*
Flowers have 4 white, petal-like sepals, long stamens. 1–6 ft.
Swamps, bogs. Manitoba, Newfoundland to Illinois, Ohio, n.
Delaware, and in mts. to Georgia.   JULY–OCT.

BLACK COHOSH, BUGBANE   *Cimicifuga racemosa*
BUTTERCUP FAMILY   (Ranunculaceae)
The stalked leaf is usually divided into 3's and further subdivided into 3's. Petals and sepals fall early, leaving bushy
tufts of stamens (1 pistil). 3–8 ft. Woods. Wisconsin, s. Ontario south to Missouri, Georgia.   JUNE–SEPT.
AMERICAN BUGBANE, *C. americana* (not shown), has several
pistils in each flower. Pennsylvania south in mts.

CULVER'S-ROOT   *Veronicastrum virginicum*
SNAPDRAGON FAMILY   (Scrophulariaceae)
The slender, sharp-toothed leaves are in *whorls of 3 to 7* around
the stem. Flowers tubelike, with 2 projecting stamens. 2–7 ft.
Moist meadows, woods, thickets. Manitoba, s. Ontario, Massa-
chusetts south.   JUNE–SEPT.

POKEWEED, POKE   *Phytolacca americana*
POKEWEED FAMILY   (Phytolaccaceae)
Note the coarse *reddish stems* of this weedy, large-leaved plant.
Greenish-white sepals look like petals. Flower clusters often
paired with leaves, fruiting clusters droop; berries purple-black,
with *red stalks.* 4–10 ft. Damp thickets, clearings, roadsides.
Minnesota, Ontario, Maine south.   JULY–SEPT.

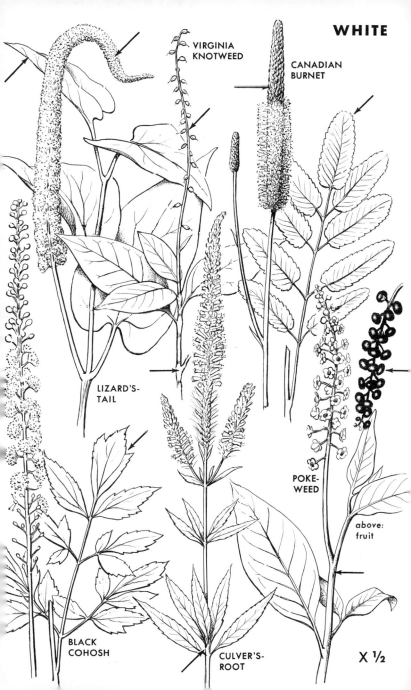

WHITE

VIRGINIA KNOTWEED

CANADIAN BURNET

LIZARD'S-TAIL

POKE-WEED

above: fruit

BLACK COHOSH

CULVER'S-ROOT

X ½

TAPERING, TIGHT CLUSTERS;
NUMEROUS SMALL FLOWERS

ENGLISH PLANTAIN Alien   *Plantago lanceolata*
PLANTAIN FAMILY   (Plantaginaceae)
A familiar dooryard weed with *slender* 3-ribbed leaves and a long, grooved stalk topped by a *short*, bushy flower head. 9–24 in. Waste places. Throughout.   APRIL–NOV.

SEASIDE PLANTAIN   *Plantago juncoides*
PLANTAIN FAMILY   (Plantaginaceae)
A seaside species with *fleshy*, linear leaves (1-nerved). Resembles preceding but flower stalk shorter, head longer. 2–8 in. Shores, cliffs. Coast south to New Jersey.   JUNE–SEPT.

COMMON PLANTAIN Alien   *Plantago major*
PLANTAIN FAMILY   (Plantaginaceae)
A low dooryard weed. Note the *broad* basal leaves and *long tight* flower head. Leaves ovate or spade-shaped; strongly ribbed and with troughlike stems. 6–18 in. Roadsides, waste places. Throughout. PALE PLANTAIN, *P. rugellii* (not shown), is similar, but the leaves are thinner and brighter green; stalks reddish at base, flower heads less dense, more attenuated at tip. Throughout.   JUNE–OCT.

GALAX, BEETLEWEED   *Galax aphylla*
DIAPENSIA FAMILY   (Diapensiaceae)
Note the glossy, *roundish*, *evergreen* leaves; also the red scaly bracts at base and reddish roots. 1–2 ft. Mt. woods. W. Virginia, Virginia south.   MAY–JULY

WHORLED MILKWORT   *Polygala verticillata*
MILKWORT FAMILY   (Polygalaceae)
Note the short linear leaves in *whorls of 3 to 6*. Flowers white, greenish, or pinkish. 6–12 in. Fields, open places. Manitoba, south to Maine and Ontario south.   JUNE–OCT.

SENECA SNAKEROOT   *Polygala senega*
MILKWORT FAMILY   (Polygalaceae)
The small pealike blossoms are in a looser cluster than in the preceding. Leaves attached *singly*. 6–18 in. Rocky woods. Alberta, Quebec, New Brunswick south.   MAY–JULY

WHITE VERVAIN   *Verbena urticifolia*
VERVAIN FAMILY   (Verbenaceae)
Note the paired, toothed, nettle-like leaves and the very small white flowers that bloom sparingly along the very slender, branched spikes. 3–5 ft. Thickets, wood edges. S. Ontario, w. Maine south.   JUNE–SEPT.

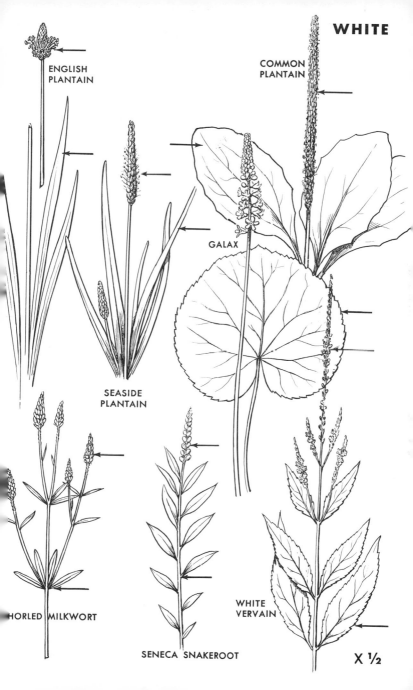

WHITE

ENGLISH PLANTAIN

COMMON PLANTAIN

GALAX

SEASIDE PLANTAIN

HORLED MILKWORT

SENECA SNAKEROOT

WHITE VERVAIN

X ½

SHOWY CLUSTERS; NARROW LINEAR LEAVES
LILY FAMILY (Liliaceae)
Flowers 6-parted; leaves most numerous near base.

STAR-OF-BETHLEHEM Alien   *Ornithogalum umbellatum*
Note the *green stripe* on the underside of the waxy petals
(flowers 1¼ in.; open only in sunshine). The grasslike leaves
often have a *whitish midrib*. 4–12 in. Fields, roadsides, near
houses. Ontario, Newfoundland south.   APRIL–JUNE

BUNCHFLOWER   *Melanthium virginicum*
Numerous flowers, creamy white at first, dull green to purplish
later. Note petal shape (*narrow at base*). Long rough leaves
mostly basal, may be 1 in. wide. 3–5 ft. Meadows, wet thickets.
Illinois, Ohio, s. New York south.   JUNE–JULY

FLY-POISON   *Amianthium muscaetoxicum*
Similar to Bunchflower but note different petal structure, more
compact cluster. 1½–4 ft. Sandy woods. Coastal plain, Long
Island south; mts. from Pennsylvania south.   MAY–JULY

FEATHERBELLS   *Stenanthium gramineum*
Note the *long points* on the starlike flowers. The myriad blossoms may form a cluster 1 to 2 ft. long. The grasslike leaves are
keeled (folded lengthwise); most numerous near base but some
ascend stem. 3–5 ft. Woods, thickets. Illinois, Indiana, Pennsylvania to Missouri, se. Virginia; south in mts.   JUNE–SEPT.

TURKEYBEARD (not shown)   *Xerophyllum asphodeloides*
Another large many-flowered cluster. Flowers lack the slender
points of Featherbells. Note the tussock of long dry grasslike
leaves (up to 2 ft.) at base and the much shorter, rigid leaves
ascending stem. 2–5 ft. Pine barrens of New Jersey; also mt.
woods of Virginia, Tennessee, N. Carolina.   MAY–JULY

DEVIL'S-BIT   *Chamaelirium luteum*
Note the graceful *tightly packed spike*, often drooping at tip.
Inset shows staminate flower. Pistillate flowers on separate
plants. Smooth leaves in basal rosette; narrower leaves ascend
stem. 1–3 ft. Moist meadows, thickets, woods. Illinois,
Michigan, s. Ontario, New York, Massachusetts south.
                                                        MAY–JULY

COLICROOT, STARGRASS   *Aletris farinosa*
The rough, *swollen-based* flowers hug the nearly leafless flowering stalk. The leaves, narrowing at base and tip, form a basal
rosette. 1½–3 ft. Dry or peaty soil. Wisconsin, Michigan, s.
Ontario, sw. Maine south.   MAY–AUG.

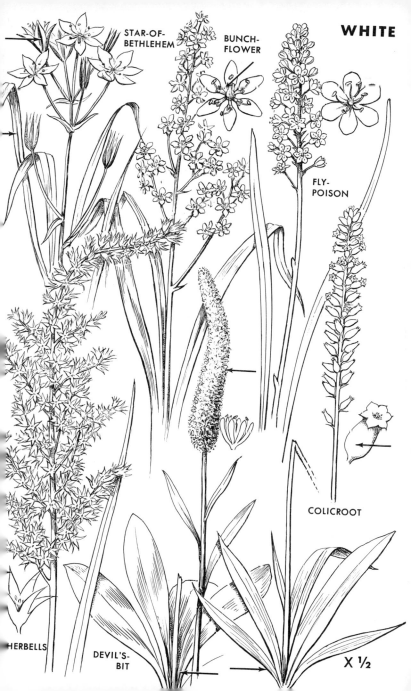

STAR-OF-
BETHLEHEM

BUNCH-
FLOWER

WHITE

FLY-
POISON

COLICROOT

HERBELLS

DEVIL'S-
BIT

X ½

TERMINAL CLUSTERS;
BROAD PARALLEL-VEINED LEAVES
LILY FAMILY (Liliaceae)

FALSE SOLOMON'S-SEAL *Smilacina racemosa*
The oval, pointed leaves alternate along the gracefully reclining stem, which is tipped with a spirea-like cluster of creamy-white flowers. Fruit a berry, at first whitish speckled with brown, later ruby-red. **Note:** The true Solomon's-seals (p. 102) have their flowers *in the leaf axils*, not in terminal clusters. Woods. Across Canada to Nova Scotia and south to Missouri, mts. of N. Carolina. MAY–JULY

STARRY FALSE SOLOMON'S-SEAL *Smilacina stellata*
Smaller than preceding, with larger, starry flowers. Leaves *clasp* the zigzag stem and are closer together (overlapping in coastal variety *crassa*). Berries become *nearly black*. Moist open places, dunes. Across s. Canada and south to Kansas, Missouri, Illinois, Ohio, s. Virginia (uplands), New Jersey.
MAY–AUG.

THREE-LEAVED FALSE SOLOMON'S-SEAL
Smilacina trifolia
A small species, usually with 3 leaves (or 2 or 4); resembles next species, but *leaf bases taper* and sheathe the stem. Flowers *6-pointed*. Berries turn *deep red*. 2–6 in. Cool woods, bogs. N. Canada south to Minnesota, n. Illinois, Michigan, n. Ohio, Pennsylvania, n. New Jersey. MAY–AUG.

WILD LILY-OF-THE-VALLEY, CANADA MAYFLOWER
Maianthemum canadense
Much like the preceding species but leaves usually 2 (sometimes 3). Note the deeply cleft, *heart-shaped leaf bases* and *4-pointed* flowers. Berries *white* with spots, later turning *pale red*. Often forms large beds. 3–6 in. Woods and clearings. Manitoba, Labrador south to Iowa, Tennessee (uplands), Georgia (uplands), and Delaware. MAY–JULY

WHITE CLINTONIA *Clintonia umbellulata*
The tight umbel of fragrant flowers, dotted with green and purple, is born at the tip of a downy stalk, to be succeeded by round black berries. The 2 to 5 wide basal leaves are similar to those of yellow Clintonia (p. 102). 8–20 in. Woods. E. Ohio, w. New York; south in mts. to Georgia. MAY–JULY

WILD LEEK *Allium tricoccum*
The 2 or 3 broad, smooth, onion-scented leaves (8–10 in.) wither before the spokelike umbel of flowers comes into bloom. Note the onion-reeking bulb (see other wild onions, p. 296). 6–18 in. Rich woods. Minnesota, s. Quebec, Nova Scotia south to Iowa, Illinois, Maryland; in mts. to Georgia. JUNE–JULY

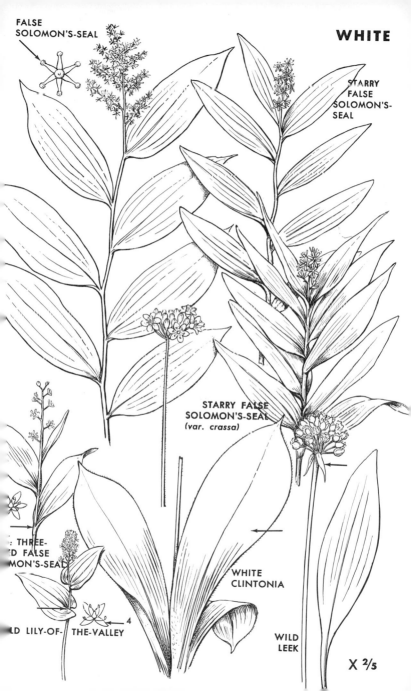

FALSE
SOLOMON'S-SEAL

WHITE

STARRY
FALSE
SOLOMON'S-
SEAL

STARRY FALSE
SOLOMON'S-SEAL
(var. crassa)

THREE-
D FALSE
MON'S-SEAL

WHITE
CLINTONIA

LD LILY-OF- THE-VALLEY

4

WILD
LEEK

X ²/₅

TERMINAL CLUSTERS; FRAGILE FLOWERS; MISCELLANEOUS LEAVES

1. **LEAVES ON STEM** (enchanter's nightshades)
EVENING-PRIMROSE FAMILY   (Onagraceae)

ENCHANTER'S NIGHTSHADE   *Circaea quadrisulcata*
The tiny flowers have *2 deeply notched petals*, 2 reflexed sepals.
Leaves paired, irregularly toothed. 1–2 ft. Woods. N. Dakota,
s. Ontario, Nova Scotia south.   JUNE–AUG.

SMALLER ENCHANTER'S NIGHTSHADE   *Circaea alpina*
Smaller than the preceding. Leaves more coarsely toothed and
with a somewhat *heart-shaped* base. 3–8 in. Cold woods. N.
Canada to n. U.S. and in mts. to Georgia.   JULY–SEPT.

2. **LEAVES MOSTLY BASAL** (Miterwort also has stem leaves)
SAXIFRAGE FAMILY   (Saxifragaceae)

MITERWORT   *Mitella diphylla*
Known from the following 4 species by the *pair of stalkless
leaves* on the stem below the flowers (also has stalked basal
leaves). Note the *beautifully fringed flower*. 10–18 in. Rich
woods. Minnesota, sw. Quebec, New Hampshire south to mts.
of Missouri, S. Carolina.   APRIL–MAY

NAKED MITERWORT (not shown)   *Mitella nuda*
Similar to *M. diphylla* but smaller; usually lacks stem leaves;
basal leaves more rounded (see p. 376). Fringes on flowers more
threadlike. 3–8 in. Cool woods, bogs. N. Canada south to
Minnesota, Michigan, n. Ohio, Pennsylvania.   MAY–AUG.

FOAMFLOWER, FALSE MITERWORT   *Tiarella cordifolia*
Similar to Miterwort but lacks the stem leaves and has a very
different flower structure (no fringes; *very long stamens*). 6–12 in.
Rich woods. Minnesota, Ontario, Nova Scotia south, mainly
in mts., to Georgia.   APRIL–MAY

EARLY SAXIFRAGE   *Saxifraga virginiensis*
Gray recognizes 17 species of *Saxifraga* in our area. This and
the next are the most familiar. Note the sticky-hairy stem and
rosette of broadly toothed oval leaves (1–3 in.) nearly as wide
as long. The 5-petaled white flowers have 10 bright yellow
stamens. 4–10 in. Dry woods, rocky fields. Minnesota, New
Brunswick south.   MARCH–MAY

SWAMP SAXIFRAGE   *Saxifraga pensylvanica*
Much larger, with bluntly lance-shaped, toothless leaves (4–10
in.). Variable. Flowers may be whitish, greenish, yellowish,
or purplish. 1–3½ ft. Swamps, low meadows. Minnesota, s.
Ontario, s. Maine south to Missouri, Virginia.   MAY–JUNE

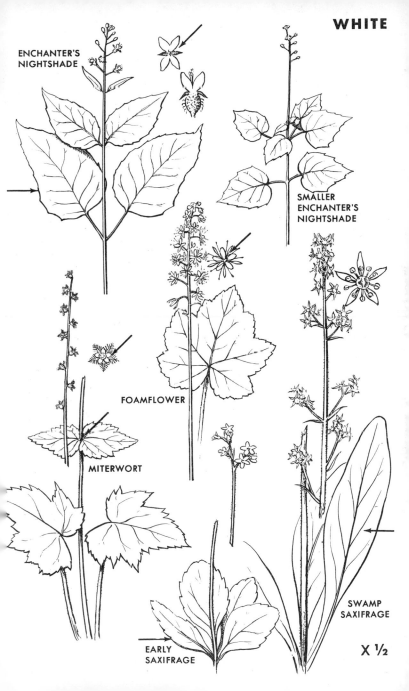

WHITE

ENCHANTER'S
NIGHTSHADE

SMALLER
ENCHANTER'S
NIGHTSHADE

FOAMFLOWER

MITERWORT

EARLY
SAXIFRAGE

SWAMP
SAXIFRAGE

X ½

LOOSE CLUSTERS: MISCELLANEOUS

 BUCKWHEAT Alien   *Fagopyrum sagittatum*
BUCKWHEAT FAMILY   (Polygonaceae)
Note the *arrowhead-shaped leaves* and the *swollen sheaths* where they are attached (upper leaf clasping). Flowers in a branching spray, greenish white or pink. Stem often reddish. 1–2 ft. Waste places. Widespread.   JUNE–SEPT.

CLIMBING FALSE BUCKWHEAT   *Polygonum scandens*
BUCKWHEAT FAMILY   (Polygonaceae)
Leaves similar to those in preceding but plant *a twining vine.* Flower spray more slender, less showy. Stems reddish, rough. Damp thickets, woods, shores. S. Canada south.   AUG.–NOV.

BIENNIAL GAURA   *Gaura biennis*
EVENING-PRIMROSE FAMILY   (Onagraceae)
The long-tubed flowers (white; pink with age) bloom 2 or 3 at a time in clusters on long wandlike spikes; petals 4, stamens 8. Note the cross-shaped stigma (inset) typical of the Evening-primrose Family. 2–5 ft. Meadows, prairies, shores. Minnesota to w. Quebec; south to Missouri, Tennessee, Virginia.
                                      JUNE–OCT.

BASTARD-TOADFLAX   *Comandra umbellata*
SANDALWOOD FAMILY   (Santalaceae)
A root parasite. A small plant with elliptical leaves attached singly; pale beneath, with pale midrib. The small blossoms are composed of a cuplike base with 5 sepals on the rim (no petals). Each sepal conceals a stamen. 6–16 in. Dry soil, thickets. Michigan to Maine and south.   APRIL–JUNE

 INTERMEDIATE DOGBANE   *Apocynum medium*
DOGBANE FAMILY   (Apocynaceae)
See Spreading Dogbane, p. 292. This species is believed by some to be a hybrid between Spreading Dogbane and Indian Hemp. Its flowers lack the strongly recurved lobes of the Spreading Dogbane and are less pink, often white. 1–4 ft. Fields, roadsides, shores. S. Canada to Missouri, Virginia.
                                      JUNE–AUG.

INDIAN HEMP   *Apocynum cannabinum*
DOGBANE FAMILY   (Apocynaceae)
Similar to the preceding but leaves narrower, with more tapering shape; flowers less showy than in it or Spreading Dogbane; smaller, greenish white. 1–4 ft. Open thickets, shores. Most of our area.   JUNE–AUG.

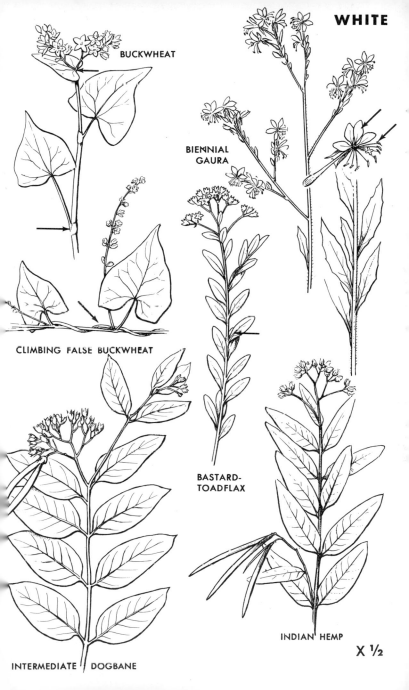

WHITE

BUCKWHEAT

BIENNIAL GAURA

CLIMBING FALSE BUCKWHEAT

BASTARD-TOADFLAX

INTERMEDIATE DOGBANE

INDIAN HEMP

X ½

LOOSE CLUSTERS OR SPRAYS OF DANGLING FLOWERS

POKE MILKWEED   *Asclepias exaltata*
MILKWEED FAMILY   (Asclepiadaceae)
Milkweeds have distinctive flowers with 5 petals bent sharply back, supporting a crown with 5 incurved horns. Juices milky. This species has drooping clusters of white flowers tinged with lavender or green. Leaves stalked, pointed at both ends, often drooping. 3–6 ft. Woods. Minnesota, s. Maine south.

                                           JUNE–AUG.

DUTCHMAN'S-BREECHES   *Dicentra cucullaria*
POPPY FAMILY   (Papaveraceae)
BLEEDING-HEART SUBFAMILY   (Fumarioideae)
A delicate spray of waxy, yellow-tipped flowers drooping in a row from an arched stem. Each flower has *2 inflated spurs* that suggest the legs of tiny pantaloons, "ankles-up." Leaves much dissected. Roots a cluster of many small white tubers. 5–9 in. Rich woods. Se. Canada, n. U.S. (west to N. Dakota); south in mts. to Georgia.   APRIL–MAY

SQUIRREL-CORN   *Dicentra canadensis*
POPPY FAMILY   (Papaveraceae)
BLEEDING-HEART SUBFAMILY   (Fumarioideae)
Similar to Dutchman's-breeches but flowers more *heart-shaped*, fragrant, and *lack elongated spurs*. Roots resemble grains of yellow corn. 6–12 in. Woods. Minnesota to sw. Quebec; south to Missouri, Tennessee, N. Carolina.   APRIL–MAY

COMMON NIGHTSHADE Alien   *Solanum nigrum*
TOMATO FAMILY   (Solanaceae)
Note reflexed petals, protruding yellow beak formed by stamens around pistil. Leaves roughly triangular, with irregular teeth. Fruit a black berry. 1–2½ ft. *S. dulcamara* (violet flower, red berry) can be white; see p. 324. Waste places. Our area.

                                         MAY–SEPT.

EARLY MEADOW-RUE   *Thalictrum dioicum*
BUTTERCUP FAMILY   (Ranunculaceae)
An *early* species, with *drooping* flowers and foliage. Flowers seem to have 4 to 5 petals (really sepals); greenish white or purple-tipped. 1–2 ft. Purple Meadow-rue, *T. dasycarpum* (see p. 390), often has purplish stem; flowers tinged with purple. SKUNK MEADOW-RUE, *T. revolutum* (not shown), has waxy glands (visible by lens) under leaflets. Woods. Minnesota, s. Ontario, sw. Quebec, Maine south.   APRIL–MAY

TALL MEADOW-RUE   *Thalictrum polygamum*
BUTTERCUP FAMILY   (Ranunculaceae)
Taller, *later* than *T. diocum*. An intricate plant; plumes of flowers lack petals. Note *starry bursts of white threadlike stamens*. Leaves divided and subdivided into many roundish 3-lobed leaflets. 3–8 ft. Swamps, streamsides. E. Canada to Indiana, Long Island; in mts. to Georgia.   JULY–SEPT.

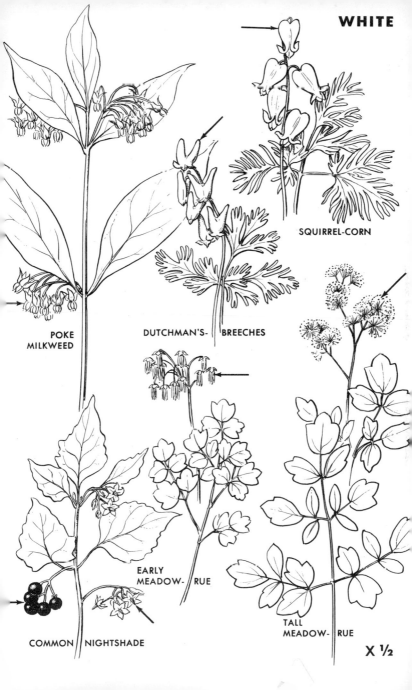

WHITE

SQUIRREL-CORN

POKE
MILKWEED

DUTCHMAN'S- BREECHES

EARLY
MEADOW- RUE

COMMON NIGHTSHADE

TALL
MEADOW- RUE

X ½

LOOSE CLUSTERS OF DANGLING BELLS:
RATTLESNAKE-ROOTS
Composite or Daisy Family (Compositae)

The rattlesnake-roots are tall, slender weeds with boldly cut, triangular or deeply lobed leaves, attached singly. The leaf shape is extremely variable. The bell-like flowers are composite, with creamy-white rays (often tinged with greenish or lilac), but unlike most composites they hang in *drooping clusters* and do not face the sun. The broken stems exude a copious milky juice. There are 10 species in our area, separable on technical characters. See also p. 292.

WHITE LETTUCE, RATTLESNAKE-ROOT *Prenanthes alba*
Note the *cinnamon-brown* pappus beneath the floral envelope (inset). Stem smooth, purplish, with a whitish bloom. 2–5 ft. Rich woods, thickets. Quebec south to Missouri and Georgia (in mts.).   Aug.–Sept.

LION'S-FOOT   *Prenanthes serpentaria*
Somewhat similar to the preceding, but the pappus is creamy and the enfolding floral bracts are rather bristly. Stem usually without bloom, leaves rougher. Flowers creamy white or pink. 1½–4 ft. Dry woods, thickets. Ohio, New York, Massachusetts south.   Sept.–Oct.

GALL-OF-THE-EARTH   *Prenanthes trifoliata*
This creamy-white species has waxy, pale green or pinkish bracts. It is a smooth plant with a waxy reddish stem. 1–5 ft. A dwarf variety (*nana*) is found on mountaintops of n. New England. Thickets, clearings, open slopes. Newfoundland south, mainly in mts., to Tennessee.   Sept.–Oct.

TALL WHITE LETTUCE   *Prenanthes altissima*
Note that the flowers have fewer bracts, *usually 5* (the other *Prenanthes* usually have about 8 principal bracts). The flowers are usually greenish white; pappus is creamy white. Leaves extremely variable. 2–7 ft. Moist woods. Manitoba and Quebec south. A variety with cinnamon pappus (*cinnamomea*) is found in the Mississippi Valley from Indiana south.
                                                        July–Oct.

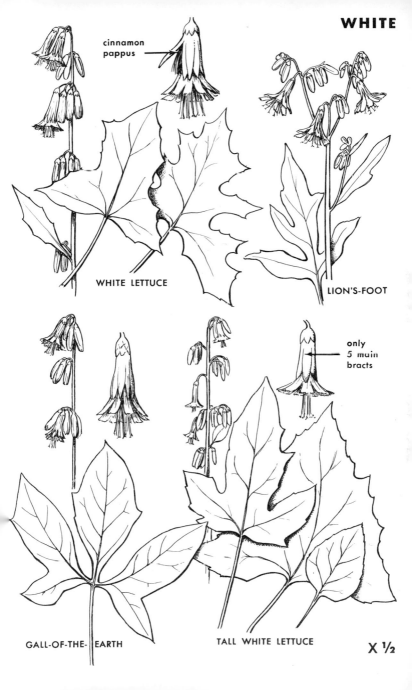

WHITE

cinnamon
pappus

WHITE LETTUCE

LION'S-FOOT

only
5 main
bracts

GALL-OF-THE- EARTH

TALL WHITE LETTUCE

X ½

CLUSTERS IN LEAF AXILS: CLIMBING PLANTS

BUR-CUCUMBER   *Sicyos angulatus*
CUCUMBER FAMILY   (Cucurbitaceae)
Note the lobed *maple-like* leaves and the tendrils and flower clusters in the axils. Distinguished from the next species by its *5-petaled* flowers and *clustered* fruits, each with a single seed. Streambanks, thickets. Minnesota, Quebec, s. Maine south.
                                       JULY–SEPT.

WILD CUCUMBER, BALSAM-APPLE   *Echinocystis lobata*
CUCUMBER FAMILY   (Cucurbitaceae)
Distinguished from the preceding species by its *6-petaled* flowers and *single*, large (up to 2 in.), fleshy fruit, which is covered with weak prickles and soon dries out; 4 flat seeds. Moist streambanks, thickets. S. Canada south.   JUNE–OCT.

VIRGIN'S-BOWER   *Clematis virginiana*
BUTTERCUP FAMILY   (Ranunculaceae)
Note the 3 sharply toothed leaflets and clusters of attractive 4-sepaled flowers in the leaf axils. These are succeeded in autumn by *gray silky plumes* adhering to the seeds (hence the name "Old Man's Beard"). Thickets, wood edges, streambanks. Manitoba, Quebec, Nova Scotia south.   JULY–SEPT.

CLIMBING HEMPWEED   *Mikania scandens*
COMPOSITE FAMILY   (Compositae)
Note the *triangular*, opposite leaves and the cluster of boneset-like flowers (also called Climbing Boneset). Flowers may be white or flesh-pink. Streambanks, moist thickets. Ontario, Maine south.   JULY–OCT.

CANADA MOONSEED   *Menispermum canadense*
MOONSEED FAMILY   (Menispermaceae)
This woody climber has large (5–10 in.) variable leaves, sometimes nearly round, with a pointed tip, but more often with 3 to 7 shallow lobes. The leaf bases are *not attached* to the stalks. The clusters of small flowers develop into black fruits resembling wild grapes. See also *A Field Guide to Trees and Shrubs*, p. 224. Streambanks. Se. Manitoba, w. Quebec, w. New England south.
                                       JUNE–JULY

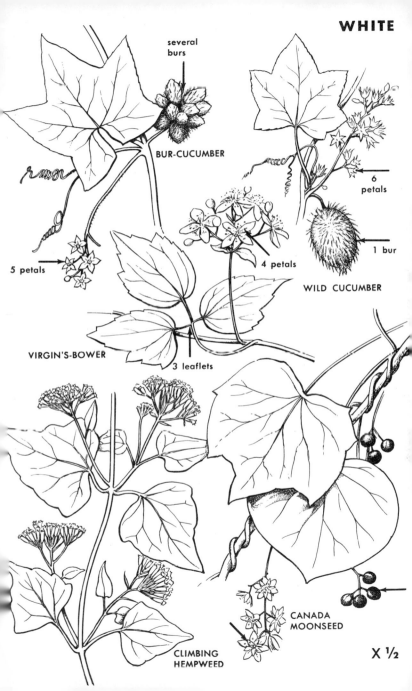

WHITE

several burs

BUR-CUCUMBER

6 petals

5 petals

4 petals

1 bur

WILD CUCUMBER

VIRGIN'S-BOWER

3 leaflets

CLIMBING HEMPWEED

CANADA MOONSEED

X ½

SQUARE STEMS, PAIRED LEAVES: MINTS
CLUSTERS OF LOBED, 2-LIPPED FLOWERS
Mint Family (Labiatae)
Lower lip usually has 3 lobes, upper 2.

MOUNTAIN-MINTS *Pycnanthemum*
Fifteen in our area; those below widespread. Most have rather flat-topped, branching clusters of roundish heads on which few florets bloom at a time. Best distinguished by leaves. 1–2½ ft. Dry woods, thickets, fields, uplands. JULY–SEPT.

VIRGINIA MT.-MINT, *P. virginiana.* Narrow, tapering, toothless leaves, broad at base. N. Dakota to Maine and south to Missouri, Ohio, Long Island; mts. to N. Carolina.

TORREY'S MT.-MINT, *P. verticillatum.* Slender leaves, slightly toothed, tapering at base. Michigan, sw. Quebec south.

HAIRY MT.-MINT, *P. pilosum.* Leaves broader, stalked; stem and leaves hairy. Sw. Ontario, s. Michigan south.

SHORT-TOOTHED MT.-MINT, *P. muticum.* Leaves broad, toothed; rounded at base. Michigan, Illinois to sw. Maine and south.

NARROW-LEAVED MT.-MINT, *P. tenuifolium.* Extremely narrow leaves. Minnesota, Wisconsin, s. Michigan, n. New York, New England south.

HOARY MT.-MINT, *P. icanum.* Broad, toothed leaves similar to *P. muticum,* but stalked and covered with white down beneath. S. Illinois, w. New York, s. New Hampshire south.

WATER-HOREHOUNDS, BUGLEWEEDS *Lycopus*
Small flowers in clusters in leaf axils. 8 species in our area; we show 2. (1) CUT-LEAVED WATER-HOREHOUND, *L. americanus.* Deeply cut, almost oaklike lobes on lower leaves. 1–2 ft. Wet places. Throughout. JULY–SEPT. (2) BUGLEWEED, *L. virginicus.* Similar, with strongly toothed but not lobed leaves. Suggestive of Wild Mint but quite smooth and without odor. 6–24 in. Wet soil. Minnesota, Wisconsin, Indiana, Ohio, New York, New England south. JULY–OCT.

WHITE DEAD-NETTLE Alien *Lamium album*
Leaves heart-shaped, toothed, suggesting nettle. Flowers in leaf axils; rather large, with wide-open mouth and 3 bristly calyx teeth. 6–12 in. Waste places. Local. MAY–OCT.

CATNIP Alien *Nepeta cataria*
Stalked, jagged, arrow-shaped leaves; whitish beneath. Minty smell attractive to cats. Flowers crowded; white with pink spots. 6–24 in. Waste places. Widespread. JUNE–SEPT.

WILD MINT *Mentha arvensis*
Note the strong mint odor. Downy or hairy. The tiny white, pale violet, or lavender flowers in leaf axils are bell-shaped. 6–24 in. Damp soil, shores. Canada, n. U.S. JULY–SEPT.

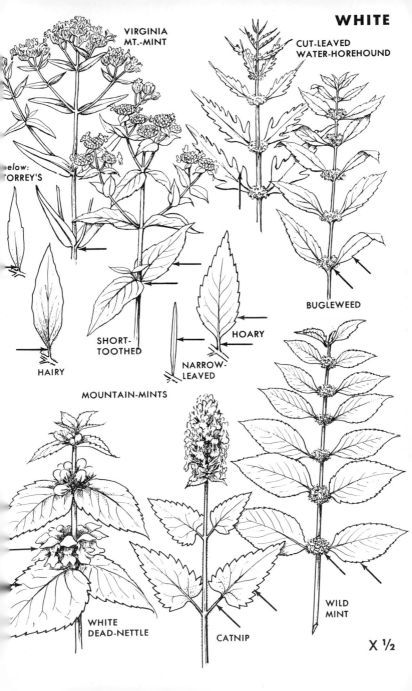

WHITE

VIRGINIA
MT.-MINT

CUT-LEAVED
WATER-HOREHOUND

below:
TORREY'S

BUGLEWEED

HAIRY

SHORT-
TOOTHED

HOARY

NARROW-
LEAVED

MOUNTAIN-MINTS

WILD
MINT

WHITE
DEAD-NETTLE

CATNIP

X ½

CLUSTERS OF SMALL PEALIKE FLOWERS; 3 LEAFLETS (CLOVERS, ETC.)
PEA FAMILY (Leguminosae)

WHITE CLOVER Alien   *Trifolium repens*
Note the *pale triangular mark* on each leaflet. Flowers and leaves grown on separate stalks from creeping runners. The heads of pealike flowers may be white or tinged with pink. 4–10 in. Fields, roadsides, lawns. Throughout.   MAY–OCT.

ALSIKE CLOVER Alien   *Trifolium hybridum*
The leaves of this clover are not marked with triangles, and they spring from branching stems. Flowers creamy white to pink. 1–2 ft. Fields, roadsides. Throughout.   MAY–OCT.

BUFFALO CLOVER   *Trifolium stoloniferum*
Note the heart-shaped leaflets (notched at tip). Leaves branch off stem. Long basal runners. Flowers white or white and red. 4–16 in. Dry woods, prairies. W. Virginia and Kentucky west to S. Dakota and e. Kansas.   MAY–JULY

WHITE SWEET CLOVER, MELILOT Alien *Melilotus alba*
The tripart leaves and shape of the flowers are cloverlike but the flowers are in *slender, tapering clusters*. Leaves fragrant. 2–8 ft. See also Yellow Sweet Clover, p. 150. Roadsides, field edges. Throughout.   MAY–OCT.

ROUND-HEADED BUSH-CLOVER   *Lespedeza capitata*
The bush-clovers, their stems crowded with short-stemmed cloverlike leaves, run the gamut of pinks, purples, yellows (see p. 246). This bushy, slender-leaved species has creamy-white flowers (pink near base) in dense, bristly clusters. 2–5 ft. Dry soil, sandy fields. Minnesota, Wisconsin, Ontario, New England south.   AUG.–SEPT.

HAIRY BUSH-CLOVER   *Lespedeza hirta*
Another creamy-white bush-clover. Note the *roundish* or oval leaflets and densely hairy stem. Variable. 2–3 ft. Dry open places, roadsides. S. Ontario, sw. Maine south.   JULY–OCT.

TICK-TREFOILS   *Desmodium*
Tick-trefoils are tall spindly plants with open flower clusters of small pealike blossoms and *jointed seedpods* (see inset). Most are pink or lavender (pp. 224, 248). The one shown here, *D. illinoense*, has white flowers and prominent stipules at the bases of the leafstalks. 3–6 ft. Prairies. Nebraska, Wisconsin, s. Michigan south to Oklahoma, Missouri, n. Ohio. Another white species, *D. pauciflorum*, has relatively few-flowered clusters that spring from the leaf axils. Woods. Kansas, Missouri, Ohio, w. New York south.   JULY–AUG.

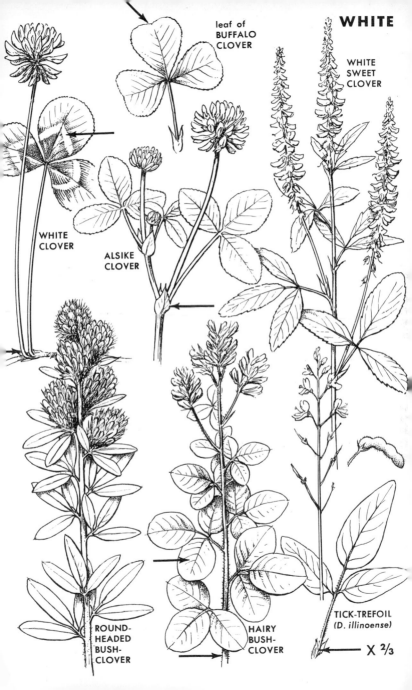

WHITE

leaf of
BUFFALO
CLOVER

WHITE
SWEET
CLOVER

WHITE
CLOVER

ALSIKE
CLOVER

ROUND-
HEADED
BUSH-
CLOVER

HAIRY
BUSH-
CLOVER

TICK-TREFOIL
(D. illinoense)

X ⅔

SLENDER CLUSTERS; 4 PETALS; SHORT PODS
MUSTARD FAMILY (Cruciferae)

SHEPHERD'S PURSE Alien　　　　　*Capsella bursa-pastoris*
Note the flat, heart-shaped pods. Flowers tiny. Basal leaves *dandelionlike*, in a rosette; stem leaves small, clasping. 8–20 in. **Note:** *C. rubella* is similar, but see shape of pod (inset). Waste ground. Throughout.　　　　　　　　　　　APRIL–SEPT.

FIELD PENNYCRESS Alien　　　　　　　*Thlaspi arvense*
Similar to Shepherd's Purse, but has wider stem leaves; lacks dandelionlike basal leaves. Note the larger size and rounder shape of the flat, *deeply notched* pods ("pennies"). 6–18 in. Waste ground. Throughout.　　　　　　　　　　　APRIL–AUG.

COW-CRESS, FIELD PEPPERGRASS　　*Lepidium campestre*
Alien
Note the shape of the flat pods, longer than broad. *Basal lobes* of leaves *embrace stem.* Seeds (1 in each pod) have peppery taste. 8–18 in. Roadsides, waste ground. Throughout.　　MAY–SEPT.

POOR-MAN'S-PEPPER, PEPPERGRASS
　　　　　　　　　　　　　　　　Lepidium virginicum
A native species, similar to *L. campestre* but leaves more deeply toothed, *stalked at base*, and not embracing stem. 6–24 in. Roadsides, waste places. Throughout.　　　　　　JUNE–NOV.

WHITLOW-GRASS Alien　　　　　　　　*Draba verna*
Very small. Note the deeply notched petals and *absence of leaves on stem.* Hairy leaves form basal rosette. 1–5 in. Roadsides, waste places. Illinois, Massachusetts south.
　　　　　　　　　　　　　　　　　　MARCH–MAY

CAROLINA WHITLOW-GRASS　　　　　*Draba reptans*
A small native, with *a pair or two of small leaves on lower stem.* Similar to *D. verna* but petals not so deeply notched; *pods longer*, stem smooth. 1–5 in. **Note:** There are 18 other native species of *Draba* in our area. Dry soil. Minnesota, Michigan, s. Ontario, n. New York, Massachusetts south.　　MARCH–JUNE

HOARY ALYSSUM Alien　　　　　　　*Berteroa incana*
Note the *pale hoary down* on leaves and stems. Petals notched as in *Draba*. Plant larger; more leaves on stems. 1–2 ft. Roadsides, waste places. Minnesota, Ontario, Massachusetts south to Missouri, Ohio, W. Virginia, New Jersey.　　JUNE–SEPT.

HORSERADISH Alien　　　　　*Armoracea lapathifolia*
Note the very large, *long-stalked basal leaves* (6–10 in.) and *tiny egg-shaped pods*. Root used as a condiment. 2–4 ft. Moist waste ground. Throughout.　　　　　　　　　MAY–JULY

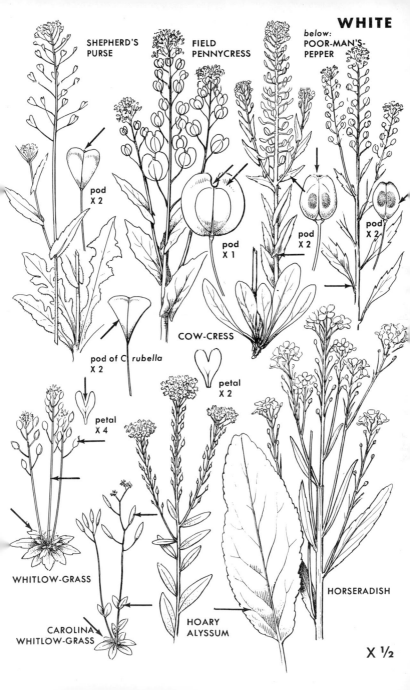

WHITE

SHEPHERD'S PURSE

FIELD PENNYCRESS

below: POOR-MAN'S-PEPPER

pod X 2

pod X 1

pod X 2

pod X 2

pod of C. *rubella* X 2

petal X 4

COW-CRESS

petal X 2

WHITLOW-GRASS

CAROLINA WHITLOW-GRASS

HOARY ALYSSUM

HORSERADISH

X ½

SMALL CLUSTERS, 4 PETALS;
MOIST OR WET PLACES
MUSTARD FAMILY (Cruciferae)
Most of these have slender, ascending seedpods.

TOOTHWORT, PEPPERWORT   *Dentaria diphylla*
Note the *pair of toothed stem leaves*, each divided into *3 broad leaflets*. Basal leaves similar, long-stalked. Flowers pink when fading. 8–14 in. Moist woods. Minnesota, s. Ontario, Gaspé south to Kentucky, S. Carolina (mts.).   APRIL–JUNE

DAME'S ROCKET Alien   *Hesperis matronalis*
Pink, purple, or white. Leaves large, toothed, alternate. See text and color plate, p. 226.

CUT-LEAVED TOOTHWORT   *Dentaria laciniata*
Note the *whorl of 3 leaves*, each divided into *3 narrow, sharply toothed segments*. 8–15 in. Rich moist woods, bottoms. Minnesota, w. Quebec, Vermont south.   APRIL–JUNE

SPRING CRESS   *Cardamine bulbosa*
Note the *roundish, long-stalked basal leaves* contrasting with the sessile, toothed stem leaves. Note also the bulblike roots. 8–20 in. Springs, low woods, wet meadows. Minnesota, Michigan, s. Ontario, New Hampshire south.   MARCH–JUNE

CUCKOO-FLOWER   *Cardamine pratensis*
Note the *small, many-paired leaflets* (roundish or oval on basal leaves, slender on stem leaves). Flowers relatively large ($\frac{1}{2}$–$\frac{3}{4}$ in.). 8–20 in. Swamps, springs, wet woods. N. Canada to Minnesota, n. Illinois, n. Ohio, W. Virginia, n. New Jersey.
                                                        APRIL–JUNE

PENNSYLVANIA BITTERCRESS   *Cardamine pensylvanica*
Similar to preceding but flowers *tiny* ($\frac{1}{16}$ in.). 8–24 in. Springs, wet ground. Nearly throughout.   APRIL–JUNE

MOUNTAIN WATERCRESS   *Cardamine rotundifolia*
A weak, fleshy plant with roundish leaves ascending the stem. Note small projections on some leafstalks. Cold springs, brooks, wet spots. Ohio, w. New York, Pennsylvania, New Jersey south.   MAY–JUNE

WATERCRESS Alien   *Nasturtium officinale*
The succulent leaves with 3 to 9 small oval leaflets and the floating or creeping habit are characteristic. Taste pungent. 4–10 in. Running water, springs, brooks. Widespread.
                                                        APRIL–JUNE

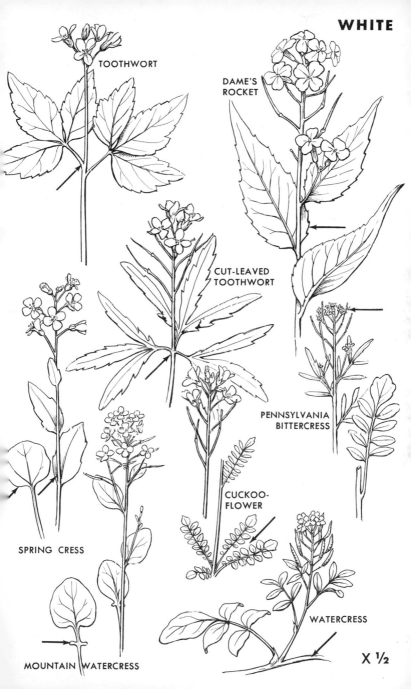

WHITE

TOOTHWORT

DAME'S ROCKET

CUT-LEAVED TOOTHWORT

SPRING CRESS

PENNSYLVANIA BITTERCRESS

CUCKOO-FLOWER

WATERCRESS

MOUNTAIN WATERCRESS

X ½

SMALL CLUSTERS, 4 PETALS;
MOSTLY WOODS, ROCKS
MUSTARD FAMILY (Cruciferae)

1. LONG, DOWNCURVED, FLAT PODS

SICKLEPOD   *Arabis canadensis*
Note the long, *deeply curved, drooping pods* and the downy, toothed, narrow-based stem leaves. 1–3 ft. Woods. Minnesota, s. Ontario, Maine south.   APRIL–JULY

SMOOTH ROCK CRESS   *Arabis laevigata*
Differs from the preceding by its smooth leaves, whose *lobed bases* clasp the stem. A pale *glaucous* (grayish-green) plant. Pods may be horizontal or curved. 1–3 ft. Woods, rocky ledges. Minnesota, sw. Quebec south.   APRIL–JULY

GREEN ROCK CRESS (not shown)   *Arabis missouriensis*
Smooth, but greener than the preceding; leaves without clasping basal lobes. Petals twice as long as in preceding ($\frac{1}{3}$ in.); twice as long as sepals. 1–2 ft. Rocky woods, ledges. Mts. from sw. Maine to Pennsylvania; also Michigan, Missouri, etc.
                                                        MAY–JULY

2. ERECT PODS (as in most mustards)
The first two species have flat pods, typical of *Arabis*.

HAIRY ROCK CRESS   *Arabis hirsuta*
Usually hairy. Basal leaves in a rosette; oblong to paddle-shaped; with or without toothed margins. Stem leaves narrow, clasping. 1–2 ft. Cliffs, ledges. N. Canada south locally to Kansas, Missouri, Georgia.   MAY–JUNE

LYRE-LEAVED ROCK CRESS   *Arabis lyrata*
Note the *deeply lobed basal leaves*. Upper leaves linear, narrowed at base. 4–12 in. Rocks or sandy soil. Minnesota, Ontario, Vermont to Missouri, Tennessee.   APRIL–MAY

GARLIC MUSTARD Alien   *Alliaria officinalis*
Note the somewhat *triangular* or heart-shaped leaves (stalked and sharply toothed), with odor of garlic. 1–3 ft. Roadsides, waste places, wood edges. Local, Ontario, Quebec south.
                                                        APRIL–JUNE

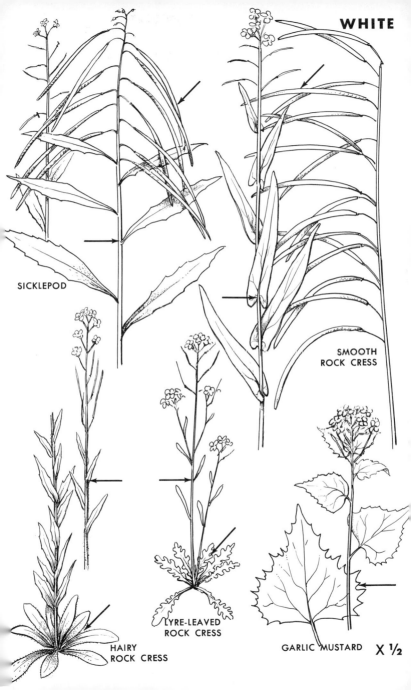

WHITE

SICKLEPOD

SMOOTH
ROCK CRESS

HAIRY
ROCK CRESS

LYRE-LEAVED
ROCK CRESS

GARLIC MUSTARD   X ½

CLUSTERS OF RAYLESS OR NEAR-RAYLESS COMPOSITES

COMPOSITE OR DAISY FAMILY (Compositae)

PILEWORT, FIREWEED *Erechtites hieracifolia*
A homely cluster of brush-shaped flowers with no rays. The white disk flowers barely peep from the *swollen-based* envelope of green bracts. Stem grooved, strong-smelling. Leaves 2 to 8 in., toothed, alternate; very variable. 1–9 ft. See also Fireweed (*Epilobium*), p. 224. Thickets, clearings, burns. Minnesota, Quebec, Maine south. JULY–OCT.

FALSE BONESET *Kuhnia eupatorioides*
A rayless composite suggesting a boneset (p. 46), but leaves *alternate* (not paired), resin-dotted. Leaves variable; toothed or not. 1–3 ft. Dry soil, open woods. Minnesota, Michigan, Pennsylvania, New Jersey south. AUG.–SEPT.

GROUNDSEL-TREE *Baccharis halimifolia*
A smooth woody shrub (not a tree) with thick, gray-green, coarsely toothed leaves. Staminate and pistillate flowers on separate plants. Pistillate flowers have conspicuous, plumelike pappus (inset). 4–10 ft. Thickets, marsh edges. Near coast, Massachusetts south. SEPT.–NOV.

HORSEWEED *Erigeron canadensis*
A rank weed with numerous linear leaves and numerous flower stalks springing from the upper leaf axils. The tiny greenish flowers (¼ in.) have short white rays' but these are compressed and do not spread. Stem bristly. 1–7 ft. Roadsides, fields, waste places. Throughout. JULY–NOV.

PALE INDIAN-PLANTAIN *Cacalia atriplicifolia*
Flowers of Indian-plantains are in flat-topped clusters and are supported by stiff slender bracts. This species is smooth and glaucous (with a whitish bloom). Leaves *irregularly fan-shaped*, coarsely toothed, or lobed. 3–6 ft. Dry woods, openings. Minnesota to New York and south. JULY–SEPT.

GREAT INDIAN-PLANTAIN *Cacalia muhlenbergii*
(not shown)
Similar to the preceding but not glaucous; leaves rounder, not as coarsely toothed or lobed. Similar habitat and range.

TUBEROUS INDIAN-PLANTAIN *Cacalia tuberosa*
Note the *large*, thick, pointed *oval* leaves with their 5 to 9 parallel veins. Flowers similar to preceding species. 2–6 ft. Prairies, marshes, wet ground. Minnesota, w. Ontario, Ohio south. JUNE–AUG.

SWEET-SCENTED INDIAN-PLANTAIN *Cacalia suaveolens*
Note the irregularly saw-toothed, *arrowhead-shaped* leaves. Flowers similar to those of preceding three species. 3–5 ft. Woods, clearings. Minnesota, Illinois, Pennsylvania, Connecticut south. JULY–SEPT.

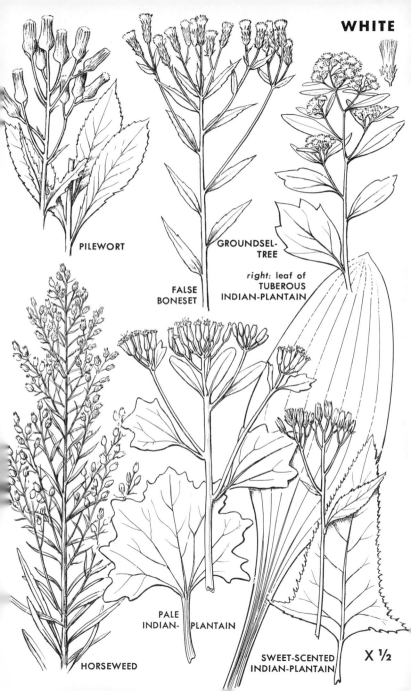

WHITE

PILEWORT

GROUNDSEL-TREE

FALSE BONESET

right: leaf of TUBEROUS INDIAN-PLANTAIN

PALE INDIAN-PLANTAIN

HORSEWEED

SWEET-SCENTED INDIAN-PLANTAIN

X 1/2

CLUSTERS OF SMALL WOOLLY EVERLASTINGS
COMPOSITE OR DAISY FAMILY (Compositae)

PEARLY EVERLASTING *Anaphalis margaritacea*
The most showy of the everlastings. Flowers in a flat cluster
of globular heads, with dry, petal-like white bracts, arranged
in series around the yellow staminate center (pistillate flowers
are on separate plants). Stem cottony. Leaves long, linear;
usually gray-green above, woolly-white beneath. Extremely
variable. 1–3 ft. Dry soil, pastures. Canada, n. U.S.; in mts.
to N. Carolina. JULY–SEPT.

SWEET EVERLASTING, CATFOOT
Gnaphalium obtusifolium
Similar to preceding; less showy, but fragrant. Flower clusters
more branched; scaly bracts tinged with yellowish, not expanding until in seed. 1–2 ft. Dry soil, clearings, fields. Most of
our area. AUG.–NOV.

CLAMMY EVERLASTING *Gnaphalium macounii*
(not shown)
More robust than preceding, more woolly. Leaves broader,
wings clasping stem. Stem sticky. 2–3 ft. S. Canada, n. U.S.

LOW CUDWEED *Gnaphalium uliginosum*
A low, branching plant with a white-woolly stem and blunt
linear leaves. Small flower clusters (brownish white) in upper
leaf axils. 4–12 in. Damp ground, ditches. Across Canada,
n. U.S.; in mts. to Virginia. JULY–OCT.

PLANTAIN-LEAVED PUSSYTOES *Antennaria plantaginifolia*
The pussytoes, *Antennaria*, are a confusing group, disputed by
specialists. Gray (Fernald) recognizes 32 species in our area;
Britton and Brown (Gleason) only 6. The pussytoes differ
from the preceding species by having the leaves mostly at the
base; stem leaves smaller. In this species the long-stalked,
spoon-shaped basal leaves have 3 to 5 main nerves. Leaves
silky, those on stem lance-shaped. Stem woolly. There are
many variants or varieties. 3–16 in. Dry soil, woods, pastures.
Canada south. APRIL–JUNE

FIELD PUSSYTOES *Antennaria neglecta*
This common species is usually smaller than *A. plantaginifolia*,
with smaller, narrower leaves. The basal leaves have only
1 main nerve. Often forms dense mats. Extremely variable;
many varieties have been named. 4–12 in. Dry fields, open
slopes. Widespread. APRIL–MAY

SOLITARY PUSSYTOES (not shown) *Antennaria solitaria*
This species, like *A. plantaginifolia*, has 3 to 5 main nerves. It
has a nearly naked stem, with stem leaves much reduced, and
only 1 flower head. Woods, clearings. Indiana, w. Pennsylvania,
Maryland south. APRIL–MAY

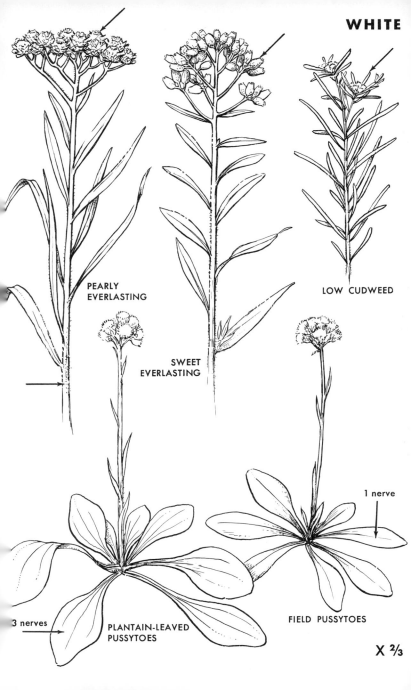

WHITE

PEARLY EVERLASTING

SWEET EVERLASTING

LOW CUDWEED

3 nerves

PLANTAIN-LEAVED PUSSYTOES

1 nerve

FIELD PUSSYTOES

X ⅔

DAISYLIKE FLOWERS, ETC.

COMPOSITE OR DAISY FAMILY (Compositae)

SNEEZEWEED YARROW Alien   *Achillea ptarmica*
Note the *linear*, pointed, *saw-toothed* leaves and flat clusters of
yarrowlike flowers (rays short, 3-lobed), but flower heads fewer,
larger ($\frac{1}{2}$–$\frac{3}{4}$ in.) than in *A. millefolium*, p. 44. 1–2 ft. Damp
roadsides, fields. E. Canada to Michigan, New York, New
England.   JULY–SEPT.

FEVERFEW Alien   *Chrysanthemum parthenium*
A bushy plant with broadly toothed pinnate leaves. Pungently
aromatic. Flower heads have *relatively large buttons, stubby
white rays*. 1–2 ft. A roadside escape.   JUNE–SEPT.

MAYWEED Alien   *Anthemis cotula*
The numerous, fine, thrice-dissected leaves have a very dis-
agreeable odor and acrid taste. Disk flowers interspersed with
chaff (next two have no chaff). 8–20 in. Roadsides, waste
ground. Throughout.   JUNE–OCT.

SCENTLESS CHAMOMILE Alien   *Matricaria maritima*
Flowers larger than in Mayweed, but scentless; leaf segments
more threadlike; disk flowers with no chaff. Often half prostrate.
6–18 in. Waste places. Local.   JULY–OCT.

WILD CHAMOMILE Alien   *Matricaria chamomilla*
Similar to the preceding (but *pineapple-scented*) and leaves
sparser, more apple-green; flowers smaller. Roadsides, etc.
E. Canada and n. U.S.   MAY–OCT.

WILD QUININE   *Parthenium integrifolium*
Ray flowers (5) are tiny ($\frac{1}{12}$ in.). Basal leaves large, toothed,
rough, long-stalked. 1$\frac{1}{2}$–3 ft. Dry woods, prairies. Minnesota,
Wisconsin, Michigan, Ohio, se. New York south.   JUNE–SEPT.

GALINSOGA Alien   *Galinsoga*
Inconspicuous, each flower head $\frac{1}{4}$ in. across, with 5 tiny 3-
lobed rays. Leaves broad, coarsely toothed; lower leaves stalked.
2 species widespread: (1) *G. ciliata*, coarsely hairy; (2) less
common *G. parviflora*, nearly hairless stems, shorter rays.
6–18 in. Waste places.   JUNE–NOV.

OX-EYE DAISY Alien   *Chrysanthemum leucanthemum*
The familiar large white daisy; flowers 2 in. across; yellow disk
depressed in center. Leaves dark, narrow, much lobed. 1–3 ft.
Fields, roadsides. Nearly throughout.   JUNE–AUG.

CHICORY Alien   *Cichorium intybus*
Usually blue, but sometimes white (forma *album;* shown here)
or pink (forma *roseum*). See also p. 362.

SPOTTED KNAPWEED Alien   *Centaurea maculosa*
Pink, purple, or white. See p. 306.

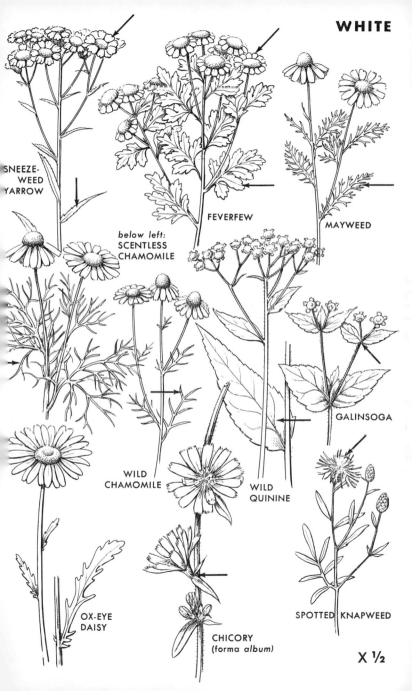

WHITE

SNEEZE-
WEED
YARROW

FEVERFEW

MAYWEED

below left:
SCENTLESS
CHAMOMILE

WILD
CHAMOMILE

WILD
QUININE

GALINSOGA

OX-EYE
DAISY

CHICORY
(forma *album*)

SPOTTED KNAPWEED

X ½

ASTERS AND ASTERLIKE FLOWERS
Composite or Daisy Family (Compositae)

DAISY FLEABANE *Erigeron annuus*
This asterlike flower, unlike the asters, starts blooming in spring.
Rays more numerous (40–70). It is hairy and leafy; leaves
strongly toothed. A similar species, *E. strigosus* (not shown),
has fewer leaves, most of which are not toothed or only slightly
toothed. The hairs lie closer to the stem, do not spread. Field,
roadsides, waste land. Throughout. MAY–OCT.

WHORLED WOOD ASTER *Aster acuminatus*
The large, narrow-based, sharp-toothed leaves are often scattered up the stem in such a way as to appear *whorled*. The
downy stem is often zigzag, may be reddish at base. 1–3 ft.
Woods, clearings. E. Canada and south in mts. JULY–OCT.

WHITE WOOD ASTER *Aster divaricatus*
Note the *stalked heart-shaped leaves*. Clusters flat-topped; relatively few rays. 1–3 ft. Dry woods. Ohio to s. Maine and south
to s. New England; in mts. to Georgia. JULY–OCT.

LOWRIE'S ASTER *Aster lowrieanus*
The *wing or flange* on the petiole (leafstalk) is distinctive.
Flowers pale blue (usually) or white. Woods. S. Michigan, sw.
Ontario to Connecticut and south in mts. AUG.–OCT.

PANICLED ASTER *Aster simplex*
A tall, smooth aster with slender, short-stalked willowlike leaves
which are toothless or few-toothed. Flowers ¾ in., may be
tinged with violet; rays numerous (20–40). 3–8 ft. Damp open
ground, wet meadows. Across Canada and south to Missouri,
Illinois, Ohio, N. Carolina (mts.). AUG.–OCT.

TOOTHED WHITE-TOPPED ASTER *Seriocarpus asteroides*
Note the *sparse rays* (usually 4–5) and the spatulate, narrow-
based leaves with several teeth beyond the middle. 6 in.–2 ft.
See also *S. linifolius*, p. 96. Dry woods. Michigan to s. Maine
and south. JUNE–OCT.

SCHREBER'S ASTER *Aster schreberi*
Best identified by the *very large* heart-shaped basal leaves with
their *broad angular sinuses* (basal notches). Variable. 1–4 ft.
Woods, thickets. Wisconsin, Illinois, Michigan, Ohio, New
York, and New Hampshire; south in mts. to Kentucky, Vir-
ginia. JULY–SEPT.

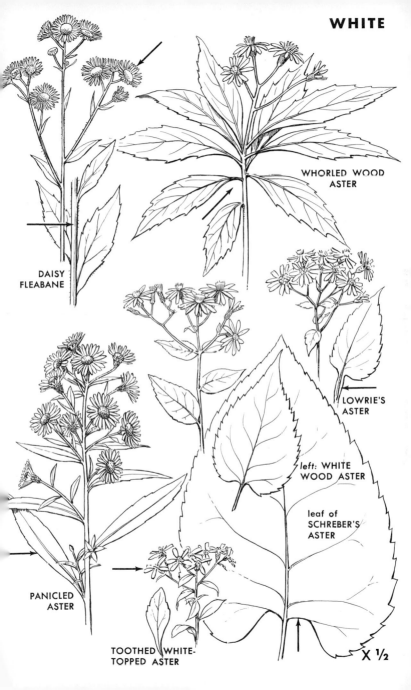

WHITE

WHORLED WOOD ASTER

DAISY FLEABANE

LOWRIE'S ASTER

left: WHITE WOOD ASTER

leaf of SCHREBER'S ASTER

PANICLED ASTER

TOOTHED WHITE-TOPPED ASTER

X ½

ASTERS

COMPOSITE OR DAISY FAMILY (Compositae)
The small white asters are numerous, extremely variable,
and may intergrade. Many can be recognized with
certainty only by technical characters not given here.

FLAT-TOPPED WHITE ASTER *Aster umbellatus*
Note the *flat-topped cluster* of few-rayed (2–15) flowers. Yellow
disk turns purplish with age. Leaves lance-shaped, toothless,
rough-margined. 2–7 ft. Thickets, edges. Minnesota, e.
Canada south to Iowa, Georgia (mts.). AUG.–SEPT.

UPLAND WHITE ASTER (not shown) *Aster ptarmicoides*
Similar but flowers a bit larger (up to 1 in.); leaves more *grasslike*, rigid, shining. Rocks, sand. S. Canada, n. U.S. JUNE–SEPT.

RUSH ASTER *Aster junciformis*
Note the linear, *grasslike* leaves ascending the single slender
stem, the nearly vertical flower stalks, and the habitat. White,
pale blue, or lavender; see also p. 360. 1–3 ft. Cold bogs,
swamps, shores. Across Canada and south to Iowa, Wisconsin,
n. Indiana, Ohio, n. Pennsylvania, n. New Jersey. JUNE–SEPT.

PERENNIAL SALT-MARSH ASTER *Aster tenuifolius*
The sparse, *extremely slender (2–6 in.)*, *fleshy leaves* and the
habitat identify this slim white or lavender aster; see also
p. 360. 1–2 ft. Salt marshes. Coast, New Hampshire south.
SEPT.–OCT.

SMALL WHITE ASTER *Aster vimineus*
Note the smooth purple stems and the small crowded flowers on
this wide-branched aster. Leaves slender, lower ones toothed,
with smaller leaflets in axils. 2–5 ft. Fields, meadows. Michigan, s. Ontario, s. Maine south. AUG.–OCT.

CALICO or STARVED ASTER *Aster lateriflorus*
This small species has wider, more coarsely toothed leaves than
A. vimineus; disk florets deeper purple. Variable. 1–5 ft.
Fields, thickets. W. Ontario, Nova Scotia south. AUG.–OCT.

NARROW-LEAVED WHITE-TOPPED ASTER
Seriocarpus linifolius
Note the flat cluster of *sparse-rayed (4–5) flowers* and firm
linear leaves. See also *S. asteroides*, p. 94. 1–2½ ft. Sandy soil.
Ohio to Maine and south. JUNE–SEPT.

TRADESCANT'S ASTER *Aster tradescanti*
Flower heads ½–⅔ in. across, white or purplish on branches
springing from leaf axils. Leaves lanceolate, lower slightly
toothed. 2–5 ft. Wet fields, shores. Quebec south to n. Michigan, n. New York, n. New England. JULY–SEPT.

HEATH ASTER *Aster ericoides*
Note the numerous, tiny, rigid heathlike leaves. Variable;
one form is so densely crowded with tiny blossoms that the
plant takes the plumelike shape of a goldenrod. Rays sometimes tinged pink. 1–3 ft. Dry open places. Minnesota, s.
Ontario, Maine south. JULY–OCT.

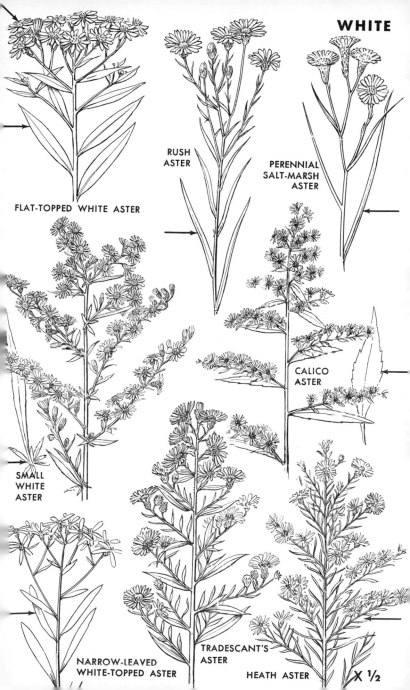

WHITE

RUSH
ASTER

PERENNIAL
SALT-MARSH
ASTER

FLAT-TOPPED WHITE ASTER

CALICO
ASTER

SMALL
WHITE
ASTER

NARROW-LEAVED
WHITE-TOPPED ASTER

TRADESCANT'S
ASTER

HEATH ASTER

X ½

Yellow
Flowers

Yellow flowers and orange flowers separate
out fairly well, so we have put them in separate sections. Greenish-yellow and yel-
lowish-green flowers may merge impercepti-
bly, so if in doubt, look here and also in the
green section, which starts on page 366.

LARGE CUPLIKE FLOWERS AND OTHERS

PRICKLY-PEAR   *Opuntia humifusa*
CACTUS FAMILY   (Cactaceae)
Our only widespread eastern cactus (2 similar species in Midwest). Jointed pads equipped with tufts of bristles; showy flower often has a reddish center. Variable; usually prostrate. Fruit red, pulpy. Rocks, sandy soil. Minnesota, s. Ontario, Massachusetts south.   JUNE–AUG.

TRUMPETS   *Sarracenia flava*
PITCHER-PLANT FAMILY   (Sarraceniaceae)
Note the strange drooping flowers and *long green trumpets* with their *raised hoods*. 1–3 ft. See also Pitcher-plant, p. 230, which may rarely have yellow flowers. Bogs, wet pine barrens. Se. Virginia south.   APRIL–MAY

YELLOW IRIS Alien   *Iris pseudacorus*
IRIS FAMILY   (Iridaceae)
The only *yellow* iris likely to be found growing wild. A European escape from gardens; now established but locally in our area. 1–3 ft. Marshes, streamsides.   MAY–JULY

AMERICAN LOTUS, NELUMBO   *Nelumbo lutea*
WATER-LILY FAMILY   (Nymphaeaceae)
Note the huge pale blossoms (4–8 in.) and great bowl-shaped leaves (1–2 ft.) usually held a foot or two above the water. Sluggish rivers, ponds. Local, Minnesota, s. Ontario, New York, Massachusetts south.   JULY–SEPT.

BULLHEAD-LILY   *Nuphar variegatum*
WATER-LILY FAMILY   (Nymphaeaceae)
The familiar *floating* yellow water-lily of the Northeast. The globular yellow flowers are made up of fleshy sepals; the stamenlike petals are concealed. Note the disklike stigma in center. Leaves with rounded basal lobes, narrow notch. Ponds, sluggish water. Across Canada and south to Iowa, n. Illinois, n. Indiana, Ohio, Maryland.   MAY–SEPT.

SMALL POND-LILY (not shown)   *Nuphar microphyllum*
WATER-LILY FAMILY   (Nymphaeaceae)
Similar to preceding but much smaller; flowers less than 1 in. across, with *red* stigmatic disk. Notch of leaf *very narrow* (more than ⅓ length of leaf). Ponds. Manitoba, Newfoundland south to Minnesota, Michigan, Pennsylvania, New Jersey.
                                              JUNE–OCT.

SPATTERDOCK (not shown)   *Nuphar advena*
WATER-LILY FAMILY   (Nymphaeaceae)
More southern than Bullhead-lily; coarser, with leaves *erect* above water, rarely floating. Notch of leaf wider (45°). Ponds, swamps, tidewater. S. U.S. north to Wisconsin, s. Michigan, Ohio, c. New York, coastal New England.   MAY–OCT.

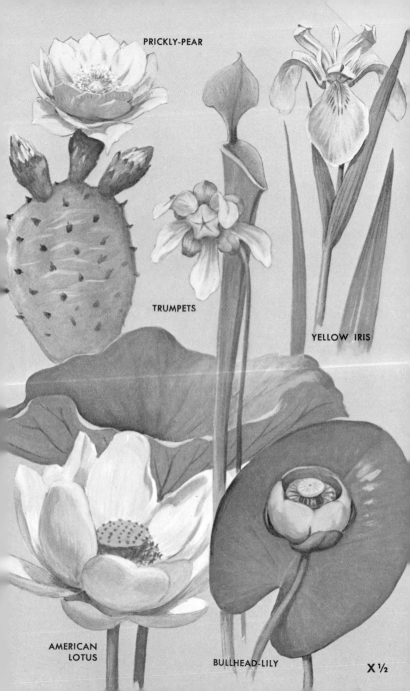

PRICKLY-PEAR

TRUMPETS

YELLOW IRIS

AMERICAN LOTUS

BULLHEAD-LILY

X ½

NODDING, BELL-LIKE, 6-POINT FLOWERS
LILY FAMILY (Liliaceae)

TROUT-LILY, ADDER'S-TONGUE *Erythronium americanum*
Note the reflexed yellow petals (often brown-purple beneath)
and 2 broad, mottled basal leaves. 4–10 in. Woods. Minnesota,
Ontario, Nova Scotia south. MARCH–MAY

CLINTONIA, CORN-LILY *Clintonia borealis*
Note the 2 or 3 broad shining basal leaves and the yellowish-
green bells on a leafless stalk. Berries deep blue. 6–16 in. See
White Clintonia, p. 66. Cool woods; open slopes on mts.
Canada, n. U.S.; south in mts. to Georgia. MAY–JULY

CANADA or WILD YELLOW LILY *Lilium canadense*
The yellowest of our large, spotted lilies; leaves in whorls. Also
orange or red (p. 206). 2–5 ft. Meadows. Se. Canada, ne. U.S.,
southward mainly in highlands. JUNE–JULY

YELLOW DAY-LILY, LEMON LILY *Hemerocallis flava*
Alien (not shown)
Blossoms unspotted, *erect,* yellow; leaves bladelike. Smaller
than orange Day-lily (p. 206). Asiatic; locally escaped.

SOLOMON'S-SEAL *Polygonatum biflorum*
Paired greenish-yellow flowers dangle beneath the leaves, ar-
ranged alternately on the stem. Berries blue black. 1–3 ft.
Woods, thickets. Great Lakes, Connecticut south. APRIL–JUNE

GREAT SOLOMON'S-SEAL *Polygonatum canaliculatum*
(not shown)
Similar, but blossoms usually in larger clusters (2–10). See
p. 370.

INDIAN CUCUMBER-ROOT *Medeola virginiana*
Note the *2 whorls* of leaves and dangling greenish-yellow flowers
with reflexed tips, reddish stamens. 1–3 ft. Woods. Minnesota,
Ontario, Nova Scotia south. MAY–JUNE

LARGE-FLOWERED BELLWORT *Uvularia grandiflora*
Somewhat stouter than next species. Flower larger, yellower,
smooth inside. Leaves clasp stem; whitish-downy beneath.
6–20 in. Woods. Ontario, Quebec south. APRIL–JUNE

PERFOLIATE BELLWORT *Uvularia perfoliata*
A single yellowish, fragrant flower droops at the tip of a forking
leafy stem; stem appears to *pierce* leaves. To tell from last
species, note inside of flower, which is *rough* with orange grains.
6–18 in. Moist woods. Ontario, Quebec south. MAY–JUNE

WILD OATS, SESSILE BELLWORT *Uvularia sessilifolia*
The creamy, drooping flowers differ from the preceding two by
having tips less pointed and spreading. Leaves *sessile,* not surrounding stem; stem angled. 6–13 in. Woods, thickets. Minnesota, Ontario, New Brunswick south. MAY–JUNE

MOUNTAIN BELLWORT (not shown) *Uvularia pudica*
Similar to preceding but stem slightly downy; leaves brighter
green and rounded at base. Pine barrens (New Jersey south)
and mt. woods (Virginia south). APRIL–MAY

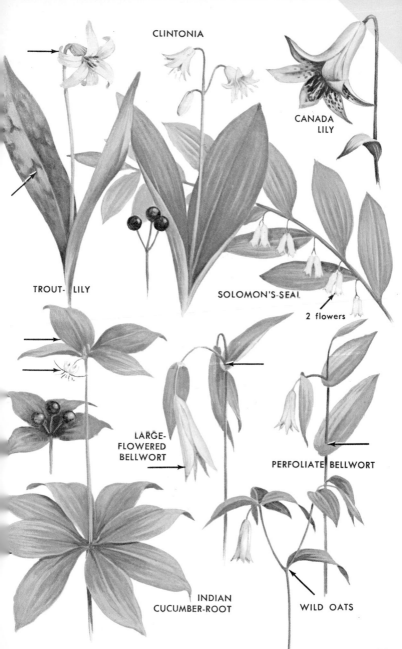

CLINTONIA

CANADA
LILY

TROUT-LILY

SOLOMON'S-SEAL

2 flowers

LARGE-
FLOWERED
BELLWORT

PERFOLIATE BELLWORT

INDIAN
CUCUMBER-ROOT

WILD OATS

X ½

POUCHLIKE OR BELL-SHAPED FLOWERS

BUTTER-AND-EGGS, TOADFLAX Alien *Linaria vulgaris*
SNAPDRAGON FAMILY (Scrophulariaceae)
Note the clublike spikes of snapdragonlike flowers with orange palates, thin drooping spurs. Leaves narrow, numerous. 1–3 ft. A coarser species, *L. dalmatica* (not shown), has oblong clasping leaves. Roadsides, waste places, dry fields. Throughout.
JUNE–OCT.

YELLOW LADY'S-SLIPPER *Cypripedium calceolus*
ORCHID FAMILY (Orchidaceae)
Note the inflated saclike lip, or "slipper," and spirally twisted petals. Variable; 3 forms: (1) var. *parviflorum* (SMALL YELLOW LADY'S-SLIPPER), shown here; (2) var. *pubescens* (LARGE YELLOW LADY'S-SLIPPER), larger, with yellower, less twisted petals, less fragrant blossoms; and (3) var. *planipetalum*, a flat-petaled form of the Gulf of St. Lawrence. 1½–2 ft. Bogs, wet woods, shady swamps. Quebec, Newfoundland south to Missouri, Georgia (in mts.). MAY–JULY

PALE TOUCH-ME-NOT, JEWELWEED *Impatiens pallida*
TOUCH-ME-NOT FAMILY (Balsaminaceae)
Blossoms pendent, similar to Spotted Touch-me-not (p. 208) but *pale yellow*, spur shorter. Stems watery when broken; ripe pods pop when touched. 3–5 ft. Wet shady places, calcareous mt. woods. Saskatchewan, Newfoundland south to Kansas, Missouri, Georgia (in mts.). JULY–OCT.

DOWNY FALSE FOXGLOVE *Gerardia virginica*
SNAPDRAGON FAMILY (Scrophulariaceae)
False foxgloves are recognized by their full-tubed, bell-shaped golden flowers with 5 wide-spreading lobes. They are said to be parasitic on roots of oaks. This species has deeply lobed *downy* leaves, downy stems. 3–6 ft. Dry oak woods. Michigan, Ontario, New Hampshire south. JULY–SEPT.

SMOOTH FALSE FOXGLOVE *Gerardia laevigata*
SNAPDRAGON FAMILY (Scrophulariaceae)
Similar but *smooth;* leaves with much *shorter* petioles, not so deeply cut (mostly without lobes). 2–6 ft. Open woods, mainly in mts. Ohio, Pennsylvania south. JULY–SEPT.

YELLOW FALSE FOXGLOVE (not shown) *Gerardia flava*
SNAPDRAGON FAMILY (Scrophulariaceae)
Intermediate, with a smooth (often purplish) stem, but deeply lobed, smoothish leaves. S. Minnesota, s. Maine south.

FERN-LEAVED FALSE FOXGLOVE *Gerardia pedicularia*
SNAPDRAGON FAMILY (Scrophulariaceae)
Note the lacy, *fernlike* leaves. Bushy, branching, downy; stems sticky. 1–4 ft. Dry oak woods, uplands. Minnesota, Ontario, Maine south, chiefly in mts. AUG.–SEPT.

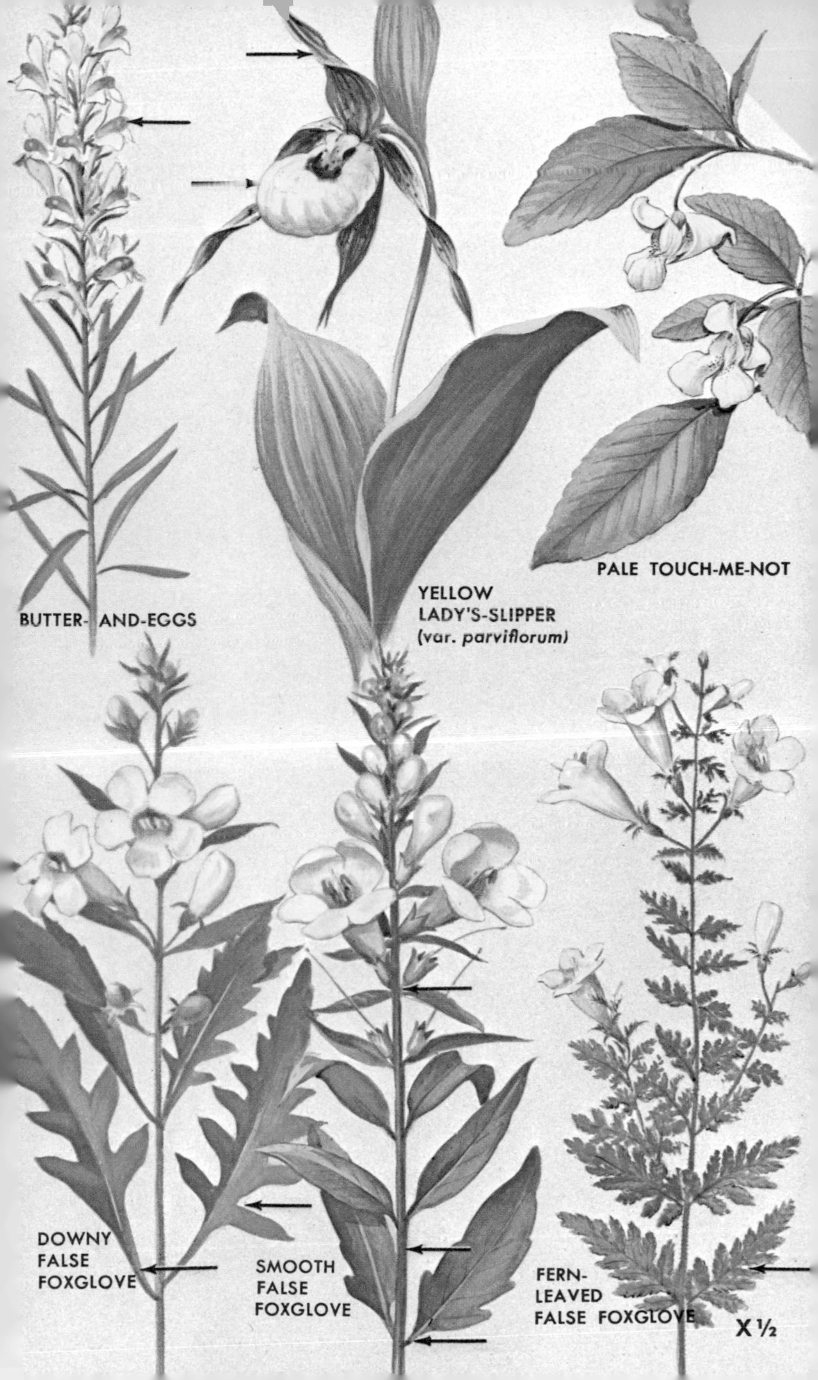

BUTTER- AND-EGGS

YELLOW
LADY'S-SLIPPER
(var. parviflorum)

PALE TOUCH-ME-NOT

DOWNY
FALSE
FOXGLOVE

SMOOTH
FALSE
FOXGLOVE

FERN-
LEAVED
FALSE FOXGLOVE

X ½

SPIKES AND CLUSTERS; 4 OR 5 PETALS
All except Evening-primrose have 5 petals

YELLOW LOOSESTRIFE, SWAMP CANDLES
PRIMROSE FAMILY (Primulaceae)   *Lysimachia terrestris*
A slender spike of small starlike flowers. Note the circle of red
spots on petals. Leaves usually paired. 8–10 in. See other yellow loosestrifes, p. 140. Swampy spots, grassy shores. Minnesota, Ontario, Newfoundland south to Georgia.   JUNE–SEPT.

COMMON EVENING-PRIMROSE   *Oenothera biennis*
EVENING-PRIMROSE FAMILY   (Onagraceae)
Note the 4 broad petals, *cross-shaped* stigma, reflexed sepals.
1–5 ft. See other evening-primroses, etc., p. 156. Roadsides,
waste places. Throughout.   JUNE–SEPT.

COMMON ST. JOHNSWORT Alien *Hypericum perforatum*
ST. JOHNSWORT FAMILY   (Guttiferae)
Note the bushy stamens, *black dots on margins of petals*, trans-
lucent dots on leaves. 1–2½ ft. See other St. Johnsworts, p. 138.
Roadsides, fields, waste places. Throughout.   JUNE–SEPT.

MOTH MULLEIN Alien   *Verbascum blattaria*
SNAPDRAGON FAMILY   (Scrophulariaceae)
Smooth and slender; often white-flowered. Note the scant
leafage, *buttonlike buds*, *orange anthers*, and *purplish beards*
on the stamens. 1–3 ft. Roadsides, vacant lots, waste places.
Throughout (north to Quebec).   JUNE–OCT.

CLASPING-LEAVED MULLEIN Alien *Verbascum phlomoides*
SNAPDRAGON FAMILY   (Scrophulariaceae)
Similar to Common Mullein but with a more open flower spike
(suggesting Moth Mullein). Leaves woolly as in Common
Mullein, but do not flow into stem.   JULY–AUG.

COMMON MULLEIN Alien   *Verbascum thapsus*
SNAPDRAGON FAMILY   (Scrophulariaceae)
Note the clublike flower head and the large *flannel-textured*
leaves that flow into the stem. 2–6 ft. Roadsides, poor fields,
waste places. Nearly throughout.   JUNE–SEPT.

PARTRIDGE-PEA   *Cassia fasciculata*
PEA FAMILY   (Leguminosae)
Note the drooping dark anthers and the finely cut compound
leaves, somewhat sensitive to the touch. 1–2 ft. See also Wild
Senna and Wild Sensitive-plant, p. 152. Sandy soil. Minnesota,
s. Ontario, Massachusetts south.   JULY–SEPT.

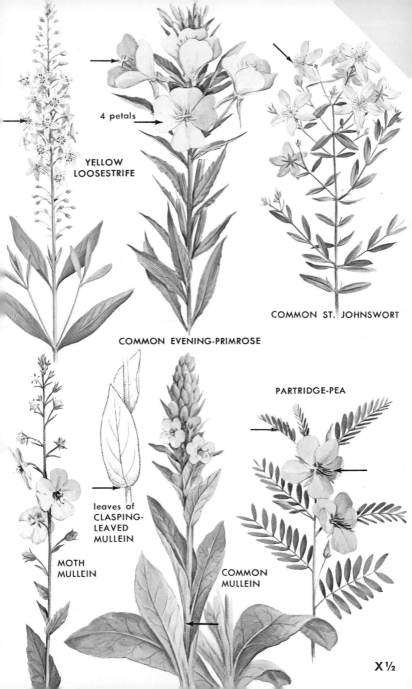

YELLOW
LOOSESTRIFE

4 petals

COMMON ST. JOHNSWORT

COMMON EVENING-PRIMROSE

PARTRIDGE-PEA

leaves of
CLASPING-
LEAVED
MULLEIN

MOTH
MULLEIN

COMMON
MULLEIN

X ½

SMALL ASTERLIKE FLOWERS
COMPOSITE OR DAISY FAMILY (Compositae)
See also p. 176.

MARYLAND GOLDEN-ASTER *Chrysopsis mariana*
Golden-asters (or "silkgrasses"), like the true asters, bloom in late summer. This one has *broader* leaves, larger flowers than the other 2 eastern species. Stems silky; bracts below flowers sticky. 1–2 ft. Barrens, sandy soil. S. Ohio, Pennsylvania, Long Island south.   AUG.–OCT.

GRASS-LEAVED GOLDEN-ASTER *Chrysopsis graminifolia*
Similar to preceding, but with soft *grasslike* leaves. 1–3 ft. Dry, sandy soil, pine barrens. S. Ohio, Delaware south.
JULY–SEPT.

PRAIRIE GOLDEN-ASTER *Chrysopsis camporum*
Similar to Maryland Golden-aster but western. Smaller leaves; very variable. 6–24 in. Other golden-asters are found in the western parts of our area. Sandy prairies, barrens. Wisconsin to w. Indiana, e. Missouri.   JULY–OCT.

SICKLE-LEAVED GOLDEN-ASTER *Chrysopsis falcata*
A small coastal species with stiff, narrow, *curved* leaves; stems white-woolly. 8–15 in. Pine barrens, sandy soil near coast from se. Massachusetts to New Jersey.   JULY–SEPT.

CAMPHORWEED *Heterotheca subaxillaris*
Similar to golden-asters, but note the broad-based, wavy-edged leaves that *clasp* the stem. 1–3 ft. Dry sandy soil. Kansas, Illinois, Pennsylvania, s. New Jersey south (a recent arrival from farther south).   AUG.–NOV.

GUMWEED *Grindelia squarrosa*
Note the *very gummy bracts* with their recurved tips. Leaves toothed. Variable. ½–3 ft. Prairies, plains of U.S., Canada; adventive locally to Atlantic states.   JULY–SEPT.

GOLDEN RAGWORT *Senecio aureus*
The ragworts with their flat-topped clusters bloom much earlier than the above flowers and may be known from them by their sparse rays (8–12) and finely cut leaves. Basal leaves of this species *heart-shaped*, long-stemmed. Variable. 1–3 ft. See other ragworts, p. 176. Wet ground, low woods, swamps, meadows. Most of our area.   MAY–JULY

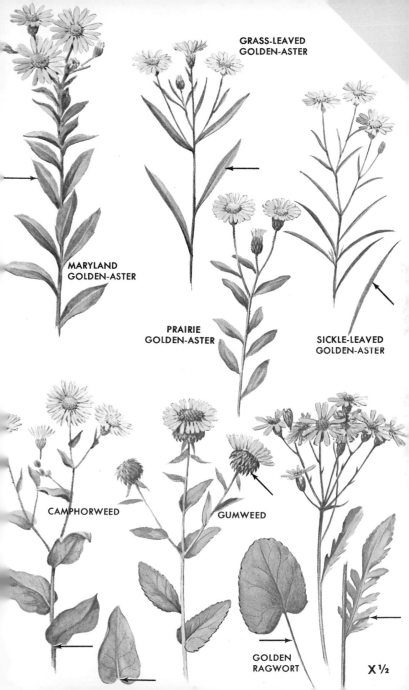

GRASS-LEAVED
GOLDEN-ASTER

MARYLAND
GOLDEN-ASTER

PRAIRIE
GOLDEN-ASTER

SICKLE-LEAVED
GOLDEN-ASTER

CAMPHORWEED

GUMWEED

GOLDEN
RAGWORT

X ½

DANDELIONLIKE FLOWERS
Composite or Daisy Family (Compositae)

FIELD SOW-THISTLE Alien   *Sonchus arvensis*
Sow-thistles have prickly-edged leaves, dandelionlike blossoms.
To separate from the following sow-thistles, note the glandular
hairs on the bracts and stalks. The spines are weak. 1½–4 ft.
Fields, waste places, roadsides. Ontario, Newfoundland south
to Missouri, Ohio, Maryland.   July–Oct.

COMMON SOW-THISTLE Alien   *Sonchus oleraceus*
This species has smooth bracts and stalks and has sharp,
pointed lobes where the leaves embrace the stem. Stem smooth,
angled. 1–8 ft. Waste places,.fields, roadsides. Ontario, Newfoundland south.   June–Oct.

SPINY-LEAVED SOW-THISTLE Alien   *Sonchus asper*
Note the *very spiny*, curled leaves and how their *eared bases*
enfold the smooth, angled stem. (Preceding species has pointed
lobes.) 1–5 ft. Waste places, roadsides. Ontario, Newfoundland south.   June–Oct.

COLTSFOOT Alien   *Tussilago farfara*
Note the stalk with its reddish scales and the bristly flower with
its numerous yellow rays in layers. The flowers appear first,
the large leaves later. 6–18 in. Waste places, roadsides, railroad
shoulders. Minnesota, Quebec, Nova Scotia south to Ohio,
Pennsylvania, New Jersey.   March–June

TWO-FLOWERED CYNTHIA   *Krigia biflora*
Note the deep *orange-yellow* flower and *clasping* upper leaves
(embracing secondary flower stalks). Plant smooth; basal
leaves vary. 1–2 ft. Woodlands, fields. Manitoba, Massachusetts south.   May–Aug.

COMMON DANDELION Alien   *Taraxacum officinale*
The familiar lawn weed with jagged-lobed leaves, hollow milky
stem, *reflexed outer bracts*, fluffy globular white seedballs.
2–18 in. See other dandelions, p. 170. Lawns, fields, roadsides.
Throughout.   March–Sept.

YELLOW GOAT'S-BEARD Alien   *Tragopogon pratensis*
Note the grasslike leaves that embrace the smooth stem and
also the *long-pointed bracts* that support the pale yellow rays.
Juice of stem milky. Flowers close at midday. 1–3 ft. See also
Oyster-plant, *T. porrifolius*, p. 308 (hybrids are frequent).
Waste places, roadsides. Manitoba, Nova Scotia to Ohio, New
Jersey.   June–Oct.

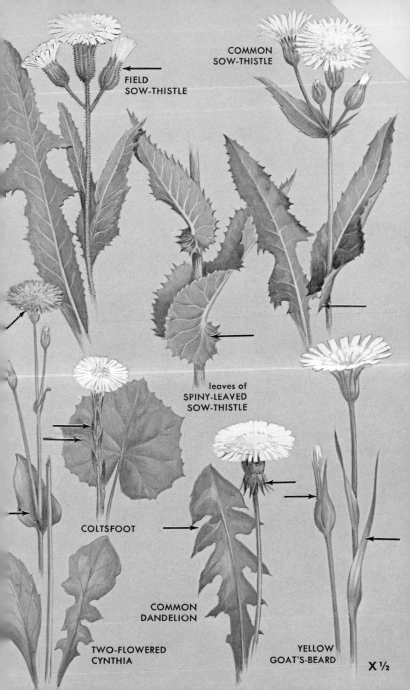

FIELD
SOW-THISTLE

COMMON
SOW-THISTLE

leaves of
SPINY-LEAVED
SOW-THISTLE

COLTSFOOT

COMMON
DANDELION

TWO-FLOWERED
CYNTHIA

YELLOW
GOAT'S-BEARD

X ½

DAISYLIKE FLOWERS
COMPOSITE OR DAISY FAMILY (Compositae)
See also p. 188.

BLACK-EYED SUSAN *Rudbeckia hirta*
Note the big, single, slender-stemmed blossom with its numerous (10–20) long, daisylike rays and *chocolate-colored* center disk. Leaves and stem very bristly-hairy. 1–3 ft. Dry fields, roadsides, open woods, waste places. Manitoba, Nova Scotia south (invader in East).   JUNE–OCT.

SNEEZEWEED *Helenium autumnale*
Note the *turned-back rays* (each with 3 scallops at tip), and the globular, ocher-yellow button. 2–5 ft. Thickets, swamps, wet meadows. Minnesota, Quebec, w. New England south.
                                                       AUG.–OCT.

FINE-LEAVED SNEEZEWEED *Helenium tenuifolium*
Similar to the preceding but leaves *grasslike* or stringlike, much branched. 1–2 ft. Roadsides, fields, sandy soil. Se. U.S., locally spreading in ne. U.S.   JULY–OCT.

PURPLE-HEADED SNEEZEWEED *Helenium nudiflorum*
Similar to Sneezeweed (*H. autumnale*), but button *deep purplish,* upper leaves smaller, less toothed. 1–3 ft. Damp thickets, rich meadows, roadsides. Michigan, New York, s. New England south. Local in North; spreading.   JUNE–OCT.

THIN-LEAVED CONEFLOWER *Rudbeckia triloba*
Distinguished from Black-eyed Susan by smaller, more numerous flowers with shorter, fewer (8–10) rays. Note also the *3-lobed* lower leaves. Plant much branched; stems hairy, but less bristly than in *R. hirta.* 2–5 ft. Open woods, thickets. Minnesota, Michigan, Ohio, e. New York, New Jersey south.
                                                       JUNE–OCT.

CHRYSOGONUM *Chrysogonum virginianum*
Note the *5 rounded rays* and the long-stalked, heart- or spade-shaped leaves. Low, usually less than 1 ft. (2–20 in.). Moist shady woodlands. Se. Ohio, s. Pennsylvania south.
                                                    APRIL–JUNE

LANCE-LEAVED COREOPSIS, TICKSEED
                                                Coreopsis lanceolata
Note the 8 rays, each with *4 deep lobes* at the tip. Leaves lance-shaped or with 2 basal prongs. 1–2 ft. Poor soils, dry sandy places, roadsides. Wisconsin, Michigan, Ontario south; local escape in Northeast.   MAY–AUG.

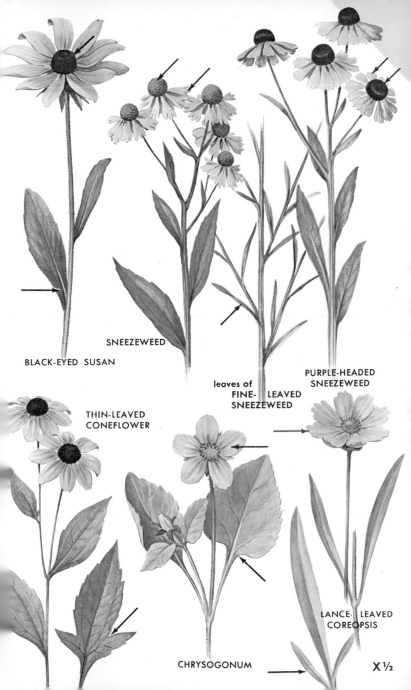

BLACK-EYED SUSAN

SNEEZEWEED

leaves of
FINE- LEAVED
SNEEZEWEED

PURPLE-HEADED
SNEEZEWEED

THIN-LEAVED
CONEFLOWER

CHRYSOGONUM

LANCE- LEAVED
COREOPSIS

X ½

SUNFLOWERLIKE FLOWERS

COMPOSITE OR DAISY FAMILY (Compositae)
See also pp. 180–86.

NARROW-LEAVED SUNFLOWER *Helianthus angustifolius*
Note the *purplish-black* disk (suggesting Black-eyed Susan)
and the thin, hard, *rigid* leaves. 1½–5 ft. Bogs, pine barrens.
S. Indiana, Long Island south. AUG.–OCT.

GREEN-HEADED CONEFLOWER *Rudbeckia laciniata*
Note the greenish, buttonlike disk, *reflexed* golden rays, deeply
cut 3- or 5-parted leaves. Stems tall, branched, smooth. 3–12
ft. Moist rich ground, thickets. Manitoba, Quebec south.
JULY–SEPT.

TICKSEED-SUNFLOWER *Bidens aristosa*
One of the showier members of the sticktight (*Bidens*) group.
Note the deeply divided, toothed leaves, showy flowers. 3–4 ft.
For a comparison of other *Bidens* and their achenes ("seeds")
see p. 186. Wet meadows, swampy spots. Minnesota, Maine
south. AUG.–OCT.

COMMON SUNFLOWER *Helianthus annuus*
A miniature of the domesticated form (which may have a
flower 10 in. across); *disk brownish*, rays golden. *Leaves heart-
or spade-shaped*, alternate, rough, toothed, with slender stalks.
Stem rough-hairy. 3–12 ft. Prairies, bottoms, roadsides.
Minnesota to Missouri; locally established in East.
JULY–OCT.

ELECAMPANE Alien *Inula helenium*
Note the slender, scraggly rays and the broad floral bracts.
The broad, toothed leaves (woolly beneath) clasp the coarse,
hairy stem. 2–6 ft. Clearings, roadsides. Ontario, Nova
Scotia south. JULY–SEPT.

GRAY-HEADED CONEFLOWER *Ratibida pinnata*
Note the longish, dull-colored button (with anise scent when
bruised) and *extremely reflexed* rays. Leaves deeply cut, whitish-hairy; stems hairy. 3–5 ft. Fields, prairies. Minnesota to
w. New York and south in interior. JUNE–SEPT.

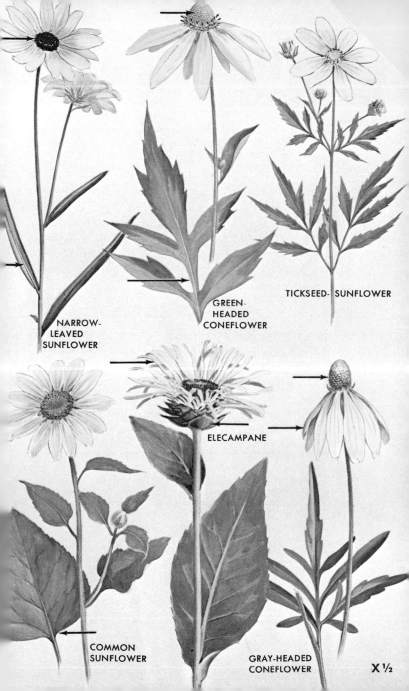

NARROW-LEAVED SUNFLOWER

GREEN-HEADED CONEFLOWER

TICKSEED- SUNFLOWER

ELECAMPANE

COMMON SUNFLOWER

GRAY-HEADED CONEFLOWER

X ½

SLENDER PLANTS OF WET PLACES, MEADOWS;
LINEAR OR PARALLEL-VEINED LEAVES

GOLDEN CLUB   *Orontium aquaticum*
ARUM FAMILY   (Araceae)
The golden *clublike spadix* is covered with tiny bright yellow
flowers containing both pistils and stamens. The spathe, or
floral leaf, is very small, soon falling. The long-stalked leaves
are elliptical and often float on the water. 1–2 ft. Swamp water,
ponds, shores. Kentucky, W. Virginia, c. New York, Massachusetts south.   APRIL–JUNE

SWEETFLAG, CALAMUS   *Acorus calamus*
ARUM FAMILY   (Araceae)
Note the rigid *swordlike leaves* and the *spadix* of small tightly
packed florets jutting *at an angle* from the flat bladelike stem.
1–4 ft. Wet meadows, pond edges, shores. Most of our area.
                              MAY–AUG.

WATER-STARGRASS   *Heteranthera dubia*
PICKERELWEED FAMILY   (Pontederiaceae)
The flaccid, grasslike leaves are submerged. The solitary, 6-
parted, pale yellow flower has a very long tube (1–1½ in.) and
just reaches surface of the water. Shallow, quiet water. Minnesota, s. Ontario, sw. Quebec south.   JUNE–SEPT.

STARGRASS   *Hypoxis hirsuta*
DAFFODIL FAMILY   (Amaryllidaceae)
The hairy, grasslike leaves and 6-pointed starlike flowers are
distinctive. 3–7 in. Meadows (moist or dry), open woods.
Manitoba to s. Maine and south.   MAY–AUG.

YELLOW-EYED GRASSES   *Xyris*
YELLOW-EYED GRASS FAMILY   (Xyridaceae)
Note the grasslike leaves and the small *3-petaled* flowers that
spring from a *conelike head* of leathery scales. Gray (Fernald)
lists 12 species in our area; variable, separated on technical
characters. Larger species may be 1 to 3 ft. high. Bogs, wet
pine barrens, sandy swamps, shores. Minnesota, Ontario, Newfoundland south, especially on coastal plain.   JUNE–SEPT.

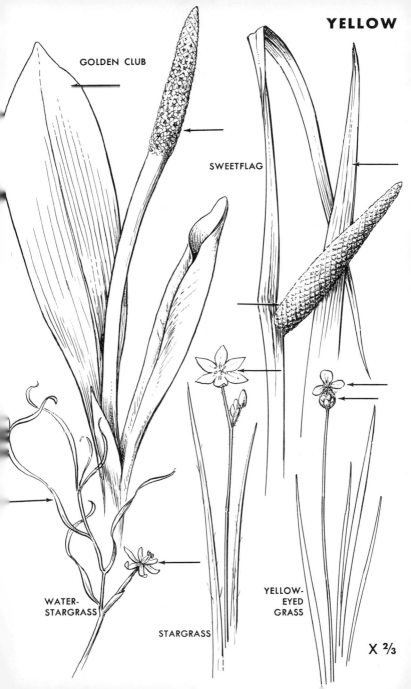

YELLOW

GOLDEN CLUB

SWEETFLAG

WATER-
STARGRASS

STARGRASS

YELLOW-
EYED
GRASS

X ²/₃

LIPPED FLOWERS: ORCHIDS
BROAD, PARALLEL-VEINED LEAVES

ORCHID FAMILY (Orchidaceae)
See also Yellow Lady's-slipper, p. 104.

WHORLED POGONIA　　　　　　　　*Isotria verticillata*
Note the whorl of 5 (or 6) wide stalkless leaves just below the
single, lipped, greenish-yellow flower and the *3 long madder-
purple sepals*. Lip streaked with purple. 6–12 in. Moist acid
woods and thickets. Wisconsin, s. Michigan, New England
south.　　　　　　　　　　　　　　　　　　　　　　MAY–JUNE

SMALL WHORLED POGONIA　　　　　*Isotria medeoloides*
Differs from the preceding by its *relatively short, arching sepals*.
Lip whitish or pale green. This plant remains dormant under-
ground for as much as 10 to 20 years before reappearing. 3–6 in.
Leaf mold of dry woods. Local, very rare from New Hampshire
and Vermont to N. Carolina.　　　　　　　　　　　MAY–JUNE

BROAD-LIPPED TWAYBLADE　　*Listera convallarioides*
Note the *pair* of broad, roundish leaves midway on the stem and
the *long, wedge-shaped*, shallowly notched lip of the greenish-
yellow flowers. Sepals purplish. 4–10 in. Damp soil, swamps,
glades, woods. Across Canada and northern edge of U.S. and
south in mts.　　　　　　　　　　　　　　　　　　JUNE–AUG.

PUTTYROOT　　　　　　　　　　　*Aplectrum hyemale*
The single large leaf develops in summer, lasts over winter, and
withers before flowering. Flowers yellowish, greenish, or whitish. The whitish lip is crinkly-edged and marked with purplish.
10–16 in. Rich deciduous woods, wet soil. S. Canada south
locally through much of our area.　　　　　　　　MAY–JUNE

YELLOW

WHORLED POGONIA

SMALL WHORLED POGONIA

BROAD-LIPPED TWAYBLADE

X 2

PUTTYROOT

X 2

X ⅔

LIPPED, SPURRED FLOWERS: ORCHIDS
LINEAR, PARALLEL-VEINED LEAVES
ORCHID FAMILY (Orchidaceae)
See similar whitish species of the genus *Habenaria*, p. 16.

CRESTED YELLOW ORCHIS *Habenaria cristata*
Note the fringed beards and the *relatively short spurs* on this deep yellow-orange species. Spur shorter than the deeply fringed lip. Sepals rounded and curved inward. 10–30 in. Open thickets, bogs. New Jersey, Tennessee south; formerly se. Massachusetts. JULY–AUG.

YELLOW FRINGED ORCHIS *Habenaria ciliaris*
See also color plate, p. 208. Yellow to deep orange. Differs from the preceding species by larger flowers, with *much longer spurs* that exceed the fringed lip. 1–2 ft. Peaty soil, grassy bogs. Michigan, New York south. JULY–AUG.

YELLOW FRINGELESS ORCHIS *Habenaria integra*
The tongue-shaped lip, *not fringed*, but toothed at the edge, separates this orchid from the preceding more showy fringed species. The spike of golden flowers is almost cylindrical. Usually 2 larger lance-shaped leaves on lower part of stem. 10–24 in. Wet pine barrens of New Jersey (now very rare); e. N. Carolina south. AUG.–SEPT.

RAGGED FRINGED ORCHIS *Habenaria lacera*
This *deeply fringed* species has a more filamentous beard than the first two shown here and is not rich yellow or orange; its color ranges from whitish or creamy to greenish yellow. 8–32 in. Swamps, marshes, bogs, glades, thickets. Minnesota, Ontario, Gulf of St. Lawrence south. JULY–AUG.

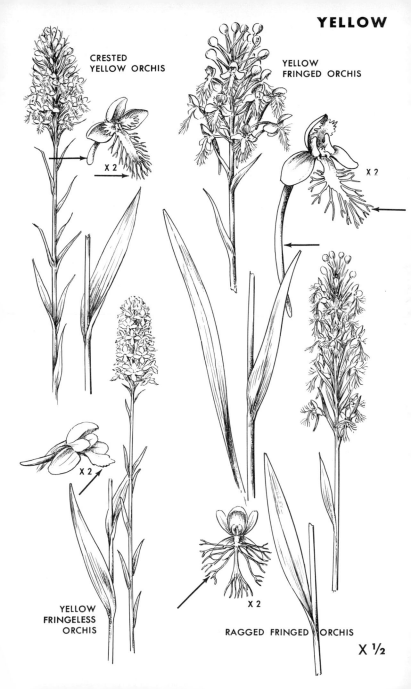

YELLOW

CRESTED
YELLOW ORCHIS

X 2

YELLOW
FRINGED ORCHIS

X 2

YELLOW
FRINGELESS
ORCHIS

X 2

RAGGED FRINGED ORCHIS

X 2

X ½

LIPPED FLOWERS; NAKED OR SCALED STALKS: MISCELLANEOUS AQUATICS & PARASITICS

1. AQUATICS

BLADDERWORTS   *Utricularia*
BLADDERWORT FAMILY   (Lentibulariaceae)
The small yellow flowers suggest the snapdragonlike flowers of
Butter-and-eggs (*Linaria*) — 2 lips and a spur. Flowering stalk
several inches tall, naked; filamentlike leaves submerged in mud
or shallow water, usually adorned with tiny bladders. At least
a dozen species in our area.   MAY–AUG.
HORNED BLADDERWORT, *U. cornuta.* Note the *long drooping spur* (½ in.). Terrestrial, with simple linear or grasslike
leaves embedded in mud. Bladders minute or absent.
GREATER BLADDERWORT, *U. vulgaris.* Spur shorter than
lower lip. Filamentlike leaves float horizontally below surface
of water; bladders scattered throughout.
FLAT-LEAVED BLADDERWORT, *U. intermedia.* Here the
bladders are not among leaf segments, but *on separate stalks.*
SWOLLEN BLADDERWORT, *U. inflata.* Note the whorl of
leaves whose *swollen stalks* act as floats. Ponds near coast.
HUMPED BLADDERWORT, *U. gibba.* Tiny, 2 to 3 in. tall,
with ¼-in. flower. Stems creep in mud; filaments few, short;
bladders few.

2. PARASITICS

BEECHDROPS   *Epifagus virginiana*
BROOMRAPE FAMILY   (Orobanchaceae)
Plants of this family lack green pigment, have scale-like leaves.
The *freely branching* habit distinguishes this species from all
others except Branched Broomrape, *Orobanche ramosa* (p. 324;
an alien, parasitic on tomato, tobacco, hemp, etc.). Yellowish,
reddish, or brown. 6–24 in. Parasitic; found under beech trees.
Ontario, Gulf of St. Lawrence south.   AUG.–OCT.

SQUAWROOT   *Conopholis americana*
BROOMRAPE FAMILY.   (Orobanchaceae)
Note the stubby, fleshy, scaly, *conelike yellow-brown stalk* sur-
mounted by a spike of lipped and hooded yellowish flowers.
3–8 in. Parasitic on roots of trees, especially oaks. Wisconsin,
Michigan, New England, Nova Scotia south.   MAY–JUNE

PINESAP   *Monotropa hypopithys*
WINTERGREEN FAMILY   (Pyrolaceae)
Similar to Indian-pipe (p. 20), but with *several* (not 1) nodding
flowers that are dull yellow or reddish (not white). Seedpod
erect. See also Sweet Pinesap, *Monotropsis odorata*, p. 232.
Woods. Throughout.   JUNE–OCT.

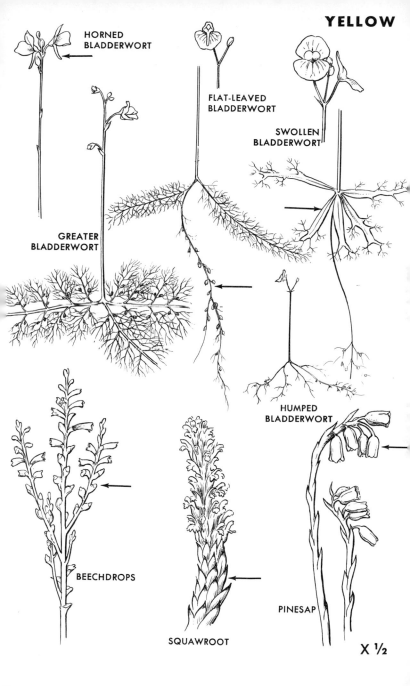

YELLOW

HORNED BLADDERWORT

FLAT-LEAVED BLADDERWORT

SWOLLEN BLADDERWORT

GREATER BLADDERWORT

HUMPED BLADDERWORT

BEECHDROPS

SQUAWROOT

PINESAP

X ½

LIPPED, LOBED, TUBULAR FLOWERS
SNAPDRAGON FAMILY (Scrophulariaceae)
See also color plate, p. 104.

WOOD-BETONY, LOUSEWORT *Pedicularis canadensis*
Yellow, red, or both. A low hairy plant topped by a broad whorl of tubular, hooded flowers. The long, soft-hairy leaves, many of them basal, are deeply incised and toothed, often reddish. 5–14 in. Woods, clearings. Manitoba, s. Quebec, Maine south. APRIL–JUNE

SWAMP LOUSEWORT *Pedicularis lanceolata*
Similar, but smooth or nearly smooth. Leaves more often *opposite*. Flowers always yellow; upper lip shorter, *not toothed* (as in Wood-betony). Note the toothed leaflike calyx embracing flower. 1–2 ft. Wet meadows, shores. Manitoba, Minnesota, Michigan, s. Ontario, Massachusetts south. AUG.–OCT.

YELLOW-RATTLE *Rhinanthus crista-galli*
Note the calyx (joined sepals), which forms a *flat bladderlike envelope* around the base of the flower; much inflated when in fruit. Seeds rattle in pod. Flowers in upper leaf axils; upper lip often tinged with violet, lower lip spotted. Leaves in pairs. 8–20 in. Fields, thickets. Canada, n. New England.
JUNE–SEPT.

COW-WHEAT *Melampyrum lineare*
A slender, smooth, parasitic plant with linear, paired leaves, the upper ones characteristically with *1 or 2 pointed teeth* near base. Flowers small, solitary, in upper leaf axils; whitish or pale yellow, upper lip arched, lower 3-lobed. 4–12 in. Woods, bogs, peaty soil, rocks. Canada south to n. Wisconsin, n. Michigan, n. New England (high mts.), e. Maine. JULY–AUG.

GOLDEN HEDGE-HYSSOP, GOLDEN PERT *Gratiola aurea*
The hedge-hyssops (6 in our area) are low plants of swampy spots. Most species are whitish or white-lobed, with a yellowish tube. This is the only bright yellow species. Leaves paired, usually 3-nerved, toothless, stalkless or semiclasping, with a broad base. Flowers appear 4-lobed (actually 2-lipped, lower lip 3-lobed). 3–15 in. Shores, swamps. Near coast from Quebec and Newfoundland south; also locally inland through Great Lakes area to N. Dakota. JUNE–SEPT.

WOOD- BETONY

SWAMP LOUSEWORT

YELLOW-RATTLE

COW- WHEAT

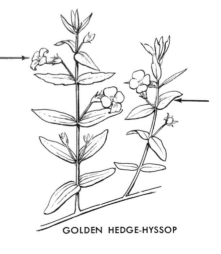

GOLDEN HEDGE-HYSSOP

X ½

LIPPED, TUBULAR FLOWERS:
MINTS AND CORYDALIS

☐ **HORSEMINT**   *Monarda punctata*
MINT FAMILY   (Labiatae)
Note the rosettes of *wide-jawed*, yellowish, purple-spotted flowers in the upper leaf axils, and the *showy white or lilac bracts* at their base. 1–3 ft. Sandy soil, coastal plain. Long Island south.   JULY–OCT.

☐ **YELLOW GIANT HYSSOP**   *Agastache nepetoides*
MINT FAMILY   (Labiatae)
Square stem indicates a mint, stalked arrowhead-shaped leaves and dense terminal cluster suggest Catnip, but the yellow flowers are distinctive. (Catnip has violet flowers.) Smooth. 2–4 ft. Thickets, wood edges. S. Dakota, w. Ontario, sw. Quebec south.   JULY–SEPT.

☐ **HORSE-BALM, RICHWEED**   *Collinsonia canadensis*
MINT FAMILY   (Labiatae)
The square stem indicates a mint; the loose, branching, pyramidal head of lemon-scented flowers identifies this species. The lower lip of the flower is long and slightly fringed, the stamens and pistil are long and projecting. 2–3 ft. Damp woods. Wisconsin, Ontario, New York, Vermont, Massachusetts south.   JULY–SEPT.

 CORYDALIS   *Corydalis*
POPPY FAMILY   (Papaveraceae)
BLEEDING-HEART SUBFAMILY   (Fumarioideae)
Closely related to Dutchman's-breeches and Bleeding-heart, as indicated by the finely cut leaves and flower structure, the genus *Corydalis* numbers 6 or 7 in our area. All but Pale Corydalis, *C. sempervirens* (p. 290), are yellow, and are very similar. All below are small plants (6–16 in.) with finely dissected leaves and narrow flowers about ½ in. long having a hollow spur. Most grow on rocks, sand, or gravel.
YELLOW CORYDALIS, *C. flavula*, has a *crest* on the upper petal, which is toothed. Spur stubby, depressed. Minnesota to Connecticut and south.   APRIL–MAY
GOLDEN CORYDALIS, *C. aurea*, has a longer spur than *C. flavula*, lacks crest. Blooms later. Sandy or rocky soil; shores, open woods. Across Canada and south to Missouri, Illinois, Ohio, W. Virginia (mts.), New York.   MAY–JUNE
SLENDER CORYDALIS, *C. micrantha*, has a *straight or slightly upturned spur*. Crest not toothed. Sandy or gravelly soil. Minnesota to Illinois and south.   MARCH–MAY

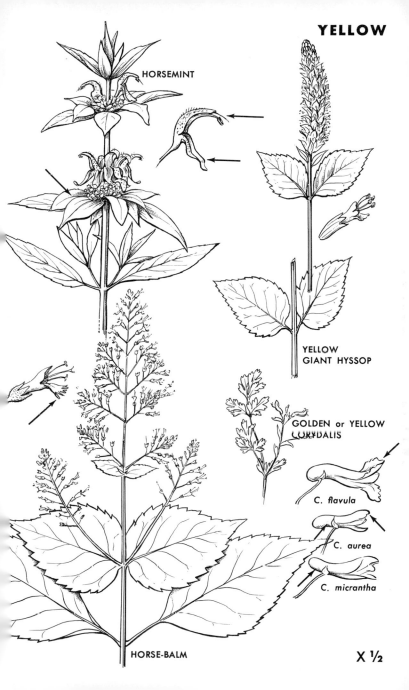

YELLOW

HORSEMINT

YELLOW
GIANT HYSSOP

GOLDEN or YELLOW
CORYDALIS

C. flavula

C. aurea

C. micrantha

HORSE-BALM

X ½

LIPPED, TUBULAR FLOWERS; PAIRED LEAVES

HONEYSUCKLE FAMILY (Caprifoliaceae)

Vines or erect shrubs. For more complete treatment see
A Field Guide to Trees and Shrubs (Field Guide No. 11).

TRUMPET HONEYSUCKLE *Lonicera sempervirens*
See also color plate, p. 216. A vine. *Long tubular flowers* yellow
inside, red outside. Upper leaves *perfoliate* (seemingly per-
forated by stem). Woods, thickets. Iowa, Ohio, New York,
Massachusetts south. APRIL–SEPT.

JAPANESE HONEYSUCKLE Alien *Lonicera japonica*
A weedy vine, difficult to eradicate; covers ground and bushes.
Flowers with long, curved stamens projecting, may be white or
buffy yellow. Some lower leaves may be lobed in White Oak
manner. Foliage evergreen. Fruit a black berry. Thickets,
wood edges, roadsides. Indiana, Ohio, New York, Massachusetts south. APRIL–JULY

HAIRY HONEYSUCKLE *Lonicera hirsuta*
A vine; higher-climbing than Japanese Honeysuckle, and not
evergreen. Upper leaves *perfoliate* (united around stem).
Flowers orange-yellow, sticky-hairy. Berries red, not black.
Thickets, shores. S. Canada, n. U.S. MAY–JULY

FLY-HONEYSUCKLE *Lonicera canadensis*
A shrub; mostly hairless. Leaves stalked, egg or heart-shaped.
Flowers *short-lobed;* yellowish to yellow-green. 2–5 ft. Woods.
Across s. Canada, n. U.S.; south in mts. JUNE–AUG.

SWAMP FLY-HONEYSUCKLE *Lonicera oblongifolia*
A hairless shrub with rather blunt oblong leaves. Note flower
type. Berries orange to red. 2–5 ft. Acid bogs, White Cedar
swamps. Manitoba, se. Quebec, New Brunswick to Minnesota,
Michigan, w. Pennsylvania, e. Maine. JULY–AUG.

NORTHERN FLY-HONEYSUCKLE *Lonicera villosa*
A small hairy honeysuckle with hairy oval leaves. Berries *blue*.
1–3 ft. Rocky or peaty soil, swamps, bogs. Manitoba to Newfoundland and south to northern tier of states. MAY–AUG.

NORTHERN BUSH-HONEYSUCKLE *Diervilla lonicera*
The bush-honeysuckles differ from other honeysuckles (*Lonicera*)
in having *toothed* leaves. The yellow funnel-form flowers may
be tinged with red; lower lobe more deeply colored. 1–4 ft.
Wood openings, dry soils. Manitoba to Newfoundland and
south to Iowa, Ohio, w. N. Carolina, Delaware. MAY–AUG.

Note: Flame Azalea, *Rhododendron calendulaceum* (not shown
here), is often called a honeysuckle. It belongs to the Heath
Family (Ericaceae). See color plate, p. 208.

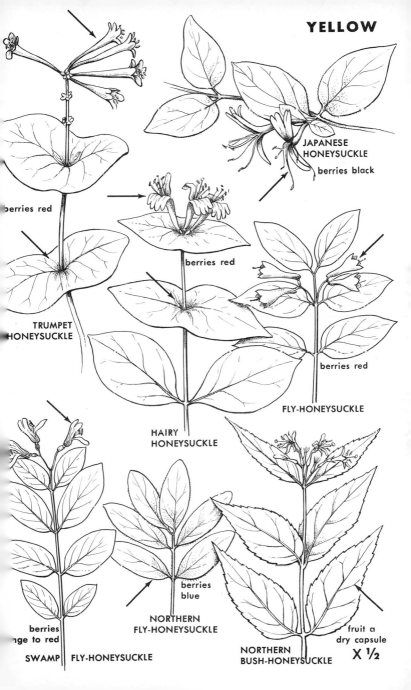

YELLOW

JAPANESE
HONEYSUCKLE

berries black

berries red

TRUMPET
HONEYSUCKLE

berries red

FLY-HONEYSUCKLE

berries red

HAIRY
HONEYSUCKLE

berries
orange to red

SWAMP FLY-HONEYSUCKLE

berries
blue

NORTHERN
FLY-HONEYSUCKLE

fruit a
dry capsule

NORTHERN
BUSH-HONEYSUCKLE

X ½

4 to 9 PETALS: BUTTERCUPLIKE FLOWERS, POPPIES, ETC.

MARSH-MARIGOLD, COWSLIP *Caltha palustris*
Buttercup Family (Ranunculaceae)
Flowers larger than in true buttercups (1–1½ in.); the 5 to 9 deep yellow "petals" are really sepals. Leaves glossy; *roundish* or kidney-shaped. Stem thick, hollow, succulent. 8–24 in. Swamps, brooksides. Most of our area. April–June

GLOBE-FLOWER *Trollius laxus*
Buttercup Family (Ranunculaceae)
The 5 to 7 greenish-yellow sepals form a large solitary buttercuplike blossom (1–1½ in.) terminating a leafy stem. Leaves buttercuplike, upper 2 sessile, *surrounding stem*. 12–20 in. Swampy spots. Rare; Michigan, Ohio, New York, w. Connecticut to Pennsylvania, Delaware. April–June

SPEARWORTS *Ranunculus*
Buttercup Family (Ranunculaceae)
Mud-loving buttercups with *lance-shaped* leaves. *R. ambigens*, shown here, has narrow petals as long as sepals. *R. flammula* (Maritime Provinces) has sepals only half as long as petals. *R. pusillus* has inconspicuous flowers and small ovate basal leaves on long stalks. Swamps, marshes, shores. June–Sept.

CELANDINE-POPPY, WOOD-POPPY
Stylophorum diphyllum
Poppy Family   Poppy Subfamily (Papaveroideae)
Note the 4 fragile, round petals and *pair* of pale, deeply lobed stem leaves (whitish bloom on underside). Juice yellow. Seedpod *ovoid, hairy*. 10–16 in. Damp woods. Mainly west of mts., Wisconsin to w. Pennsylvania and south. March–May

CELANDINE Alien *Chelidonium majus*
Poppy Family   Poppy Subfamily (Papaveroideae)
Similar to Celandine-poppy but flowers smaller (¾ in.), leaves attached *singly*. Seedpod *slender, smooth*. 1–2 ft. Moist ground, towns, wood edges. Much of area. April–Aug.

LESSER CELANDINE Alien *Ranunculus ficaria*
Buttercup Family (Ranunculaceae)
Eight glossy petals, long-stalked, *heart-shaped* leaves. Flower solitary. 2–6 in. Damp shade. Local. April–June

HORN-POPPY, SEA-POPPY Alien *Glaucium flavum*
Poppy Family   Poppy Subfamily (Papaveroideae)
Note the large (2-in.), solitary, 4-petaled flower and deeply cut, gray-green leaves, upper ones clasping. Seedpod very long (6–12 in.), *sickle-shaped*. 2–3 ft. Waste places, especially near coast. Massachusetts to Virginia. June–Aug.

PRICKLY POPPY Alien *Argemone mexicana*
Poppy Family   Poppy Subfamily (Papaveroideae)
Note the prickly, *thistle-like* leaves and bristly stems. Flowers large (over 2 in.) with 4 to 6 yellow or orange petals. Seedpod ovoid, prickly. Occasional in waste places. May–Sept.

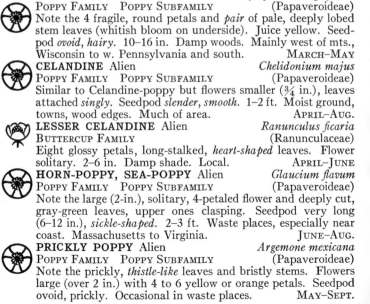

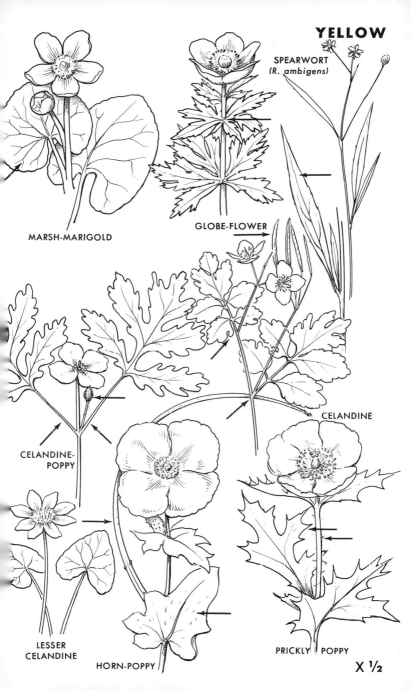

YELLOW

SPEARWORT
(R. ambigens)

MARSH-MARIGOLD

GLOBE-FLOWER

CELANDINE

CELANDINE-
POPPY

LESSER
CELANDINE

HORN-POPPY

PRICKLY POPPY

X 1/2

5 (to 7) GLOSSY PETALS: BUTTERCUPS

BUTTERCUP FAMILY (Ranunculaceae)
Note the bushy stamens, deeply cut, palmate leaves;
36 species in our area; most familiar ones below.

COMMON or TALL BUTTERCUP Alien *Ranunculus acris*
The most familiar buttercup. Erect, branching, hairy. Basal
leaves deeply cut into 5 to 7 unstalked segments. Petals overlap.
2–3 ft. Fields, meadows. Most of our area. MAY–SEPT.

BULBOUS BUTTERCUP Alien *Ranunculus bulbosus*
Small, hairy; flowers deep yellow. Note bulbous root, *reflexed*
sepals. Basal leaves in 3 segments, end one stalked. 6–18 in.
Fields, roadsides. Widespread. APRIL–JUNE

CREEPING BUTTERCUP Alien *Ranunculus repens*
Note *pale blotches* on leaves; also creeping *runners,* which send
up leaves. 1–3 ft. Roadsides, vacant lots, old gardens, wet
meadows. Most of our area. MAY–AUG.

SWAMP BUTTERCUP *Ranunculus septentrionalis*
Weak, hollow, smoothish stem often reclines. Leaves in 3 segments, *each* short-stalked. Achenes ("seeds") flat, flanged, with
long beak. 1–3 ft. Moist meadows, thickets. S. Canada south
to Missouri, Kentucky, Maryland. APRIL–JULY

HISPID BUTTERCUP *Ranunculus hispidus*
Similar to preceding but more erect, stem hairy, petals narrower.
Achenes ("seeds") not flanged. 1–2 ft. Woods. Illinois, In-
diana, Ohio, New York south. MARCH–MAY

KIDNEYLEAF BUTTERCUP *Ranunculus abortivus*
Note the *kidney-shaped* basal leaves of this inconspicuous
species. Petals very small, reflexed or drooping. 6–24 in.
Woods, damp thickets. Most of area. APRIL–AUG.

EARLY BUTTERCUP *Ranunculus fascicularis*
The earliest buttercup. Silky basal leaves *longer than wide;*
narrowly and *bluntly lobed.* The 5 to 7 petals are relatively
narrow. 6–12 in. Open woods, hillsides, prairies. Minnesota,
Ontario, s. New Hampshire south. APRIL–MAY

HOOKED BUTTERCUP *Ranunculus recurvatus*
Hairy; small petals, shorter than recurved sepals. Hooked
beaks on achenes. 1–2 ft. Woods. Most of area. MAY–JULY

BRISTLY BUTTERCUP *Ranunculus pensylvanicus*
Similar to *R. recurvatus,* but note leaf shape (stalked outer
segment). 1–2 ft. Wet ground. Most of area. JULY–SEPT.

CURSED BUTTERCUP (not shown) *Ranunculus sceleratus*
Elongated flower heads (thimble-shaped in fruit); petals shorter
than sepals. Leaves and stems watery, juice causes blisters.
8–24 in. Swamps. Widespread. MAY–AUG.

YELLOW WATER-BUTTERCUP *Ranunculus flabellaris*
Leaves submerged, filamentous. See White Water-buttercup,
p. 6. Quiet water. S. Canada, Maine south. MAY–JUNE

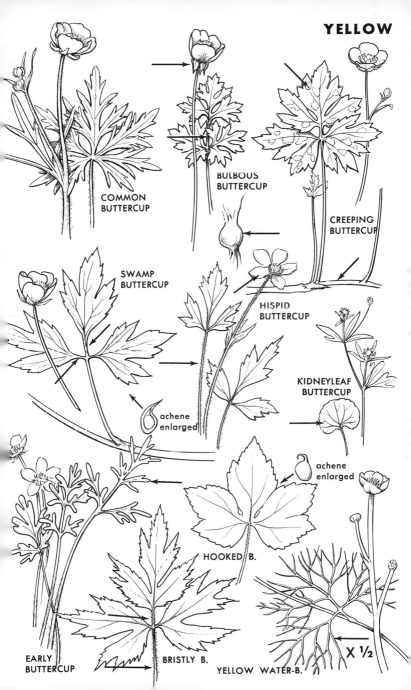

YELLOW

COMMON BUTTERCUP

BULBOUS BUTTERCUP

CREEPING BUTTERCUP

SWAMP BUTTERCUP

HISPID BUTTERCUP

achene enlarged

KIDNEYLEAF BUTTERCUP

achene enlarged

EARLY BUTTERCUP

HOOKED B.

BRISTLY B.

YELLOW WATER-B.

X ½

5 PETALS: CINQUEFOILS
5-PART AND PINNATE LEAVES
Rose Family (Rosaceae)
See other cinquefoils, pp. 28, 44, 148.

COMMON CINQUEFOIL   *Potentilla simplex*
Cinquefoils suggest yellow-flowered wild strawberries, but most species have radially 5-parted leaves (hence the name). This familiar species has prostrate stems, rooting at the nodes. Flowers and leaves rise from runners on separate stalks. Runners 6 to 20 in. Fields, dry woods. Minnesota, s. Ontario, Nova Scotia south.   APRIL–JUNE

DWARF CINQUEFOIL   *Potentilla canadensis*
A more petite species than *P. simplex*, with more *wedge-shaped* leaflets. Toothed leaflets *rounded;* without teeth below middle. Stems densely silver-hairy. There is a cream-colored form. 2–4 in. (runners 6–20 in.). Fields, woods. Minnesota, s. Ontario, w. Nova Scotia south.   MARCH–JUNE

ROUGH-FRUITED CINQUEFOIL Alien   *Potentilla recta*
Erect, hairy, very leafy, many-branched. Leaflets 5 to 7, relatively narrow. Flowers rather large (½–1 in.), *pale* yellow, in flat terminal cluster. 1–2 ft. Roadsides, fields. Most of our area.   JUNE–AUG.

SILVERY CINQUEFOIL Alien   *Potentilla argentea*
The 5 wedge-shaped leaflets are narrow, with relatively few deep, blunt, *oaklike teeth;* edges *rolled inward; silvery-woolly* beneath. Flowers clustered at ends of white-woolly branches. 5–12 in. Dry soil, fields. Most of our area.   JUNE–SEPT.

SHRUBBY CINQUEFOIL   *Potentilla fruticosa*
Note the toothless leaf segments. A *bushy shrub* with larger flowers than in Common Cinquefoil. Leaves silky, whitish beneath. Stems *woody*, often with loose bark. 1–3 ft. Meadows, shores. Across Canada and south to n. Iowa, Illinois, Indiana, Ohio, Pennsylvania, n. New Jersey.   JUNE–OCT.

PRAIRIE CINQUEFOIL   *Potentilla pensylvanica*
Note the *pinnate* leaves with *White Oak-like* lobes. Densely woolly. Stipules at base of leaves large, arrow-shaped. 1–2 ft. Shores, bluffs, calcareous rocks. N. Canada to Minnesota, n. Michigan.   JUNE–AUG.

BUSHY CINQUEFOIL   *Potentilla paradoxa*
Bushy, with bluntly toothed, pinnate leaves. 1–2 ft. Prairies, shores. Ontario to Missouri, Ohio, w. New York.   JUNE–SEPT.

SILVERWEED   *Potentilla anserina*
A prostrate species that sends up flowers and leaves on separate stalks. Leaves strikingly *silvery beneath*, divided into 7 to 25 paired, sharp-toothed leaflets, *increasing in size* upward. 1–3 ft. Wet sandy shores. Canada south to Iowa, Great Lakes, coastal New England.   JUNE–AUG.

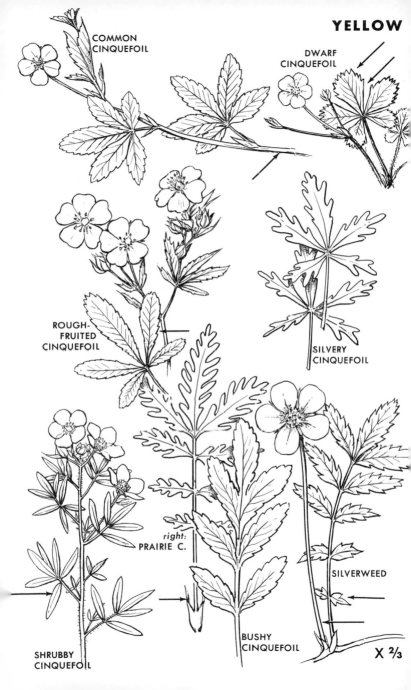

YELLOW

COMMON CINQUEFOIL

DWARF CINQUEFOIL

ROUGH-FRUITED CINQUEFOIL

SILVERY CINQUEFOIL

SHRUBBY CINQUEFOIL

right: PRAIRIE C.

BUSHY CINQUEFOIL

SILVERWEED

X ⅔

5 PETALS: AVENS, AGRIMONIES, ETC.
UNEQUAL LEAFLETS, PAIRED LATERALLY
ROSE FAMILY (Rosaceae)

SILVERWEED *Potentilla anserina*
A prostrate potentilla that sends up flowers and leaves on separate stalks. Leaves strikingly *silvery beneath*, divided into 7 to 25 paired, sharp-toothed leaflets, *increasing in size* upward. 1–3 ft. Wet sandy beaches, shores. Canada south to Iowa, Great Lakes, coastal New England. JUNE–AUG.

MOUNTAIN AVENS *Geum peckii*
A showy buttercuplike flower (1 in.) *of the high mts.* Note the smooth, much-toothed, roundish basal leaves, usually with small leaflets on the leafstalk. 6 in.–2 ft. Alpine slopes of White Mts., New Hampshire. JUNE–SEPT.

ROUGH AVENS *Geum virginianum*
Most leaves are divided into 3 large terminal leaflets, the center one larger than the 2 others; coarsely toothed. Stem hairy. Petals pale yellow or cream-colored, *shorter* than long sepals. 12–30 in. Low ground, woods, thickets. Indiana, New York, Massachusetts south. JUNE–JULY

LARGE-LEAVED AVENS *Geum macrophyllum*
A hairy species with basal leaves that end in a *very large* rounded segment; lateral leaves much smaller. Petals *longer* than the reflexed sepals. 1–3 ft. Woods, thickets. Across Canada and northern edge of U.S. MAY–JULY

YELLOW AVENS *Geum aleppicum* var. *strictum*
Another hairy species, differing from *G. macrophyllum* in having more *wedge-shaped* leaflets; variable, large leaflets often interspersed with small ones. 2–5 ft. Low ground, thickets. S. Canada south to Iowa, Illinois, Ohio, Pennsylvania, New Jersey. JUNE–AUG.

AGRIMONIES *Agrimonia*
The agrimonies have compound leaves somewhat resembling avens (*Geum*), with large leaflets interspersed with smaller ones. The flowers are much smaller, borne in a *slender spikelike wand.* Hooked seed receptacles adhere to clothing. There are 7 similar species in our area, accurately identified only by technical characters. 1–6 ft. Thickets, woods. Most of our area. JULY–SEPT.

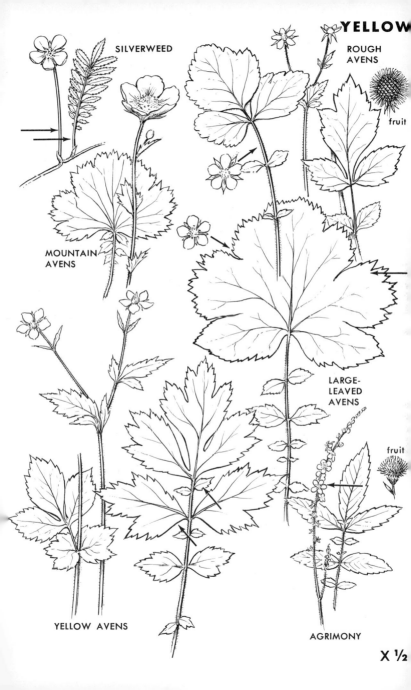

YELLOW

SILVERWEED

ROUGH
AVENS

fruit

MOUNTAIN
AVENS

LARGE-
LEAVED
AVENS

fruit

YELLOW AVENS

AGRIMONY

X ½

5 PETALS, BUSHY STAMENS; PAIRED LEAVES:
ST. JOHNSWORTS

ST. JOHNSWORT FAMILY (Guttiferae)

Leaves toothless, dotted with tiny translucent or black glands.

COMMON ST. JOHNSWORT Alien *Hypericum perforatum*
See color plate, p. 106. This, the most familiar, weedy St.
Johnswort, has *black dots on margins of petals*, translucent dots
on leaves. Flowers about 1 in. 1–2½ ft. Roadsides, fields,
waste places. Throughout. JUNE–SEPT.

GREAT ST. JOHNSWORT *Hypericum pyramidatum*
A very large species with *large elliptic leaves* (2–3 in.). Flowers
(2 in.) with very bushy stamens and *5 styles* spreading from
united base (most other species have 3 styles). 2–6 ft. Wet
places, streambanks. Manitoba, Quebec, Maine south to
Kansas, Indiana, Pennsylvania. JUNE–AUG.

SHRUBBY ST. JOHNSWORT *Hypericum spathulatum*
A much-branched *shrub* with *woody 2-edged twigs* crowned with
a mass of golden flowers. A similar shrubby species, *H. kal-
mianum* (not shown), with narrower leaves, *5 styles*, is found on
shores of Great Lakes. 1–4 ft. Pastures, fields. Minnesota,
Ontario, New York south. JULY–SEPT.

SPOTTED ST. JOHNSWORT *Hypericum punctatum*
In this species both leaves and flowers are *conspicuously dotted*
with black glands. 1–3 ft. Thickets, damp places. Minnesota,
s. Ontario, s. Quebec south. JUNE–SEPT.

COPPERY ST. JOHNSWORT *Hypericum denticulatum*
Note the coppery yellow flowers and 4-angled stem. Leaves
may be narrow and pointed or elliptic. 8–20 in. Pine barrens,
sandy soil, shores. New Jersey south. JUNE–AUG.

PALE ST. JOHNSWORT *Hypericum ellipticum*
Flowers (½ in.) on simple, unbranched stems arising from a
rhizome (prostrate stem). 8–20 in. Marshes, shores. S. Canada,
n. U.S. JULY–AUG.

DWARF ST. JOHNSWORT *Hypericum mutilum*
Small blossoms (less than ¼ in.), broadly oval leaves. 1–3 ft.
Low wet ground. Manitoba, Quebec south. JULY–SEPT.

CANADIAN ST. JOHNSWORT *Hypericum canadense*
Small blossoms (less than ¼ in.), very narrow leaves. 6–20 in.
Wet soil. Manitoba, Newfoundland south. JULY–SEPT.

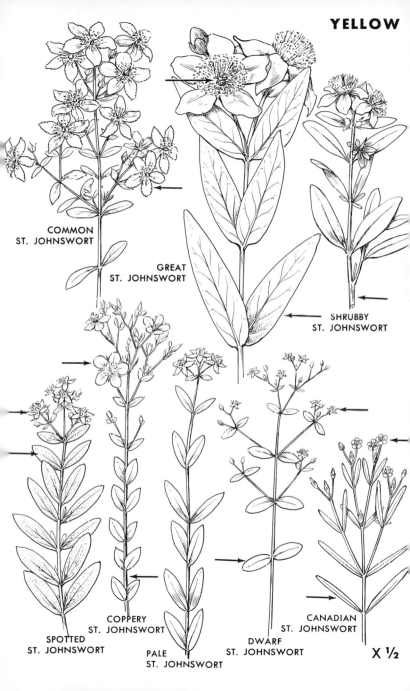

YELLOW

COMMON
ST. JOHNSWORT

GREAT
ST. JOHNSWORT

SHRUBBY
ST. JOHNSWORT

SPOTTED
ST. JOHNSWORT

COPPERY
ST. JOHNSWORT

PALE
ST. JOHNSWORT

DWARF
ST. JOHNSWORT

CANADIAN
ST. JOHNSWORT

X ½

5 PETALS; PAIRED OR WHORLED LEAVES:
YELLOW LOOSESTRIFES (*Lysimachia*)
PRIMROSE FAMILY (Primulaceae)

1. FLOWERS IN UPPER LEAF AXILS
FRINGED LOOSESTRIFE *Lysimachia ciliata*
Note the *nodding flowers* (face downward), the fringed or
slightly toothed petals, and the broad, paired leaves with *fringed*
leafstalks. 1–4 ft. Swamps, wet thickets, shores. Nearly
throughout.   JUNE–AUG.

WHORLED LOOSESTRIFE *Lysimachia quadrifolia*
A delicate species with most leaves and flowers *in whorls of
4 (3–6)*. Flowers are dotted around center with *red*. 1–3 ft.
Open woods, thickets, shores. Wisconsin, s. Ontario, Maine
south to Illinois and in uplands to Georgia.   JUNE–AUG.

GARDEN LOOSESTRIFE Alien   *Lysimachia vulgaris*
A coarser, *bushier* species with leaves sometimes black-dotted,
mostly in whorls of 3 or 4. Densely downy. Some flowers in
upper leaf axils but most in a terminal panicle. Stamens red.
Petals hairless at edge. 2–3 ft. Roadsides, thickets. Quebec
to Illinois, Ohio, Maryland. A similar garden escape, *L. punctata* (not shown), has most flowers in axils; petals edged with
minute hairs.   JUNE–SEPT.

PRAIRIE LOOSESTRIFE   *Lysimachia quadriflora*
Leaves *very narrow, stiff*. The slightly toothed flowers spring
from leaf axils mostly near summit. 1–3 ft. Wet soil, prairies,
shores. West of mts., Manitoba, s. Ontario, w. New York south
to Missouri, Kentucky, w. Virginia.   JULY–AUG.

LANCE-LEAVED LOOSESTRIFE   *Lysimachia lanceolata*
Similar to preceding but leaves wider, tapering narrowly at
both ends, *not* distinctly stalked. Note *runners* at base of plant.
1–2 ft. Woods, thickets, prairies. Wisconsin, Michigan, Ohio,
Pennsylvania south.   JUNE–AUG.

HYBRID LOOSESTRIFE   *Lysimachia hybrida*
Not really a hybrid. Similar to *L. lanceolata* but leaves *stalked*.
No runners at base of plant. 1–3 ft. Swamps, shores. Minne-
sota, sw. Quebec, w. Ontario south.   JULY–AUG.

2. FLOWERS IN ELONGATED TERMINAL CLUSTER
YELLOW LOOSESTRIFE, SWAMP CANDLES
                                   Lysimachia terrestris
See text and color plate, p. 106.

3. TRAILING VINES
MONEYWORT Alien   *Lysimachia nummularia*
Note the *small, round*, shining, paired leaves and pairs of
slender-stalked flowers in the leaf axils. *Trailing*. Moist ground,
lawns, roadsides. Throughout.   JULY–SEPT.

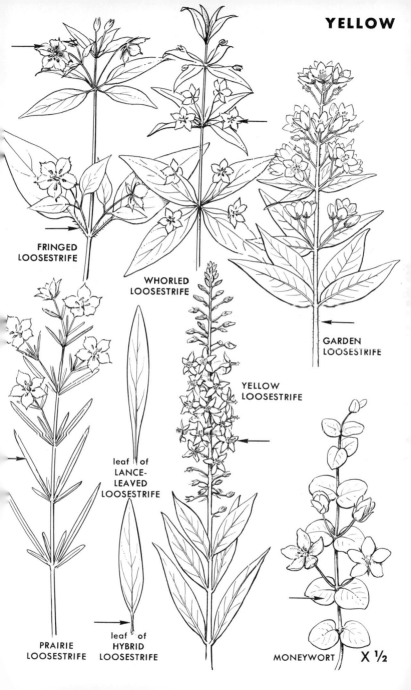

YELLOW

FRINGED
LOOSESTRIFE

WHORLED
LOOSESTRIFE

GARDEN
LOOSESTRIFE

YELLOW
LOOSESTRIFE

leaf of
LANCE-
LEAVED
LOOSESTRIFE

PRAIRIE
LOOSESTRIFE

leaf of
HYBRID
LOOSESTRIFE

MONEYWORT   X ½

5 PETALS; ALTERNATE LEAVES

Most flowers borne singly in leaf axils.

VELVET-LEAF Alien   *Abutilon theophrasti*
MALLOW FAMILY   (Malvaceae)
Note the *very large* (4–10 in.), velvety, *heart-shaped* leaves.
Yellow, mallow-like flowers (1–1½ in.) borne singly in leaf axils.
3–5 ft. Waste ground, fields. Minnesota, Great Lakes region,
New England south.   JULY–OCT.

FLOWER-OF-AN-HOUR Alien   *Hibiscus trionum*
MALLOW FAMILY   (Malvaceae)
Note the *dark purple eye* of the pale yellow flower, which
quickly wilts. Calyx inflated, bladderlike. Leaves deeply 3-
parted, coarsely toothed. 1–2 ft. Waste ground, roadsides.
Local, Minnesota, Michigan, Nova Scotia south.   JULY–SEPT.

CREEPING PRIMROSE-WILLOW   *Jussiaea repens*
EVENING-PRIMROSE FAMILY   (Onagraceae)
This semiaquatic plant has creeping or floating stems, often
rooting at the nodes. Note the *rose-colored or purplish* stems
and long-stalked shiny flowers. Leaves untoothed, alternate,
with narrow stalks. Shallow water, mud, swamps. Missouri,
s. Illinois, s. Indiana south; also introduced locally in lower
Delaware River below Philadelphia.   JUNE–OCT.

UPRIGHT PRIMROSE-WILLOW   *Jussiaea decurrens*
(not shown)
EVENING-PRIMROSE FAMILY   (Onagraceae)
Similar to preceding but erect, stems *4-angled*. Leaves *stalkless*
or nearly so, flowing into stem. 1–2 ft. Swamps, ditches.
Missouri, s. Illinois, s. Indiana, W. Virginia, Virginia south.
                                       JULY–SEPT.

MOTH MULLEIN Alien   *Verbascum blattaria*
SNAPDRAGON FAMILY   (Scrophulariaceae)
See text and color plate, p. 106.

FROSTWEED   *Helianthemum canadense*
ROCKROSE FAMILY   (Cistaceae)
Note the narrow, toothless, alternate leaves and single, 5-
petaled flower (about 1 in.) with many stamens. Later, clusters
of flowers without petals appear on branches. 6–20 in. Sandy
soil, rocky woods. Wisconsin, s. Ontario, sw. Quebec, s. Maine,
Nova Scotia south.   MAY–JUNE

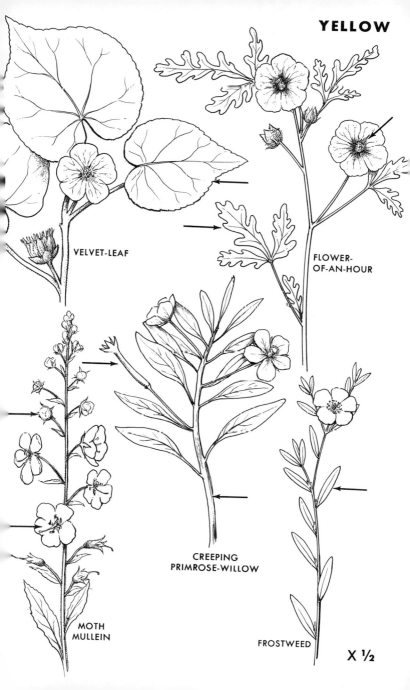

YELLOW

VELVET-LEAF

FLOWER-OF-AN-HOUR

CREEPING PRIMROSE-WILLOW

MOTH MULLEIN

FROSTWEED

X ½

5 PETALS OR LOBES; ALTERNATE LEAVES

1. FLAT OR CURLED CLUSTERS
FORGET-ME-NOT FAMILY   (Boraginaceae)

HOARY PUCCOON   *Lithospermum canescens*
Puccoons have flattish or curled-over clusters of yellow or
orange flowers. The 5 flat forget-me-not-like lobes flare from a
tube that conceals the stamens. Leaves alternate, slender,
toothless. 2–20 in. Dry or sandy soil, prairies, roadsides, open
woods. Saskatchewan to s. Ontario and south through Mississippi Valley.   APRIL–JUNE
HAIRY PUCCOON, *L. croceum,* has larger flowers (up to 1 in.);
leaves more numerous, wider, coarsely hairy.
NARROW-LEAVED PUCCOON, *L. incisum,* has *toothed* petals,
very narrow leaves.

COMFREY Alien   *Symphytum officinale*
Note the broad, rough-hairy, lanceolate leaves *flowing into the
winged stem.* Flowers bell-like, yellow, whitish, or pinkish fading to bluish; in a 1-sided, curled cluster, accompanied by a
pair of winglike leaves. 2–3 ft. Roadsides, ditches, waste places.
Much of our area.   JUNE–SEPT.

2. NODDING, BELL-LIKE FLOWERS, SHALLOW LOBES
TOMATO FAMILY   (Solanaceae)

GROUND-CHERRIES   *Physalis*
These coarse-leaved plants have bell-like flowers, often with
a dark center, which hang singly from leaf axils, or forks, in
stem. Fruit enclosed in a papery bladder formed by sepals.
Chinese Lantern Plant, *P. alkekengi,* is cultivated. 18 or 19
species in our area.
SMOOTH GROUND-CHERRY, *P. subglabrata,* is quite
smooth, with diamond-shaped leaves tapering into petioles,
often with 1 or 2 blunt teeth. Flower yellow with purplish
throat. 3–5 ft. Minnesota, Ontario, s. New England south.
                                                  JULY–SEPT.
VIRGINIA GROUND-CHERRY, *P. virginiana.* Indistinctly
toothed or toothless leaves taper at both ends. Stem with long
soft hairs. Flower yellow with purplish spots. Fruiting bladder
deeply dented at base. 18–36 in. Woods, clearings. S. Manitoba, s. Ontario, s. New England south.   MAY–AUG.
STRAWBERRY-TOMATO, *P. pruinosa.* Covered with hoary
down, giving a gray-green look. Leaves heart-shaped at base,
with coarse teeth. Dry soil, fields. Wisconsin, Indiana, Ohio,
New York, sw. Maine south.   JULY–OCT.
CLAMMY GROUND-CHERRY, *P. heterophylla.* Note rounded
leaf base, few teeth. Stems with sticky hairs. Variable. Flower
greenish yellow, brown center. 1–3 ft. Dry woods, clearings.
Saskatchewan, s. Quebec, New England south.   JUNE–SEPT.

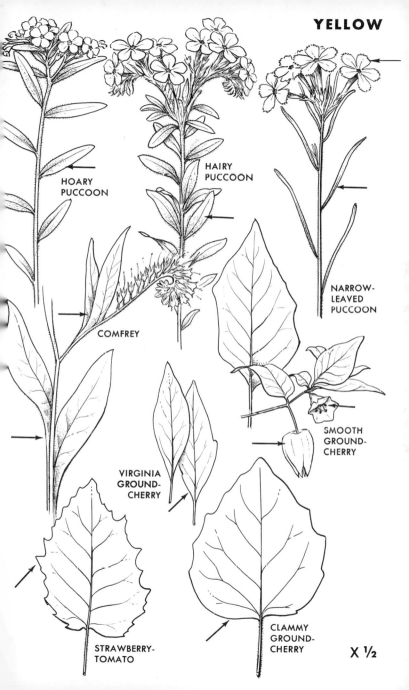

YELLOW

HOARY
PUCCOON

HAIRY
PUCCOON

NARROW-
LEAVED
PUCCOON

COMFREY

SMOOTH
GROUND-
CHERRY

VIRGINIA
GROUND-
CHERRY

STRAWBERRY-
TOMATO

CLAMMY
GROUND-
CHERRY

X ½

5 PETALS AND A SPUR: VIOLETS

VIOLET FAMILY (Violaceae)

Violets suggest tiny pansies. There are 2 categories: (1) "stem-less" violets, with leaves and flowers arising on separate stalks; and (2) "stemmed" violets, whose erect stems bear both leaves and flowers. See other violets on pp. 24 (white), 318, 328–32 (violet–blue), 366 (green).

1. "STEMLESS" YELLOW VIOLETS

ROUND-LEAVED YELLOW VIOLET   *Viola rotundifolia*
In spring flowering stage *our only "stemless" yellow violet*. Note small size, roundish leaves close to ground. 2–5 in. Rich woods. Minnesota, s. Ontario, Maine south.   APRIL–MAY

2. "STEMMED" YELLOW VIOLETS

DOWNY YELLOW VIOLET   *Viola pubescens*
Note the *downy* stems and leaves (especially along veins, margins); leaves heart-shaped; occasionally 1 basal leaf. Stipules *toothed*. 6–16 in. Dry woods. Minnesota, Ontario, Nova Scotia to Virginia.   APRIL–MAY

SMOOTH YELLOW VIOLET   *Viola pensylvanica*
Differs from preceding (may hybridize) by *1 to 5 basal leaves, untoothed* stipules. Stems *smooth* (or nearly). Leaves broad, *smooth*. 4–12 in. Meadows, low woods. Manitoba, N. Scotia south.   APRIL–JUNE

PRAIRIE YELLOW VIOLET   *Viola nuttallii*
Note the *lance-shaped*, wavy-margined leaf. Blossoms often hidden below the leaves. 2–5 in. Sandy, arid prairies, plains. W. Minnesota, w. Missouri west to Rockies.   APRIL–MAY

THREE-PART-LEAVED VIOLET   *Viola tripartita*
The only yellow violet with *cut leaves* in our area. Leaves variable; some little-cut. 6–10 inches. Rich, wooded slopes. S. Ohio, West Virginia and south in mts.   APRIL–MAY

HALBERD-LEAVED VIOLET   *Viola hastata*
Note the *long triangular leaf*. The deeply buried rootstock is long, white, and brittle. 4–10 in. Deciduous woods, ravines. Ohio, Pennsylvania and south in mts.   APRIL–MAY

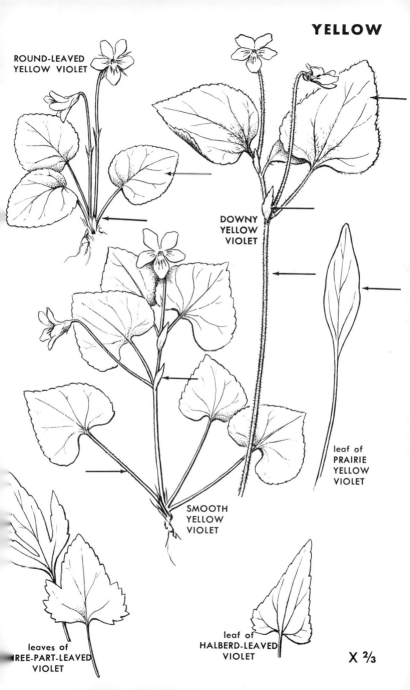

YELLOW

ROUND-LEAVED
YELLOW VIOLET

DOWNY
YELLOW
VIOLET

leaf of
PRAIRIE
YELLOW
VIOLET

SMOOTH
YELLOW
VIOLET

leaves of
THREE-PART-LEAVED
VIOLET

leaf of
HALBERD-LEAVED
VIOLET

X ⅔

5 PETALS; 3 LEAFLETS

BARREN STRAWBERRY *Waldsteinia fragarioides*
ROSE FAMILY (Rosaceae)
Suggests a strawberry with *yellow* flowers, but *lacks runners;* leaflets *blunter*, more rounded. Leaves and flowers on separate stalks. Fruit *not a berry*. 3–8 in. Woods, clearings. Minnesota, w. Quebec, Maine south to Indiana, Pennsylvania; in mts. to N. Carolina. APRIL–JUNE

INDIAN STRAWBERRY Alien *Duchesnea indica*
ROSE FAMILY (Rosaceae)
Differs from preceding in *more pointed* leaflets, *trailing habits.* Single yellow flowers spring from leaf nodes. Note the *3-toothed bracts* exceeding petals and sepals. Fruit *strawberrylike* but inedible. Moist waste ground. Iowa, Indiana, Ohio, New York, s. Connecticut south. APRIL–JULY

ROUGH CINQUEFOIL *Potentilla norvegica*
ROSE FAMILY (Rosaceae)
A cinquefoil with 3 leaflets; suggests a yellow-flowered strawberry but *much taller* (1–3 ft.), with leaves *springing at intervals from stalk.* See 5-leaflet cinquefoils, p. 134. Clearings, thickets, roadsides. Most of our area. JUNE–OCT.

YELLOW WOOD-SORREL *Oxalis stricta*
WOOD-SORREL FAMILY (Oxalidaceae)
Note the delicate, heart-shaped, cloverlike leaflets of this and the following species. This species is known by the *sharp angle* formed by the erect seedpods and their bent stalks. Flowers sometimes reddish at base. 6–15 in. Dry soil, roadsides. Most of our area. MAY–OCT.

CREEPING WOOD-SORREL Alien *Oxalis corniculata*
(not shown)
WOOD-SORREL FAMILY (Oxalidaceae)
Similar to *O. stricta* (seedpods deflexed) but hairier; flowers and leaves spring from a creeping stem. Stipules large, brown. Lawns, roadsides. Widespread. APRIL–NOV.

YELLOW WOOD-SORREL *Oxalis europaea*
WOOD-SORREL FAMILY (Oxalidaceae)
Similar to *O. stricta* but more variable, greener; seedpod stalks *not deflexed.* Has underground runners up to 2 ft. Roadsides, fields, waste ground. Widespread. MAY–OCT.

LARGE YELLOW WOOD-SORREL *Oxalis grandis*
WOOD-SORREL FAMILY (Oxalidaceae)
Coarser, with larger blossoms (to 1 in.). Leaves much larger, often with purple margin. Seedpod stalks not deflexed. 1–3 ft. Woods. S. Illinois, Ohio, Pennsylvania south. JUNE–SEPT.

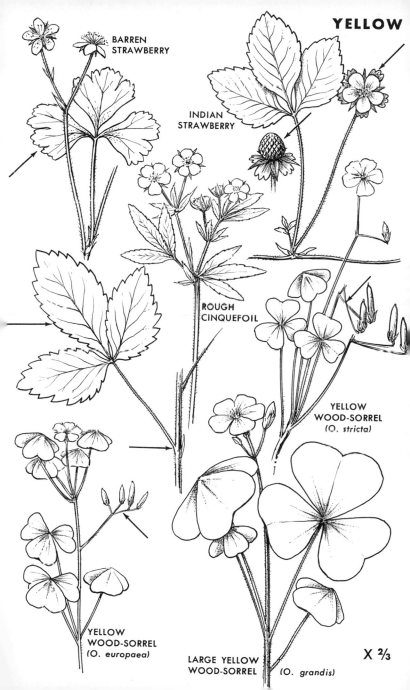

YELLOW

BARREN
STRAWBERRY

INDIAN
STRAWBERRY

ROUGH
CINQUEFOIL

YELLOW
WOOD-SORREL
(O. stricta)

YELLOW
WOOD-SORREL
(O. europaea)

LARGE YELLOW
WOOD-SORREL   (O. grandis)

X ⅔

CLOVERLIKE FLOWERS; 3 LEAFLETS
PEA FAMILY (Leguminosae)

HOP CLOVER Alien   *Trifolium agrarium*
Similar to the medicks (below) but mostly erect; leafstalks less than ½ in. When flower heads (½–¾ in.) wither, florets *fold down*, become brownish, suggesting dried hops. 6–16 in. Roadsides, waste places. Throughout.   JUNE–SEPT.

SMALLER HOP CLOVER Alien   *Trifolium procumbens*
Similar to preceding but *usually prostrate*, more pubescent. Flower heads smaller (less than ½ in.). Note that the terminal leaflet is *stalked* and often *notched* at tip. Roadsides, waste places. Widespread.   MAY–SEPT.

LEAST HOP CLOVER Alien   *Trifolium dubium*
Smaller than preceding two. Leaves as in *T. procumbens*, but flower heads *tiny*, with only 5 to 15 florets. Roadsides, waste places. Most of our area.   APRIL–OCT.

BLACK MEDICK Alien   *Medicago lupulina*
A prostrate plant suggestive of hop clovers (above), but note downy stems and *twisted black seedpods* that soon replace flowers. Leaflets often minutely spine-tipped. Roadsides, waste places. Throughout.   MARCH–DEC.

SPOTTED MEDICK Alien   *Medicago arabica*
Note small *dark spot* near center of leaflet, *large toothed stipules* at base of leafstalk, *burry seedpod*. Prostrate. Sandy soil, waste ground. Local, New England, etc.   APRIL–OCT.

YELLOW SWEET CLOVER Alien   *Melilotus officinalis*
A tall smooth plant with narrow tripartite leaves and long tapering spikes of yellow pealike flowers. Sweet odor when crushed. Very similar to White Sweet Clover, p. 80. 2–5 ft. Roadsides, waste ground. Throughout.   JUNE–AUG.

BIRDFOOT TREFOIL Alien   *Lotus corniculatus*
Note 5-part leaves (3 cloverlike leaflets and *2 more at base*, appearing like large stipules). Flowers in cluster of 3 to 6, yellow to red. Slender pod suggests bird's foot. Erect or prostrate. 6–24 in. Waste places, roadsides.   JUNE–SEPT.

WILD INDIGO   *Baptisia tinctoria*
A smooth plant with stalkless or almost stalkless gray-green leaves *that turn black* when dried. Stems, leaves may have bluish bloom. Attractive pealike flowers in loose racemes at branch tips. 1–3 ft. Dry woods, clearings. Minnesota, Michigan, s. Ontario, s. Maine south.   MAY–SEPT.

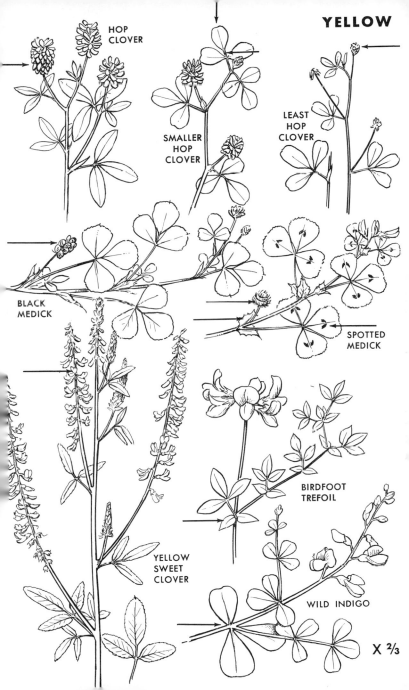

YELLOW

HOP CLOVER

SMALLER HOP CLOVER

LEAST HOP CLOVER

BLACK MEDICK

SPOTTED MEDICK

YELLOW SWEET CLOVER

BIRDFOOT TREFOIL

WILD INDIGO

X ⅔

PEALIKE FLOWERS; PINNATE LEAVES
SMALL, OVAL, PAIRED LEAFLETS
PEA FAMILY (Leguminosae)

GOAT'S-RUE *Tephrosia virginiana*
Hoary, covered with silky whitish hairs. Note the large, *bicolored* pealike flowers (yellow standards, pink wings). Leaves with 8 to 14 pairs of leaflets plus 1 leaflet at tip. 1–2 ft. Sandy woods, openings. Manitoba, Wisconsin, s. Michigan, s. Ontario, New York, c. New England south.   MAY–AUG.

MILK-VETCH *Astragalus canadensis*
The milk-vetches are a large confusing genus. To separate the 25 species in our area, see the technical manuals. The one shown here may be pale yellow or whitish, lacks hoary hairiness of Goat's-rue. Flowers slender, pealike. Leaflets in 7 to 15 pairs. 1–4 ft. Shores, thickets. Widespread except Atlantic seaboard.
                                                    JUNE–AUG.

PARTRIDGE-PEA *Cassia fasciculata*
See also color plate, p. 106. The 6 to 15 finely cut pairs of oval leaflets, each tipped with a tiny bristle, are sometimes sensitive to the touch. The large single flowers tucked in the leaf axils have 5 unequal broad petals and *dark drooping anthers.* 1–2 ft. Sandy soil. Minnesota, s. Ontario, Massachusetts south.
                                                    JULY–SEPT.

SICKLEPOD *Cassia tora*
Flowers similar to Wild Senna (below), borne singly in upper leaf axils. Leaflets in 2 or 3 pairs. Note the *long sickle-shaped seedpod.* 1½–2 ft. Riverbanks, etc. Kansas, Illinois, Indiana, Michigan, Pennsylvania south.   JULY–SEPT.

WILD SENSITIVE-PLANT *Cassia nictitans*
Similar to Partridge-pea but much smaller; more sensitive to touch. Flowers much smaller (¼ in.), with only 5 stamens. 6–15 in. Sandy soil. Kansas, Illinois, Indiana, Ohio, New York, Massachusetts south.   JULY–SEPT.

WILD SENNA *Cassia hebecarpa*
A coarse plant with 5 to 10 pairs of oval leaflets and large clusters of loosely constructed flowers in leaf axils. Note the unequal stamens and dark brown anthers. Note also the club-shaped gland on leafstalk. 3–6 ft. Roadsides, thickets. Wisconsin to New England and south. A similar, more southern species, *C. marilandica* (not shown), has larger leaflets (4–8 pairs), flatter seedpods, fewer flowers. Similar habitat. Iowa to Pennsylvania and south.   JULY–AUG.

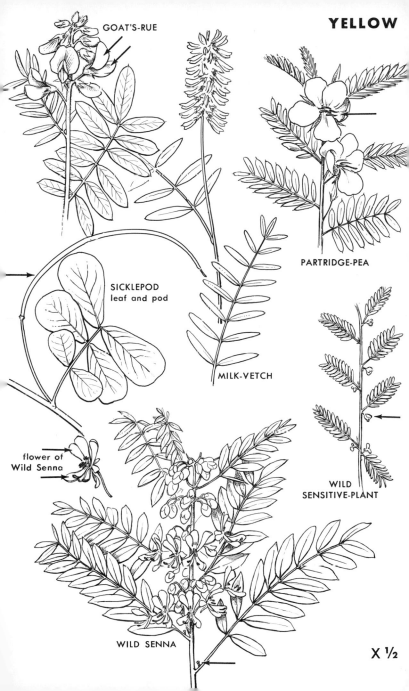

YELLOW

GOAT'S-RUE

PARTRIDGE-PEA

SICKLEPOD
leaf and pod

MILK-VETCH

WILD
SENSITIVE-PLANT

flower of
Wild Senna

WILD SENNA

X ½

PEALIKE FLOWERS; MISCELLANEOUS LEAVES
PEA FAMILY (Leguminosae)

BROOM Alien   *Cytisus scoparius*
Suggests a slender spineless Gorse (below). Stems angled;
leaves very small (¼–½ in.), lanceolate or trefoil, often dropping
early. Flowers showy (1 in.), style curled. Pods longer than
those of Gorse. 3–5 ft. Sandy soil, roadsides, pine barrens. W.
New York, sw. Maine, Nova Scotia south, especially near coast.
                                                        MAY–JUNE

RATTLEBOX   *Crotalaria sagittalis*
Note the *stipules that form arrowheads* pointing down the stem.
A small hairy plant with alternate, toothless leaves. Seeds rattle
in black pod when dry. 12–16 in. Sandy soil. Minnesota, Wisconsin, s. Michigan, s. Ohio, s. New York, Massachusetts south.
                                                        JUNE–SEPT.

DYER'S GREENWEED Alien   *Genista tinctoria*
A bushy shrub suggesting a small leafy Broom (above). Leaves
small, shining, alternate, on angled, woody stems. Flowers in
showy spikes. Dry soil. Local, New England to Michigan and
D.C.   JUNE–SEPT.

GORSE, FURZE Alien   *Ulex europaeus*
A dense, spiny, evergreen bush or shrub. Stems furrowed, leaves
replaced by *rigid spines*. Flowers (½–⅔ in.) showy. 2–6 ft.
Sandy soil; an escape from cultivation. Se. Massachusetts to
Virginia.   MAY–SEPT.

YELLOW VETCHLING Alien   *Lathyrus pratensis*
Note the pair of pointed leaflets accompanied by a *tendril* and
the similar *pair of stipules* at the base of the leafstalk which
simulate a 2nd pair of leaflets. Flowers in long cluster from leaf
axil. 1–3 ft. Roadsides, meadows, shores. E. Canada, south to
Illinois, Michigan, Ohio, New York, New England. JUNE–AUG.

YELLOW

BROOM

RATTLEBOX

GORSE

DYER'S
GREENWEED

YELLOW
VETCHLING

X ⅔

4 SHOWY PETALS

1. LEAVES ALTERNATE, CROSSLIKE STIGMA
EVENING-PRIMROSE FAMILY (Onagraceae)

The genus *Oenothera* numbers at least 15 in our area. Identification is complex, partly because of hybridization. They divide roughly into (1) evening-primroses, which open toward evening and wilt next day, and (2) sundrops, which open in sunshine. The 4 petals surmount a slender calyx tube rising from a swollen ovary. The 4-branched stigma forms a cross. Dry or sandy soil, open places. JUNE–SEPT.

COMMON EVENING-PRIMROSE, *O. biennis.* Typical of genus (4 petals, X-shaped stigma, reflexed sepals). Leafy, rough-hairy; often reddish-stemmed, branched. 1–5 ft. See color plate, p. 106. Dry soil, open places. Throughout.

SMALL-FLOWERED EVENING-PRIMROSE, *O. parviflora* (not shown). Smaller, usually unbranched; flowers about 1 in.; sepal tips spread in bud (do not form tube). Canada, n. U.S.

CROSS-SHAPED EVENING-PRIMROSE, *O. cruciata.* Narrow-petaled (forming cross). Michigan to New England.

CUT-LEAVED EVENING-PRIMROSE, *O. laciniata.* Note incised leaves. S. Dakota, Illinois, Pennsylvania, New Jersey south.

SEABEACH EVENING-PRIMROSE, *O. humifusa.* A small whitish-hoary species of dunes, beaches. New Jersey south.

MISSOURI PRIMROSE, *O. missouriensis.* Very large flowers; calyx tube up to 6 in. Pod 4-winged. Missouri to Texas.

SUNDROPS, *O. fruticosa.* Sundrops are day-blooming. Note orange stamens, strongly ribbed pods. Leaves lance-shaped, plain-edged. Variable; several similar species. 1–3 ft. Meadows, fields. Minnesota, Nova Scotia south. JUNE–AUG.

SEEDBOX *Ludwigia alternifolia*
Superficially like a small evening-primrose, but the *wide sepals,* as long as petals, are *not reflexed.* Flowers on short stalks in leafstalks. "Seedbox" refers to short, squarish pods. 2–3 ft. Swamps. Iowa, Illinois, s. Michigan, s. Ontario, New York, Massachusetts south. JUNE–AUG.

2. PAIRED LEAVES, PAIRED UNEQUAL SEPALS
ST. JOHNSWORT FAMILY (Guttiferae)

ST. PETERSWORT *Ascyrum stans*
Flowers terminal; *2 pairs of unequal sepals* — 1 pair broad, 1 pair narrow. *Styles 3 or 4.* 1–2½ ft. Sandy soil, pine barrens. Long Island, New Jersey south. JULY–SEPT.

ST. ANDREW'S CROSS *Ascyrum hypericoides*
Narrower petals than in *A. stans,* forming oblique cross. Sepals very unequal, 1 pair very large, the other tiny or lacking. *Styles 2.* 5–10 in. Sandy or rocky soil. Illinois, Pennsylvania, New Jersey south; Nantucket I., Massachusetts. JULY–AUG.

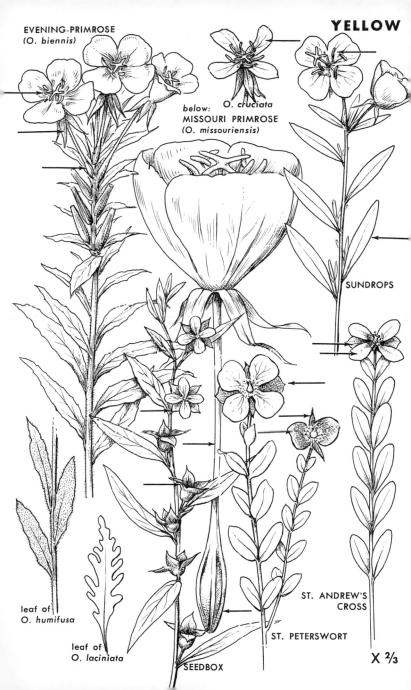

EVENING-PRIMROSE
(O. biennis)

O. cruciata

below:
MISSOURI PRIMROSE
(O. missouriensis)

YELLOW

SUNDROPS

leaf of
O. humifusa

leaf of
O. laciniata

SEEDBOX

ST. PETERSWORT

ST. ANDREW'S CROSS

X ⅔

4 SMALL PETALS; TERMINAL CLUSTERS
Mustard Family (Cruciferae)
Most species have ascending seedpods.

HARE'S-EAR MUSTARD Alien   *Conringia orientalis*
Note the *pale, ovate*, untoothed leaves, upper ones *clasping* the
stem. Plant somewhat succulent, covered with whitish bloom.
Flowers pale yellow. 12–32 in. Waste places. Locally, most
of our area.   JUNE–AUG.

TOWER MUSTARD   *Arabis glabra*
Note the gray-green waxy look. Slender, unbranched. Upper
leaves narrowly *arrowhead-shaped*, clasping stem with earlike
lobes. Rosette of downy yellowish leaves at base withers early.
Flowers pale creamy yellow. Seedpods long, *bushy*, hug stem.
1–3 ft. Dry banks, ledges, sandy soil. Canada, ne. U.S.; south
in mts.   MAY–JULY

HEDGE MUSTARD Alien   *Sisymbrium officinale*
Typical leaves are roughly halberd-shaped (*with basal lobes
spreading widely*). Note also the way the seedpods closely hug
the stem. Flowers tiny, light yellow. 1–3 ft. Waste places.
Throughout.   MAY–OCT.

TUMBLE MUSTARD Alien   *Sisymbrium altissimum*
Note the *extremely narrow*, linear segments of the leaves, especially the upper ones. Much branched. 2–3 ft. Roadsides,
waste places. Throughout.   MAY–AUG.

WINTER CRESS Alien   *Barbarea vulgaris*
Suggests *Brassica* mustards (p. 160) but with shorter beak on
seedpod. Note the rounded "ears" on the lower leaves and the
broad, toothed, clasping, uppermost leaves. Variable. The
typical variety shown here has erect seedpods hugging the stem;
other varieties have spreading seedpods. 1–2 ft. Wet meadows,
fields, brooksides. E. Canada to Missouri, Illinois, Ohio, Virginia.   APRIL–AUG.

EARLY WINTER CRESS Alien   *Barbarea verna*
Similar to the preceding but usually with *more lobes* (4–10 pairs)
on lower leaves. Pods much longer. 1–2 ft. Fields. Indiana,
Michigan, Ohio, New York, Connecticut south.   APRIL–MAY

YELLOW CRESS   *Rorippa islandica*
Note the tiny flowers and *short, roundish pods*. The leaves are
lobed, each lobe *coarsely toothed*. Variable. Wet places. Shores
throughout.   MAY–SEPT.
R. sinuata (not shown) has similar leaves but strongly curved,
hooklike pods. Sandy soil. *R. sylvestris* (not shown), an alien,
has slender, slightly curved, more erect pods (½–⅔ in.), sharply
toothed leaves.

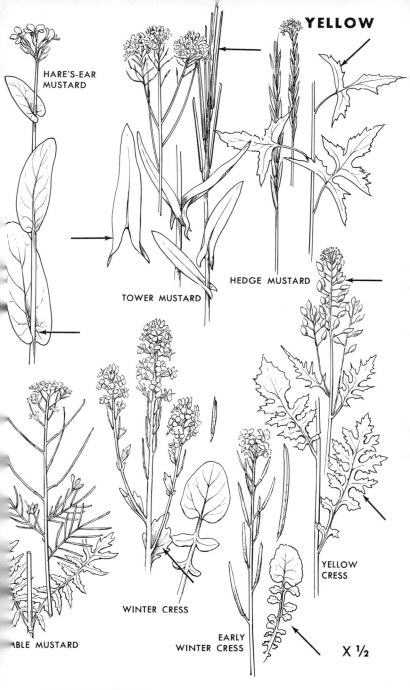

HARE'S-EAR
MUSTARD

YELLOW

TOWER MUSTARD

HEDGE MUSTARD

WINTER CRESS

YELLOW
CRESS

ABLE MUSTARD

EARLY
WINTER CRESS

X ½

4 PETALS; TERMINAL CLUSTERS

MUSTARD FAMILY (Cruciferae)

Most of these have broad, deeply lobed lower
leaves and slender ascending seedpods that
end in a conspicuous pointed beak.

WILD RADISH Alien   *Raphanus raphanistrum*
Note the conspicuous *lilac veins* in the pale yellow or whitish
petals. Note also the large rounded lobe at the end of the hairy,
pinnately lobed leaves. Seedpod conspicuously beaded. 1–2½ ft.
Waste places, vacant lots. Most of our area.   APRIL–NOV.

WHITE MUSTARD Alien   *Brassica hirta*
Similar to the preceding, but note the *bristling pod* that ends in a
flattened beak often longer than the stubby pod. 1–2 ft.
Fields, waste places. Widespread.   JUNE–AUG.

CHARLOCK Alien   *Brassica kaber*
Bristly, similar to the preceding but leaves less deeply lobed.
The conical beak is shorter than the hairless or nearly hairless
seedpod. 1–2 ft. Widespread weed of waste ground, roadsides.
                                              MAY–JULY

BLACK MUSTARD Alien   *Brassica nigra*
Note the way the seedpods hug the stem. Lower leaves coarsely
lobed and bristly; upper leaves lanceolate, hairless. 2–3 ft.
Waste places, fields. Throughout.   JUNE–OCT.

CHINESE or INDIAN MUSTARD Alien   *Brassica juncea*
Similar to the preceding brassicas but quite smooth, with a
whitish bloom. Lower leaves variously lobed; upper leaves tapering to short petioles. 1–4 ft. Fields. Widespread.
                                              JUNE–SEPT.

FIELD MUSTARD, RAPE Alien   *Brassica rapa*
A smooth, succulent, gray-green species with a whitish bloom;
recognized by the *clasping earlike* lobes of the stem leaves.
24–32 in. Cultivated fields. Widespread.   JUNE–OCT.

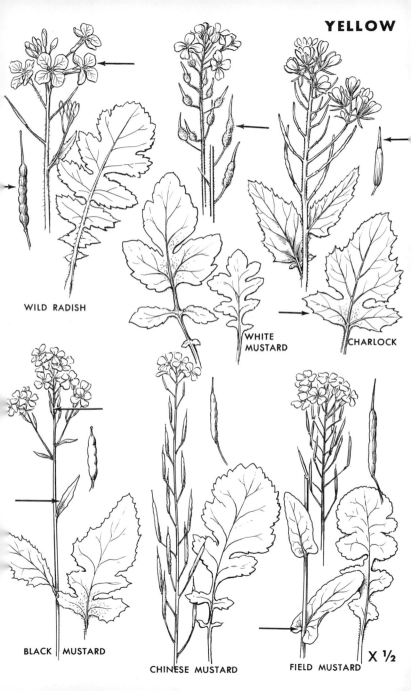

YELLOW

WILD RADISH

WHITE
MUSTARD

CHARLOCK

BLACK MUSTARD

CHINESE MUSTARD

FIELD MUSTARD

X ½

UMBRELLALIKE CLUSTERS (UMBELS)

See similar white species, pp. 48, 50, 52.

MEADOW-PARSNIP   *Thaspium trifoliatum*
PARSLEY FAMILY   (Umbelliferae)
The short-stalked (or stalkless), toothed stem leaves are divided into 3 leaflets. Basal leaves *heart-shaped or rounded.*
1–3 ft. **Note:** A species of GOLDEN ALEXANDERS, *Zizia aptera*
(not shown), resembles this species closely (tripartite stem leaves, heart-shaped basal leaves), but in *Zizia* the central flower of each secondary umbel is *stalkless;* the fruits are *ribbed*, not winged. Wood edges, thickets, banks. Mainly Mississippi Valley, Minnesota to New York and south.
MAY–JULY

WILD PARSNIP Alien   *Pastinaca sativa*
PARSLEY FAMILY   (Umbelliferae)
Stem stout, deeply grooved. Leaves divided into 5 to 15 sessile, sharply toothed, ovate leaflets. 2–5 ft. Roadsides, waste places. Throughout.
MAY–OCT.

GOLDEN ALEXANDERS   *Zizia aurea*
PARSLEY FAMILY   (Umbelliferae)
Leaves doubly compound: 3 divisions are divided again into 3 to 7 narrow (or sometimes ovate), toothed leaflets. Stem often red-tinged. See also *Z. aptera* in note under Meadow-parsnip. Meadows, wet thickets, swamps. Saskatchewan, Quebec, New Brunswick south.
APRIL–JUNE

YELLOW PIMPERNEL   *Taenidia integerrima*
PARSLEY FAMILY   (Umbelliferae)
The *untoothed* leaflets separate this species from the preceding three. Each leaf is divided into 3 to 5 parts and again divided. The slender smooth stem often has a whitish bloom. 1–3 ft. Dry woods, rocky hillsides, thickets. Minnesota to w. Quebec and south.
MAY–JULY

CYPRESS SPURGE Alien   *Euphorbia cyparissias*
SPURGE FAMILY   (Euphorbiaceae)
Note the *numerous, linear, pale green leaves* that suggest its name. The pair of yellowish or greenish "petals" are really bracts. The flowers are inconspicuous (inset). 6–12 in. There are a number of other introduced spurges as well as native species in our area (see also p. 374). Roadsides, cemeteries, vacant lots. Throughout.
APRIL–AUG.

LEAFY SPURGE Alien   *Euphorbia esula*
SPURGE FAMILY   (Euphorbiaceae)
Similar to preceding but leaves more scattered, longer, broader. Variable. 8–24 in. Waste places, roadsides. S. Canada to Iowa, Illinois, Indiana, Pennsylvania.
MAY–SEPT.

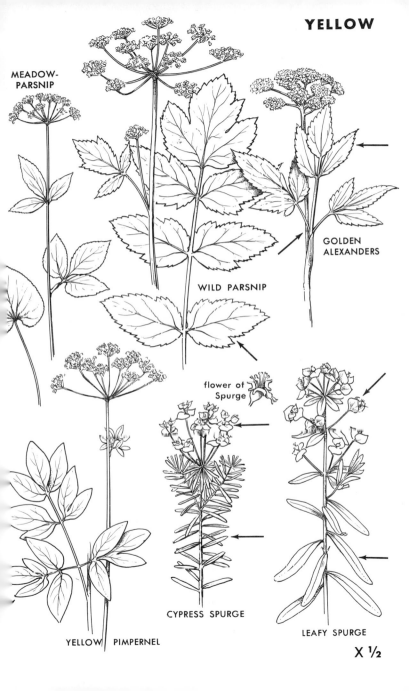

YELLOW

MEADOW-PARSNIP

GOLDEN ALEXANDERS

WILD PARSNIP

flower of Spurge

CYPRESS SPURGE

LEAFY SPURGE

YELLOW PIMPERNEL

X ½

MISCELLANEOUS INCONSPICUOUS FLOWERS

STONECROP Alien   *Sedum sarmentosum*
SEDUM FAMILY   (Crassulaceae)
A fleshy, pale green plant, grows in low mats. Most leaves *in 3's*. Starlike flowers yellow-green. A garden escape.   JUNE

MOSSY STONECROP, WALLPEPPER Alien   *Sedum acre*
SEDUM FAMILY   (Crassulaceae)
Mosslike mats of *tiny fat leaves* taste of pepper. Starlike flowers. 2–4 in. Walls, rocks, dunes. E. Canada, n. U.S.   JUNE–JULY

FALSE HEATHER, HUDSONIA   *Hudsonia tomentosa*
ROCKROSE FAMILY   (Cistaceae)
Scale-like leaves suggest heather. Shrubby, covered with whitish down. Flowers (¼ in.) at twig tips. 4–8 in. Dunes, beaches. E. Canada, Great Lakes, coast from Gaspé south.
                                                       MAY–JULY

GOLDEN-HEATHER   *Hudsonia ericoides*
ROCKROSE FAMILY   (Cistaceae)
Similar to preceding but with more spreading leaves; greener. 4–8 in. Dunes, pine barrens, rocks. Maritime Canada to mts. of n. New England; south locally along coast.   MAY–JULY

PURSLANE Alien   *Portulaca oleracea*
PURSLANE FAMILY   (Portulacaceae)
Note rosettes of fleshy, paddle-shaped leaves, each with a tiny flower. Prostrate, succulent. Waste places.   JUNE–OCT.

BARTONIA   *Bartonia virginica*
GENTIAN FAMILY   (Gentianaceae)
Wiry *leafless* stem with paired scales. Tiny flowers, 4-lobed. 4–12 in. Bogs. Most of area.   JULY–SEPT.

YELLOW FLAX   *Linum virginianum*
FLAX FAMILY   (Linaceae)
Fine-stemmed, branching with small oval, alternate leaves. Flowers about ⅓ in., mostly single. Several other yellow species in our area. 1–2 ft. Thickets, clearings.   JULY–AUG.

PRICKLY MALLOW, SIDA Alien   *Sida spinosa*
MALLOW FAMILY   (Malvaceae)
Stalked, toothed, arrowhead-shaped leaves *often have a spine at base*. Flowers (¼ in.) in leaf axils. 1–3 ft. Waste ground. Michigan, Massachusetts south.   JUNE–OCT.

YELLOW BEDSTRAW Alien   *Galium verum*
BEDSTRAW FAMILY   (Rubiaceae)
Note linear leaves *in rosettes of 6 to 8;* also the fragrant 4-lobed flowers in dense clusters. 8–30 in. See white bedstraws, p. 40. Fields. S. Canada, n. U.S.   JUNE–AUG.

YELLOW WILD LICORICE   *Galium lanceolatum*
BEDSTRAW FAMILY   (Rubiaceae)
Wide 3-nerved leaves *in rosettes of 4*; clusters of tiny 4-lobed yellowish flowers. 1–2 ft. See White Wild Licorice, p. 40. Woods. Minnesota, w. Quebec, s. Maine south.   JUNE–JULY

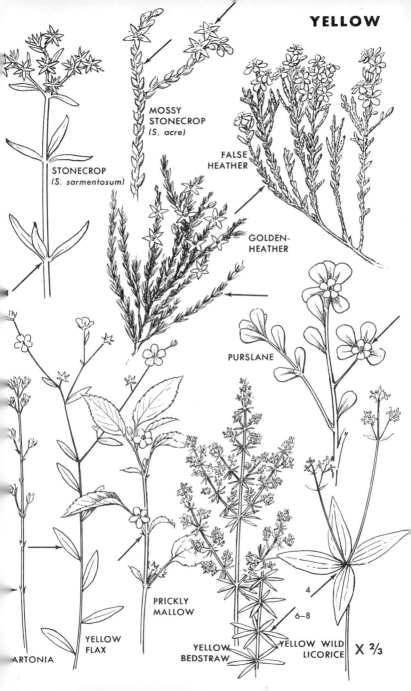

YELLOW

STONECROP
(S. sarmentosum)

MOSSY
STONECROP
(S. acre)

FALSE
HEATHER

GOLDEN-
HEATHER

PURSLANE

ARTONIA

YELLOW
FLAX

PRICKLY
MALLOW

YELLOW
BEDSTRAW

4

6–8

YELLOW WILD
LICORICE

X 2/3

RAYLESS OR NEAR-RAYLESS COMPOSITES

COMMON TANSY Alien   *Tanacetum vulgare*
Note the showy flat-topped cluster of *golden buttons* (each like
the center button of a daisy minus the white rays). Leaves
fernlike, strongly scented. 1–3 ft. Roadsides, waste ground.
Most of our area.   JULY–SEPT.

HURON TANSY   *Tanacetum huronense*
A native species, similar to Common Tansy but shorter; *soft-
hairy or woolly*, especially when young; flower heads *fewer*,
larger, and they often have short, inconspicuous rays.
16–32 in. Sandy or gravelly shores of Lakes Superior, Michigan,
and Huron. Varieties also occur about Hudson Bay, Gulf of
St. Lawrence, Maritime Provinces of Canada.   JUNE–AUG.

PINEAPPLE-WEED Alien   *Matricaria matricarioides*
Similar to the familiar Wild Chamomile (p. 92) but lacking the
white daisylike rays. Branching, leafy; leaves finely cut into
linear segments. When bruised, *smells like pineapple*. 6–18 in.
Roadsides, waste places. S. Canada south to Missouri, Indiana,
Ohio, Pennsylvania, Delaware.   JUNE–OCT.

COMMON GROUNDSEL Alien   *Senecio vulgaris*
The coarsely lobed and toothed leaves are similar to other
senecios (ragworts, p. 176), but this species lacks the showy
yellow rays. Outer bracts *black-tipped*. Branched, leafy. 6–16
in. Waste places. Throughout.   MAY–OCT.

STINKING GROUNDSEL Alien   *Senecio viscosus*
Similar to the preceding but plant very sticky-hairy, odorous.
This species does have yellow rays, but so very short as to be
inconspicuous. 1–2 ft. Waste places. Near coast from Newfoundland to New Jersey.   JULY–SEPT.

DUSTY MILLER Alien   *Artemisia stelleriana*
A matted and creeping *whitish plant*. Note the deeply lobed
white-woolly leaves. 8–24 in. Sea beaches, dunes. Gulf of St.
Lawrence to Virginia; also locally on Great Lakes.   MAY–AUG.

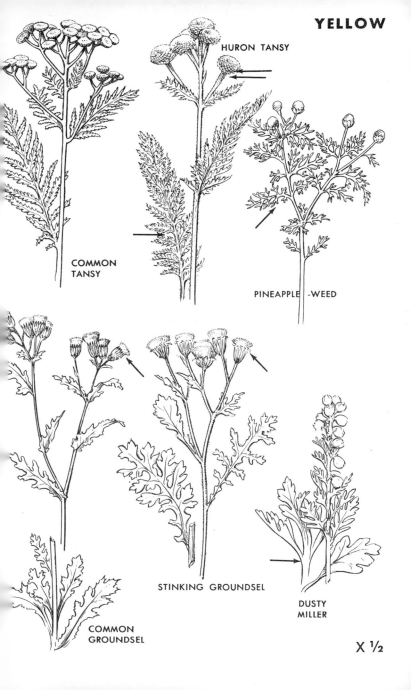

YELLOW

HURON TANSY

COMMON TANSY

PINEAPPLE-WEED

STINKING GROUNDSEL

COMMON GROUNDSEL

DUSTY MILLER

X ½

RAYLESS COMPOSITES: BEGGAR-TICKS
COMPOSITE OR DAISY FAMILY (Compositae)

These inconspicuous flowers, lacking rays, make themselves known by their barbed achenes (see insets), or "seeds," which adhere to clothing. See other *Bidens* (with rays) on p. 186. **Note:** There is so much variation in *Bidens* that exact determination of many plants can be made only on basis of technical characters.

SPANISH NEEDLES *Bidens bipinnata*
Note the *much-dissected*, fernlike leaves and the rayless flowers that develop into a divergent cluster of *slender* achenes, each tipped with 4 short barbs. 1–3 ft. Roadsides, waste places. Kansas, Missouri, Illinois, Indiana, Ohio, New York, Massachusetts south. AUG.–OCT.

BEGGAR-TICKS, STICKTIGHT *Bidens frondosa*
The stalked leaves are divided into 3 to 5 lance-shaped, toothed, divisions. The leafy bracts support and exceed the dull yellowish flower head. The achenes are flat, armed with 2 long barbed awns. 1–4 ft. Damp ground, fields, waste places. Throughout. AUG.–OCT.

EUROPEAN or TRIFID BEGGAR-TICKS *Bidens tripartita*
Alien
Typical specimens have the leaves divided into *3 segments*, middle one much the longest, stalk of leaf *winged*. Stems often purplish. The flat or somewhat quadrangular achenes are tipped with 2 to 4 barbed awns. The unrayed flower heads are surrounded by *blackish sepal-like bracts*. 1–2 ft. Wet waste places. Locally, e. Canada, ne. U.S. The following two very variable species, or forms, are regarded by some botanists as American varieties of this species. AUG.–OCT.

SWAMP BEGGAR-TICKS *Bidens connata*
Similar to preceding but most leaves *undivided*, lanceolate, toothed, *well stalked* (lower leaves may be 3-cleft). Stem smooth, reddish. Occasionally has 1 to 5 inconspicuous rays. Variable. 1–7 ft. Achenes somewhat quadrangular, with 2 to 4 barbed awns. Swamps, moist soil. Minnesota, Wisconsin, s. Ontario, s. Quebec, Nova Scotia south. AUG.–OCT.

LEAFY-BRACTED BEGGAR-TICKS *Bidens comosa*
Similar to *B. connata* but leaves tapering to *wing-margined stalks, or leaves stalkless*. Bracts of flower heads *much leafier*, often with serrate teeth. Achenes flat, usually with 3 barbed awns. 1–4 ft. Moist soil. N. Dakota to Maine and south. AUG.–OCT.

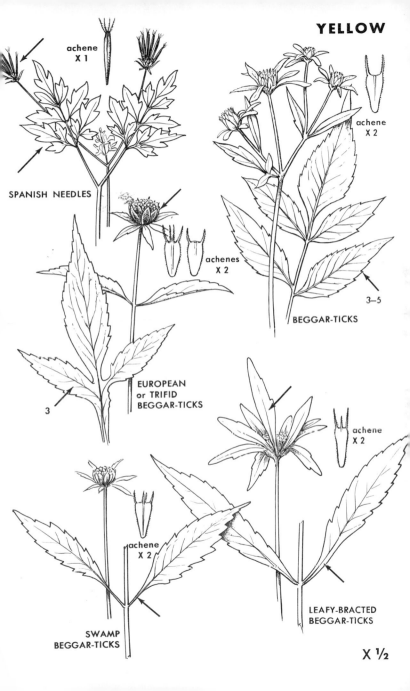

YELLOW

achene
X 1

SPANISH NEEDLES

achene
X 2

achenes
X 2

BEGGAR-TICKS

3–5

EUROPEAN
or TRIFID
BEGGAR-TICKS

3

achene
X 2

SWAMP
BEGGAR-TICKS

achene
X 2

LEAFY-BRACTED
BEGGAR-TICKS

X ½

DANDELIONS, ETC.

COMPOSITE OR DAISY FAMILY (Compositae)
Note the rosette of lobed basal leaves
See also color plate, p. 110.

COMMON DANDELION Alien   *Taraxacum officinale*
See color plate, p. 110. The familiar lawn weed with jagged, lobed leaves, hollow milky stem, *reflexed outer bracts*, fluffy globular white seedballs. Seeds olive or brown. 2–18 in. Lawns, fields, roadsides. Throughout.   MARCH–SEPT.

RED-SEEDED DANDELION   *Taraxacum erythrospermum*
Alien
Differs from preceding in following ways: (1) smaller heads, much less than 2 in.; (2) seeds *red;* (3) leaves *more deeply cut;* (4) outer bracts shorter, usually *not reflexed*. 2–8 in. Dry soil, fields. S. Canada, n. U.S.   APRIL–JUNE

FALL DANDELION Alien   *Leontodon autumnalis*
Taller than the preceding; leaves narrowly cut, shiny, with lobes pointing forward or backward. Stem wiry, *without milky juice*, sometimes branched. Outer rays usually *reddish beneath*. Seeds have plumed bristles. 5–15 in. Fields, roadsides. S. Canada to Michigan, Pennsylvania.   JUNE–NOV.

DWARF DANDELION   *Krigia virginica*
A small, slender species with single small hawkweedlike blossom (½–¾ in.) and a dandelionlike rosette of basal leaves; sometimes branched. 2–12 in. Dry soil, sandy fields. Wisconsin, Michigan, s. Ontario, New York, c. New England south.
          APRIL–AUG.

CAT'S-EAR Alien   *Hypochoeris radicata*
Note the *very hairy leaves*. Flowers about 1 in. Scale-like bracts scattered on slender, smooth, sometimes branched stem. 8–16 in. Grassy places, lawns, fields. S. Canada, n. U.S.
          MAY–AUG.

LAMB SUCCORY Alien   *Arnoseris minima*
Note the *swollen stem* below the flower heads. Flowers with very short rays. Leaves coarsely toothed. 6–12 in. Roadsides, sandy fields. Local, s. Canada, n. U.S.   MAY–SEPT.

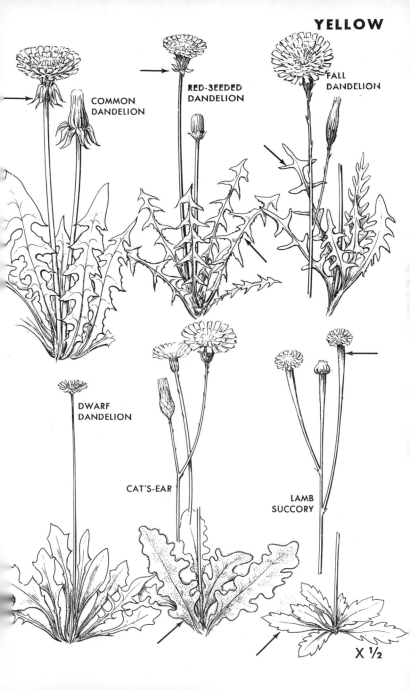

YELLOW

COMMON DANDELION

RED-SEEDED DANDELION

FALL DANDELION

DWARF DANDELION

CAT'S-EAR

LAMB SUCCORY

X ½

TALL, BRANCHED, DANDELIONLIKE FLOWERS

Composite or Daisy Family (Compositae)

Most of these have deeply cut dandelionlike leaves scattered along stem, not in basal rosette (except in *Crepis*).

WILD LETTUCE   *Lactuca canadensis*
A very tall branched plant, smooth, with whitish bloom; many pale, small, insignificant dandelionlike flowers in long, narrow clusters. Each flower head has 12 to 20 florets. Extremely variable; a number of forms have been named on basis of leaf shape (deeply lobed to lance-shaped; see opposite). Lower leaves up to 10 in. 4–10 ft. Thickets, roadsides, clearings in woods. Most of our area. See also blue lettuces (p. 362). JULY–SEPT.

PRICKLY LETTUCE Alien   *Lactuca scariola*
Similar to preceding but with *prickly leaves* (weakly spiny on margins; prickles on midrib); also prickly on lower stem. Flower head (5–12 florets) yellow, drying to bluish. 2–7 ft. Waste places, roadsides. S. Canada, New England south.
JULY–OCT.

HAIRY LETTUCE   *Lactuca hirsuta*
Similar to *L. scariola*, but note the *red or purplish stems and flower bracts*. In typical form this species has a hairy lower stem and leaves. However, a relatively hairless variety (hairy only on midrib of leaf) is more frequent. 1–6 ft. Dry open woods, clearings. S. Canada south.   JULY–OCT.

SMOOTH HAWKSBEARD Alien   *Crepis capillaris*
A branched dandelionlike composite, with a basal rosette of shiny dandelionlike leaves. Note the narrow upper leaves *clasping the stem* with arrowlike lobes. Flower heads ½ in., on slender stalks. Outer bracts shorter than inner series. 6–15 in.
Note: Several similar species of *Crepis*, varying in leaf shape, are sometimes found as escapes in our area. See LARGE ROUGH HAWKSBEARD, *C. biennis*, and NARROW-LEAVED HAWKSBEARD, *C. tectorum*, opposite. Fields, waste places. N. U.S.
JULY–SEPT.

NIPPLEWORT Alien   *Lapsana communis*
Stiff leathery stems, smooth and branched above, hairy near base. No basal rosette; leaves alternate, pointed-oval, toothed; lower ones *often with small lobes* at base and a winged stalk, upper ones sessile. Main flower bracts smooth, with pale bloom; outer bracts tiny. 1–2 ft. Roadsides, waste places. S. Canada to Missouri, Virginia.   JUNE–SEPT.

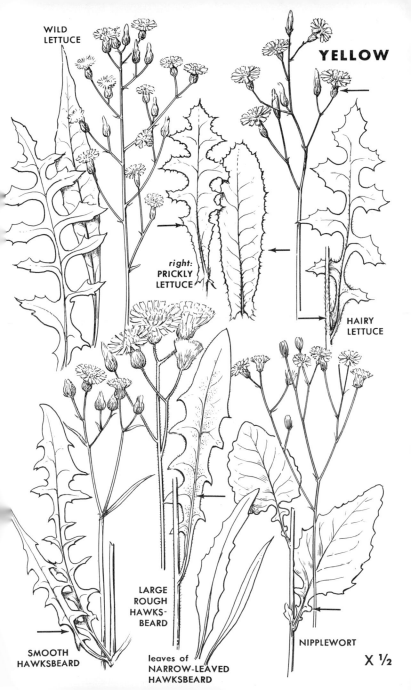

WILD LETTUCE

YELLOW

right: PRICKLY LETTUCE

HAIRY LETTUCE

SMOOTH HAWKSBEARD

LARGE ROUGH HAWKS-BEARD

leaves of NARROW-LEAVED HAWKSBEARD

NIPPLEWORT

X ½

SMALL DANDELIONLIKE FLOWERS: HAWKWEEDS

COMPOSITE OR DAISY FAMILY (Compositae)
Flowers like but leaves unlike small dandelions.
A highly variable group; 19 or 20 occur in our area.

1. LEAVES ASCEND STEM (native species)

CANADA HAWKWEED *Hieracium canadense*
Note the *numerous sessile, toothed leaves* on stem. Blossoms largish (1 in.). 2–5 ft. Wood edges, thickets. Canada to Illinois, Ohio, Pennsylvania, New Jersey. JULY–SEPT.

ROUGH HAWKWEED *Hieracium scabrum*
A coarse, rough-hairy plant with a stout red-tinged stem. Elliptical *leaves smaller as they ascend stem;* basal leaves usually absent. 1–5 ft. Woods, clearings. Minnesota, Ontario, Quebec south to mts. of Georgia. JUNE–SEPT.

HAIRY HAWKWEED *Hieracium gronovii*
More slender than preceding, with several hairy leaves on lower half of stem and at base, *none higher up.* Flowers in *longer cluster.* 1–5 ft. Dry woods, thickets. Michigan, Ohio, New York, Massachusetts south. JULY–OCT.

PANICLED HAWKWEED *Hieracium paniculatum*
Note the small blossoms on slender stalks *branching horizontally* from main stalk in open panicles. Leaves slightly toothed, ascend stem. Nearly smooth; the only hairless species in Group 1. 1–3½ ft. Open woods. S. Ontario, s. Quebec, Nova Scotia south. JULY–SEPT.

2. LEAVES MAINLY IN BASAL ROSETTE (mostly alien)

MOUSE-EAR HAWKWEED Alien. *Hieracium pilosella*
Note the solitary blossom (rarely 2 or 3). Basal leaves *white-woolly below. Forms mats of creeping runners.* 4 in.–1 ft. Fields. Newfoundland to n. U.S. JUNE–SEPT.

SMOOTHISH HAWKWEED Alien *Hieracium floribundum*
Similar to next species but leaves smooth on upper side, with whitish bloom. Fields. Newfoundland to Ohio, Connecticut. JUNE–AUG.

KING DEVIL Alien *Hieracium pratense*
A hairy yellow hawkweed resembling a yellow version of Orange Hawkweed (p. 208). *Stems and bracts bristly with blackish hairs.* Leaves hairy on both sides. 1–3 ft. Fields, roadsides. E. Canada south to ne. U.S. and south into mts. MAY–AUG.

RATTLESNAKE-WEED *Hieracium venosum*
Note the *heavy purple-red veining* in the leaves; leaves purplish beneath. Variable. 1–2½ ft. Open woods, clearings. S. Ontario, s. Maine south. MAY–OCT.

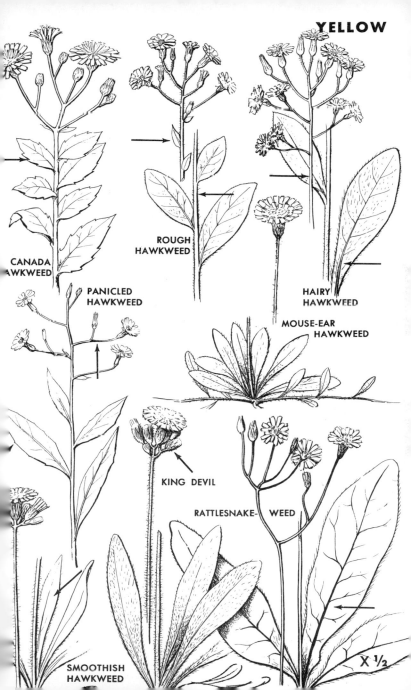

YELLOW

CANADA HAWKWEED

ROUGH HAWKWEED

HAIRY HAWKWEED

PANICLED HAWKWEED

MOUSE-EAR HAWKWEED

SMOOTHISH HAWKWEED

KING DEVIL

RATTLESNAKE- WEED

X ½

ASTERLIKE FLOWERS: RAGWORTS (*Senecio*)

COMPOSITE OR DAISY FAMILY (Compositae)

See also color plate, p. 108.

Flat-topped clusters of small yellow-rayed flowers. Small leaves attached to flowering stem; also, larger, long-stalked basal leaves (note the main differences here). Most are woolly when expanding, smooth later. See also rayless or near rayless senecios, on p. 166. Do not confuse name ragwort with ragweed (*Ambrosia*), p. 374.

GOLDEN RAGWORT   *Senecio aureus*
See also color plate, p. 108. Note the *heart-shaped*, long-stalked basal leaves; often reddish beneath. Variable. 1–3 ft. Wet meadows, swamps, boggy woods. Ontario, Quebec, Newfoundland south.   APRIL–JULY

TANSY RAGWORT Alien   *Senecio jacobaea*
Note the *finely cut, tansy-like leaves*. Lacks heart-shaped basal leaves of *S. aureus*. 1–3½ ft. Fields, roadsides. Maritime Provinces of Canada south to e. Massachusetts; occasionally elsewhere.   JULY–AUG.

ROUNDLEAF RAGWORT   *Senecio obovatus*
Note oval leaf, wider above middle, tapering into a slender stalk. 6 in.–1½ ft. Woods, banks, calcareous rocks. Michigan, s. Ontario, s. New Hampshire south.   APRIL–JUNE

ROBBINS' RAGWORT   *Senecio robbinsii*
Note the long-bladed basal leaves of this northern species; *long-oval or long arrowhead-shaped*, with pointed tip. Flowers paler than Golden Ragwort's. 1–3 ft. Wet meadows, swamps, wood edges, mts. Quebec, Nova Scotia, to ne. New York, n. New England; also high Smokies.   JUNE–AUG.

BALSAM RAGWORT   *Senecio pauperculus*
Note the *small, slender-oval* basal leaves; sometimes woolly beneath. Variable. 4–18 in. Rocky places, ledges, bogs. N. Canada to n. U.S. and south in mts.   LATE MAY–AUG.

WOOLLY RAGWORT   *Senecio tomentosus*
Note the *dense, matted, whitish wool* on underside of leaves and on stems (other ragworts may have woolly hairs when young, and, unfolding, soon lose them). 1–2 ft. Open woods, pine barrens, clearings. Mainly coastal plain, s. New Jersey south.   APRIL–JUNE

PRAIRIE RAGWORT (not shown)   *Senecio plattensis*
Similar to preceding; smaller-leaved, lower, less woolly. Note range. 6–16 in. Dry soil, calcareous rocks. Saskatchewan, s. Ontario south (mainly west of mts.).   MAY–JULY

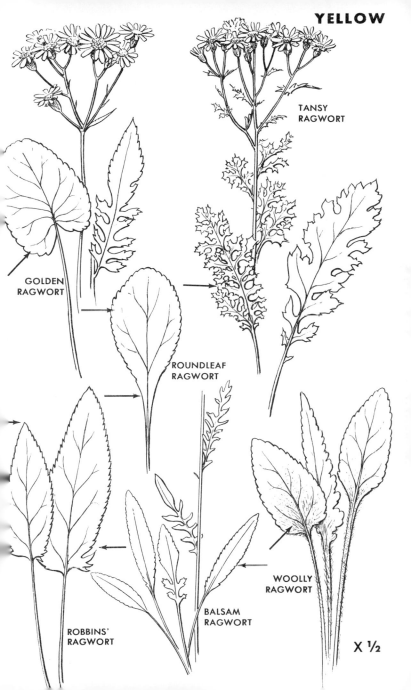

YELLOW

TANSY
RAGWORT

GOLDEN
RAGWORT

ROUNDLEAF
RAGWORT

ROBBINS'
RAGWORT

BALSAM
RAGWORT

WOOLLY
RAGWORT

X ½

THISTLES AND OTHER PRICKLY PLANTS
See also Gorse, p. 154, and Prickly-pear, p. 100.

 YELLOW THISTLE   *Cirsium horridulum*
COMPOSITE FAMILY   (Compositae)
Our native yellow thistle. Note the *deeply incised, extremely
bristly leaves*. Flower head large (3 in.) supported by spiny
bracts, sometimes purple or white. 1–3 ft. Sandy soil, fields,
shores, salt marshes. Near coast from s. Maine south.
MAY–AUG.

 BLESSED THISTLE Alien   *Cnicus benedictus*
COMPOSITE FAMILY   (Compositae)
A hairy, deep yellow thistle. Note the *large leafy bracts* that
surround the flower head. Leaves not as spiny as in preceding
species, broader at base. 10–30 in. Roadsides, waste places.
Local, s. Canada, U.S.   MAY–AUG.

BARNABY'S THISTLE Alien   *Centaurea solstitialis*
COMPOSITE FAMILY   (Compositae)
Note the *very long spines* at the base of the 1-in. flower head;
no leafy bracts. Leaves woolly, *without spines.* 10–30 in.
Fields, waste places, roadsides. Local, s. Ontario, New York,
Massachusetts south.   JULY–OCT.

SPINY-LEAVED SOW-THISTLE Alien   *Sonchus asper*
COMPOSITE FAMILY   (Compositae)
The sow-thistles have dandelionlike flowers and leaves edged
with prickles. See p. 110 and accompanying color plate for
further discussion and distinctions between 3 species of *Sonchus.*

PRICKLY POPPY Alien   *Argemone mexicana*
POPPY FAMILY   (Papaveraceae)
POPPY SUBFAMILY   (Papaveroideae)
The large *cuplike yellow flower* with 4 to 6 petals in conjunction
with the somewhat *thistle-like leaves* identifies this species.
Seedpod ovoid, prickly. Waste places. Escaped from cultiva-
tion locally.   MAY–SEPT.

YELLOW

YELLOW THISTLE

BLESSED THISTLE

SOW-THISTLE
(S. asper)

BARNABY'S THISTLE

PRICKLY POPPY

X ½

SUNFLOWERS, ETC.

COMPOSITE OR DAISY FAMILY (Compositae)
Species with many or most leaves *not in pairs*. All
except the Whorled Rosinweed and Saw-toothed
Sunflower have rough or hairy stems.

WHORLED ROSINWEED   *Silphium trifoliatum*
This sunflower*like* plant has a smooth stem (often with a
whitish bloom) and rough leaves usually in *whorls of 3 or 4.*
3–9 ft. See other silphiums, p. 184. Open woods, thickets.
Indiana, Pennsylvania south.   JULY–SEPT.

JERUSALEM ARTICHOKE   *Helianthus tuberosus*
A large sunflower with broad, thick, hard, rough leaves and
rough, hairy stems. Lower leaves often opposite but upper
leaves alternate; sometimes in whorls of 3. 6–10 ft. Thickets,
fields. Saskatchewan, Ontario south.   AUG.–OCT.

TALL or GIANT SUNFLOWER   *Helianthus giganteus*
Note the rough, *stalkless or short-stalked*, lance-shaped leaves.
These are usually attached alternately to the rough dull reddish
stem, but lower ones may be in pairs. 4–10 ft. Thickets,
swamps. Saskatchewan, Ontario, Maine south.   AUG.–OCT.

SAW-TOOTHED SUNFLOWER   *Helianthus grosseserratus*
Leaf shape similar to preceding but more strongly toothed,
more tapering at base. Stem *smooth*, often with a whitish
bloom. Leaves often whitish-downy beneath; attached alternately. Prairies, roadsides. N. Dakota, Minnesota, Ohio south;
local in East.   JULY–OCT.

COMMON SUNFLOWER   *Helianthus annuus*
See also color plate, p. 114. A miniature of the domesticated
form (which may have 10-in. flower); *disk large, brownish;* rays
golden. *Leaves heart- or spade-shaped*, rough, toothed, with
slender stalks. They are attached singly. Stem rough-hairy.
3–12 ft. Prairies, bottoms, roadsides. Minnesota to Missouri;
locally established in East.   JULY–OCT.

PRAIRIE SUNFLOWER   *Helianthus petiolaris*
Similar to the preceding but smaller; blossoms also smaller.
Note the narrower leaf (usually without teeth), with longer
stalk; sometimes may be slightly toothed. 1–3 ft. Dry prairies.
Saskatchewan, Minnesota south.   JUNE–SEPT.

WEAK SUNFLOWER Alien (not shown)   *Helianthus debilis*
Like a weak edition of the preceding with a semireclining,
mottled stem and usually much smaller and narrower leaves.
Roadsides, waste places. Southern; has spread locally north to
Maine.   JUNE–OCT.

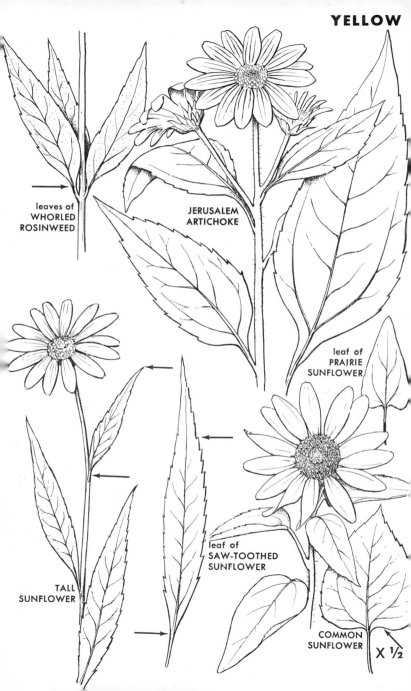

YELLOW

leaves of
WHORLED
ROSINWEED

JERUSALEM
ARTICHOKE

leaf of
PRAIRIE
SUNFLOWER

leaf of
SAW-TOOTHED
SUNFLOWER

TALL
SUNFLOWER

COMMON
SUNFLOWER

X ½

SUNFLOWERS, ETC.

COMPOSITE OR DAISY FAMILY (Compositae)
Species with most of their leaves *in pairs*. All but
3 of these also have relatively smooth, hairless stems.

OX-EYE *Heliopsis helianthoides*
Not a true sunflower. Note the relatively short arrowhead-
shaped leaves attached in pairs to the smooth stem. There is
a smooth-leaved and also a rough-leaved variety. Both ray
and disk flowers form achenes ("seeds"), thus differing from
true sunflowers. 2–5 ft. Woodland openings, thickets, riverbanks. Minnesota, s. Ontario south. JULY–SEPT.

THIN-LEAVED SUNFLOWER *Helianthus decapetalus*
Note the way the larger leaves *narrow abruptly into long, winged
petioles*. Upper leaves sometimes alternate. Leaves thin; stem
smooth. Rays often 10, as scientific name hints. 2–5 ft. Moist
woods, banks, thickets. Minnesota, sw. Quebec, Maine south.
AUG.–OCT.

WOODLAND SUNFLOWER *Helianthus divaricatus*
A smooth-stemmed sunflower with slender, thick leaves (very
rough above, hairy below). Leaves with very short stalks or
stalkless. 2–6½ ft. Open woods, dry thickets. Saskatchewan,
Ontario, Maine south. JULY–OCT.

STIFF-HAIRED SUNFLOWER *Helianthus hirsutus*
(not shown)
Similar to preceding but stems covered with stiff hairs. Dry
soil. Wisconsin, Ohio, Pennsylvania south. JULY–OCT.

SMALL WOOD SUNFLOWER *Helianthus microcephalus*
Note the numerous *small blossoms*, scarcely more than 1 in.
across. Leaves shaped somewhat like those of Woodland Sunflower; thin, rough above, pale downy below. Stem smooth.
3–6 ft. Woods, banks of streams. Missouri, Ohio, Pennsylvania
south. JULY–SEPT.

WESTERN SUNFLOWER *Helianthus occidentalis*
Note the *very long stalks* on the large basal leaves. Most of
flowering stem is almost naked; leaves few and small. 1–3 ft.
Dry soil, oak woods. Minnesota, Ohio south. AUG.–SEPT.

PALE-LEAVED WOOD SUNFLOWER *Helianthus strumosus*
Note the smooth stem, sometimes with a whitish bloom and the
downy hoary underside of the broad basal leaves. 3–7 ft. Dry
woods. Minnesota, Ontario, Maine south. JULY–SEPT.

HAIRY SUNFLOWER *Helianthus mollis*
Note the *heart-shaped stalkless leaves* that clasp the stem.
Entire plant *whitish-hairy or downy*. 2–3½ ft. Dry soil, open
woods. Michigan, Ohio south; local in East. AUG.–OCT.

SHOWY SUNFLOWER *Helianthus laetiflorus* var. *rigidus*
Note the *dark purple center disk*, the harsh, rough stem, and
the *stiff narrow leaves*. 2–6 ft. Prairies. Minnesota, w. Ontario,
Michigan south; locally eastward. AUG.–OCT.

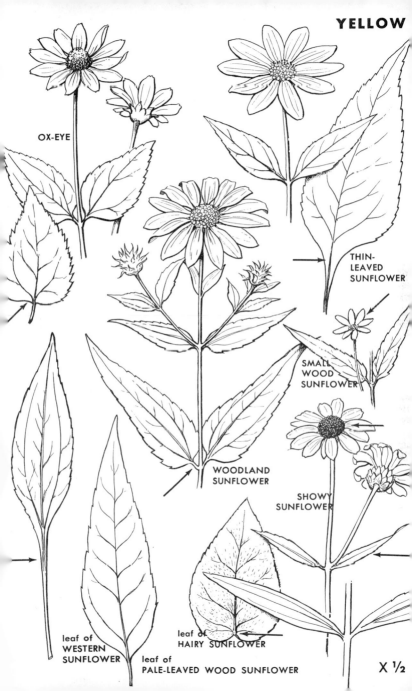

YELLOW

OX-EYE

THIN-LEAVED SUNFLOWER

WOODLAND SUNFLOWER

SMALL WOOD SUNFLOWER

SHOWY SUNFLOWER

leaf of WESTERN SUNFLOWER

leaf of PALE-LEAVED WOOD SUNFLOWER

leaf of HAIRY SUNFLOWER

X ½

SUNFLOWERLIKE PLANTS WITH LARGE LEAVES
COMPOSITE OR DAISY FAMILY (Compositae)

COMPASS-PLANT   *Silphium laciniatum*
Note the *very large, deeply pinnatified leaves;* very stiff and
rough-bristly. Leaves alternate on stem. 4–10 ft. Prairies.
N. Dakota, Minnesota, Michigan south.   JULY–SEPT.

CUP-PLANT   *Silphium perfoliatum*
Note the way the 2 upper leaves surround the flowering stalks
to *form a shallow cup;* leaves rough; stem smooth, 4-angled.
4–8 ft. Open woodlands, meadows, prairies. S. Dakota, Ontario
south in interior; locally introduced eastward.   JULY–SEPT.

ROSINWEED   *Silphium integrifolium*
The rosinweeds (*Silphium*) are large, coarse plants named for
their resinous juices. This species has rough, stalkless, paired
leaves, with or without teeth. 2–6 ft. Prairies, roadsides.
Minnesota, Ohio south in prairies.   JULY–SEPT.

LARGE-FLOWERED LEAFCUP   *Polymnia uvedalia*
Note the *somewhat maple-shaped*, hairy leaves that flow into
their *winged stalks.* Distinguished from next species by larger
flowers (1½–3 in.). 3–10 ft. Woods, thickets. Illinois, New
York south.   JULY–AUG.

SMALL-FLOWERED LEAFCUP   *Polymnia canadensis*
(not shown)
Similar to preceding but stalks of leaves usually not winged.
Rays of flowers few or absent (0–5); very short when present.
2–5 ft. Damp woods, ravines. Minnesota, Ontario, w. Vermont
south to Louisiana and Georgia.   JUNE–OCT.

PRAIRIE-DOCK   *Silphium terebinthinaceum*
Note the *huge, oval or somewhat heart-shaped, docklike leaves*
near the base of the plants (leaves may reach 2 ft. in length).
4–10 ft. Prairies. Minnesota, s. Ontario south.   AUG.–OCT.

YELLOW

leaf of
COMPASS-
PLANT

CUP-PLANT

ROSINWEED

PRAIRIE-
DOCK

LARGE-FLOWERED
LEAFCUP

X ½

SUNFLOWERLIKE OR DAISYLIKE FLOWERS
COMPOSITE OR DAISY FAMILY (Compositae)

Note: Plants of genus *Bidens* can be roughly divided into:
(1) tickseed-sunflowers — with showy rays; divided leaves;
(2) bur-marigolds — without or with rays; undivided leaves;
(3) beggar-ticks, etc. (see p. 168) — with no rays.

TICKSEED-SUNFLOWERS   *Bidens*
Tickseed-sunflowers have deeply divided, toothed leaves and
showy rays, 1 in. or more long. 3 similar species are separated on technical characters: (1) *B. aristosa* and (2) *B. polylepis* are very similar; leaves subdivided into toothed segments.
The achenes ("seeds") are flat, oval (inset). In *aristosa* the
8 to 10 smooth outer bracts are *shorter* than the inner. In *polylepis* the *12 to 20 hairy* outer bracts are *longer* than the inner.
1–4 ft. Wet places. *Aristosa* is found from Minnesota to
Maine and south; *polylepis* is found mainly in Midwest; adventive eastward. (3) *B. coronata* has leaves very deeply divided
into lobes. *Outer bracts 6 to 8.* The spined achenes are wedge-
shaped. 1–4 ft. Wet ground. Nebraska, s. Ontario, Connecticut south.   AUG.–OCT.

BUR-MARIGOLDS or STICKTIGHTS   *Bidens*
Bur-marigolds have smooth, stalkless, lance-shaped leaves;
coarsely toothed. The 2 following forms, often regarded as
species, intergrade and may be considered as one. *B. laevis*
is showy, with 2-in. flowers. 1–3 ft. Swamps. Mainly coastal,
New England south; locally inland. *B. cernua* is similar, but
rays *short or absent. Flowers nod* as they age. Wet places.
Most of our area except Southeast.   JULY–OCT.

WINGSTEM   *Actinomeris alternifolia*
Note the way the alternating leaves flow into "wings" on the
stem. Rays few (2–8), *reflexed backward* from moplike center.
3–8 ft. Wood edges, thickets. Iowa, s. Ontario, New York
south.   AUG.–SEPT.

CROWN-BEARD   *Verbesina occidentalis*
Similar to Wingstem, but *leaves opposite*. Rays few (1–5).
3–6 ft. Woods, thickets. Missouri, Pennsylvania south.
                                                        AUG.–OCT.
Another crown-beard, *V. helianthoides* (not shown), has alternate leaves; differs from Wingstem in having more rays (8–15),
not reflexed; disk flowers in tighter cluster. 2–3 ft. Prairie
thickets. Iowa, Illinois, Ohio south.   JUNE–OCT.

WATER-MARIGOLD   *Megalodonta beckii*
Like a *Bidens* that has gone aquatic. Note the yellow composite flower (6–10 rays) in association with the *finely dissected
submerged leaves.* Often 2 to 3 firm emergent leaves. Ponds,
streams. S. Canada, n. U.S.   AUG.–OCT.

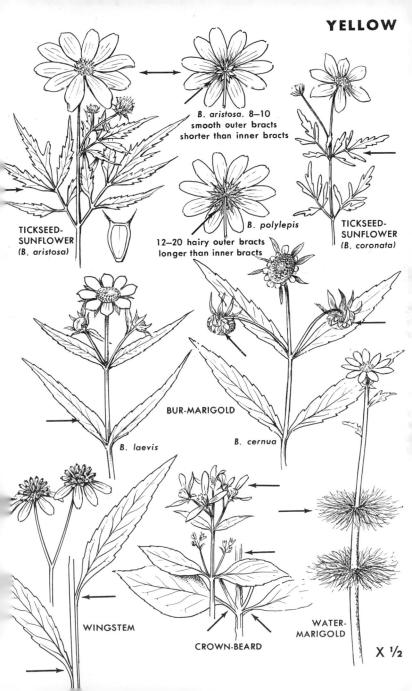

YELLOW

TICKSEED-
SUNFLOWER
(B. aristosa)

B. aristosa. 8–10
smooth outer bracts
shorter than inner bracts

B. polylepis
12–20 hairy outer bracts
longer than inner bracts

TICKSEED-
SUNFLOWER
(B. coronata)

BUR-MARIGOLD

B. laevis

B. cernua

WINGSTEM

CROWN-BEARD

WATER-
MARIGOLD

X ½

DAISYLIKE FLOWERS

COMPOSITE OR DAISY FAMILY (Compositae)
See also color plate, p. 112.

SWEET CONEFLOWER *Rudbeckia subtomentosa*
Similar to Black-eyed Susan (p. 112). Downy; *lower leaves 3-cleft.* 1–4 ft. Prairies, riverbanks. Wisconsin, Illinois, Indiana south. AUG.–SEPT.

ORANGE CONEFLOWER *Rudbeckia fulgida*
Similar to Black-eyed Susan (p. 112), but note *orange base of rays.* Flower heads 1 to 1½ in., rays 8 to 15. Variable. 1–3 ft. Woods. Indiana, Pennsylvania, New Jersey south. AUG.–OCT.

SHOWY CONEFLOWER (not shown) *Rudbeckia speciosa*
Similar to Orange Coneflower (orange base of rays) but flower heads larger (2–3 in.), more rays (12–20). Lower leaves often coarsely incised. 1–3 ft. Woods, wet soil, swamps. Michigan, Ohio, New York south. JULY–SEPT.

ARNICA *Arnica mollis*
A large-flowered (2 in.), hairy, yellow composite found *above treeline.* 10 to 14 rays tipped with 2 to 3 small teeth. Leaves paired, mostly sessile, shallow-toothed. 1–2½ ft. Cliffs, high slopes. Gaspé to high mts. of New England. Other species to north and west of our area. JULY–SEPT.
LEOPARD'S-BANE, *Arnica acaulis* (not shown), is similar but note stemless oval basal leaves. 1–3 ft. Sandy soil, woods. Se. Pennsylvania, Delaware south near coast. APRIL–JUNE

COREOPSIS or TICKSEEDS *Coreopsis*
Most *coreopsis* have 8 showy rays which in most (but not all) species are tipped with 3 to 4 teeth.
LANCE-LEAVED COREOPSIS, TICKSEED, *C. lanceolata.* This is the most familiar *Coreopsis.* See color plate, p. 112.
STIFF COREOPSIS, *C. palmata.* Note the *rigid 3-lobed, crowfootlike leaves.* 1–3 ft. Prairies, thickets. Manitoba, Wisconsin to Oklahoma, Missouri, Indiana. JUNE–JULY
WHORLED COREOPSIS, *C. verticillata.* Note whorls of 3-forked *filamentlike leaves.* Rays not toothed. 1–2 ft. Dry soil, clearings. Maryland and D.C. south. JUNE–JULY
TALL COREOPSIS, *C. tripteris.* Very tall, smooth; stalked leaves divided into 3 lanceolate segments. Rays rounded at tip. Anise-like odor. 3–9 ft. Thickets, wood edges. Wisconsin, s. Ontario south. JULY–OCT.
GARDEN COREOPSIS, *C. tinctoria.* Note brown base of rays. 1–3 ft. Manitoba, Minnesota west; garden escape eastward. JUNE–SEPT.

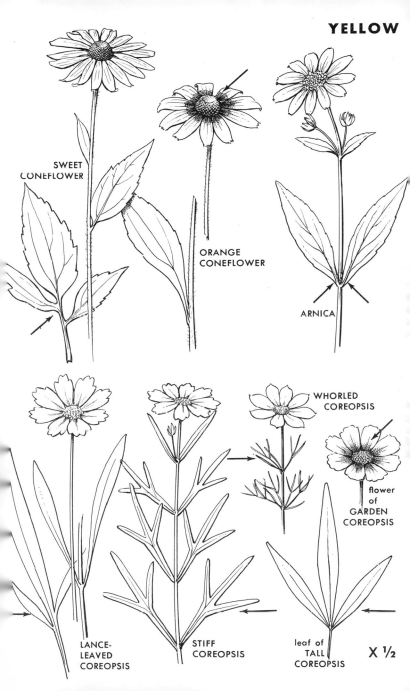

YELLOW

SWEET CONEFLOWER

ORANGE CONEFLOWER

ARNICA

WHORLED COREOPSIS

flower of GARDEN COREOPSIS

LANCE-LEAVED COREOPSIS

STIFF COREOPSIS

leaf of TALL COREOPSIS

X ½

GOLDENRODS
PLUMELIKE; LEAVES PARALLEL-VEINED
<small>COMPOSITE OR DAISY FAMILY</small> (Compositae)

Familiar composites whose tiny yellow-rayed blossoms are massed in showy clusters. Gray (Fernald) lists 69 species in our area; Britton and Brown (Gleason) downgrades the number to 62. Most of the more widespread species are illustrated in the following pages.

Identification, often difficult, is simplified by: (1) assigning the plant to one of the categories below; (2) noting whether the leaves are feather-veined or parallel-veined (see drawings, p. 192).

| plumelike, graceful | elm-branched | clublike, showy | wandlike, slender | flat-topped |

TALL GOLDENROD   *Solidago altissima*
Note the *rough* texture of the leaves (finely downy beneath) and the *downy* grayish stem. Leaves usually toothed; often few or no serrations. Rays 9–15. Plant 3–6 ft. Roadsides, open woods, clearings. S. Ontario and s. Quebec south. AUG.–NOV.

SWEET GOLDENROD   *Solidago odora*
Note the sweet, *anise-like odor* of the crushed leaves. The slender leaves are *toothless*, smooth, and show transparent dots. Rays 3–5. Plant 1½–3 ft. Dry open woods. Missouri, Ohio, New York, s. New Hampshire south. JULY–SEPT.

LATE GOLDENROD   *Solidago gigantea*
Note the *smooth* pale green or *purplish* stem, often covered with a whitish *bloom.* Leaves usually smooth or with soft hairs; toothed. Rays 8–15. Plant 2–7 ft. Moist open thickets. Quebec and Nova Scotia south throughout our area.

                 AUG.–OCT.

CANADA GOLDENROD   *Solidago canadensis*
Stem smooth at base, closely downy near top. Leaves dense; usually smooth, edges *sharply* toothed. Rays 9–15. Plant 1–5 ft. Roadsides, thickets, clearings. Manitoba and Newfoundland to Minnesota, Illinois, N. Carolina. JULY–SEPT.

<small>190</small>

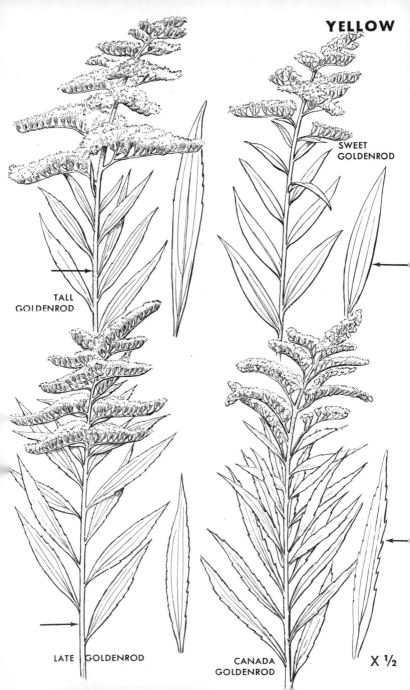

YELLOW

SWEET
GOLDENROD

TALL
GOLDENROD

LATE GOLDENROD

CANADA
GOLDENROD

X ½

GOLDENRODS
PLUMELIKE; LEAVES FEATHER-VEINED
Composite or Daisy Family (Compositae)

parallel-veined (or nerved)   feather-veined

EARLY GOLDENROD   *Solidago juncea*
Note the *tiny winglike leaflets* in the axils of the *slim toothless*
upper leaves. Lower leaves large, broad, toothed and tapering
into a long, margined stalk. Stem and leaves smooth. This
species may take an elmlike shape. Rays 7–12. Plant 1½–4 ft.
Dry soil, roadsides, rocky banks, open woods. Saskatchewan,
New Brunswick, and Nova Scotia south to Missouri, Georgia
(mts.), Maryland.   JULY–SEPT.

ROUGH-STEMMED GOLDENROD   *Solidago rugosa*
Note the *wrinkled, very hairy aspect* of the *deeply toothed* leaves.
Stem densely hairy. The rough lower leaves (jagged-toothed)
are rather broad, tapering into a long margined stalk. Variable;
often assuming an elmlike shape. Rays 6–10. Plant 1–7 ft.
Thickets, roadsides, banks, open places. Widespread, Michigan,
Ontario, Newfoundland south.   JULY–OCT.

SHARP-LEAVED or CUT-LEAVED GOLDENROD
                                                      Solidago arguta
The smooth stem is often reddish brown. The deep green,
double-toothed leaves are usually rough. They are broad, especially the lower ones, and narrow into a *slender tip* and a slender,
margined leafstalk. Rays 5–8. Plant 2–6 ft. Open woods, dry
thickets. S. Ontario, s. Maine south to Illinois, N. Carolina.
                                                        JULY–SEPT.

BOOTT'S GOLDENROD   *Solidago boottii*
Very similar to *S. arguta* and often difficult to separate; it
may hybridize. More southern. Leaves usually smoother, less
sharply serrate. *A rosette or tuft of basal leaves* is often distinctive. Rays 2–8. Plant 1½–4½ ft. Dry woodlands, slopes.
Missouri, Virginia, Maryland south.   JULY–OCT.

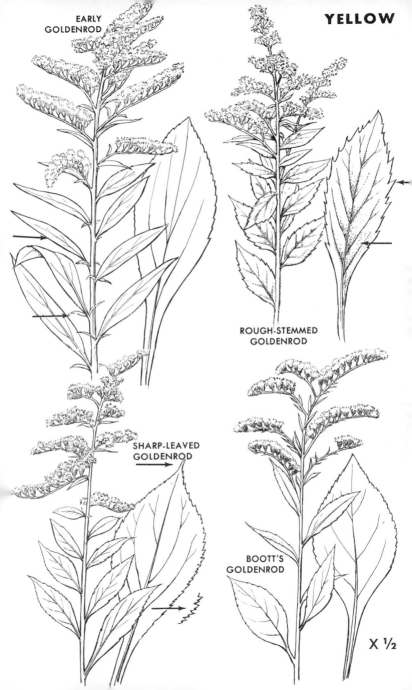

EARLY
GOLDENROD

YELLOW

ROUGH-STEMMED
GOLDENROD

SHARP-LEAVED
GOLDENROD

BOOTT'S
GOLDENROD

X ½

GOLDENRODS
PLUMELIKE; LEAVES FEATHER-VEINED
COMPOSITE OR DAISY FAMILY (Compositae)

GRAY GOLDENROD   *Solidago nemoralis*
Note the slender, rather *1-sided* plumes of this small species.
Note also the *tiny leaflets in the axils* of the leaves where they
join the stem. The grayish stem is *densely covered with fine
hairs*, as are the rough green-gray leaves. Rays 5–9. Plant
½–2 ft. Dry or sandy soil, old pastures, dry open woods.
Minnesota, s. Ontario, and Nova Scotia south throughout our
area.   JULY–NOV.

BOG GOLDENROD   *Solidago uliginosa*
A smooth-stemmed, smooth-leaved species of swamps, bogs.
Lower leaves *lance-like* (up to 12 in. long); shallowly toothed.
The long leafstalk clasps the stem. Rays 1–8. Plant 2–5 ft.
Swamps, bogs, wet meadows. Minnesota, Wisconsin, s. On-
tario, and Gulf of St. Lawrence south to N. Carolina (mts.)
and Maryland.   AUG.–SEPT.

PINE-BARREN GOLDENROD   *Solidago fistulosa*
This goldenrod of the coastal plain can be told from Elliott's
Goldenrod (below) by its *hairy* stem and its leaves, which are
often *hairy beneath*, especially on the midrib. The crowded
elliptical leaves ascend and slightly clasp the stem. Rays 7–12.
Plant 2½–6 ft. Moist sandy soil, pine barrens. Coastal plain
from New Jersey south.   AUG.–OCT.

ELLIOTT'S GOLDENROD   *Solidago elliottii*
Note the *smooth, elliptical, short-pointed leaves.* These are
crowded and not much reduced in size as they climb the *smooth*
stem. Flower clusters usually dense and crowded. Rays 6–12.
Plant 2–6 ft. Fresh and brackish swamps and wet thickets
near coast. Nova Scotia, Massachusetts to Florida.
                                                    SEPT.–OCT.

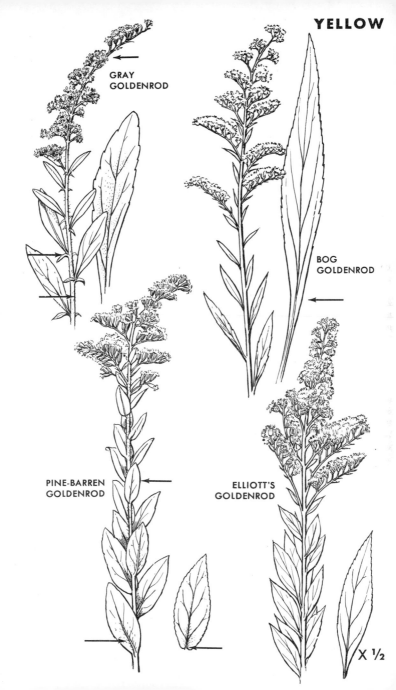

YELLOW

GRAY
GOLDENROD

BOG
GOLDENROD

PINE-BARREN
GOLDENROD

ELLIOTT'S
GOLDENROD

X ½

GOLDENRODS
2 ELM-BRANCHED, 1 ZIGZAG SPECIES
COMPOSITE OR DAISY FAMILY (Compositae)

ROUGH-LEAVED GOLDENROD   *Solidago patula*
Note the smooth, sharply *4-angled stem* and the *very large lower leaves*, which are often more than 12 in. long and taper toward the base to a long, rather broadly margined petiole. Note, too, the *harsh roughness* of the upper surface of the leaves; the lower surface is smooth and veiny. Rays 6–12. Plant 2–7 ft. Swamps, bogs, wet meadows. Minnesota, s. Ontario, Vermont, Maine south to highlands of s. U.S.   AUG.–OCT.

ZIGZAG or BROAD-LEAVED GOLDENROD
                Solidago flexicaulis
Note the *zigzag* stem (angled in cross section). The leaves (both upper and lower) are *very broad* and well pointed at both ends. The flowers (only 3–4 rays) are in small clusters in the upper leaf axils and at the summit. Plant 1–3 ft. Woodlands, rich thickets. N. Dakota, Minnesota, Quebec (Gaspé) south to Arkansas, Georgia.   JULY–OCT.

ELM-LEAVED GOLDENROD   *Solidago ulmifolia*
Note the spreading *elmlike shape* of the flower clusters and the thin coarsely toothed leaves, which usually have soft hairs beneath. Stem smooth and slender, but flower branches hairy. Rays 3–5. Plant 2–4½ ft. Dry woodlands, thickets. S. Minnesota, Vermont, Nova Scotia south.   AUG.–OCT.

Note: Two other goldenrods may also take an elmlike shape: (1) Rough-stemmed Goldenrod (p. 192). The *wrinkled leaves* and *very hairy stem* separate it from those species above. (2) Early Goldenrod (p. 192). Note the *tiny winglike leaflets* in the axils of the *slim toothless* upper leaves.

Goldenrods of certain species are given to regional variation in form and might not look precisely like the examples shown. In addition, hybrids occur, confounding even the specialist. However, goldenrods in general seem not quite as prone to variation and hybridization as are the asters.

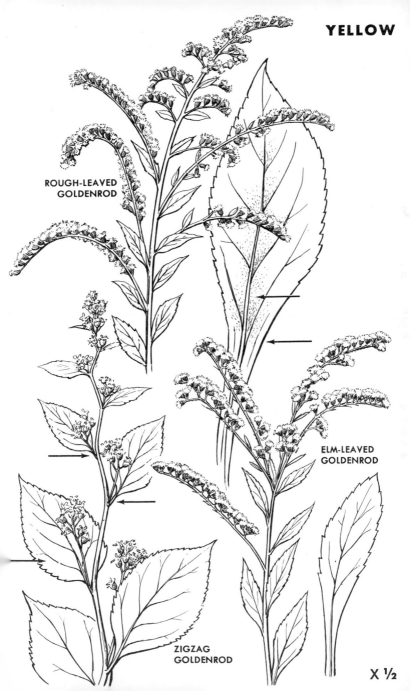

YELLOW

ROUGH-LEAVED
GOLDENROD

ELM-LEAVED
GOLDENROD

ZIGZAG
GOLDENROD

X ½

GOLDENRODS
CLUBLIKE; SHOWY FLOWERS

COMPOSITE OR DAISY FAMILY (Compositae)

STOUT GOLDENROD   *Solidago squarrosa*
Note the *stiff, recurved bracts* at the base of the rather large flowers. Basal leaves *very large*, strongly toothed, often forming a *rosette*. Stem stout, often reddish. Rays 10–16. Plant 1½–5 ft. Dry or rocky woodland openings, edges, thickets. S. Ontario, e. Quebec, and New Brunswick to s. Indiana, Ohio, and N. Carolina (mts.).   AUG.–OCT.

SEASIDE GOLDENROD   *Solidago sempervirens*
Note the slim, *smooth, often fleshy leaves.* All leaves are *toothless,* including the long lower ones that clasp the stem. Stem smooth and stout. Blossoms rather showy. Rays 7–10. Plant 1½–8 ft. **Note:** This species varies and often assumes a more graceful plumelike head. It also frequently hybridizes with the Rough-stemmed Goldenrod (*S. rugosa*); see p. 192. Mainly coastal; salt marshes, dunes, beaches. The typical showy form is found from the Gulf of St. Lawrence to New Jersey (occasionally Virginia). A narrower-leaved, less showy form is found southward (New York to Florida).   AUG.–NOV.

SHOWY GOLDENROD   *Solidago speciosa*
This rather showy species with the stout, smooth, reddish stem and smooth leaves can be told from the Stout Goldenrod (above) by the lack of strong teeth on the margins of its lower leaves. These have *irregular edges,* or may be obscurely toothed. Rays 5–6 (Stout Goldenrod has 10–16 rays). Plant 2–6 ft. Rich thickets, woodland openings, fields, prairies. S. Minnesota, Michigan, New York, s. New Hampshire, and Massachusetts south.   AUG.–OCT.

LARGE-LEAVED GOLDENROD   *Solidago macrophylla*
This showy species can be told from the others on this page by the slim leafstalk on all but the topmost leaves. The broad, *coarsely toothed* lower leaves are usually *rather rounded* where they join the broadly margined leafstalk. In the other species they narrow more gradually into the leafstalk. Rays 8–10. Plant 1–4 ft. Damp woods, rocky thickets, mts. Northern. Hudson Bay, Labrador, Newfoundland south to n. Michigan, New York (Catskills), w. Massachusetts (Mt. Greylock).
JULY–SEPT.

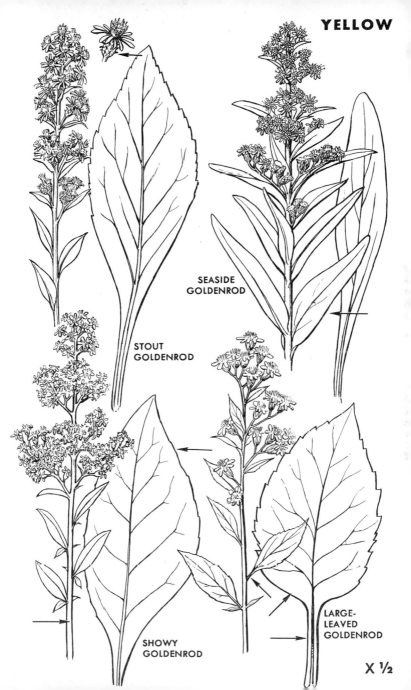

YELLOW

SEASIDE
GOLDENROD

STOUT
GOLDENROD

SHOWY
GOLDENROD

LARGE-
LEAVED
GOLDENROD

X ½

GOLDENRODS
WANDLIKE, SLENDER
COMPOSITE OR DAISY FAMILY (Compositae)

WANDLIKE GOLDENROD   *Solidago stricta*
Note the very small *bractlike leaves that hug the stem* of this
smooth, slender species. Basal leaves longer, more willowlike,
not toothed. Rays 5–7. Plant 2–7 ft. Moist sand, pine barrens.
Coastal plain, New Jersey to Louisiana.   AUG.–OCT.

BLUE-STEMMED GOLDENROD   *Solidago caesia*
Note the *well-spaced flower tufts* in the axils of the smooth
slender leaves where they join the stem. Note also the plumlike
bloom on the smooth bluish or purplish stem. Rays 3–5. Plant
1–3 ft. Woodlands, thickets. Wisconsin, s. Ontario, Maine,
Nova Scotia south.   AUG.–OCT.

HAIRY GOLDENROD   *Solidago hispida*
Note the *very hairy* stem and leaves. The Gray Goldenrod (p.
194), which is also somewhat hairy, lacks the erect flower head,
and has a bending, 1-sided plume. In the Gray Goldenrod note
also the tiny leaflets in the leaf axils. Rays 7–14. Plant 1–3 ft.
Rocky slopes, limestone. Manitoba, s. Quebec, Newfoundland
south to Arkansas, Georgia.   JULY–OCT.

ERECT or SLENDER GOLDENROD   *Solidago erecta*
Very similar in structure to the preceding species, but stem and
leaves usually *smooth*, devoid of hair; blossoms paler. Rays 6–9.
Plant 1–4 ft. Dry soil, woodlands. Indiana, s. Ohio, s. Pennsylvania, n. New Jersey, Cape Cod south to Alabama, Georgia.
                                                   AUG.–OCT.

ALPINE GOLDENROD   *Solidago cutleri*
This dwarf goldenrod of the mountaintops has a distinctive
shape, with its tuft of rather large blossoms *at the summit* of its
short, angled stem and a *rosette* of coarsely toothed leaves at
the base. Rays 12–15. Plant 2–12 in. Alpine summits of
Maine, Vermont, New Hampshire, New York.   JULY–SEPT.

DOWNY GOLDENROD   *Solidago puberula*
Note under a hand glass the *minute, spreading hairs* on the
stem and leaves. The stem is often purplish. Rays 9–16.
Plant 1–3 ft. Dry sandy or sterile soils, barrens. From Gulf
of St. Lawrence south, mainly near coast.   AUG.–OCT.

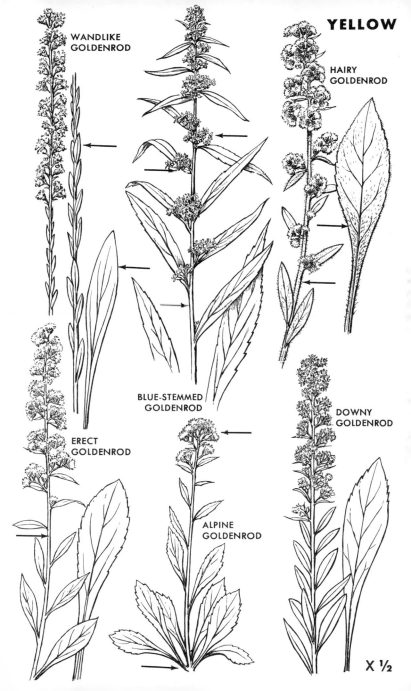

YELLOW

WANDLIKE
GOLDENROD

HAIRY
GOLDENROD

BLUE-STEMMED
GOLDENROD

ERECT
GOLDENROD

ALPINE
GOLDENROD

DOWNY
GOLDENROD

X ½

GOLDENRODS: FLAT-TOPPED

COMPOSITE OR DAISY FAMILY (Compositae)
Note the venation of the leaves.

LANCE-LEAVED GOLDENROD   *Solidago graminifolia*
This is the common flat-topped goldenrod with the linear
leaves. The slender willowlike leaves have rough, untoothed
edges and have *3 to 5 (sometimes 7) parallel nerves*. Fragrant.
Rays 12–25. Plant 1–4 ft. Damp places, thickets, roadsides,
streambanks. Saskatchewan, Quebec, and Newfoundland south
throughout most of our area.   JULY–OCT.

SLENDER FRAGRANT GOLDENROD   *Solidago tenuifolia*
Similar to the preceding but smoother, more delicate and
finely cut. The small, very slender grasslike leaves usually
show *only 1 nerve* and are minutely dotted with resin dots.
Fragrant. Rays 6–15. Plant 1–2 ft. Sandy soil and edges of
salt marshes. Nova Scotia and s. Maine to Florida, mainly
near the coast. **Note:** A similar species, *S. remota* (not shown),
is found in swampy situations near the southern shores of Lake
Michigan and Lake Erie.   AUG.–OCT.

HARD-LEAVED GOLDENROD   *Solidago rigida*
Note the *extremely rigid oval upper leaves*, which slightly clasp
the hairy stem. Unlike those of the previous two flat-topped
species, the leaves are broad, feather-veined, and thick, not
linear and grasslike. The lower leaves are large and rough,
with long petioles. Flowers relatively large. Rays 6–14. Plant
1–5 ft. Dry thickets, sandy soil, prairies. S. Saskatchewan,
Minnesota, New York, and Massachusetts south (mainly west
of Appalachians).   AUG.–OCT.

OHIO GOLDENROD   *Solidago ohioensis*
The flat top and slender leaves may suggest the Lance-leaved
Goldenrod (above), but note that the long-petioled basal leaves
are *feather-veined*. Note also the *erect* way in which the smaller
leaves climb the stem. Rays 6–8. Plant 2–3 ft. Bogs, moist
prairies, sandy beaches. Great Lakes and upper Mississippi
Valley; Minnesota, s. Ontario, and w. New York south to
Missouri, Illinois, Indiana.   AUG.–SEPT.

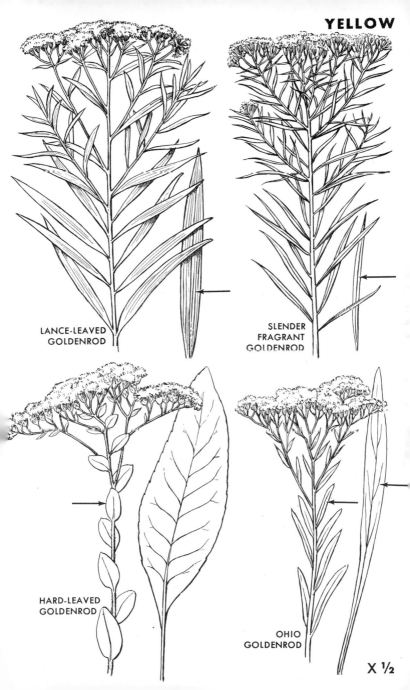

YELLOW

LANCE-LEAVED
GOLDENROD

SLENDER
FRAGRANT
GOLDENROD

HARD-LEAVED
GOLDENROD

OHIO
GOLDENROD

X ½

Orange
Flowers

Flowers that are truly orange are relatively few and are covered almost in their entirety in the two following color plates.

ORANGE LILIES
Lily Family (Liliaceae)

The lily family has a flower plan of 3 and 6. Fruit a pod. True lilies, *Lilium*, have spotted blossoms and leaves in whorls or alternate on the stem. The introduced Day-lily, *Hemerocallis*, has unspotted blossoms, swordlike leaves. Flowers of lilies come in 2 styles: (1) bell-like, nodding; (2) cuplike, upright. See also Blackberry-lily, p. 208.

CANADA or WILD YELLOW LILY *Lilium canadense*
Note the nodding orange or yellow bells. A red form is sometimes found. Leaves usually in whorls. See also next species. 2–5 ft. Moist meadows, bogs, openings. Se. Canada, ne. U.S., southward in highlands. JUNE–AUG.

TURK'S-CAP LILY *Lilium superbum*
Differs from preceding (which is usually more yellow) by more completely reflexed petals (forming "turk's cap"), *green central star*; stamens *project* much farther. 3–8 ft. Meadows, wet ground. New York, New Brunswick south. JULY–AUG.

TIGER LILY Alien *Lilium tigrinum*
Suggests Turk's-cap, but note the leaves *alternate* along the stem, with dark *bulblets in the axils*. 2–5 ft. Native of e. Asia. Escaped from gardens locally. JULY–AUG.

MICHIGAN LILY *Lilium michiganense*
Somewhat intermediate between Canada and Turk's-cap Lilies (replaces latter in Midwest). Examine illustration. Meadows, low spots, open woods. Manitoba, s. Ontario to Arkansas, Tennessee. JUNE–JULY

DAY-LILY Alien *Hemerocallis fulva*
Note the *upward-facing*, tawny, *unspotted* blossoms (open 1 day only). Unlike flowering stem in true lilies, it is *leafless* here. Leaves *long, swordlike*. 3–6 ft. An escape from gardens. New Brunswick to Virginia. **Note:** YELLOW DAY-LILY, LEMON LILY, *H. flava* (not shown), a smaller yellow species, is another escape of Asiatic origin. JUNE–AUG.

GRAY'S or BELL LILY *Lilium grayi*
Small, southern. Suggests Canada Lily but deep red-orange; less reflexed, more heavily spotted. 2–3 ft. Meadows, swamps among mts. Virginia to N. Carolina. JUNE–JULY

WOOD LILY *Lilium philadelphicum*
Note the brilliant orange to scarlet, *upward-facing*, spotted blossoms (other spotted lilies nod). Day-lily is *unspotted*. 1–3 ft. Sandy or acid soil, meadows, wood openings. S. Canada, Maine to c. U.S., N. Carolina (mts.). **Note:** 2 varieties: (1) eastern form (*philadelphicum*) with leaves in whorls; (2) western form (*andinum*) with leaves *scattered* along stem. These intergrade west of Appalachians. JUNE–JULY

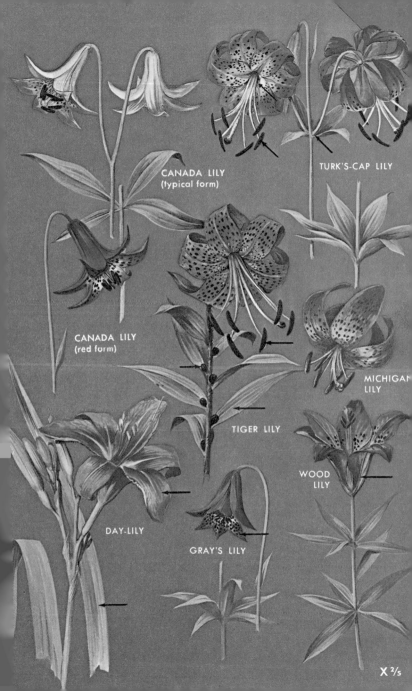

CANADA LILY
(typical form)

TURK'S-CAP LILY

CANADA LILY
(red form)

MICHIGAN
LILY

TIGER LILY

WOOD
LILY

DAY-LILY

GRAY'S LILY

X ²/₅

MISCELLANEOUS ORANGE FLOWERS

SPOTTED TOUCH-ME-NOT,   *Impatiens capensis*
JEWELWEED   TOUCH-ME-NOT FAMILY   (Balsaminaceae)
The spotted blossom hangs like a pendent jewel; succulent
stems exude juice when broken. Ripe seedpod pops at a touch.
2–5 ft. Wet, shady places. Most of our area.   JULY–SEPT.

FLAME AZALEA   *Rhododendron calendulaceum*
HEATH FAMILY   (Ericaceae)
A mountain shrub. Note the hairy-tubed blossoms, very long
style, hoary down under leaves. Our only orange azalea. 4–12
ft. Appalachians; s. Pennsylvania south.   MAY–JUNE

YELLOW MILKWORT   *Polygala lutea*
MILKWORT FAMILY   (Polygalaceae)
Suggests an orange clover head. Alternate leaves climb smooth
stem; also a basal rosette. 6–12 in. Pine barrens, wet sandy
soil. Coastal plain, Long Island south.   JUNE–OCT.

ORANGE HAWKWEED Alien   *Hieracium aurantiacum*
COMPOSITE FAMILY   (Compositae)
Whereas similar hawkweeds are yellow, the "Devil's Paintbrush" is *deep orange*. Plant very hairy; leaves form a basal
rosette. 8–24 in. Roadsides, fields. Minnesota, Newfoundland
south to Iowa, Ohio, n. Virginia.   JUNE–SEPT.

BUTTERFLY-WEED   *Asclepias tuberosa*
MILKWEED FAMILY   (Asclepiadaceae)
A variable milkweed. Stems hairy, not milky when broken.
Seedpod spindle-shaped (4–5 in.). Plant 1–2 ft. Fields, dry
soil. Minnesota, s. Ontario, s. Maine south.   JUNE–SEPT.

LANCEOLATE MILKWEED   *Asclepias lanceolata*
MILKWEED FAMILY   (Asclepiadaceae)
Resembles Butterfly-weed but note the *smooth* slender stem,
linear leaves, scant number of flowers. 2–4 ft. Brackish coastal
marshes. New Jersey south.   JUNE–AUG.

BLACKBERRY-LILY Alien   *Belamcanda chinensis*
IRIS FAMILY   (Iridaceae)
Six-petaled, rather lily-like (flower smaller, flatter); leaves iris-
like. Fruit pod holds a mass of black seeds resembling a black-
berry. 1½–4 ft. See true lilies, p. 206. Thickets, roadsides.
Indiana, Connecticut south.   JUNE–JULY

YELLOW FRINGED ORCHIS   *Habenaria ciliaris*
ORCHID FAMILY   (Orchidaceae)
Note the *fringed* "beards," *long* drooping spurs. Crested Yellow
Orchis (p. 120) has much shorter spurs. 1–2 ft. Peaty soil,
grassy bogs. Michigan, New York south.   JULY–AUG.

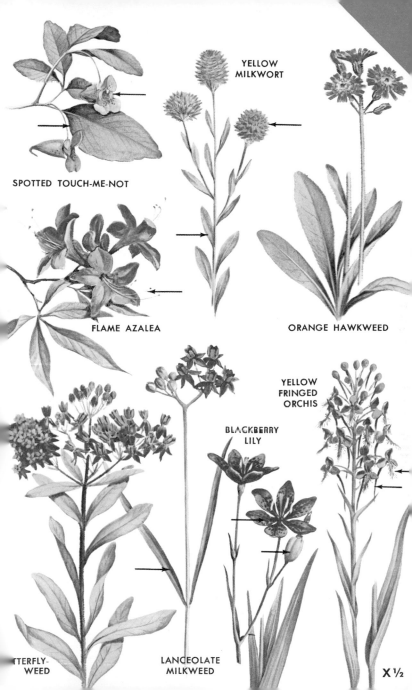

SPOTTED TOUCH-ME-NOT

YELLOW MILKWORT

ORANGE HAWKWEED

FLAME AZALEA

YELLOW FRINGED ORCHIS

BLACKBERRY LILY

TTERFLY-WEED

LANCEOLATE MILKWEED

X ½

Pink to Red Flowers

In this category we include not only the unmistakably pink or red flowers but also those of the variable lavender, lilac, and purple shades that lean toward the red side of the spectrum. There is a very difficult-to-define middle range which is so close to the dividing line between the red–purple and the violet categories that we have no recourse but to repeat some species — such as the ironweeds — in both sections. And then there are those species that may vary across the line in different individuals. Indeed, the same blossom may even change color perceptibly within a day or two. If in doubt, look also in the violet–blue section, which starts on page 314.

SHOWY FLOWERS; BROAD LEAVES:
RED AND BICOLORED TRILLIUMS, ORCHIDS

RED or PURPLE TRILLIUM, WAKEROBIN
LILY FAMILY (Liliaceae)   *Trillium erectum*
In trilliums all parts are in 3's. In this species the ill-scented, liver-red flower is on a short stalk. Occasionally pink, salmon, greenish, white, etc. 7–16 in. See other red trilliums, p. 240. Rich woods. Michigan, Ontario, Quebec to Pennsylvania, n. Delaware, and south in mts.   APRIL–JUNE

PAINTED TRILLIUM   *Trillium undulatum*
LILY FAMILY   (Liliaceae)
The *crimson blaze* at the base of the wavy white petals renders this species unique. 8–20 in. Acid woods, bogs. Manitoba, Ontario, e. Quebec south to Wisconsin, Michigan, Pennsylvania, n. New Jersey and in mts. to Georgia.   APRIL–JUNE

MOCCASIN-FLOWER, PINK LADY'S-SLIPPER
ORCHID FAMILY (Orchidaceae)   *Cypripedium acaule*
The heavily veined, deeply cleft pink pouch is distinctive. Rarely white (p. 14). Note also the 2 oval basal leaves (giving rise to the name Stemless Lady's-slipper). 6–15 in. Acid woods; sometimes bogs. Manitoba, Newfoundland south to n. U.S. and in mts. to Georgia.   MAY–JUNE

SHOWY LADY'S-SLIPPER   *Cypripedium reginae*
ORCHID FAMILY   (Orchidaceae)
Our largest and most beautiful northern orchid. The white sepals and petals are in striking contrast to the rose-mouthed pouch. The stout, hairy flowering stem is leafy to the top. 1–3 ft. Swamps, wet woods. Ontario, Newfoundland to n. U.S. and locally in mts. southward.   JUNE–JULY

RAM'S-HEAD LADY'S-SLIPPER   *Cypripedium arietinum*
ORCHID FAMILY   (Orchidaceae)
A small, rare lady's-slipper. Note the small *conical* pouch veined with crimson and lined with silky white hairs. Flowers solitary, short-lived. Leaves 3 to 5 on stem. 6–12 in. Bogs, damp woods. Manitoba, sw. Quebec south locally to Minnesota, Michigan, New York, Massachusetts.   MAY–JUNE

SHOWY ORCHIS   *Orchis spectabilis*
ORCHID FAMILY   (Orchidaceae)
The purple or rose hood (sepals and lateral petals) contrasts strikingly with the white lip and spur. 2 wide, smooth, basal leaves. 4–12 in. Rich woods. Ontario, Quebec south to Missouri and in mts. to Georgia.   APRIL–JUNE

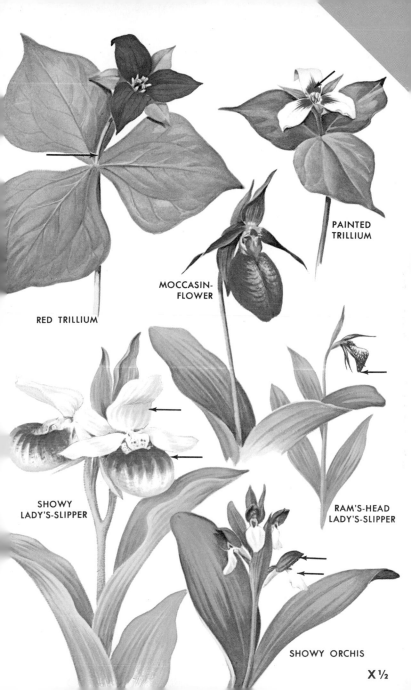

RED TRILLIUM

PAINTED
TRILLIUM

MOCCASIN-
FLOWER

SHOWY
LADY'S-SLIPPER

RAM'S-HEAD
LADY'S-SLIPPER

SHOWY ORCHIS

X ½

FLOWERS WITH CRESTED LIPS: ORCHIDS
ORCHID FAMILY (Orchidaceae), except Fringed Polygala

ROSE POGONIA, SNAKE-MOUTH *Pogonia ophioglossoides*
The crested and fringed lip is distinctive. Flowers borne singly; petals and sepals of similar shape. A broad, sheathing leaf midway on stem. 4–20 in. Acid soil of wet meadows, sphagnum bogs. Minnesota, w. Ontario, Newfoundland south locally to n. Illinois, Indiana, Tennessee, and on coastal plain to Florida. JUNE–AUG.

NODDING POGONIA, THREE-BIRDS
Triphora trianthophora
Note the nodding buds and blossoms (usually 3) borne in upper leaf axils. Lip marked with 3 green lines. Leaves stubby, ovate, sheathing stem. 3–10 in. Humus, rotten wood, of hardwood forests. Very local from s. Wisconsin, s. Michigan, Ohio, New York, Vermont, and sw. Maine south. JULY–SEPT.

CALOPOGON, GRASS-PINK *Calopogon pulchellus*
Note that the yellow-crested lip is held *uppermost* in this orchid. A loose cluster of 2 to 10 flowers. A single slender leaf sheathes the stem near the base. 4–20 in. Wet acid soil, bogs, peat meadows, swamps. Minnesota, Ontario, Quebec, Newfoundland to s. U.S. JUNE–AUG.

CALYPSO, FAIRY-SLIPPER *Calypso bulbosa*
Note the slipperlike lip with its translucent cover, yellow crest, and 2 tiny horns at the "toe." The broad solitary leaf survives the winter and withers after the plant flowers, to be replaced by another leaf. 3–8 in. Mossy, coniferous woods. Across Canada and south rarely to Minnesota, n. Michigan, New York, n. New England. MAY–JULY

SPREADING POGONIA, ROSEBUD ORCHID
Cleistes divaricata
The *extraordinary sepals* (1½–2½ in.) flare above the petals and lip, which join to form a slender pink tube. A slender clasping leaf midway on stem. 1–2 ft. Coastal bogs, moist pine barrens. S. New Jersey (very rare) south. Also sandy uplands, Kentucky south. JUNE–JULY

ARETHUSA, DRAGON'S-MOUTH *Arethusa bulbosa*
The illustration best explains this bizarre flower with its *3 erect sepals* and the hood over its blotched and crested lip. A single grasslike leaf develops after the flowering season. 5–10 in. Sphagnum bogs, swamps. Minnesota, Ontario, Quebec, Newfoundland south to the central and lake states and in mts. to N. Carolina. MAY–JULY

FRINGED POLYGALA, GAYWINGS *Polygala paucifolia*
MILKWORT FAMILY (Polygalaceae)
Not an orchid. See p. 244.

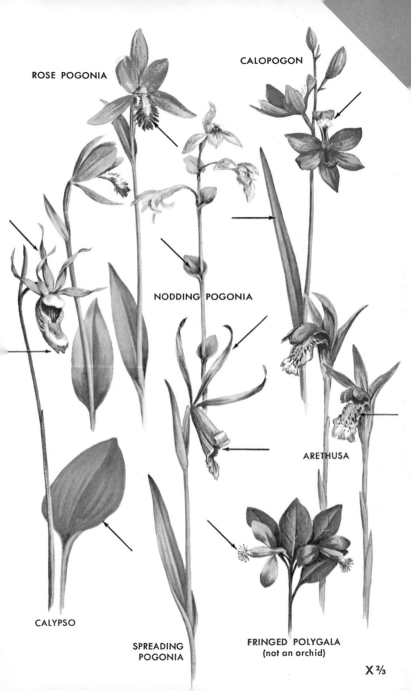

ROSE POGONIA

CALOPOGON

NODDING POGONIA

ARETHUSA

CALYPSO

SPREADING POGONIA

FRINGED POLYGALA
(not an orchid)

X ⅔

TUBED FLOWERS

TRUMPET-CREEPER   *Campsis radicans*
BIGNONIA FAMILY   (Bignoniaceae)
A climbing vine with swollen, 3-inch, trumpetlike flowers.
Leaves *compound*, with 7 to 11 *toothed* leaflets. Low thickets,
woods. Illinois, e. Pennsylvania, New Jersey south; naturalized
north to Michigan, Connecticut.   JULY–SEPT.

CROSS-VINE (not shown)   *Bignonia capreolata*
BIGNONIA FAMILY   (Bignoniaceae)
Resembles Trumpet-creeper but leaves consist of 2 large, *paired*,
oval leaflets. Stem in section reveals cross. Low woods. S.
Missouri, s. Ohio, Maryland south.   MAY–JUNE

COLUMBINE   *Aquilegia canadensis*
BUTTERCUP FAMILY   (Ranunculaceae)
The drooping bells with *5 long, curved spurs* are characteristic.
Compound leaves divided and subdivided into 3's. 1–2 ft.
Rocky woods, slopes. Manitoba, Ontario, Quebec south.
                                        APRIL–JULY

TRUMPET HONEYSUCKLE   *Lonicera sempervirens*
HONEYSUCKLE FAMILY   (Caprifoliaceae)
A smooth climbing vine. Note the *whorls of slender trumpets;*
roundish upper leaves often *join around stem.* Woods, thickets.
Iowa, Ohio, New York, Massachusetts south.   APRIL–SEPT.

BEE-BALM, OSWEGO-TEA   *Monarda didyma*
MINT FAMILY   (Labiatae)
The ragged *scarlet pompon* of tubular flowers is easily recog-
nized. Note also the red bracts. Leaves paired on the square
stem. 2–3 ft. Wet places, thickets, streambanks. Michigan,
New York south, chiefly in uplands.   JULY–SEPT.

WILD BERGAMOT   *Monarda fistulosa*
MINT FAMILY   (Labiatae)
Similar to Bee-balm but *pinkish or pale lilac.* Bracts often
tinged with lilac. A similar species, *M. clinopardia* (not shown),
is paler, often whitish, with whitish bracts. 2–3 ft. Dry edges,
thickets, clearings. Minnesota, sw. Quebec, w. New England
south (mainly in uplands southward).   JULY–AUG.

PURPLE BERGAMOT   *Monarda media*
MINT FAMILY   (Labiatae)
Similar to Wild Bergamot but *red-purple.* Bracts purplish.
Indiana, Ontario, New York south (in mts.); often cultivated.

CARDINAL-FLOWER   *Lobelia cardinalis*
BLUEBELL FAMILY   (Campanulaceae)
LOBELIA SUBFAMILY   (Lobelioideae)
America's favorite. A slender spike of intense scarlet flowers.
Our illustration explains form better than description. 2–4 ft.
Wet places, streambanks, swamps. Minnesota, Michigan, s.
Ontario, s. New Brunswick south.   JULY–SEPT.

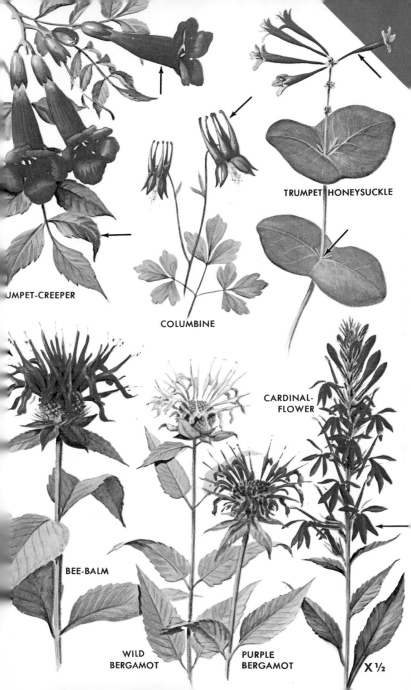

TRUMPET HONEYSUCKLE

TRUMPET-CREEPER

COLUMBINE

CARDINAL-
FLOWER

BEE-BALM

WILD
BERGAMOT

PURPLE
BERGAMOT

X ½

5 SHOWY, ROSE-LIKE PETALS

CRIMSON-EYED ROSE-MALLOW
MALLOW FAMILY (Malvaceae)   *Hibiscus palustris* forma *peckii*
A white form of the next species, with a *red center*. Very similar
to *H. moscheutos* (p. 258) but with a wider leaf. Perhaps should
be regarded as conspecific. Coastal marshes, especially southward.   AUG.–SEPT.

SWAMP ROSE-MALLOW   *Hibiscus palustris*
MALLOW FAMILY   (Malvaceae)
This large pink *hollyhocklike* bloom is unmistakable. Like
other species of *Hibiscus* it has the characteristic long style
tipped with 5 round stigmas. 5–7 ft. Brackish or salt marshes
near coast from e. Massachusetts to e. N. Carolina; also fresh
marshes locally in Great Lakes region.   AUG.–SEPT.

WILD GERANIUM   *Geranium maculatum*
GERANIUM FAMILY   (Geraniaceae)
Note the deeply 5-parted hairy leaves and the *long beak*, or
"cranesbill," in the center of the flower. 1–2 ft. See other
geraniums (cranesbills), p. 260. Woods, shady roadsides. Manitoba, s. Ontario, Maine south.   APRIL–JUNE

MUSK MALLOW Alien   *Malva moschata*
MALLOW FAMILY   (Malvaceae)
Note the *notched petals* (pink-lavender or white) and the in-
tricately cut leaves. As in other mallows there is a bushy
center column of stamens. 1–2 ft. See other mallows, p. 258.
Fields, roadsides. Ontario, Newfoundland south to Tennessee,
Delaware.   JUNE–SEPT.

PASTURE or CAROLINA ROSE   *Rosa carolina*
ROSE FAMILY   (Rosaceae)
This low, slender wild rose has rather thin, straight (not recurved) thorns. 1–3 ft. For comparison with other pink roses
see p. 256. Sandy or rocky pastures, open woods. Minnesota,
Wisconsin, Michigan, s. Ontario, New York, New England
south.   JUNE–JULY

PURPLE-FLOWERING RASPBERRY   *Rubus odoratus*
ROSE FAMILY   (Rosaceae)
A shrub with *maple-shaped* leaves and rose-like flowers (1–2 in.)
having curious long sepals. The reddish-brown stems are
sticky-hairy. The shallow, cup-shaped red berry is rather dry
and acid. 3–6 ft. Rocky woods, ravines, thickets. S. Ontario,
s. Quebec, Nova Scotia south.   JUNE–AUG.

CRIMSON-EYED
ROSE-MALLOW

SWAMP
ROSE-MALLOW

WILD
GERANIUM

MUSK MALLOW

PASTURE
ROSE

PURPLE-FLOWERING
RASPBERRY

X ½

PINK FLOWERS OF MARSH AND MEADOW

 MARSH- or SEA-PINK *Sabatia stellaris*
GENTIAN FAMILY (Gentianaceae)
A yellow eye with border of red marks the marsh-pinks. *Wider leaves, shorter sepals* separate this species from next. 6–20 in. Coast marshes. Se. Massachusetts south. JULY–OCT.

SLENDER MARSH-PINK *Sabatia campanulata*
GENTIAN FAMILY (Gentianaceae)
Similar, but note the *linear leaves and much longer sepals*. 8–24 in. Sandy or peaty soil. Coastal plain north to se. Massachusetts; inland to Virginia, Indiana. JULY–SEPT.

 ROSE-PINK *Sabatia angularis*
GENTIAN FAMILY (Gentianaceae)
Note the paired flowering branches and thick, 4-angled stem. Leaves broad. 1–3 ft. Moist fields, roadsides. Wisconsin, Michigan, s. Ontario, se. New York south. JULY–SEPT.

 LARGE MARSH-PINK *Sabatia dodecandra*
GENTIAN FAMILY (Gentianaceae)
This large *Sabatia* has 8–12 petals. 1–2 ft. Brackish coastal marshes north to Connecticut, Long Island. A similar species, *S. kennedyana* (not shown), is found in fresh marshes near coast in Rhode Island, Massachusetts, Nova Scotia. JULY–AUG.

SHOOTING-STAR *Dodecatheon meadia*
PRIMROSE FAMILY (Primulaceae)
Note the *swept-back* petals. Stamens join to form a *pointed beak*. Leaves in rosette, red at base. 10–24 in. Meadows, open woods, prairies. Wisconsin, w. Pennsylvania, D.C. south. *D. amethystinum* (not shown), with pale leaves (no red), is local in e. Pennsylvania and in Mississippi Valley. APRIL–JUNE

 PURPLE GERARDIA *Gerardia purpurea*
SNAPDRAGON FAMILY (Scrophulariaceae)
The purple gerardias may be known by the inflated bell-like flowers in the leaf axils, and the paired linear leaves. 1–3 ft. See p. 268 for comparison of similar species. Wet, sandy soil, damp meadows. Minnesota, Wisconsin, s. Michigan, n. Ohio, New York, s. New England south. AUG.–OCT.

 MARYLAND MEADOW-BEAUTY *Rhexia mariana*
MEADOW-BEAUTY FAMILY (Melastomataceae)
Note the 4 lopsided petals and slender curved anthers. This species is *pale pink* and quite hairy. Leaves *narrow* at base. 1–2 ft. Wet sands, pine barrens. Coastal plain north to s. Massachusetts; inland to Virginia, Kentucky. JULY–SEPT.

VIRGINIA MEADOW-BEAUTY *Rhexia virginica*
MEADOW-BEAUTY FAMILY (Melastomataceae)
Similar to *R. mariana* but *deeper rose;* less hairy; leaves wider, *broad* at base; stem with 4 thin lengthwise ridges. 1–1½ ft. Wet sandy soil. S. Ontario, Nova Scotia south. JULY–SEPT.

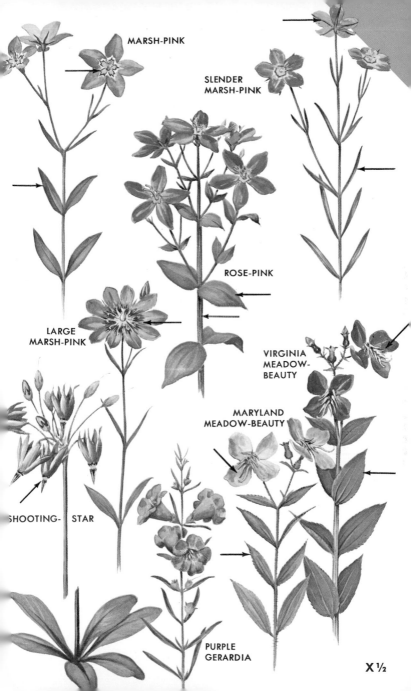

MARSH-PINK

SLENDER
MARSH-PINK

ROSE-PINK

LARGE
MARSH-PINK

VIRGINIA
MEADOW-
BEAUTY

MARYLAND
MEADOW-BEAUTY

SHOOTING- STAR

PURPLE
GERARDIA

X ½

5 PETALS, TUBED CALYX; PAIRED LEAVES: PINKS, ETC.

PINK FAMILY (Caryophyllaceae), except Moss Phlox
See also p. 266 (other pinks) and p. 226 (phlox).

RAGGED-ROBIN Alien   *Lychnis flos-cuculi*
Note the *deeply 4-cleft* petals, giving a ragged aspect. Sometimes white. 1–2 ft. Fields, wet meadows. Local, Quebec, Nova Scotia to New York, Pennsylvania.   JUNE–JULY

MAIDEN PINK Alien   *Dianthus deltoides*
Differs from the following by *solitary* flowers; petals rounder, much toothed (inset). 6–16 in. Dry fields, roadsides. Vermont to New Jersey; west to Michigan, Illinois.   JUNE–AUG.

DEPTFORD PINK Alien   *Dianthus armeria*
Very slender, with a stiff stem and needlelike leaves. Note the petal shape and white spotting of the small (½ in.) flowers and the long bristly bracts. 8–20 in. Dry fields, roadsides. Quebec, Ontario south.   MAY–JULY

FIRE PINK   *Silene virginica*
Note the *narrow, deep scarlet* petals, double-toothed at the tip, and the long flower stalks. 1–2 ft. Open woods, rocky slopes. Minnesota, s. Ontario, New Jersey south.   APRIL–JUNE

WILD PINK   *Silene caroliniana* var. *pensylvanica*
The wedge-shaped pink petals and sticky upper stem and calyx are easily recognized. A tuft of slender leaves at base. 4–10 in. Dry or rocky woods, openings. E. Ohio, New York, s. New Hampshire south, mainly in mts.   APRIL–JUNE

CORN-COCKLE Alien   *Agrostemma githago*
Note the *strongly ribbed calyx* and the wide, veined, purplish-pink petals. The hairy sepals greatly exceed the petals. 1–3 ft. Grainfields, waste places. Throughout.   JUNE–SEPT.

SCARLET LYCHNIS Alien   *Lychnis chalcedonica*
Note the congested flower head and *Y-shaped* red, rose, or white petals. Leaves broad. 2–3 ft. Red Campion, *L. dioica* (p. 266), has less crowded flowers, long-stalked basal leaves. Both aliens are established locally.   JUNE–SEPT.

MOSS PHLOX, MOSS-PINK   *Phlox subulata*
PHLOX FAMILY   (Polemoniaceae)
Not a true pink. Flowers pink, violet, or white. See text and plate, p. 322. See also Moss Campion, p. 266.

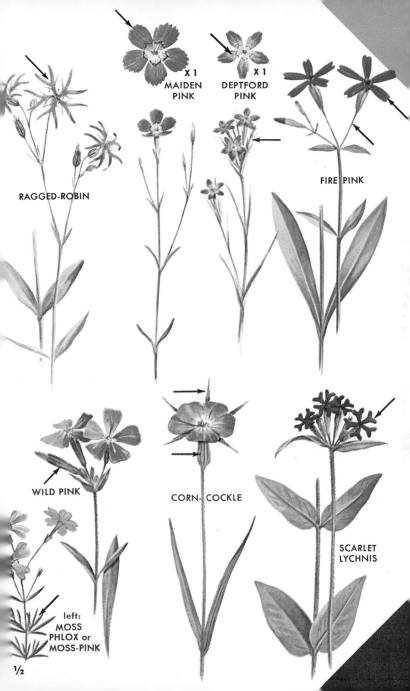

X 1
MAIDEN
PINK

X 1
DEPTFORD
PINK

RAGGED-ROBIN

FIRE PINK

WILD PINK

CORN-COCKLE

SCARLET
LYCHNIS

left:
MOSS
PHLOX or
MOSS-PINK

1/2

SLENDER SPIKES OF MANY FLOWERS

 PURPLE or SPIKED LOOSESTRIFE Alien *Lythrum salicaria*
LOOSESTRIFE FAMILY (Lythraceae)
The slender spikes of *6-petaled* blossoms carpet swampy
meadows with magenta. Leaves stalkless, downy, opposite or
in 3's. 2–4 ft. See other loosestrifes, p. 140 (yellow), p. 288
(purple). Swamps, wet meadows. Minnesota, Quebec, Newfoundland to Missouri, Ohio, Virginia. JUNE–SEPT.

 FIREWEED *Epilobium angustifolium*
EVENING-PRIMROSE FAMILY (Onagraceae)
Note the *4 roundish petals*, drooping flower buds, and reddish seedpods angling upward. Leaves alternate. 3–7 ft. See
other epilobiums, p. 270. Clearings, fire-desolated areas. Subarctic south to Iowa, Indiana, n. Ohio, and in mts. to Georgia.
JULY–SEPT.

 STEEPLEBUSH, HARDHACK *Spiraea tomentosa*
ROSE FAMILY (Rosaceae)
Note the *woolly brownish underside* of the leaves and the fuzzy
steeple shaped cluster of tiny 5-petaled flowers. Blooms from
top downward. Stems woody. 2–4 ft. Meadows, pastures.
Minnesota, Quebec, Nova Scotia south. JULY–SEPT.

 PURPLE FRINGED ORCHIS *Habenaria fimbriata*
ORCHID FAMILY (Orchidaceae)
Note the 3-part, *fringed lip* of this many-flowered orchis.
Flower cluster *more than 2 in. thick.* Lower leaves large, upper
small. 1–4 ft. Woods, meadows. Se. Ontario, s. Newfoundland
south to Pennsylvania, New Jersey, and in mts. to N. Carolina.
JUNE–AUG.

 SMALL PURPLE FRINGED ORCHIS *Habenaria psycodes*
ORCHID FAMILY (Orchidaceae)
A smaller version; intergrades frequent. Flower cluster *less
than 2 in. thick,* lip less deeply fringed. 1–3 ft. Swamps,
meadows. Ontario, Quebec, Newfoundland to Iowa, Illinois,
Ohio, New Jersey, and in mts. to Georgia. JULY–AUG.

 SHOWY TICK-TREFOIL *Desmodium canadense*
PEA FAMILY (Leguminosae)
Pealike blossoms (½ in.) in clusters at the summit of a hairy,
leafy stem. Leaves cloverlike (3 long-oval leaflets). Hairy, 3- to
5-jointed seedpods. 2–6 ft. See other tick-trefoils, p. 248. Open
woods, edges. Saskatchewan, Nova Scotia south to Missouri,
Illinois, Ohio, Maryland. JULY–AUG.

DENSE BLAZING-STAR *Liatris spicata*
COMPOSITE FAMILY (Compositae)
Note the dense wand of small thistle-like blossoms and the
linear grasslike leaves on the stem. 1–5 ft. See other blazing-
stars, p. 282. Wet meadows. Wisconsin, Michigan, sw. Ontario,
Pennsylvania, n. New Jersey south. JULY–SEPT.

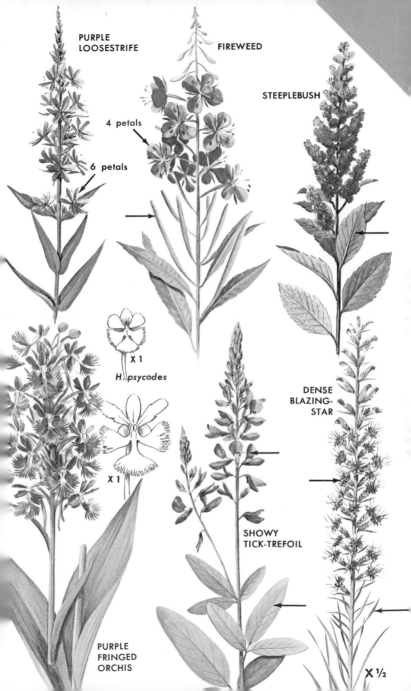

PURPLE
LOOSESTRIFE

FIREWEED

STEEPLEBUSH

4 petals

6 petals

H. psycodes

X 1

X 1

DENSE
BLAZING-
STAR

SHOWY
TICK-TREFOIL

PURPLE
FRINGED
ORCHIS

X ½

SHOWY CLUSTERS; TUBED COROLLAS

 RED TURTLEHEAD Alien *Chelone lyoni*
SNAPDRAGON FAMILY (Scrophulariaceae)
The large snapdragonlike flowers resemble *heads of turtles.*
Leaves broad, coarsely toothed. 1–2½ ft. Wet woods. S. U.S.;
introduced locally in s. New England. A similar red species,
C. obliqua (not shown), with narrower leaves, is found in the in-
terior from s. Minnesota south and on coastal plain from Mary-
land south. See white Turtlehead (may be pink-tinged), p. 58.
AUG.–OCT.

FALSE DRAGONHEAD *Physostegia virginiana*
MINT FAMILY (Labiatae)
Although suggestive of a snapdragon, this plant is a mint (note
square stem and spotted 3-lobed lip). When flowers are pushed
right or left they *stay* that way (hence nickname "Obedient-
plant"). 1–4 ft. Riverbanks, thickets. Minnesota, s. Quebec
to Missouri, N. Carolina (mts.). JUNE–SEPT.

DAME'S ROCKET Alien *Hesperis matronalis*
MUSTARD FAMILY (Cruciferae)
This garden escape resembles a phlox, but note the *4 petals* (not
5) and long seedpods of a mustard. Pink, purple, or white.
1–3 ft. Roadsides, wood edges. Ontario, Newfoundland south
to n. U.S., and in mts. to Georgia. MAY–JULY

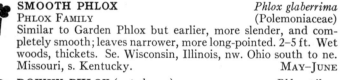 **SMOOTH PHLOX** *Phlox glaberrima*
PHLOX FAMILY (Polemoniaceae)
Similar to Garden Phlox but earlier, more slender, and com-
pletely smooth; leaves narrower, more long-pointed. 2–5 ft. Wet
woods, thickets. Se. Wisconsin, Illinois, nw. Ohio south to ne.
Missouri, s. Kentucky. MAY–JUNE

DOWNY PHLOX (not shown) *Phlox pilosa*
PHLOX FAMILY (Polemoniaceae)
A smaller downy species with stamens completely hidden inside
corolla tube. Dry woods, sandhills, prairies. Wisconsin, s. Ontario, New York south. MAY–JUNE

GARDEN or FALL PHLOX *Phlox paniculata*
PHLOX FAMILY (Polemoniaceae)
The familiar cultivated phlox. Stouter than similar species
with wider, more veiny leaves (lateral veins branch from central
vein). 2–6 ft. Woods, thickets. Interior from n. Iowa, c. New
York south; widely escaped elsewhere. JULY–OCT.

 WILD SWEET-WILLIAM *Phlox maculata*
PHLOX FAMILY (Polemoniaceae)
Similar to the familiar Garden Phlox but note the *purple-spotted*
stems and longer corolla tubes. Flowers in a longer, more
cylindrical cluster. 1½–3 ft. Riverbanks, low woods. S. Minnesota, sw. Quebec, New York, sw. Connecticut south to Missouri, Virginia (mts.), n. Delaware. MAY–SEPT.

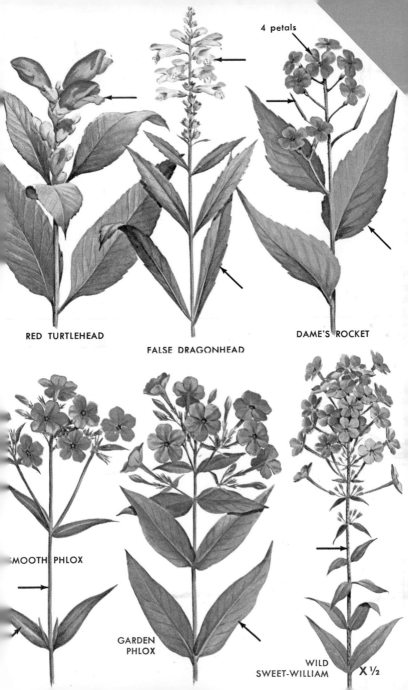

4 petals

RED TURTLEHEAD

FALSE DRAGONHEAD

DAME'S ROCKET

SMOOTH PHLOX

GARDEN PHLOX

WILD SWEET-WILLIAM

X ½

SHOWY FLOWERING SHRUBS
HEATH FAMILY (Ericaceae)

MOUNTAIN LAUREL   *Kalmia latifolia*
A showy shrub, often forming dense thickets. Leaves shiny, leathery, evergreen. The bowl-shaped flower clusters are composed of many small cup-shaped pink flowers, each with 10 anthers, forming *arching spokes* from the center to 10 pits in sides. Buds strongly ribbed. 13–15 ft: Rocky woods. Indiana, Ohio, New York, New England south   MAY–JULY

SHEEP LAUREL   *Kalmia angustifolia*
Smaller than Mountain Laurel, with narrow *drooping* leaves. Flowers crimson-pink, *not terminal;* surmounted by newer, upright leaves. 1–3 ft. Pastures, rocky slopes, swamps. Canada south to Michigan, New England; in mts. to Georgia.
                                        JUNE–JULY

PALE LAUREL   *Kalmia polifolia*
Similar to Sheep Laurel but flower cluster *terminal.* Leaves in pairs, rolled at edges and *whitened beneath.* Twigs 2-edged. 6–24 in. Bogs, peat. Canada south to Minnesota, Michigan, Pennsylvania, New Jersey.   MAY–JULY

GREAT RHODODENDRON   *Rhododendron maximum*
Larger than Mountain Laurel, with much larger leaves that are dark beneath. Flowers pink *spotted with green or orange.* Flower stems sticky. 5–40 ft. Wet woods, swamps. Ohio, s. Ontario, New York, s. New England south.   JUNE–JULY

CATAWBA RHODODENDRON   *Rhododendron catawbiensis*
(not shown)
Similar to Great Rhododendron but usually smaller. Flowers pale purple or lilac. Leaves more oval; paler beneath. 3–6 ft. Mts. from Virginia south.   MAY–JUNE

EARLY AZALEA, HONEYSUCKLE   *Rhododendron roseum*
Very fragrant, pink flowers often appear before leaves. Stamens and pistil project from tubed corolla that is as long as petals. Leaves *whitish woolly beneath.* Twigs, buds woolly. WOOLLY AZALEA, *R. canescens* (not shown), more southern, has flower tubes twice as long as petals. 2–10 ft. Woods. Sw. Quebec, sw. Maine to mts. of Missouri, Virginia.   MAY–JUNE

PINK AZALEA, PINXTER-FLOWER
                                    Rhododendron nudiflorum
Similar to *R. roseum* but stamens and pistil longer; flowers rather *odorless.* Buds, twigs, and leaves (beneath) lack woolliness of *roseum*. 2–8 ft. Woods, swamps. S. Ohio, New York, Massachusetts south.   MARCH–MAY

RHODORA   *Rhododendron canadense*
Note the shallowly 3-lobed upper lip and 2 narrow lobes, or petals, below. Curving stamens and pistils almost fully exposed. Magenta flowers bloom before leaves unfold. 1–3 ft. Bogs, rocky slopes. Quebec, Newfoundland to c. New York, ne. Pennsylvania, n. New Jersey.   MARCH–JUNE

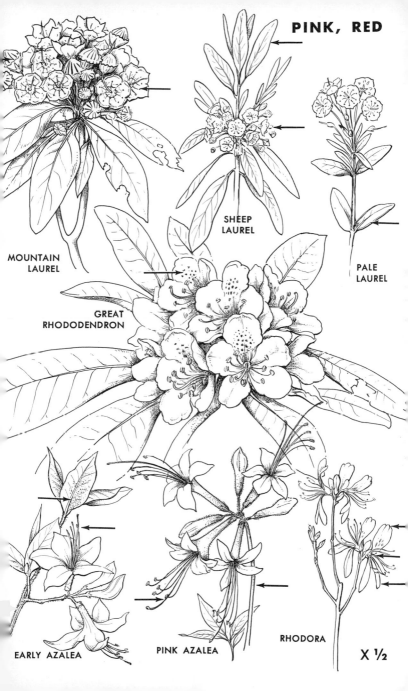

PINK, RED

MOUNTAIN
LAUREL

SHEEP
LAUREL

PALE
LAUREL

GREAT
RHODODENDRON

EARLY AZALEA

PINK AZALEA

RHODORA

X ½

MISCELLANEOUS PINK OR RED FLOWERS

PITCHER-PLANT *Sarracenia purpurea*
PITCHER-PLANT FAMILY (Sarraceniaceae)
Unmistakable. The *pitcherlike*, heavily veined red or green leaves are usually half filled with water; the flaring lips are lined with downward-pointing bristles that help trap insects. The nodding, globular dull red flower is on a separate stalk. Note the *very large flattened pistil*. 8–24 in. Sphagnum bogs. Canada south to Minnesota, Great Lakes, Ohio, Maryland and along coast to Florida. MAY–JULY

WATER-SHIELD *Brassenia schreberi*
WATER-LILY FAMILY (Nymphaeaceae)
Note the oval (2–4 in.), floating, *water-lily-like leaves* on long, slimy, submerged stems. The small (¾ in.) dull purple flowers have 3 (or 4) petals. Ponds, sluggish streams. Minnesota, s. Ontario, s. Quebec south. JUNE–SEPT.

PURPLE BLADDERWORT *Utricularia purpurea*
BLADDERWORT FAMILY (Lentibulariaceae)
Small, lipped, pealike lavender or pink flowers on a naked 2- to 6-inch stalk. Leaves *filamentlike, with tiny bladders;* submerged in mud or water. Other bladderworts (p. 122) are *yellow.* Ponds, muddy streams. Wisconsin, s. Michigan, sw. Quebec, New England, Nova Scotia south. JUNE–SEPT.

PAINTED-CUP, INDIAN PAINTBRUSH *Castilleja coccinea*
SNAPDRAGON FAMILY (Scrophulariaceae)
Note the *3-lobed, scarlet-tipped bracts* that all but hide the small 2-lipped greenish-yellowish flowers and their protruding pistils. 1–2 ft. Fields, meadows, prairies. Manitoba, Ontario to s. Maine and south. MAY–JULY

RED or COPPER IRIS *Iris fulva*
IRIS FAMILY (Iridaceae)
A spectacular orange-red species, the only *red* iris in our area. 1–3 ft. Ditches, shores, swamps. Lower Mississippi Valley from se. Missouri and s. Illinois south. MAY–JUNE

LEATHER-FLOWER *Clematis viorna*
BUTTERCUP FAMILY (Ranunculaceae)
A vine climbing on bushes. Flowers dull reddish, bell-like (leathery "petals" are really sepals). Note also heart-shaped leaves, *Medusa-like fruit clusters.* Woods, thickets. Illinois, s. Indiana, Ohio, Pennsylvania south. MAY–AUG.

SPIDER-FLOWER Alien *Cleome spinosa*
CAPER FAMILY (Capparidaceae)
Note the *extraordinarily long stamens* projecting beyond the 4 narrow-stalked pink or white petals. Sticky-downy. Lower leaves palmate. 2–4 ft. A garden escape. Indiana, Ohio, New York, Massachusetts south. JULY–SEPT.

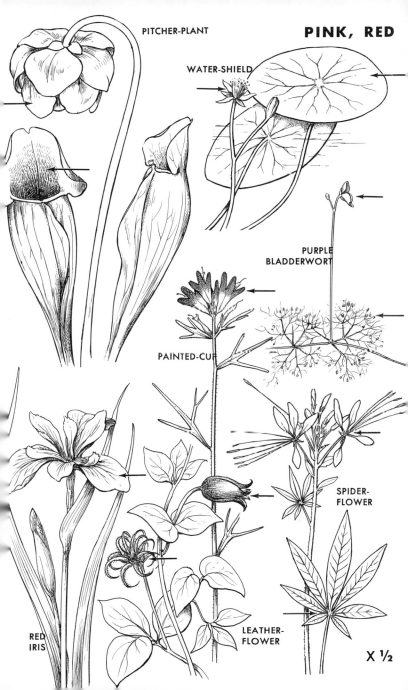

PITCHER-PLANT

PINK, RED

WATER-SHIELD

PURPLE
BLADDERWORT

PAINTED-CUP

SPIDER-
FLOWER

RED
IRIS

LEATHER-
FLOWER

X ½

SMALL PLANTS WITH SPECIALIZED HABITS

1. **INSECT-EATING PLANTS** (see also Pitcher-plant, p. 230)

ROUND-LEAVED SUNDEW *Drosera rotundifolia*
SUNDEW FAMILY (Droseraceae)
Note the rosette of small *round* leaves, each on a slender stalk
and covered with *reddish glandular hairs* that exude a sticky
juice, like tiny dewdrops. Flowers, pink or white in a 1-sided
cluster, open 1 at a time. 4–9 in. Acid or peaty bogs. Most of
our area. JUNE–AUG.

THREAD-LEAVED SUNDEW *Drosera filiformis*
SUNDEW FAMILY (Droseraceae)
This sundew has its sticky glandular hairs on *erect stringlike
leaves*. The small purplish flowers, which open 1 or 2 at a time,
are borne on a separate curved stalk. 8–10 in. See other sun-
dews, p. 20. Damp sand. Coastal plain, se. Massachusetts to s.
New Jersey. JUNE–SEPT.

2. **PARASITIC OR SAPROPHYTIC PLANTS; NO GREEN
COLOR**

BEECHDROPS *Epifagus virginiana*
BROOMRAPE FAMILY (Orobanchaceae)
Yellowish, reddish, or brown. Scale-like leaves, lack of green
pigment, are typical of this family. The *branching habit* distinguishes this species from all others except Branched Broomrape, *Orobanche ramosa* (p. 324; an alien parasitic on tomato,
tobacco, hemp, etc.). 6–24 in. Parasitic; under beech trees.
Ontario, Gulf of St. Lawrence south. AUG.–OCT.

ONE-FLOWERED CANCER-ROOT *Orobanche uniflora*
BROOMRAPE FAMILY (Orobanchaceae)
A single, downy white, pale lavender, or violet flower is borne at
the summit of a naked, sticky, pale stalk. 3–10 in. Parasitic;
damp woods. Nearly throughout. APRIL–JUNE

INDIAN-PIPE *Monotropa uniflora*
WINTERGREEN FAMILY (Pyrolaceae)
Usually white but may be pink; turns blackish later. Note the
single, nodding, translucent, waxy pipes. Leaves scale-like.
4–10 in. Shady woods. Most of our area. JUNE–SEPT.

PINESAP *Monotropa hypopithys*
WINTERGREEN FAMILY (Pyrolaceae)
Similar to Indian-pipe, but with *several* nodding flowers that
are dull yellow or reddish (not white). Seedpod erect. 4–14 in.
Woods, leaf mold. Throughout. JUNE–OCT.

SWEET PINESAP, PYGMY-PIPES *Monotropsis odorata*
WINTERGREEN FAMILY (Pyrolaceae)
A smaller, scarcer, southern species often hidden by fallen
leaves. At first much recurved. Light rose to purple. Very
fragrant (of violets). 2–4 in. Pine woods. W. Virginia, Maryland south. MARCH–APRIL

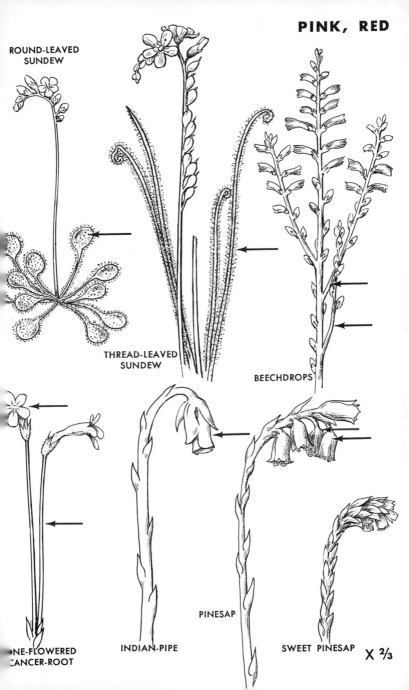

PINK, RED

ROUND-LEAVED SUNDEW

THREAD-LEAVED SUNDEW

BEECHDROPS

ONE-FLOWERED CANCER-ROOT

INDIAN-PIPE

PINESAP

SWEET PINESAP

X ⅔

SMALL, WAXY, NODDING, 5-PETALED FLOWERS

WINTERGREEN FAMILY (Pyrolaceae)

Mostly evergreen, often under conifers. Leaves in basal rosettes or in whorls of 3 to 6 toothed leaves on stem. See also p. 26.

SPOTTED WINTERGREEN   *Chimaphila maculata*
Note the *whitish pattern* on the midribs of the deeply toothed, tapering leaves. The leaves all are arranged in whorls on the stem, much as in Pipsissewa. The nodding waxy flowers may be white or pink. 4–10 in. Woods. Michigan, Ontario, Maine south, especially in uplands.   JUNE–AUG.

PIPSISSEWA   *Chimaphila umbellata*
Note the terminal cluster of waxy white or pinkish flowers, each with its ring of reddish anthers. The dark, shiny, toothed leaves are in 2 or 3 tiers, which radiate in whorls around the stem. 6–12 in. Dry woods. Ontario, Quebec south to n. U.S.; in mts. to Georgia.   JULY–AUG.

PINK PYROLA   *Pyrola asarifolia*
Note the *indented*, or heart-shaped, leaf base. Leaves in basal rosette. Flowers in a slender cluster or spike similar to those of most other pyrolas (p. 26) but always pink or crimson. 6–15 in. Rich woods. Canada to Great Lakes states, c. New York, n. New England.   JUNE–AUG.

ONE-FLOWERED WINTERGREEN   *Moneses uniflora*
Note the *single*, nodding, waxy white or pink flower and basal rosette of small roundish leaves. 2–5 in. Cool woods, bogs. N. Canada to Minnesota, Michigan, Pennsylvania, Connecticut.
     JUNE–AUG.

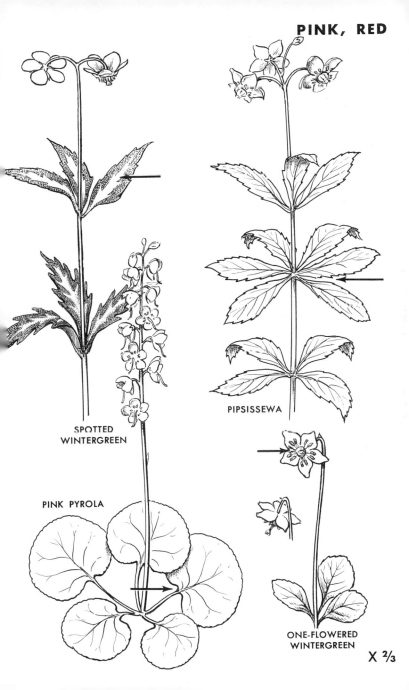

PINK, RED

SPOTTED
WINTERGREEN

PINK PYROLA

PIPSISSEWA

ONE-FLOWERED
WINTERGREEN

X ⅔

CREEPING OR MATTED EVERGREEN PLANTS

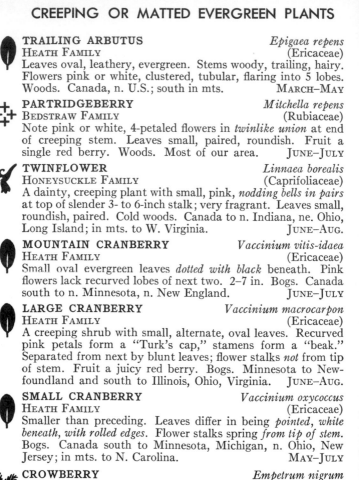

TRAILING ARBUTUS   *Epigaea repens*
HEATH FAMILY   (Ericaceae)
Leaves oval, leathery, evergreen. Stems woody, trailing, hairy.
Flowers pink or white, clustered, tubular, flaring into 5 lobes.
Woods. Canada, n. U.S.; south in mts.   MARCH–MAY

PARTRIDGEBERRY   *Mitchella repens*
BEDSTRAW FAMILY   (Rubiaceae)
Note pink or white, 4-petaled flowers in *twinlike union* at end
of creeping stem. Leaves small, paired, roundish. Fruit a
single red berry. Woods. Most of our area.   JUNE–JULY

TWINFLOWER   *Linnaea borealis*
HONEYSUCKLE FAMILY   (Caprifoliaceae)
A dainty, creeping plant with small, pink, *nodding bells in pairs*
at top of slender 3- to 6-inch stalk; very fragrant. Leaves small,
roundish, paired. Cold woods. Canada to n. Indiana, ne. Ohio,
Long Island; in mts. to W. Virginia.   JUNE–AUG.

MOUNTAIN CRANBERRY   *Vaccinium vitis-idaea*
HEATH FAMILY   (Ericaceae)
Small oval evergreen leaves *dotted with black* beneath. Pink
flowers lack recurved lobes of next two. 2–7 in. Bogs. Canada
south to n. Minnesota, n. New England.   JUNE–JULY

LARGE CRANBERRY   *Vaccinium macrocarpon*
HEATH FAMILY   (Ericaceae)
A creeping shrub with small, alternate, oval leaves. Recurved
pink petals form a "Turk's cap," stamens form a "beak."
Separated from next by blunt leaves; flower stalks *not* from tip
of stem. Fruit a juicy red berry. Bogs. Minnesota to Newfoundland and south to Illinois, Ohio, Virginia.   JUNE–AUG.

SMALL CRANBERRY   *Vaccinium oxycoccus*
HEATH FAMILY   (Ericaceae)
Smaller than preceding. Leaves differ in being *pointed, white
beneath, with rolled edges*. Flower stalks spring *from tip of stem*.
Bogs. Canada south to Minnesota, Michigan, n. Ohio, New
Jersey; in mts. to N. Carolina.   MAY–JULY

CROWBERRY   *Empetrum nigrum*
CROWBERRY FAMILY   (Empetraceae)
Mat-forming. Flowers minute, pinkish, at base of *short needle-
like leaves*. Berry turns purple, then black. Open peaty soil.
Arctic south to n. Minnesota, n. Michigan, n. New York, n.
New England; also Montauk Point, L.I.   JULY–AUG.

HEATHER, LING Alien   *Calluna vulgaris*
HEATH FAMILY   (Ericaceae)
A low fernlike evergreen shrub with tiny sharp needlelike
leaves in 4 rows along twigs. Flowers pink, in long clusters.
5–15 in. Peat or sand. Local, Newfoundland south to Michigan;
mts. of W. Virginia, New Jersey.   JULY–NOV.

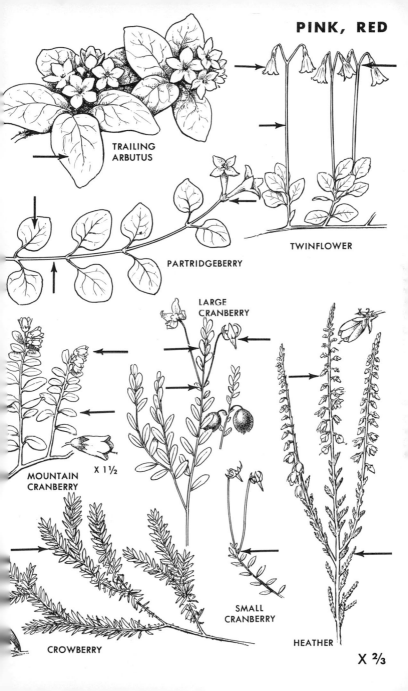

PINK, RED

TRAILING ARBUTUS

TWINFLOWER

PARTRIDGEBERRY

LARGE CRANBERRY

MOUNTAIN CRANBERRY

X 1½

SMALL CRANBERRY

CROWBERRY

HEATHER

X ⅔

LOW FLOWERS OF WOODLANDS

VIOLET WOOD-SORREL   *Oxalis violacea*
WOOD-SORREL FAMILY   (Oxalidaceae)
Note the inversely heart-shaped leaflets with their cloverlike arrangement of 3, typical of *Oxalis;* they often fold along a center crease. Leaflets reddish or purplish underneath. In this species the 5 flaring petals are *rose-purple or purplish violet.* 4–8 in. Open woods, banks. Minnesota, Wisconsin, Indiana Ohio, New York, Massachusetts south.   APRIL–JULY

SPRING-BEAUTY   *Claytonia virginica*
PURSLANE FAMILY   (Portulacaceae)
Note the pair of smooth *linear leaves* midway up the stem. Petals white or pink, with darker pink veins. 6–12 in. Moist woods. Minnesota, s. Ontario, s. Quebec, s. New England south.   MARCH–MAY

CAROLINA SPRING-BEAUTY   *Claytonia caroliniana*
PURSLANE FAMILY   (Portulacaceae)
Similar to preceding but leaves *much wider, with slender petioles.* Woods, uplands. S. Canada south through Appalachians and westward.   MARCH–MAY

COMMON WOOD-SORREL   *Oxalis montana*
WOOD-SORREL FAMILY   (Oxalidaceae)
The leaves of *Oxalis* are divided into 3 inversely heart-shaped leaflets suggesting clover. In this species the 5 white or pink petals are *strongly veined with pink.* 3–4 in. Woods. Canada, northern edge of U.S.; south in mts.   MAY–JULY

ROUND-LOBED HEPATICA   *Hepatica americana*
BUTTERCUP FAMILY   (Ranunculaceae)
Note the *rounded lobes of the 3-lobed leaves.* Stalks hairy. Flowers white, pink, lavender, or blue. The 6 to 10 "petals" are really sepals. There are 3 bracts below each flower. 4–6 in. Leafy woods. S. Canada south.   MARCH–MAY

SHARP-LOBED HEPATICA   *Hepatica acutiloba*
BUTTERCUP FAMILY   (Ranunculaceae)
Similar to the preceding but lobes of leaves *pointed;* occasionally 5 to 7 lobes. Hybridizes. 4–9 in. Upland woods. Appalachians from Maine south; west to Minnesota, Missouri.
                                          MARCH–APRIL

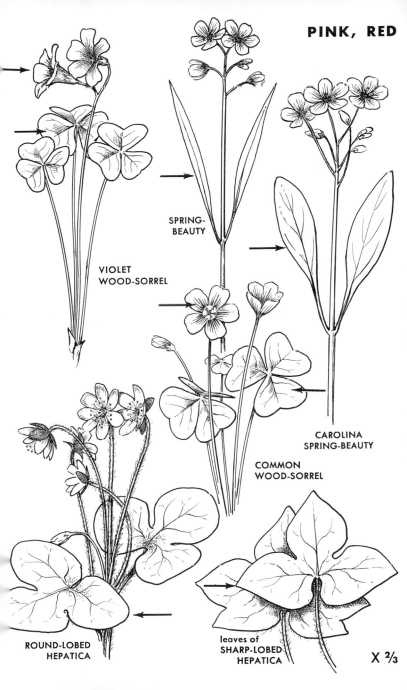

PINK, RED

VIOLET
WOOD-SORREL

SPRING-
BEAUTY

CAROLINA
SPRING-BEAUTY

COMMON
WOOD-SORREL

ROUND-LOBED
HEPATICA

leaves of
SHARP-LOBED
HEPATICA

X ⅔

3 PETALS OR LOBES; BROAD LEAVES

TOADSHADE, SESSILE TRILLIUM   *Trillium sessile*
LILY FAMILY   (Liliaceae)
Trilliums have leaves, petals, and sepals in whorls of 3. This species has sessile (stalkless) flowers with *erect petals* and *erect-spreading* sepals. Maroon or purplish; also a yellow-green form. 4–12 in. Woods. Missouri, Illinois, Indiana, Ohio, w. New York, Pennsylvania south.   APRIL–JUNE

PRAIRIE TRILLIUM   *Trillium recurvatum*
LILY FAMILY   (Liliaceae)
Similar to Toadshade but leaves *with petioles* (narrow stalks) and sepals *recurved* or drooping. 6–16 in. Woods. Iowa to Ohio and south.   APRIL–MAY

PAINTED TRILLIUM   *Trillium undulatum*
LILY FAMILY   (Liliaceae)
Note the *red blaze* in the center of the white flower. See text and color plate, p. 212.

RED or PURPLE TRILLIUM, WAKEROBIN
LILY FAMILY (Liliaceae)   *Trillium erectum*
See text and color plate, p. 212. The maroon or purple flower (rarely yellowish or white) is on a slender stalk above the leaves. Ill-scented. 7–16 in. Woods. Michigan, Ontario, Quebec south to Pennsylvania, n. Delaware; in mts. to Georgia.
                                                 APRIL–JUNE

LARGE-FLOWERED or WHITE TRILLIUM
LILY FAMILY (Liliaceae)   *Trillium grandiflorum*
Usually white but often turns deep pink with age. See p. 10.

DUTCHMAN'S-PIPE   *Aristolochia durior*
BIRTHWORT FAMILY   (Aristolochiaceae)
A climbing vine often grown as an ornamental on porches, arbors. Leaves large, heart-shaped. Flower a hook-shaped, pipe-like structure with 3 short purple-brown calyx lobes. Woods, streambanks. Sw. Pennsylvania and W. Virginia south in mts. to Georgia. Cultivated in North.   MAY–JUNE

WILD GINGER   *Asarum canadense*
BIRTHWORT FAMILY   (Aristolochiaceae)
The curious flower in the crotch between 2 leafstalks is at ground level. It is somewhat cup-shaped, with 3 pointed red-brown calyx lobes. Leaves large, heart-shaped, with hairy stalks. 6–12 in. Rich woods. Minnesota to the Gaspé, and south to Arkansas and N. Carolina.   APRIL–MAY

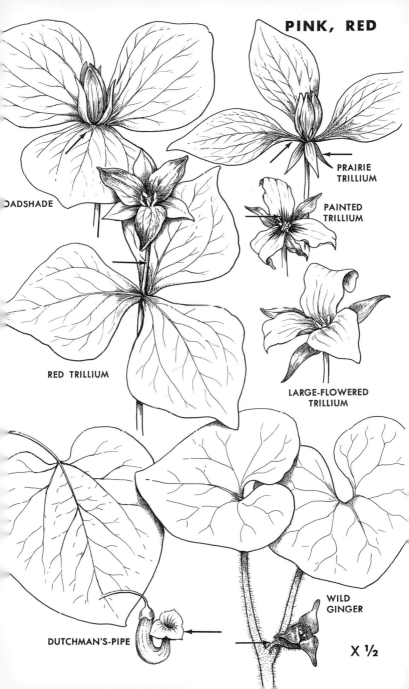

PINK, RED

TOADSHADE

PRAIRIE
TRILLIUM

PAINTED
TRILLIUM

RED TRILLIUM

LARGE-FLOWERED
TRILLIUM

DUTCHMAN'S-PIPE

WILD
GINGER

X ½

LIPPED FLOWERS; PARALLEL-VEINED LEAVES: MISCELLANEOUS ORCHIDS

Orchid Family (Orchidaceae)

SMALL PURPLE FRINGED ORCHIS *Habenaria psycodes*
See color plate, p. 224. Note the 3-part, fringed lips of this many-flowered phlox-purple orchid. Flower cluster *less than 2 in. thick.* 1–3 ft. Swamps, meadows. Ontario, Quebec, Newfoundland to Iowa, Illinois, Ohio, New Jersey; in mts. to Georgia.   July–Aug.

PURPLE FRINGED ORCHIS *Habenaria fimbriata*
See color plate, p. 224. Often regarded as a larger version of the preceding; intergrades frequent. Flower cluster *more than 2 in. thick.* Lip usually more deeply fringed. 1–4 ft. Woods, meadows. Se. Ontario, s. Newfoundland; south in Appalachians to N. Carolina.   June–Aug.

PURPLE FRINGELESS ORCHIS *Habenaria peramoena*
Similar to the preceding but flowers *fringeless* or nearly so. Rich rose-purple. 1–3 ft. Moist meadows, open swampy woods. Local, Illinois, Indiana, Ohio, w. New York, Pennsylvania, w. New Jersey south.   June–Aug.

LARGE TWAYBLADE *Liparis lilifolia*
Note the broad paired basal leaves and the dull mauve flowers with their broad lip, *threadlike side petals* and narrow greenish sepals. 4–10 in. Mossy woods, ravines. S. Minnesota through Great Lakes states to c. New England and south.   May–July

HEARTLEAF TWAYBLADE *Listera cordata*
Note the pair of *heart-shaped* leaves midway on stem. Flowers small, dull purple; note long forked lip suggesting snake's tongue. 3–10 in. Mossy woods, bogs. Canada, colder parts of n. U.S.; south in mts. to N. Carolina.   June–Aug.

SMALL ROUND-LEAVED ORCHIS *Orchis rotundifolia*
Note the *solitary, oval* or roundish leaf near base. Pale rose; lip white, spotted with magenta. There is a small spur. 8–10 in. Mossy swamps and woods. N. Canada south very locally to n. Minnesota, n. Wisconsin, n. Michigan, n. New York, n. New England.   June–July

PUTTYROOT *Aplectrum hyemale*
See p. 118. Yellowish, greenish, or whitish. Lip marked with purplish.

SPOTTED CORALROOT *Corallorhiza maculata*
Coralroots lack green pigment and bear their flowers on a leafless stalk. This, the largest, has dull purple flowers; the lobed lip is white spotted with red. 8–20 in. Woods. Canada south to n. U.S.; in mts. to N. Carolina.   July–Aug.
See insets: Striped Coralroot, *C. striata*, mainly Canadian, has *purple-striped* petals; Wister's Coralroot, *C. wisteriana*, is early, has magenta spots on lip; Northern Coralroot, *C. trifida*, is usually white, unspotted, blooms early (May–June).

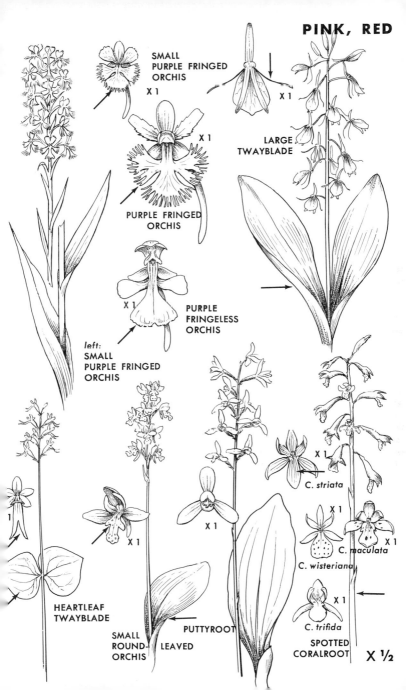

PINK, RED

SMALL PURPLE FRINGED ORCHIS
X 1

PURPLE FRINGED ORCHIS
X 1

LARGE TWAYBLADE
X 1

PURPLE FRINGELESS ORCHIS
X 1

left:
SMALL PURPLE FRINGED ORCHIS

HEARTLEAF TWAYBLADE

SMALL ROUND-LEAVED ORCHIS
X 1

PUTTYROOT
X 1

C. striata
X 1

C. maculata
X 1

C. wisteriana

C. trifida
X 1

SPOTTED CORALROOT

X ½

CLOVERLIKE HEADS; LINEAR LEAVES:
MILKWORTS OR POLYGALAS
Milkwort Family (Polygalaceae)
Note whether leaves are in whorls or attached singly
(Fringed Polygala has broad leaves).

CROSS-LEAVED MILKWORT *Polygala cruciata*
The narrow leaves, in *whorls of 4*, form *crosses*. Flower heads
dense, oblong, purplish (or greenish white). 4–12 in. Sandy
soil, bogs, pinelands, marsh edges. Coast from Maine south;
inland from Minnesota, n. Ohio south. July–Oct.

FIELD MILKWORT *Polygala sanguinea*
Leaves attached singly (alternately). Flower head oblong, rose-
purple (or greenish or whitish). 6–15 in. Fields, meadows.
Minnesota, s. Ontario, Nova Scotia south. June–Oct.

FRINGED POLYGALA, GAYWINGS *Polygala paucifolia*
Also called Flowering Wintergreen, because of *broad evergreen
leaves*. A low, dainty flower with *2 flaring pink-purple wings*
(lateral sepals). Petals united into tube, lower one tipped with
bushy fringe. 3–6 in. See also color plate, p. 214. Woods.
Manitoba to the Gaspé, and south to Minnesota, n. Illinois,
New England; in uplands to Georgia. May–June

RACEMED MILKWORT *Polygala polygama*
Leaves attached singly (often very leafy); flowers in a *loose
slender raceme*, pink or rose. 4–12 in. Sandy woods, open sandy
soil. Minnesota, Wisconsin, Michigan, s. Ontario, sw. Quebec,
New England south. June–July

WHORLED MILKWORT *Polygala verticillata*
Leaves in whorls of 3 to 6. Flowers tiny, in *tapering* clusters,
usually whitish but sometimes pinkish. 6–12 in. Sterile soil,
fields. Michigan, s. Ontario, Maine south. June–Oct.

SHORT-LEAVED MILKWORT *Polygala brevifolia*
Suggests a weak, miniature variety of Cross-leaved Milkwort,
but leaves *shorter* (in whorls of 3–5). 2–12 in. Sandy swamps.
New Jersey south on coastal plain. July–Sept.

CURTISS' MILKWORT *Polygala curtissii*
Similar to Field Milkwort (leaves attached singly) but more
loosely flowered; flower head pointed at first, blunt later. 6–10
in. Dry soil, pinelands. Ohio, W. Virginia, Maryland, Delaware south. June–Oct.

PINK MILKWORT (not shown) *Polygala incarnata*
A very slender, smooth, glaucous species with narrow alternate
leaves that are *few and distant*, sometimes absent. Pink or rose.
1–2 ft. Dry soil, open ground. Iowa, s. Wisconsin, s. Michigan,
Ontario, Pennsylvania, Long Island south. June–Nov.

CROSS-LEAVED MILKWORT

FIELD MILKWORT

FRINGED POLYGALA

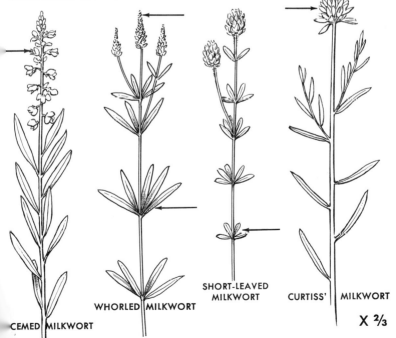

CEMED MILKWORT

WHORLED MILKWORT

SHORT-LEAVED MILKWORT

CURTISS' MILKWORT

X ⅔

PEALIKE FLOWERS; LEAFLETS IN 3'S: CLOVERS, BUSH-CLOVERS

Pea Family (Leguminosae)

RED CLOVER Alien   *Trifolium pratense*
This is the familiar, round-headed, purple-red clover of field and wayside. Leaflets often show pale chevrons. 6–16 in. Roadsides, fields. Throughout.   May–Sept.

ZIGZAG CLOVER Alien (not shown)   *Trifolium medium*
Similar to Red Clover but flowers longer-stalked, deeper-colored. Leaflets more slender, unmarked. Stem often zigzag. Local in e. Canada, New England.   June–Aug.

CRIMSON or ITALIAN CLOVER   *Trifolium incarnatum*
Alien
Note the *deep blood-red* shade of the *longish flower head;* also the *very blunt* leaflets. 6–30 in. Cultivated.   May–July

ALSIKE CLOVER Alien   *Trifolium hybridum*
Creamy white to pink. See also White Clover, *T. repens*, p. 80. Leaves *branch from stems;* not marked with pale triangles. 1–2 ft. Fields, roadsides. Throughout.   May–Oct.

RABBIT'S-FOOT CLOVER Alien   *Trifolium arvense*
The soft silky foliage and the *fuzzy, grayish-pink heads* of bloom are unmistakable. Leaflets relatively narrow. 4–16 in. Waste fields, roadsides. Throughout.   May–Oct.

TRAILING BUSH-CLOVER   *Lespedeza procumbens*
A *trailing or reclining* species with more or less erect flowering branches rising from leaf axils. *Downy or woolly.* Flowers purplish. Dry woods, clearings. S. Wisconsin, Indiana, Ohio, New York, Massachusetts south.   Aug.–Oct.

CREEPING BUSH-CLOVER (not shown)   *Lespedeza repens*
Similar to *L. procumbens* but more slender, *smooth* or nearly so. Range similar.   June–Sept.

BUSH-CLOVER   *Lespedeza violacea*
A tall, upright or spreading species; much branched. Leaflets small, oval; leaves with longish stalks. Flowers purple, few, on slender stalks. 1–3 ft. Dry woods, clearings. S. Wisconsin, s. Michigan, Ohio, New York, s. New Hampshire south.
                                                          July–Sept.

SLENDER BUSH-CLOVER   *Lespedeza virginica*
Erect, with crowded, *narrow leaflets.* Flowers purple, in short clusters in upper leaf axils. 1–3 ft. Dry woods, openings. Wisconsin, Michigan, s. Ontario, s. Maine south.   July–Sept.

WANDLIKE BUSH-CLOVER   *Lespedeza intermedia*
An erect, smoothish, wandlike species. Similar to the last but leaflets oval. 1–3 ft. Woods, openings. Wisconsin, Michigan, s. Ontario, New York, c. New England south.   July–Sept.

STUEVE'S BUSH-CLOVER (not shown)   *Lespedeza stuevei*
Similar to preceding but *densely downy.* 2–4 ft. Dry woods. Illinois, Ohio, New York, Massachusetts south.   Aug.–Sept.

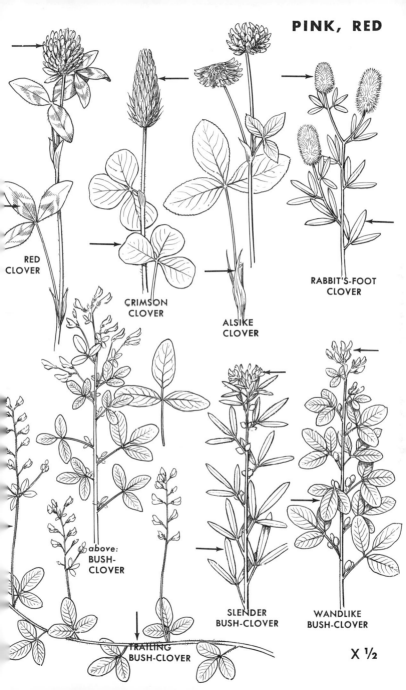

PINK, RED

RED
CLOVER

CRIMSON
CLOVER

ALSIKE
CLOVER

RABBIT'S-FOOT
CLOVER

above:
BUSH-
CLOVER

TRAILING
BUSH-CLOVER

SLENDER
BUSH-CLOVER

WANDLIKE
BUSH-CLOVER

X ½

PEALIKE FLOWERS; LEAFLETS IN 3'S: TICK-TREFOILS

PEA FAMILY (Leguminosae)

Slender plants with small pink, lavender, purplish, or white flowers in loose racemes. Note the jointed pods, which adhere to clothing (tick-trefoils are often called sticktights).

SHOWY TICK-TREFOIL (not shown) *Desmodium canadense* See text and color plate, p. 224. The most showy species. *Flower spikes more crowded* than those of species shown here.

POINTED-LEAVED TICK-TREFOIL *Desmodium glutinosum* Leaves in a *cluster or whorl* at tip of short stem *from which slender flower stalk rises*. 1–4 ft. Woods. Minnesota, sw. Quebec, Maine south.   JULY–AUG.

NAKED-FLOWERED TICK-TREFOIL

Desmodium nudiflorum

Tall, slender flower stalk (18–36 in.) is *leafless*. Leaves crowded in whorl at top of shorter (6–8 in.) *separate stalk*. Woods. Minnesota to Quebec, s. Maine and south.   JULY–AUG.

LARGE-BRACTED TICK-TREFOIL *Desmodium cuspidatum* Similar to *D. glutinosum* but leaves scattered up and down stem. Triangular joints on pods. 2–4 ft. Woods. S. Wisconsin, Michigan to Vermont, New Hampshire and south. JULY–AUG.

HOARY TICK-TREFOIL *Desmodium canescens* *Much branched*. The racemes of pink flowers (which soon turn green) branch from the upper leaf axils. *Finely hairy* or pubescent, often sticky, especially on petioles and stems. 3–5 ft. Woods, sandy soil. Wisconsin, sw. Ontario to w. Massachusetts and south.   JULY–SEPT.

SESSILE TICK-TREFOIL *Desmodium sessilifolium* Nearly *stalkless, narrow* leaflets. Dry soil. Local, Illinois, Michigan, s. Ontario, se. Massachusetts south.   JULY–AUG.

STIFF TICK-TREFOIL *Desmodium strictum* Note the *extremely slender, stiff* leaflets. Petioles *short* but distinct. Pods with 1 to 3 joints. Pine barrens. Coastal plain, New Jersey south.   JULY–AUG.

PANICLED TICK-TREFOIL *Desmodium paniculatum* Another species with *relatively slender* leaflets of variable width; *leafstalks fairly long*. Note the *horizontal branchlets* on the compound flower racemes. Pods 3 to 6 joints. Wood edges, clearings. Michigan, Ontario, s. Maine south.   JULY–AUG.

SMALL-LEAVED TICK-TREFOIL *Desmodium ciliare* Note the *small ovate leaflets* suggesting a bush-clover. Stems *downy*. Pods with only 1 to 2 joints. There is a *smooth* species, *D. marilandicum* (not shown). Sandy soil. Oklahoma, Indiana, Michigan, New York, Massachusetts south.   JULY–AUG.

PROSTRATE TICK-TREFOIL *Desmodium rotundifolium* *Prostrate*, trailing. Note *round leaflets*. Dry woods. Michigan, s. Ontario, New York, c. New England south.   JULY–SEPT.

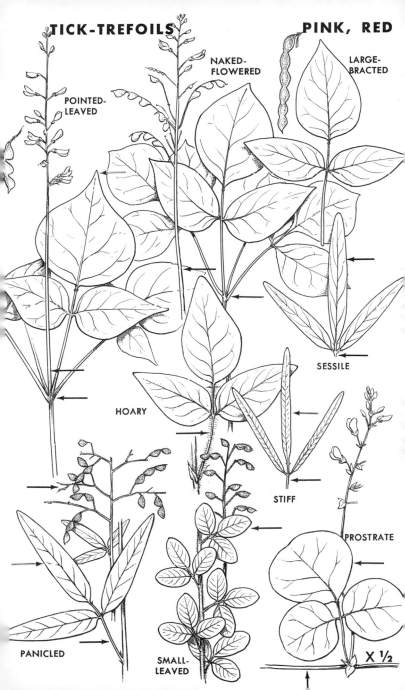

TICK-TREFOILS

PINK, RED

POINTED-
LEAVED

NAKED-
FLOWERED

LARGE-
BRACTED

SESSILE

HOARY

STIFF

PROSTRATE

PANICLED

SMALL-
LEAVED

X ½

PEALIKE FLOWERS; LEAFLETS IN 3'S: WILD BEANS, ETC.
PEA FAMILY (Leguminosae)

PINK WILD BEAN   *Strophostyles umbellata*
A slender twining plant. Leaflets in 3's, *relatively slender*. Flowers pink, showy, on stalks that *much exceed* leaves. Pods straight or nearly so, twisting when open. Open woods, fields, sandy soil. Missouri, Illinois, s. Indiana, Long Island south.
JULY–SEPT.

TRAILING WILD BEAN   *Strophostyles helvola*
Note the *bluntly 3-lobed* leaflets (some may be without lobes). Flower stalk much shorter than in *S. umbellata*. Pink flowers turn greenish with age. Pods straight. Shores, thickets. Minnesota, Wisconsin, Michigan, s. Ontario, Massachusetts south.
JUNE–OCT.

MILK PEA   *Galactia regularis*
Prostrate, rarely twining. Note the *long-oval* leaflets, rounded at both ends. Flowers reddish purple, usually on stalks shorter than leaves. Pods straight. Sandy soil. E. Pennsylvania, se. New York south.
JUNE–AUG.

HOG-PEANUT   *Amphicarpa bracteata*
A delicate twining vine with well-formed, pointed, light green leaflets. Flowers of 2 sorts: (1) short drooping clusters of pealike lilac flowers in the leaf axils; these produce curved pods with 3 or 4 mottled beans; and (2) flowers without petals at the base of the plant which produce fleshy 1-seeded pods. Moist woods. Manitoba to Quebec and south.   AUG.–SEPT.

WILD BEAN   *Phaseolus polystachios*
A climbing plant similar to the preceding species but coarser. Note the more *asymmetrical* shape and *deeply rounded base* of the side leaflets. Flowers on *much longer stalks* forming loose racemes; red-purple. Pods curved. Dry woods, sandy soil. Iowa, s. Illinois, Indiana, Ohio, W. Virginia, s. New Jersey south.   JULY–SEPT.

ALFALFA, LUCERNE Alien   *Medicago sativa*
Usually blue-violet but also may be purplish. See p. 352. A cultivated forage plant; has spread to waste land.   MAY–OCT.

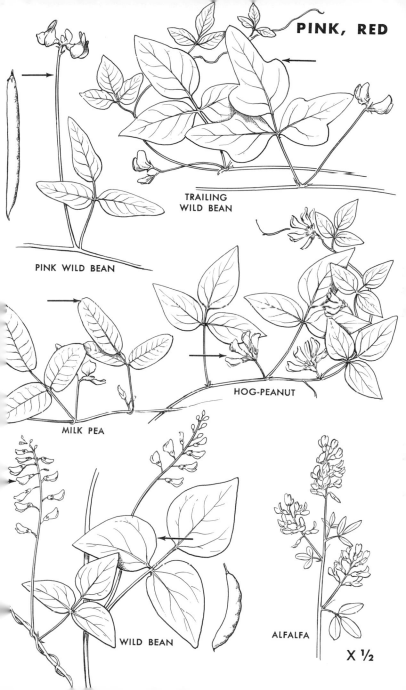

PINK, RED

TRAILING
WILD BEAN

PINK WILD BEAN

HOG-PEANUT

MILK PEA

WILD BEAN

ALFALFA

X ½

PEALIKE FLOWERS; LEAFLETS IN PAIRS

PEA FAMILY (Leguminosae)

EVERLASTING PEA Alien *Lathyrus latifolius*
Flowers very large, sweet-pea-like; pink, blue, or white. Leaflets in *single pairs*, accompanied by tendrils. Stems and petioles with *flattish wings*. A local escape. Indiana to New England and south to Missouri, Virginia. JUNE–SEPT.

GROUNDNUT *Apios americana*
A vine, climbing over bushes. Leaves divided into 5 to 7 broad, sharp-pointed leaflets. Flowers in short thick clusters in leaf axils; *maroon or chocolate;* very fragrant. Thickets. Minnesota through Great Lakes area to New Brunswick and south.
JULY–SEPT.

PRAIRIE-CLOVERS *Petalostemum*
Prairie-clovers have pinnate leaves and dense, longish pink or white flower heads on wiry stems. 7 species in our area, differing in number and width of leaflets. The one shown, *P. villosum*, is silky-downy. Prairies. Midcontinent. JULY–SEPT.

VETCHLING *Lathyrus palustris*
Slender, climbing. Typically with a *winged stem*, but some plants wingless. Leaflets long-oval, 2 to 4 pairs. Flowers red-purple. Shores, meadows, marshes. Canada to Missouri, Indiana, Ohio, New York; in mts. to N. Carolina. JUNE–SEPT.

BEACH PEA *Lathyrus japonicus*
Low, with showy purple flowers. *Large arrowhead-shaped stipules* embrace leafstalks. Oval leaflets paired or alternate. 1–2 ft. Sandy shores. Coast south to New Jersey; also shores of Great Lakes, Oneida Lake, Lake Champlain. JUNE–AUG.

GOAT'S-RUE *Tephrosia virginiana*
A hoary plant covered with silky hairs. Note the large *bicolored flowers (yellow standards, pink wings)*. Leaves with 8 to 14 pairs of leaflets and 1 leaflet at tip. 1–2 ft. Sandy woods, openings. Manitoba, Minnesota, Wisconsin, s. Michigan, s. Ontario, New York, c. New England south. MAY–AUG.

PURPLE VETCH *Vicia americana*
Note the loose raceme of 3 to 9 purple or violet flowers in the leaf axils. A smooth plant, climbing by tendrils. 2–3 ft. See other vetches, p. 352. Shores, meadows. Canada south to Illinois, Indiana, Virginia. MAY–JULY

SPRING VETCH, TARE Alien *Vicia sativa*
Note the *notched leaflets*. Flowers pink or purple, short-stalked, borne *singly or in pairs* in leaf axils. 1–3 ft. Cultivated; spread locally to roadsides. MAY–AUG.

CROWN-VETCH, AXSEED Alien *Coronilla varia*
Note the rather cloverlike cluster (really an umbel) of *bicolored (pink and white) flowers*. Stems creeping. Leaves divided into many small paired leaflets. Roadsides. Local, S. Dakota to New England and south. JUNE–AUG.

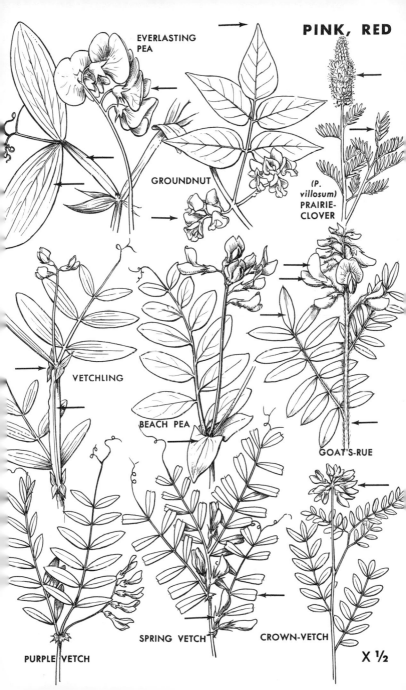

PINK, RED

EVERLASTING PEA

GROUNDNUT

(P. villosum) PRAIRIE-CLOVER

VETCHLING

BEACH PEA

GOAT'S-RUE

PURPLE VETCH

SPRING VETCH

CROWN-VETCH

X ½

LILY-LIKE AND BELL-LIKE FLOWERS

WOOD LILY   *Lilium philadelphicum*
LILY FAMILY   (Liliaceae)
Orange to scarlet. See text and color plate, p. 206.
JUNE–JULY

CANADA or WILD YELLOW LILY   *Lilium canadense*
LILY FAMILY   (Liliaceae)
Yellow to deep red. See text and color plate, pp. 102, 206.
JUNE–AUG.

PRAIRIE TROUT-LILY   *Erythronium propullans*
LILY FAMILY   (Liliaceae)
The pair of tapering basal leaves suggest the familiar yellow Trout-lily (p. 102), but the single drooping flower is much smaller, pink. 3–6 in. Rich woods. Minnesota.   MAY

ATAMASCO-LILY   *Zephyranthes atamasco*
DAFFODIL FAMILY   (Amaryllidaceae)
The large, waxy, erect, lily-like flower is white or pinkish. Leaves linear, channeled. 6–15 in. Wet woods, clearings. Se. U.S. north to Virginia.   APRIL–JUNE

ROSE TWISTED-STALK   *Streptopus roseus*
LILY FAMILY   (Liliaceae)
Note the zigzag stem and nodding 6-pointed bells in the axils of each alternate, sessile leaf. 2–3 ft. Cold woods. Canada, northern edge of U.S.; south in mts. to Georgia. APRIL–JULY

SMALL RED MORNING-GLORY Alien *Ipomoea coccinea*
MORNING-GLORY FAMILY   (Convolvulaceae)
Note the small scarlet flowers (⅔ in. across). Leaves heart-shaped or lobed. Stems twining. Waste places. Illinois, Michigan, Ohio, New York, Massachusetts.   AUG.–OCT.

COMMON MORNING-GLORY Alien *Ipomoea purpurea*
MORNING-GLORY FAMILY   (Convolvulaceae)
A twining vine; the familiar garden morning-glory with broad heart-shaped leaves. Purple, pink, blue, or white. Stems pubescent. Roadsides, cultivated ground. Widespread.
JULY–OCT.

IVY-LEAVED MORNING-GLORY Alien *Ipomoea hederacea*
MORNING-GLORY FAMILY   (Convolvulaceae)
White, pink, or blue. See p. 12.   JULY–OCT.

HEDGE BINDWEED   *Convolvulus sepium*
MORNING-GLORY FAMILY   (Convolvulaceae)
White or pink. See p. 12.   MAY–SEPT.

FIELD BINDWEED Alien   *Convolvulus arvensis*
MORNING-GLORY FAMILY   (Convolvulaceae)
White or pink. See p. 12.   JUNE–SEPT.

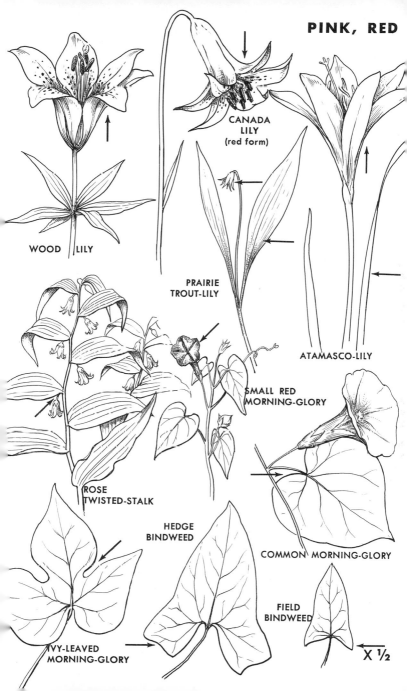

PINK, RED

WOOD LILY

CANADA LILY
(red form)

PRAIRIE
TROUT-LILY

ATAMASCO-LILY

ROSE
TWISTED-STALK

SMALL RED
MORNING-GLORY

HEDGE
BINDWEED

COMMON MORNING-GLORY

IVY-LEAVED
MORNING-GLORY

FIELD
BINDWEED

X ½

5 SHOWY PETALS: ROSES
ROSE FAMILY (Rosaceae)
Shrubs or vines; 20+ in our area.

SWAMP ROSE   *Rosa palustris*
Note the *very narrow stipules* (winged formations) at bases of leafstalks. Plant bushy. Spines *hooked*. Flowers pale pink; calyx bristly. 1–7 ft. Swamps, wet ground. Minnesota to Nova Scotia and south.   JUNE–AUG.

PASTURE or CAROLINA ROSE   *Rosa carolina*
Similar to the preceding but low and slender. Note the *slender straight prickles* below the stipules. See also color plate, p. 218. 1–3 ft. Dry soil, rocky pastures, open woods. Minnesota, Wisconsin, Michigan, s. Ontario, New York, New England south.   JUNE–JULY

NORTHEASTERN ROSE   *Rosa nitida*
Note the canes, *densely prickled* with dark purple bristles. The relatively small, crowded leaflets are also characteristic. A low, slender shrub. 1–3 ft. Swamps, bogs. Newfoundland to Connecticut.   JUNE–SEPT.

PRAIRIE ROSE   *Rosa setigera*
Climbing or trailing; canes may be up to 12 ft. long. Note that the *leaflets are in 3's*. Thorns hooked. Open woods, thickets. E. U.S. north to Missouri, Illinois, Indiana, Ohio, New York; introduced north to Michigan, s. New York.   JUNE–JULY

SMOOTH ROSE   *Rosa blanda*
A *thornless* or near-thornless rose. Leaflets blunt, pale beneath. Stems smooth, with a slight bloom. Flowers pale pink. 2–5 ft. Rocky slopes, shores. Manitoba to Quebec and south to Missouri, Illinois, Indiana, n. Ohio, Pennsylvania.   JUNE–AUG

WRINKLED ROSE Alien   *Rosa rugosa*
Note the *heavily wrinkled leaves, bristly stems*, very large deep rose or white flowers. A coarse, dense species. 2–6 ft. Sand dunes, seashores, roadsides. Minnesota through Great Lakes region to Quebec, New Brunswick, and south along coast to New Jersey.   JUNE–SEPT.

SWEETBRIER Alien   *Rosa eglanteria*
Long, arching stems bear numerous pink flowers, smaller than those of most other roses. Leaves fragrant. Leaflets roundish, double-toothed. 4–6 ft. Roadsides, clearings. Throughout.
                                      MAY–JULY

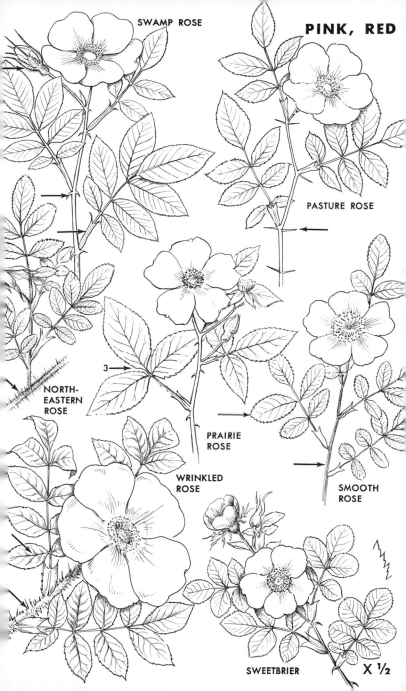

SWAMP ROSE

PINK, RED

PASTURE ROSE

NORTH-
EASTERN
ROSE

3

PRAIRIE
ROSE

WRINKLED
ROSE

SMOOTH
ROSE

SWEETBRIER

X ½

5 SHOWY PETALS: MALLOWS
MALLOW FAMILY (Malvaceae)
Note bushy column of stamens, typical of mallows.

SWAMP ROSE-MALLOW   *Hibiscus palustris*
Pink. See text and color plate, p. 218.   AUG.–SEPT.

SWAMP ROSE-MALLOW   *Hibiscus moscheutos*
Regarded by some authorities as a race of *H. palustris*. Median
leaves narrower, sometimes 3-pointed. Flowers (to 8 in. across)
tend to be white with *red or purple center* much like *H. palustris*
forma *peckii;* see color plate, p. 218. 5–7 ft. Marshes. Indiana, s. Ohio, Virginia, e. Maryland south.   JULY–SEPT.

HALBERD-LEAVED ROSE-MALLOW   *Hibiscus militaris*
Note the leaf shape. Flowers (6 in.) pale pink with purple
center. 3–5 ft. Riverbanks, swamps. Minnesota, Illinois,
Indiana, s. Ohio, s. Pennsylvania south.   JULY–SEPT.

SEASHORE MALLOW   *Kosteletzkya virginica*
Suggests a small rose-mallow (flowers 1–2 in.). Leaves 3- to 5-
pointed; somewhat maple-shaped. 1–3 ft. Brackish marshes.
Coast, from Long Island south.   JULY–SEPT.

MARSH MALLOW Alien   *Althaea officinalis*
Velvety, gray-green, soft to the touch. Leaves coarsely toothed
or shallowly lobed. Lower leaves heart-shaped or 3-lobed.
Flowers pink. 2–4 ft. Marsh edges. Coast from Connecticut
to Virginia; locally inland.   AUG.–OCT.

MUSK MALLOW Alien   *Malva moschata*
Pink or white. See text and color plate, p. 218.   JUNE–SEPT.

EUROPEAN MALLOW Alien (not shown)   *Malva alcea*
Similar to Musk Mallow but the 5-lobed leaves less deeply cut;
lobes *shallowly toothed*, not deeply cleft again. Under a hand-
glass note the short *star-shaped* hairs. Roadsides. Local,
Michigan, Ohio to Vermont, Pennsylvania.   JUNE–SEPT.

HIGH MALLOW Alien   *Malva sylvestris*
Note the *strong dark red veins* on the pink or lavender flowers.
Leaves broad, crinkly; bluntly 5-lobed, ivy-like. 1–3 ft. Road-
sides. Local but widespread in our area.   JUNE–AUG.

CHEESES, COMMON MALLOW Alien   *Malva neglecta*
A small creeping weed. *Small* (½ in.) pale rose-lavender or
white flowers in leaf axils; petals heart-shaped (notched).
Leaves roundish, with 5 to 7 shallow lobes. The name Cheeses
refers to the *flat, round fruits*. Waste places, gardens. Throughout.   APRIL–OCT.

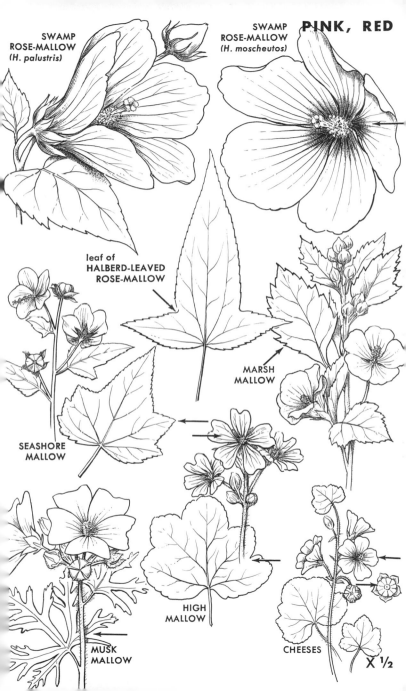

SWAMP
ROSE-MALLOW
(H. palustris)

SWAMP
ROSE-MALLOW
(H. moscheutos)

PINK, RED

leaf of
HALBERD-LEAVED
ROSE-MALLOW

MARSH
MALLOW

SEASHORE
MALLOW

HIGH
MALLOW

MUSK
MALLOW

CHEESES

X ½

5 PETALS; PALMATE OR FERNLIKE LEAVES
GERANIUM FAMILY (Geraniaceae)
Fruits end in a long beak, or "cranesbill."

WILD GERANIUM   *Geranium maculatum*
See text and color plate, p. 218.   APRIL–JUNE

MEADOW CRANESBILL Alien   *Geranium pratense*
Similar to Wild Geranium but leaves often 7-parted, with *more deeply incised* teeth. Flowers deeper in color, more *blue-purple;* stalks woolly. 1–2 ft. Grassy places. Maritime Provinces, Maine; rarely Massachusetts, New York.   JUNE–AUG.

BLOODY CRANESBILL Alien   *Geranium sanguineum*
Flower solitary on a *very long stalk; deep crimson,* 1 in. or more across. Leaves palmate, very deeply cut. 1–2 ft. An occasional garden escape.   JUNE–AUG.

HERB-ROBERT   *Geranium robertianum*
Hairy, strong-scented; stems often reddish. Leaves fernlike, divided into 3 to 5 pinnately lobed segments; end segment *well stalked.* Flowers ½ in., pink, usually paired, petals *not* notched. 8–18 in. Rocky woods, shores. Manitoba to Newfoundland and south to Illinois, Indiana, Ohio, Maryland.   MAY–OCT.

BICKNELL'S CRANESBILL   *Geranium bicknellii*
Similar to Herb-Robert (flowers in pairs), but leaves less intricately cut and lacking stalks on the 5 segments. Flowers magenta-pink, petals notched, about equal to sepals. 8–16 in. Open woods, clearings. S. Canada south to Iowa, Illinois, n. Indiana, Pennsylvania, New York, Connecticut.   MAY–SEPT.

CAROLINA CRANESBILL   *Geranium carolinianum*
In this species the short-stalked flowers are crowded in *compact clusters.* Leaves deeply 5- to 9-cleft. 8–16 in. Dry woods, sandy soil. Missouri, Illinois, s. Michigan, Ohio, New York, Massachusetts south.   MAY–JULY

DOVE'S-FOOT CRANESBILL Alien   *Geranium molle*
A low, downy species, often prostrate. Leaves relatively rounded, with short blunt lobes. Flowers about ¼ in., petals deeply notched. Seedpod stalks reflexed. 3–8 in. Waste places, lawns. S. Canada and south.   JUNE–AUG.

SMALL-FLOWERED CRANESBILL   *Geranium pusillum*
Alien
Another very small-flowered species. Flowers about ¼ in., petals more bluish lilac than those of *G. molle,* less deeply notched. Leaves more deeply cut; seedpod stalks not sharply reflexed. Reclining. 4–16 in. Waste ground, roadsides. S. Canada and south.   JUNE–OCT.

STORKSBILL, ALFILARIA Alien   *Erodium cicutarium*
The leaves, unlike the leaves of the cranesbills, are *twice-pinnate,* or fernlike, not palmate; often in prostrate rosettes. Flowers rose, less than ½ in. 3–12 in. Roadsides, sandy ground. Illinois, Michigan, Quebec south.   APRIL–OCT.

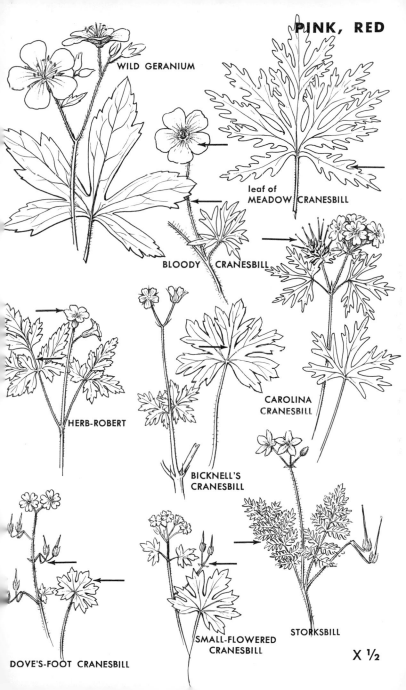

WILD GERANIUM

leaf of
MEADOW CRANESBILL

BLOODY CRANESBILL

HERB-ROBERT

CAROLINA
CRANESBILL

BICKNELL'S
CRANESBILL

DOVE'S-FOOT CRANESBILL

SMALL-FLOWERED
CRANESBILL

STORKSBILL

X ½

DEEP RED-PURPLE FLOWERS;
COMPOUND LEAVES

Rose Family (Rosaceae)

LONG-PLUMED PURPLE AVENS *Geum triflorum*
Note the *very long feathery hairs* (up to 2 in.) of the fruiting
head, which suggests a feather duster. Flowers usually in 3's,
ruddy purplish, rather globular, with *5 slender calyx lobes*.
Lower leaves divided into slender, paired, jagged, irregular
segments. 6–16 in. Rocky soil, prairies. Great Lakes are:
(local) to Nebraska, Iowa, and west.   April–June

WATER or PURPLE AVENS *Geum rivale*
In this species the end segment of the basal leaves is *broader*
than the others. Stem leaves 3-fingered. Flowers usually in 3's.
nodding, globular, brownish purple, sometimes yellow. Fruits
hooked. 1–2 ft. Bogs, wet places, meadows. Canada south to
Minnesota, n. Illinois, Ohio, W. Virginia, Pennsylvania, n. New
Jersey.   May–Aug.

MARSH CINQUEFOIL *Potentilla palustris*
The toothed 5- to 7-fingered leaves resemble those of other
cinquefoils, which are yellow (see p. 134), but the erect flowers
of this species are deep red-purple. Petals pointed, shorter and
narrower than the *wide purple sepals*. Flooded meadows,
swamps. Canada south to n. Iowa, n. Illinois, n. Indiana, Ohio,
Pennsylvania, n. New Jersey.   June–Aug.

EUROPEAN GREAT BURNET *Sanguisorba officinalis*
Alien
Note the ladder of *toothed, spade-shaped* leaves and the compact
oblong head of tiny *4-petaled* reddish-purple flowers. 10–24 in.
Local, Maine to Minnesota. Damp grassy places, low fields.
                                             June–Oct.

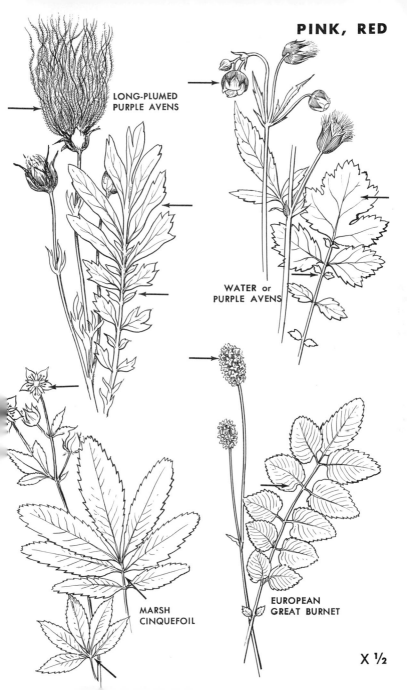

PINK, RED

LONG-PLUMED
PURPLE AVENS

WATER or
PURPLE AVENS

MARSH
CINQUEFOIL

EUROPEAN
GREAT BURNET

X ½

5 PETALS: MISCELLANEOUS SMALL FLOWERS

See also p. 310.

MARSH ST. JOHNSWORT   *Hypericum virginicum*
ST. JOHNSWORT FAMILY   (Guttiferae)
Unlike other St. Johnsworts, which are yellow, this one is *pink*.
3 groups of 3 stamens alternate with 3 large orange glands.
Stalks and sepals purplish. Oval leaves embrace stem in pairs.
12–18 in. Bogs, swamps. Mostly coastal, Nova Scotia south;
local inland to Great Lakes.   JULY–AUG.

SCARLET PIMPERNEL Alien   *Anagallis arvensis*
PRIMROSE FAMILY   (Primulaceae)
The small (¼ in.) starlike flowers, borne singly on long nodding
stalks in the leaf axils, close in dull weather. Usually *scarlet*
but may also be white or blue. Leaves ovate, stalkless, in pairs
or whorls. 4–12 in. Sandy soil, roadsides. Widespread.
     JUNE–AUG.

CENTAURY Alien   *Centaurium*
GENTIAN FAMILY   (Gentianaceae)
Note the long calyx tubes. Leaves oval, in pairs. *C. pulchellum*
has pink flowers, mostly terminal on short stalks. *C. umbellatum*
differs in having nearly stalkless rose-purple flowers that form
flat-topped clusters. 2–12 in. Waste ground. Local in s.
Canada, e. U.S.   JULY–SEPT.

SAND SPURREY Alien in part   *Spergularia rubra*
PINK FAMILY   (Caryophyllaceae)
Pink. See p. 310.   JUNE–OCT.

FAMEFLOWER   *Talinum teretifolium*
PURSLANE FAMILY   (Portulacaceae)
Note the short basal stem with its cluster of fleshy, stringlike
leaves. Leafless flowering stem bears small (½ in.) pink flowers
with 5 petals, 2 sepals, numerous stamens. 4–12 in. Rocks,
sand. W. Virginia, se. Pennsylvania south.   JUNE–SEPT.

BIRD'S-EYE PRIMROSE   *Primula mistassinica*
PRIMROSE FAMILY   (Primulaceae)
Leaves in a basal rosette, oval, slightly toothed. Flowers in an
umbel at the tip of the leafless stem; pink, lilac, or white, with
a yellow eye; petals notched. 6–10 in. Rocks, shores. N.
Canada south to Iowa, Wisconsin, n. Illinois, Michigan, New
York, New England.   MAY–AUG.

SEA-LAVENDER   *Limonium nashii*
SEA-LAVENDER FAMILY   (Plumbaginaceae)
The branching sprays often tinge salt marshes with lavender in
late summer. Sprays often flat-topped; tiny flowers line single
side of branchlets. Leaves basal, broadly lance-shaped. 1–2 ft.
Salt marshes. Gulf of St. Lawrence south. **Note:** A very
similar species, *L. carolinianum* (not shown; New York south),
differs in having a smooth calyx.   JULY–OCT.

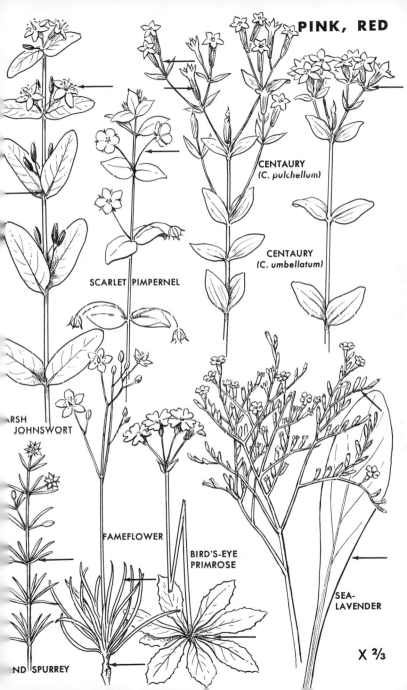

PINK, RED

CENTAURY
(C. pulchellum)

CENTAURY
(C. umbellatum)

SCARLET PIMPERNEL

MARSH ST. JOHNSWORT

FAMEFLOWER

BIRD'S-EYE PRIMROSE

SEA-LAVENDER

SAND SPURREY

X ⅔

5 PETALS, TUBED CALYX; PAIRED LEAVES

PINK FAMILY (Caryophyllaceae)
See also text and color plate, p. 222.

RED CAMPION Alien   *Lychnis dioica*
Similar to Scarlet Lychnis (p. 222) but flowers less crowded, basal leaves with long stalks. 1–2 ft. Roadsides, waste places. Ontario, Newfoundland south to n. U.S.   JUNE–SEPT.

ROUNDLEAF CATCHFLY   *Silene rotundifolia*
Similar to Fire Pink (p. 222) but petals more deeply cleft, leaves much wider. 8–28 in. Rocky slopes, cliffs. S. Ohio, W. Virginia south.   JUNE–JULY

ROYAL CATCHFLY   *Silene regia*
Similar to Fire Pink (p. 222) but the slender red petals are untoothed or only slightly toothed. Calyx sticky. Leaves rounded at base. 2–4 ft. Dry woods, prairies. Missouri, s. Illinois, Indiana, Ohio south.   JUNE–AUG.

SWEET-WILLIAM CATCHFLY Alien   *Silene armeria*
Smooth; leaves with whitish bloom. Note umbel-like clusters of small pink flowers. 10–12 in. A roadside escape. JUNE–OCT.

MULLEIN PINK Alien   *Lychnis coronaria*
Note the *dense whitish wool* covering the stems and leaves. Flowers deep rose or white. Sepals do not exceed petals as in Corn-cockle (p. 222). 1–3 ft. Roadsides, waste places, dry open woods. S. Ontario, n. U.S.   JUNE–AUG.

BOUNCING BET Alien   *Saponaria officinalis*
The clusters of ragged-looking, scallop-tipped flowers form great colonies along roadsides. Pink or whitish; petals reflexed, sometimes double; leaves smooth. Stems smooth, thick-jointed. 1–2 ft. Roadsides, railroad banks, waste places. Throughout.
     JULY–SEPT.

MOSS CAMPION   *Silene acaulis*
Tiny, forming mossy tussocks on open mountaintops. Petals notched; pink or violet. Leaves much more crowded, calyx more inflated, flower stalk much shorter than in Moss Phlox (p. 222); note also northern range. 1–3 in. Alpine areas of Canada south to White Mts., New Hampshire.   JUNE–AUG.

NIGHT-FLOWERING CATCHFLY Alien   *Silene noctiflora*
Petals deeply cleft, whitish, often pink. See p. 34. Calyx handsomely veined. Very sticky; fragrant. Note 3 styles, typical of *Silene*. Campions (*Lychnis*) have 5 styles. 1–3 ft. Waste places. Throughout.   JUNE–SEPT.

SLEEPY CATCHFLY   *Silene antirrhina*
A tiny-flowered pink or white species with an inflated bladder below the petals (which may be very small or absent). Note the black sticky zones often present on the stems. 8–30 in. Fields, open woods, waste places. Throughout.   MAY–SEPT.

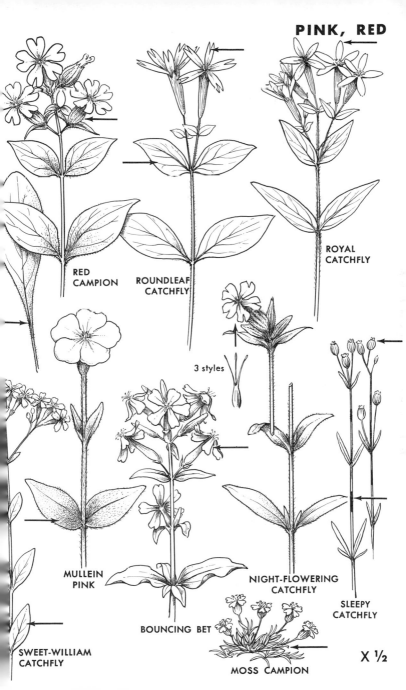

PINK, RED

RED CAMPION

ROUNDLEAF CATCHFLY

ROYAL CATCHFLY

3 styles

MULLEIN PINK

BOUNCING BET

NIGHT-FLOWERING CATCHFLY

SLEEPY CATCHFLY

SWEET-WILLIAM CATCHFLY

MOSS CAMPION

X ½

TUBED AND BELL-LIKE FLOWERS

SNAPDRAGON FAMILY (Scrophulariaceae)

HAIR BEARDTONGUE *Penstemon hirsutus*
Beardtongues get their name from a *tufted stamen* in the trumpet-shaped flower, which is 2-lipped (2 lobes above, 3 below). 17 species in our area; some pink, some white; often difficult to identify (see technical manuals). This species, tinged with magenta, has a *woolly* stem. 1–3 ft. A *smooth* species, Foxglove Beardtongue, *P. digitalis* (p. 58), is sometimes pink. Rocky woods, fields. Wisconsin, s. Ontario, s. Quebec, Maine south.
JUNE–JULY

LESSER SNAPDRAGON Alien *Antirrhinum orontium*
A small downy plant with untoothed linear leaves and small pink snapdragonlike flowers. 6–18 in. Waste places. Local; an occasional garden escape. JULY–SEPT.

WOOD-BETONY, LOUSEWORT *Pedicularis canadensis*
Red, yellow, or both. A hairy plant topped by a whorl of tubular, hooded flowers. Leaves, deeply cut, often reddish. 5–14 in. Woods, clearings. S. Canada, Maine south.
APRIL–JUNE

RED BARTSIA Alien *Odontites serotina*
A small, downy plant with toothed narrow leaves and leafy spikes of pink, 2-lipped flowers (lower lip 3-lobed, upper lip hoodlike, not folded back). 4–12 in. Roadsides. E. Canada, n. New York, n. New England. JUNE–AUG.

PURPLE GERARDIA *Gerardia purpurea*
See also color plate, p. 220. Gerardias have pink-purple bell-like flowers in leaf axils, paired linear leaves. 18 species in our area; recognition often technical. This, the largest, has downy flowers (about 1 in.), very short flower stalks (about ⅛ in.). Lowest leaves may be ⅙ in. wide. 1–3 ft. Damp acid soils. Minnesota, Wisconsin, s. Michigan, n. Ohio, Pennsylvania, New York, s. New England south. AUG.–SEPT.

SMALL-FLOWERED GERARDIA *Gerardia paupercula*
Similar to Purple Gerardia (very short flower stalks) but leaves narrower, flowers about ¾ in. 8–30 in. Damp open places, bogs. Iowa, s. Wisconsin, through Great Lakes area to Long Island, New England. AUG.–SEPT.

SEASIDE GERARDIA *Gerardia maritima*
A salt-marsh species with smooth flowers and rather *succulent* leaves. Leaf tips *blunt*, not pointed. Flowers ½–¾ in., stalks more than ¼ in. 2–12 in. Coastal marshes. Nova Scotia, Maine south. JULY–SEPT.

SLENDER GERARDIA *Gerardia tenuifolia*
This species lives in a dry habitat and has long flower stalks (½ in. or more), small flowers (½ in. or less). Teeth of calyx slight. 6–24 in. Dry woods, fields. S. Michigan to Maine and south. AUG.–OCT.

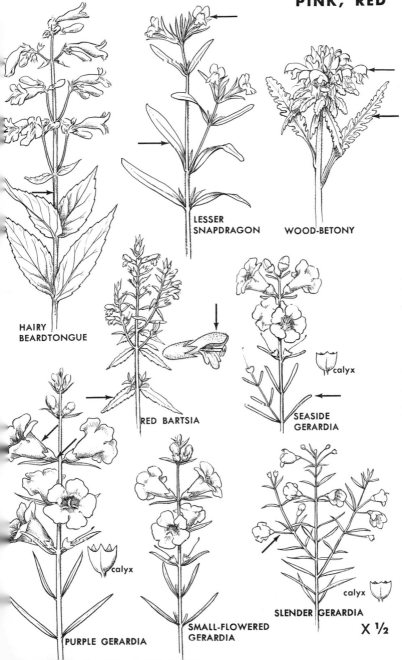

PINK, RED

LESSER
SNAPDRAGON

WOOD-BETONY

HAIRY
BEARDTONGUE

RED BARTSIA

SEASIDE
GERARDIA

calyx

PURPLE GERARDIA

calyx

SMALL-FLOWERED
GERARDIA

SLENDER GERARDIA

calyx

X ½

4 PETALS: WILLOW-HERBS

EVENING-PRIMROSE FAMILY (Onagraceae)
Note the long ascending seedpods. See also Meadow-beauties,
p. 220.

FIREWEED   *Epilobium angustifolium*
See text and color plate, p. 224.   JULY–SEPT.

HAIRY WILLOW-HERB Alien   *Epilobium hirsutum*
A bushy, large-flowered, magenta willow-herb, differing from
Fireweed in *hairy* aspect, more deeply notched petals, and
sharply toothed leaves. Leaves mostly paired, sessile. Pistil
with 4-branched stigma, as in Fireweed. 3–6 ft. Streamsides,
ditches, waste places. S. Ontario, s. Quebec south to n. Illinois,
Michigan, Ohio, New York, s. New England.   JULY–SEPT.

RIVER-BEAUTY   *Epilobium latifolium*
A showy far-northern relative of Fireweed; a short depressed
plant. Flowers magenta, relatively few, large (up to 2 in.), in
upper leaf axils; 4-branched pistil shorter than stamens. Leaves
broader than in Fireweed; fleshy, not as veiny. 4–16 in. Gravelly streambeds, shores. In our area only the Gaspé; northward
into Arctic.   JULY–AUG.

PURPLE-LEAVED WILLOW-HERB   *Epilobium coloratum*
Note the distinctly toothed leaves, which may be *marked with
purplish*. Stem often purplish. Flowers tiny (less than ¼ in.),
pink or white, often nodding. Seedpods often very numerous,
stiffly ascending. 1–3 ft. Wet ground. Most of our area.
                                                JULY–AUG.

NORTHERN WILLOW-HERB   *Epilobium glandulosum*
Leaves similar in shape to those of *E. coloratum* but broader,
less toothed, and more often sessile or nearly so. Flowers more
erect. The seeds have *whitish* hairs (cinnamon in *E. coloratum*).
1–3 ft. Wet places. N. Canada south to Wisconsin, Michigan,
Ohio, W. Virginia, Maryland.   JULY–SEPT.

NARROW-LEAVED WILLOW-HERB *Epilobium leptophyllum*
(not shown)
Much branched, with very narrow toothless leaves (⅛ in. wide);
tufts of smaller leaves in leaf axils. Plant hoary with down.
Flowers small, pink or white. 1–4 ft. Marshes, wet ground.
S. Canada south to Missouri, Illinois, Indiana, Ohio, n. Virginia.
                                                JULY–SEPT.

DOWNY WILLOW-HERB   *Epilobium strictum*
Densely white-downy; similar to *E. leptophyllum* but less
branched and with somewhat broader, ascending, sessile leaves.
4–24 in. Swamps, bogs. Minnesota to the Gaspé, and south to
n. Illinois, c. Indiana, n. Ohio, n. Virginia. JULY–SEPT.

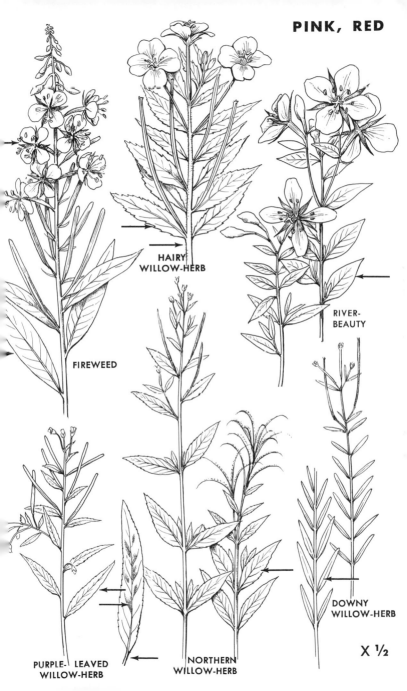

PINK, RED

HAIRY
WILLOW-HERB

RIVER-
BEAUTY

FIREWEED

DOWNY
WILLOW-HERB

PURPLE-LEAVED
WILLOW-HERB

NORTHERN
WILLOW-HERB

X ½

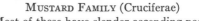

4 PETALS, TERMINAL CLUSTERS: MUSTARDS

MUSTARD FAMILY (Cruciferae)
Most of these have slender ascending pods.

CUT-LEAVED TOOTHWORT   *Dentaria laciniata*
Note the *whorl of 3 leaves*, each divided into *3 narrow, sharply
lacerated segments.* Flowers white or pale lavender. 8–15 in.
Rich moist woods, bottomlands. Minnesota, w. Quebec,
Vermont south.   APRIL–JUNE

TOOTHWORT, PEPPERWORT   *Dentaria diphylla*
Note the *pair of nearly opposite stem leaves*, each divided into
3 broad, toothed leaflets. Basal leaves similar, but long-stalked.
Flowers white; pink when fading. 8–14 in. Moist woods.
Minnesota, s. Ontario, the Gaspé south to Kentucky, S.
Carolina (mts.).   APRIL–JUNE

TOOTHWORT (not shown)   *Dentaria multifida*
The 2 opposite stem leaves are deeply cut into 3 to 7 threadlike
segments. Low woods. S. Indiana, s. Ohio south.   APRIL

LARGE TOOTHWORT   *Dentaria maxima*
Differs from the *D. diphylla* in having *3 leaves* branching off
the stem *at different levels.* Flowers white or pale purple. 6–16 in.
Woods, streambanks. Wisconsin, Michigan, to s. Maine and
south to Tennessee, W. Virginia.   APRIL–MAY

SLENDER TOOTHWORT   *Dentaria heterophylla*
The pair of *small* stem leaves are divided into 3 toothed or untoothed *lanceolate* segments quite unlike the broad, long-stalked
basal leaves. Flowers pink. 8–16 in. Rich woods. Michigan, s.
Ontario, the Gaspé south to Kentucky, S. Carolina.
       APRIL–JUNE

CUCKOO-FLOWER   *Cardamine pratensis*
Note the *many small paired leaflets* (roundish or oval on basal
leaves, slender on stem leaves). Flowers white or pink. 8–20 in.
Swamps, springs, wet woods. N. Canada to Minnesota, n.
Illinois, n. Ohio, W. Virginia, n. New Jersey.   APRIL–JUNE

RADISH Alien   *Raphanus sativus*
The broad jagged leaves, pale purple petals, and fat dark pods
distinguish the cultivated radish. Sometimes found as an escape
in dumps and waste places.

PURPLE CRESS   *Cardamine douglassii*
Basal leaves long-stalked, roundish; stem leaves stalkless,
slightly toothed. Stem hairy. Flowers pink or purple. 4–12 in.
Wet woods, springs. Wisconsin, s. Ontario, Connecticut to
Missouri, Tennessee, Virginia.   MARCH–MAY

SEA-ROCKET   *Cakile edentula*
A seaside mustard recognized by its succulent stems and small
purple flowers. Note also the distinctive pods (inset). 6–12 in.
Beaches, seacoast. Coast from s. Labrador south; also local
on shores of Great Lakes.   JULY–SEPT.

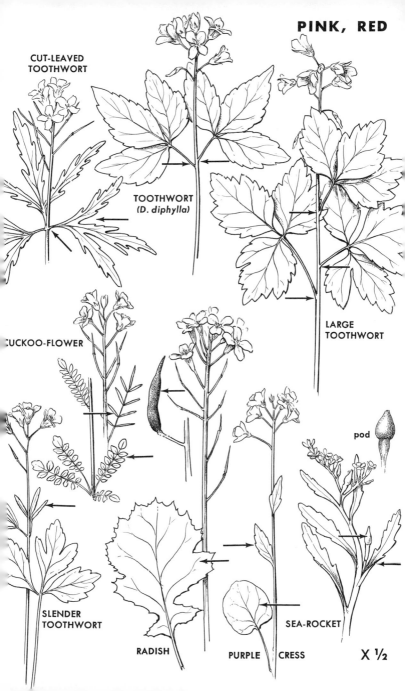

PINK, RED

CUT-LEAVED TOOTHWORT

TOOTHWORT
(D. diphylla)

LARGE TOOTHWORT

CUCKOO-FLOWER

pod

SLENDER TOOTHWORT

RADISH

PURPLE CRESS

SEA-ROCKET

X ½

TIGHT PINK CLUSTERS, TINY FLOWERS
BUCKWHEAT FAMILY (Polygonaceae)

Smartweeds are easy to recognize because on the stem at each leaf joint there is a swelling and a sheath. In our area there are 46 species in the genus *Polygonum;* most are pink or white, with tiny flowers either in tight spikelike terminal clusters or clustered in the leaf axils (knotweeds). Many are so plastic and variable as to be identified with certainty only by recourse to the technical manuals. Several of the more showy species are presented here. See also pp. 70 (white), 276 (pink), 380, 386 (green).

SWAMP SMARTWEED　　　　　　*Polygonum coccineum*
A very variable species with erect terrestrial forms, aquatic forms with floating leaves, and intermediate forms that reflect the water level. This species is most readily separated from the equally variable *P. amphibium* (below) by the longer flower clusters, usually *much longer than 1 in.* Swamps, shallow water, ditches, shores. Most of our area.　　　JULY–SEPT.

ALPINE SMARTWEED　　　　　　*Polygonum viviparum*
A small unbranched alpine species with narrow dark green leaves that have turned-down margins. Note the *very slender sheaths.* Basal leaves long-oval, long-stalked. Flowers pale pink or white, the lower ones often replaced by *tiny purple bulblets.* 4–8 in. Moist limy soil. Arctic south to n. Minnesota, n. Michigan, and mts. of Quebec and n. New England.
　　　　　　　　　　　　　　　　JULY–AUG.

WATER SMARTWEED　　　　　　*Polygonum amphibium*
Similar to *P. coccineum* (above) and as plastic, varying from aquatic forms with floating leaves to erect terrestrial forms like the one shown here, which is quite hairy. The quickest distinction is the flower cluster, which in the present species is stubby, usually *less than 1 in.* long. Swamps, shallow water, ditches. N. Canada south to Missouri, Illinois, Indiana, Ohio, Pennsylvania, New Jersey.　　　JUNE–SEPT.

PRINCE'S-FEATHER Alien　　　　*Polygonum orientale*
The most showy of all the smartweeds, readily known by its large *drooping* clusters of bright rose-colored flowers and its very large, long-stalked, *heart-shaped* leaves. 2–7 ft. A garden escape locally.　　　　　　　　　　JUNE–OCT.

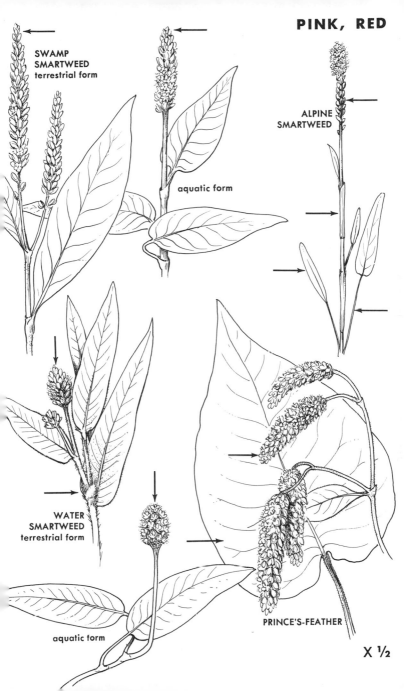

PINK, RED

SWAMP SMARTWEED
terrestrial form

aquatic form

ALPINE SMARTWEED

WATER SMARTWEED
terrestrial form

aquatic form

PRINCE'S-FEATHER

X ½

TIGHT PINK CLUSTERS, TINY FLOWERS
BUCKWHEAT FAMILY (Polygonaceae)

LADY'S-THUMB, REDLEG Alien   *Polygonum persicaria*
Smartweeds, *Polygonum*, are known by their tight, spikelike
clusters of tiny pink (or whitish) flowers and "knotted" stems
with a papery sheath at each joint. Lady's-thumb is erect or
sprawling, has narrow leaves, often with a *dark triangular*
blotch. Stems *reddish;* all sheaths *with fringes.* 6–24 in. Cultivated ground, waste places. Throughout.   JUNE–OCT.

PALE SMARTWEED   *Polygonum lapathifolium*
Similar to Lady's-thumb but stems usually *green;* most sheaths
without fringes. Flower clusters slender, with *bent tips;* pink,
or more often greenish white. 1–6 ft. Fields, waste ground, wet
places. Throughout.   JULY–NOV.

PENNSYLVANIA SMARTWEED   *Polygonum pensylvanicum*
Similar to Lady's-thumb but sheaths *without fringes.* Joints
reddish, leaves shiny. With hand lens note *tiny hairlike glands*
on upper branches and stems. Flowers rose-pink or white. 1–4
ft. Damp soil, roadsides, fields. S. Minnesota, s. Michigan, s.
Ontario, New England south.   JUNE–OCT.

LONG-BRISTLED SMARTWEED   *Polygonum cespitosum*
Alien
Similar to Lady's-thumb but sheaths at joints have *much longer bristles.* Flower spikes narrower, *about 1/4 in. wide* (in Lady's-
thumb 3/8 in.). Roadsides, wet spots. Illinois to Massachusetts
and south to Kentucky, Virginia.   JUNE–OCT.

MILD WATER-PEPPER   *Polygonum hydropiperoides*
In this species the slender pink (or white) flower spike is usually
sparse and more or less *interrupted.* Sheaths at joints have a
fringe of slender bristles. 1–3 ft. A similar species, *P. hydropiper*
(see p. 380), and usually with greenish-white nodding flowers,
lacks sheath bristles or has very short ones; its leaves have an
extremely acrid *peppery taste.* Shallow water, wet shores.
Minnesota, Michigan, se. Canada south.   JUNE–NOV.

ARROW-LEAVED TEARTHUMB   *Polygonum sagittatum*
Narrow arrow-shaped leaves have weak prickles on midrib below.
Stems prickly. Flower clusters small, pink or whitish. 2–6 ft.
Wet places, marshes. Throughout.   JUNE–OCT.

HALBERD-LEAVED TEARTHUMB   *Polygonum arifolium*
Similar to Arrow-leaved Tearthumb but even *more prickly.*
Most leaves wider, with *flaring basal lobes.* 2–6 ft. Tidal
marshes. Delaware, Maryland south.   JULY–OCT.

KNOTWEEDS   *Polygonum*
Knotweeds are small, short-leaved, erect or prostrate plants of
this genus. The tiny pink, white, or greenish flowers are tucked
singly or in 2's or 3's in the leaf axils. We cannot elaborate here
on the dozen kinds in our area. The one shown is *P. prolificum*
(coast from Maine south).

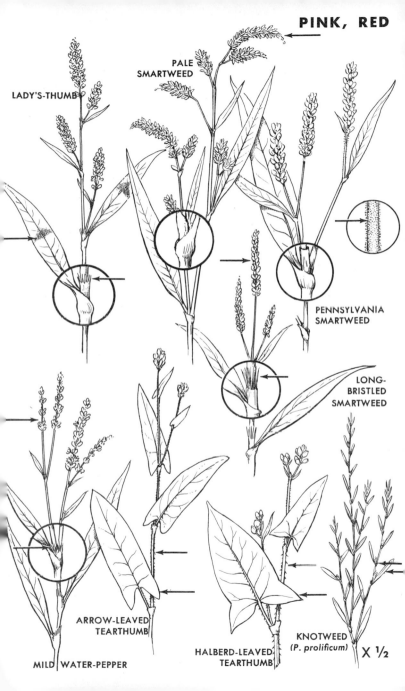

PINK, RED

LADY'S-THUMB

PALE
SMARTWEED

PENNSYLVANIA
SMARTWEED

LONG-
BRISTLED
SMARTWEED

MILD WATER-PEPPER

ARROW-LEAVED
TEARTHUMB

HALBERD-LEAVED
TEARTHUMB

KNOTWEED
(P. prolificum)

X ½

SPIKES OR TERMINAL CLUSTERS
SQUARE STEMS; LIPPED FLOWERS: MINTS
Mint Family (Labiatae)

ROUGH HEDGE-NETTLE   *Stachys tenuifolia* var. *hispida*
Flowers clustered in circles; rose-pink, *hooded;* 3-lobed lower lip
spotted with purple. Plant (including flowers) downy-hairy,
stem *bristly.* Leaves with or without short stalks. Variable.
There is also a smooth variety (see below). 1–5 ft. Wet roadsides, ditches, meadows. Canada, n. U.S.   July–Sept.

GERMANDER, WOOD-SAGE   *Teucrium canadense*
Note the flower construction (inset) with *stamens projecting
through cleft in upper lip.* Flowers pink. Leaves broad or narrow (var. *littorale*, opposite). 8–36 in. Woods, thickets, shores.
Minnesota, s. Quebec, w. New England.   July–Sept.

PURPLE GIANT HYSSOP   *Agastache scrophulariaefolia*
Flowers purplish, in a crowded spike mixed with purplish bracts.
Note the *4 protruding stamens* (inset). Most leaves coarsely
toothed, well stalked, white-hairy beneath. Stems purplish,
with whitish hairs. 2–5 ft. Wet woods, thickets. W. Ontario to
Vermont, Massachusetts, and south.   July–Sept.

CURLED MINT Alien   *Mentha crispa*
The very broad leaves have *ragged-toothed, crisped margins.*
Flowers pinkish. 1½–3 ft. Wet spots, ditches. Michigan to
Massachusetts and south to Pennsylvania, New Jersey.
                                                      June–Sept.

SMOOTH HEDGE-NETTLE   *Stachys tenuifolia*
Similar to Rough Hedge-nettle (above) but flowers mostly
smooth; leaves often smooth; stems bristly only on angles.
Leaves usually *well stalked.* Variable. 2–4 ft. Moist, shaded
soil, low woods, shores. Minnesota to New York and south.
                                                      June–Sept.

PEPPERMINT Alien   *Mentha piperita*
Note the familiar fragrance and *hot taste* of the chewed leaves.
Flowers in *interrupted clusters* forming a terminal spike. Plant
smooth, branching. Flowers pale violet or pink-purple. Stems
purplish. 1½–3 ft. Shores, wet meadows, roadsides. Throughout.   July–Sept.

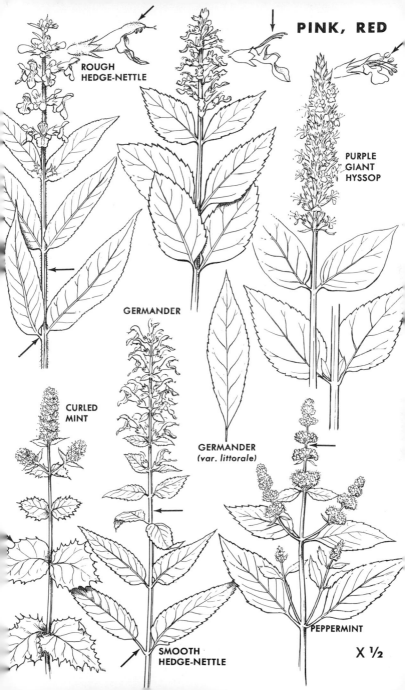

ROUGH
HEDGE-NETTLE

PINK, RED

PURPLE
GIANT
HYSSOP

GERMANDER

CURLED
MINT

GERMANDER
(var. littorale)

SMOOTH
HEDGE-NETTLE

PEPPERMINT

X ½

CLUSTERS IN LEAF AXILS;
SQUARE STEMS; LIPPED FLOWERS: MINTS
MINT FAMILY (Labiatae)

HEMP-NETTLE Alien   *Galeopsis tetrahit*
Note the *swollen area* below the joints on the bristly stem.
Flower envelope with 5 long bristles. Flowers hairy; white or
pale magenta; lower lip striped with purple. Note *humps at
base of lower lip*. 1–2 ft. Roadsides, waste places. S. Canada,
n. U.S.   JUNE–SEPT.

WOUNDWORT Alien in part   *Stachys palustris*
A downy plant with hairs on stem. Flowers magenta, in
whorled spike. Note particularly the downy calyx, which may
be green or maroon. Leaves lanceolate, toothed, stalkless or
short-stalked. 2–3 ft. Ditches, wet ground, low meadows,
shores. Canada, n. U.S.   JULY–SEPT.

BASIL Alien in part   *Satureja vulgaris*
A hairy plant with slightly toothed, pointed-oval leaves. The
cluster of pink-purple flowers looks *woolly* (white hairs on calyx
and bracts). 9–18 in. Roadsides, woods, shores. Canada, n.
U.S.; in uplands to N. Carolina.   JUNE–SEPT.

HYSSOP HEDGE-NETTLE   *Stachys hyssopifolia*
Note the smooth, *narrow, toothless* or near-toothless leaves.
Flowers pink, mottled with purple and white. 4–30 in. Bogs,
shores, damp prairies. Se. Massachusetts and Connecticut
south along coast; locally inland from Illinois, Indiana, s.
Michigan, Pennsylvania south.   JUNE–SEPT.

PURPLE or RED DEAD-NETTLE   *Lamium purpureum*
Alien
Note the way the crowded, heart-shaped leaves tend to *overlap*.
Stem often leafless below the leafy flower spike. Upper leaves
often purplish. Flowers red or purplish. 4–12 in. Roadsides,
waste places. Local but widespread.   APRIL–OCT.

DITTANY   *Cunila origanoides*
A much-branched plant with wiry stems and stalkless leaves.
The small purplish flowers are in tufts, their 5 lobes almost equal.
Note the *2 long protruding stamens* and pistil. 8–16 in. Wood
openings, clearings. Missouri, Illinois, Indiana, Ohio, e.
Pennsylvania, se. New York south.   JULY–OCT.

MOTHERWORT Alien   *Leonurus cardiaca*
The leaves, often held horizontally, are wedge-shaped at the
base and have *3 long points* and several lesser teeth. Flowers
in rosettes in axils, pink-lilac; upper lip furry. 2–4 ft. Roadsides, waste ground. Most of our area.   JUNE–AUG.

HENBIT Alien   *Lamium amplexicaule*
Leaves scalloped and rounded; lower ones long-stalked, upper
ones *half clasping* stem. Flowers purplish, erect. 2–12 in.
Roadsides, waste ground. Most of area.   MARCH–NOV.

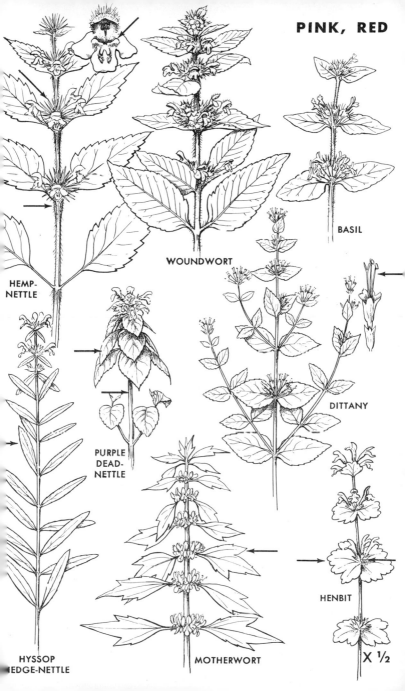

PINK, RED

HEMP-
NETTLE

WOUNDWORT

BASIL

PURPLE
DEAD-
NETTLE

DITTANY

HENBIT

HYSSOP
HEDGE-NETTLE

MOTHERWORT

X ½

CROWDED SPIKES; LINEAR LEAVES:
BLAZING-STARS (Liatris)
COMPOSITE OR DAISY FAMILY (Compositae)
Tufted rose-purple flower heads supported by scaly bracts.
18 species in our area; they often hybridize.

DENSE BLAZING-STAR   *Liatris spicata*
See also color plate, p. 224. Usually hairless, with numerous
sessile flower heads. Relatively few (5–9) florets per head.
Flower bracts few, long, blunt, sticky, purple or with purple
margins. 1–5 ft. Meadows, marsh edges. Wisconsin, Michigan,
sw. Ontario, Pennsylvania, n. New Jersey south. Locally established in Northeast.   JULY–SEPT.

PRAIRIE BLAZING-STAR   *Liatris pycnostachya*
Similar to *L. spicata* but usually *hairy*. Flower heads crowded
and sessile, but note that the *long-pointed* bracts are *reflexed*.
Florets 5 to 10 per head. 1–4 ft. Damp prairies. Minnesota,
Wisconsin, and south.   JULY–OCT.

DOTTED BLAZING-STAR   *Liatris punctata*
Most *Liatris* have resinous dots on leaves (punctate), especially this species. Similar to above two but floral bracts
pointed, flat, with hairy margins. 1–3 ft. Dry prairies. Manitoba, Minnesota, w. Iowa, and west.   JULY–SEPT.

CYLINDRIC BLAZING-STAR   *Liatris cylindracea*
Flower heads *few or solitary* (20–50 florets per head); usually
stiffly stalked (but may be sessile). Bracts in a tight cylinder;
shining, sharp-pointed, flat. 8–24 in. Dry, limy soil. Minnesota to s. Ontario and south to Missouri, Illinois, Indiana,
Ohio, w. New York.   JULY–SEPT.

NEW ENGLAND BLAZING-STAR   *Liatris borealis*
The northeastern range is a good clue. Flower heads large,
loose, well stalked. Floral bracts rounded or slightly pointed,
flat or slightly spreading. Florets 35 to 60 per head. 1–3 ft.
Open woods, clearings. E. New York to sw. Maine and south
to c. Pennsylvania and New Jersey.   AUG.–SEPT.

ROUGH BLAZING-STAR   *Liatris aspera*
Note the outflaring, *broadly rounded* floral bracts with their
crisped, curled margins. Flower head *sessile or short-stalked*.
Florets 25 to 40 per head. 6–30 in. Sandy soil. Dry open places.
N. Dakota to Ohio and south.   AUG.–SEPT.

SCALY BLAZING-STAR   *Liatris squarrosa*
Note the *pointed, spreading flower-bracts*. Flower heads large,
well stalked. Florets 20 to 40 per head. 8–30 in. Fields. S.
Illinois, Indiana, Ohio, Delaware south.   JULY–SEPT.

BLAZING-STAR   *Liatris ligulistylis*
Similar to *L. aspera* but flower heads on much longer stalks.
Florets 30 to 100 per head. 6–24 in. Prairies. S. Manitoba, n
Wisconsin, Minnesota south.   JUNE–AUG.

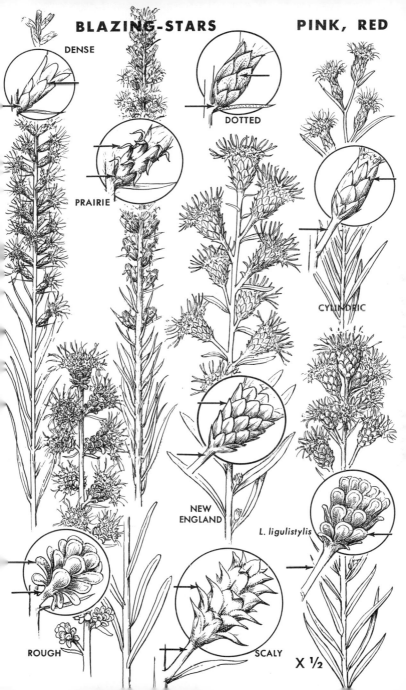

BLAZING-STARS

PINK, RED

DENSE

DOTTED

PRAIRIE

CYLINDRIC

NEW
ENGLAND

L. ligulistylis

ROUGH

SCALY

X ½

DENSE SPIKES AND CLUSTERS

STEEPLEBUSH, HARDHACK   *Spiraea tomentosa*
ROSE FAMILY   (Rosaceae)
See also color plate, p. 224. A low woody shrub. Note the
woolly, pale brownish underside of the leaves and the fuzzy,
rose or purplish steeple-shaped cluster of tiny 5-petaled flowers.
Blooms from top downward (and withers first at top). 2–4 ft.
Meadows, pastures, old fields. Minnesota, Quebec, Nova
Scotia south.   JULY–SEPT.

QUEEN-OF-THE-PRAIRIE   *Filipendula rubra*
ROSE FAMILY   (Rosaceae)
Flowers deep pink, somewhat resembling those of Steeplebush
but clusters more spreading or divergent. Note the distinctive
leaves, which are *deeply divided* and interruptedly compound.
2–8 ft. Moist prairies, meadows. Iowa, Michigan, east to w.
Pennsylvania and south.   JUNE–AUG.

MEADOWSWEET   *Spiraea latifolia*
ROSE FAMILY   (Rosaceae)
Similar to Steeplebush but pale pink or white. Flower cluster
wider, looser. Reddish or brownish stems not woolly, and the
coarsely toothed leaves lack woolly undersurface of Steeplebush. 2–5 ft. The similar NARROWLEAF MEADOWSWEET, *S.
alba* (not shown), is typically white, has hairy yellowish stems
and narrower, more finely toothed leaves. 1–4 ft. Old fields,
meadows, roadsides, low ground. Michigan to Newfoundland,
south to New England, Long Island; in mts. to Ne. Carolina.
                                           JUNE–SEPT.

SALT-MARSH FLEABANE   *Pluchea purpurascens*
COMPOSITE FAMILY   (Compositae)
A sticky, camphor-smelling plant that touches the late-summer
salt marshes with pink-purple. Leaves alternate, ovate, slightly
toothed. The rayless pink flower heads are mostly in flattish
terminal clusters. 8–36 in. Mainly salt marshes. Coast from
s. Maine south; rarely inland.   AUG.–SEPT.

SWAMP-PINK   *Helonias bullata*
LILY FAMILY   (Liliaceae)
Note the basal tuft or rosette of lanceolate, or spatulate, evergreen leaves from which rises a tall hollow stem bearing a tight
egg-shaped cluster of bright pink flowers with blue anthers.
1–3 ft. Swamps, bogs. Coastal plain from Staten Island, New
York, and New Jersey to e. Virginia; also mts. from Pennsylvania south.   APRIL–MAY

BUTTERBUR Alien   *Petasites hybridus*
COMPOSITE FAMILY   (Compositae)
Note the *huge* roundish leaves (often 2 ft. across) and the stout
hollow stems (6–12 in.) bearing clublike spikes of rayless heads
of tiny lilac-pink flowers with white anthers. Waste places.
Local, Massachusetts to Pennsylvania.   APRIL–MAY

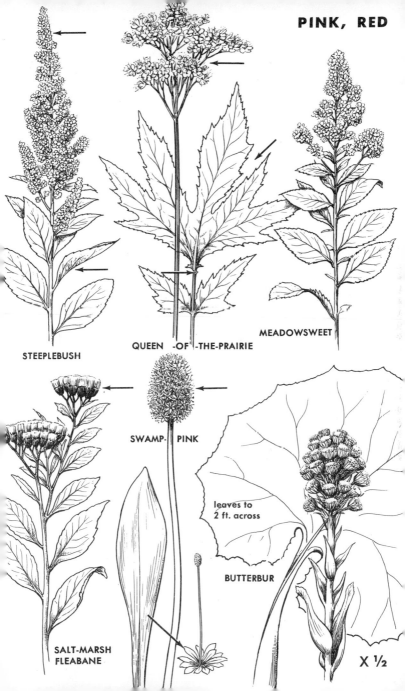

PINK, RED

STEEPLEBUSH

QUEEN -OF-THE-PRAIRIE

MEADOWSWEET

SWAMP-PINK

leaves to
2 ft. across

BUTTERBUR

SALT-MARSH
FLEABANE

X ½

SLENDER SPIKES OF SMALL FLOWERS

HOARY VERVAIN   *Verbena stricta*
VERVAIN FAMILY   (Verbenaceae)
Similar to the familiar Blue Vervain, *V. hastata* (see color plate, p. 316), but flowers larger and on the *purplish* rather than blue-violet side; sometimes *rosy pink*. Note the thick, coarsely toothed *ovate*, almost stalkless leaves that, like the stems, are *hoary* with whitish hairs. 1–4 ft. Prairies, roadsides. S. Ontario, west to Montana and south. Naturalized locally in Northeast.   JUNE–SEPT.

NARROW-LEAVED VERVAIN   *Verbena simplex*
VERVAIN FAMILY   (Verbenaceae)
This vervain with its spikes of lavender or purple flowers may be known from the others by its narrow *lanceolate* leaves, which taper to a stalkless base. 1–2 ft. Fields, dry soil. Minnesota. Ontario, sw. Quebec, Massachusetts south.   MAY–SEPT.

EUROPEAN VERVAIN Alien   *Verbena officinalis*
VERVAIN FAMILY   (Verbenaceae)
This alien species with its flimsy spikes of lilac flowers is distinguished by its paired, *deeply lobed* lower leaves. 1–2 ft. Roadsides, waste places. Local, from Massachusetts and New York south.   JUNE–OCT.

LOPSEED   *Phryma leptostachya*
LOPSEED FAMILY   (Phrymaceae)
The Lopseed enjoys individual family status; there is no other species in the Family Phrymaceae. This plant, with broad, coarsely toothed, opposite leaves, is topped by a slender spike of small lavender or pinkish-purple snapdragonlike flowers with lobed lips. These flowers are in pairs, and when going to seed *lop down* against the stem. 1–3 ft. Woods, thickets. Manitoba east to New Brunswick and south throughout our area.
       JULY–SEPT.

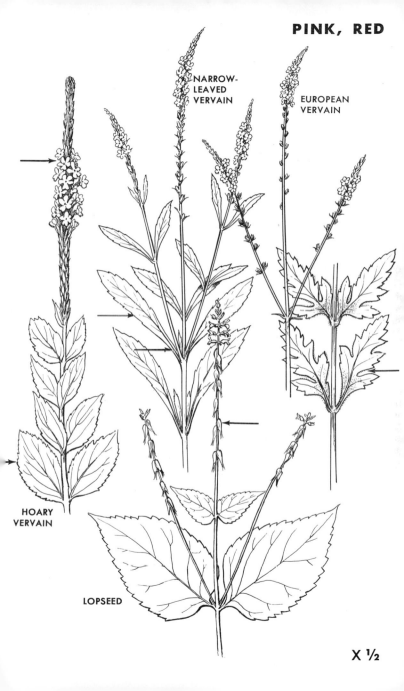

PINK, RED

NARROW-
LEAVED
VERVAIN

EUROPEAN
VERVAIN

HOARY
VERVAIN

LOPSEED

X ½

FLOWERS IN SPIKES OR IN LEAF AXILS; 5 to 6 PETALS: PURPLE LOOSESTRIFES, ETC.

LOOSESTRIFE FAMILY (Lythraceae)
See yellow loosestrifes on p. 140.

PURPLE or SPIKED LOOSESTRIFE   *Lythrum salicaria*
Alien
See also color plate, p. 224. The tapering spikes of slender-petaled flowers (4–6 petals, usually 6) often tinge swampy meadows with magenta. Leaves sessile, *wide at base, downy,* opposite or in 3's. 2–4 ft. Swamps, wet meadows. Minnesota, Quebec, Newfoundland to Missouri, Ohio, Virginia.
JUNE–SEPT.

PURPLE LOOSESTRIFE Alien   *Lythrum virgatum*
Similar to *L. salicaria* but *smooth.* Leaves more slender and *narrowed* to base. Established locally in New England.

WING-ANGLED LOOSESTRIFE   *Lythrum alatum*
Note the branching *4-angled stem* (may be slightly winged). Lower leaves paired, upper single; lanceolate to ovate. Flowers 6-petaled, pink or purple, borne singly in leaf axils. 1–4 ft. Swamps, wet prairies. S. Canada and south (mainly west of mts.). Local in Northeast.   JUNE–SEPT.

HYSSOP-LEAVED LOOSESTRIFE   *Lythrum hyssopifolia*
In this small species the leaves are narrow and *alternate.* Sometimes branched near base. Flowers tiny, 6-petaled, tucked singly in leaf axils. 6–24 in. Salt marshes. Coastal, s. Maine to New Jersey; also local in Ohio, se. Pennsylvania.
JUNE–SEPT.

NARROW-LEAVED LOOSESTRIFE   *Lythrum lineare*
Similar to *L. hyssopifolia* but leaves narrower, *opposite;* flowers paler. 1–3 ft. Salt marshes. Coastal, Long Island south.
JUNE–SEPT.

CLAMMY CUPHEA   *Cuphea petiolata*
Clammy, with sticky hairs. Note the curious saclike base of the flower and the uneven, stalked, magenta-pink petals, 2 large ones at top, 4 small at bottom. Leaves paired, ovate, well stalked. 1–2 ft. Dry soil, sandy fields. Iowa, Illinois, Indiana, Ohio, New York, s. New England south. JUNE–SEPT.

SWAMP LOOSESTRIFE, WATER-WILLOW
Decodon verticillatus
Stems long, reclining or bent, 4- to 6-sided. Flowers lavender, in tufts in upper leaf axils; bell-shaped, with 5 petals, cuplike calyx. Leaves lance-shaped, paired or in 3's. 2–8 ft. Swamps, shallow water. Minnesota, Wisconsin, s. Ontario, n. New York, New England south.   JULY–AUG.

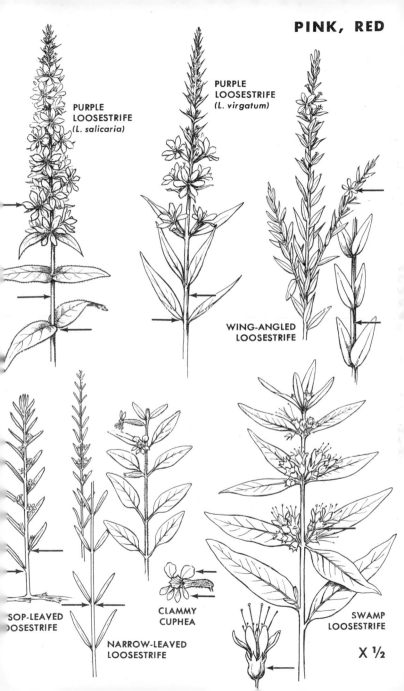

PURPLE LOOSESTRIFE
(*L. salicaria*)

PURPLE LOOSESTRIFE
(*L. virgatum*)

WING-ANGLED LOOSESTRIFE

HYSSOP-LEAVED LOOSESTRIFE

NARROW-LEAVED LOOSESTRIFE

CLAMMY CUPHEA

SWAMP LOOSESTRIFE

X ½

NODDING SPRAYS OR SPIKES OF FLOWERS WITH SHORT, ROUNDED SPURS

POPPY FAMILY (Papaveraceae)
BLEEDING-HEART SUBFAMILY (Fumarioideae)

WILD BLEEDING-HEART   *Dicentra eximia*
Similar to the garden Bleeding-heart from Asia. The 2 deeply
rounded spurs form a heart from which a "drop of blood" drips
between 2 flaring wings. Deep pink to red-purple. Leaves intricately cut. 10–16 in. Rocky woods, ledges. Appalachian
region from w. and se. New York south.   MAY–AUG.

ALLEGHENY-VINE, CLIMBING FUMITORY
                                        Adlumia fungosa
A vine that climbs over bushes by aid of its coiling leafstalks.
The flowers, drooping in clusters of 3 to 5 from the leaf axils,
have only the barest suggestion of spurs. Whitish or pale pink-
purple. Leaflets in 3's. Stems to 10 or 12 ft. long. Wooded
mountainsides, rocky slopes. Minnesota, Ontario, e. Quebec,
New England; south in mts. to N. Carolina.   JUNE–OCT.

PALE CORYDALIS   *Corydalis sempervirens*
Note the single bulbous spur on the pale pink flowers and the
yellow lips. Leaves with a whitish bloom. 6–36 in. See also
yellow species of *Corydalis*, p. 126. Rocky ground, clearings.
Canada, n. U.S.; south in mts. to Georgia.   MAY–SEPT.

FUMITORY, EARTH-SMOKE Alien   *Fumaria officinalis*
This delicate, climbing, gray-green plant has a smoky look in
the distance, hence its name. The finely cut leaflets are 3- to 5-
pronged. Note the shape of the single-spurred flower (inset).
Flowers in spikes; pinkish purple, tipped with maroon. 6–36 in.
Waste places, cultivated ground. Local in our area. MAY–AUG.

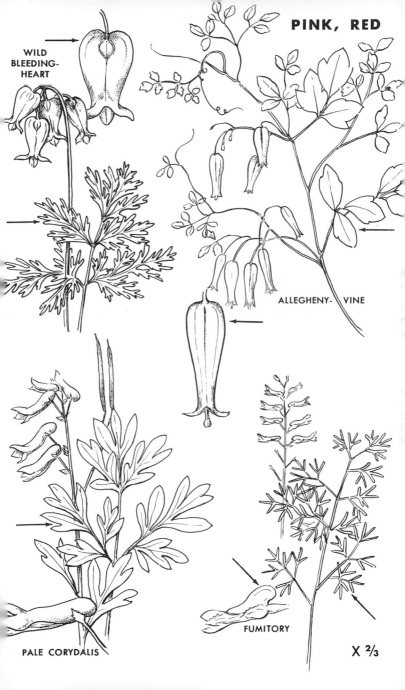

PINK, RED

WILD BLEEDING-HEART

ALLEGHENY- VINE

PALE CORYDALIS

FUMITORY

X ⅔

CLUSTERS OF NODDING BELLS, ETC.

 SPREADING DOGBANE   *Apocynum androsaemifolium*
DOGBANE FAMILY   (Apocynaceae)
Shrublike, with ruddy stems and paired, ovate, leaves. Fragrant pale pink bells dangling from curved stalks are *striped inside with deep rose.* Seedpods in pairs, narrow, 3 to 8 in. long. Note *milky juice* when stem is broken. 1–4 ft. Thickets, roadsides. Most of our area.   JUNE–JULY

INTERMEDIATE DOGBANE   *Apocynum medium*
DOGBANE FAMILY   (Apocynaceae)
Intermediate between Spreading Dogbane and Indian Hemp (p. 70). Flowers lack strongly recurved lobes of Spreading Dogbane and are less pink, often white. Leaves may be more elliptical. 1–4 ft. Fields, roadsides, shores. S. Canada to Missouri, Virginia.   JUNE–AUG.

FOUR-O'CLOCK   *Mirabilis nyctaginea*
FOUR-O'CLOCK FAMILY   (Nyctaginaceae)
Flowers pink or purple, seated in *broad, veiny, 5-lobed green cups* of joined bracts. Leaves paired, stalked, heart-shaped. 1–6 ft. Prairies, waste places. Montana, Colorado east to Wisconsin, Michigan; south to Louisiana. Local in East.   JUNE–OCT.

LION'S-FOOT   *Prenanthes serpentaria*
COMPOSITE FAMILY   (Compositae)
White or pink. Leaves usually lobed. See p. 74.

SMOOTH WHITE LETTUCE   *Prenanthes racemosa*
COMPOSITE FAMILY   (Compositae)
Similar to other rattlesnake-roots (see p. 74) but flower clusters in a narrow spike; usually *pink.* Leaves spatulate; lower ones stalked, upper ones *clasping.* Plant smooth, with a pale bloom. Pappus yellowish. 2–6 ft. Wet ground, prairies. Canada to Missouri, Illinois, Ohio, se. New York, n. New Jersey.
    AUG.–SEPT.

 HOUND'S-TONGUE Alien   *Cynoglossum officinale*
FORGET-ME-NOT FAMILY   (Boraginaceae)
Downy, with a mousy odor. *Maroon* flowers are embraced by velvety calyx scales. Fruits flattened, covered with hooked spines; adhere to clothing. 1–3 ft. Roadsides, waste places, pastures. Most of our area.   MAY–JULY

COMFREY Alien   *Symphytum officinale*
FORGET-ME-NOT FAMILY   (Boraginaceae)
A coarse, branching, hairy plant. Note the way the large, veiny leaves *flow into the winged stem.* Flowers in curled clusters may be white, cream, pink, purplish, or blue. 2–3 ft. Roadsides, waste places. Most of our area.   JUNE–SEPT.

ROSE TWISTED-STALK   *Streptopus roseus*
LILY FAMILY   (Liliaceae)
See p. 254.

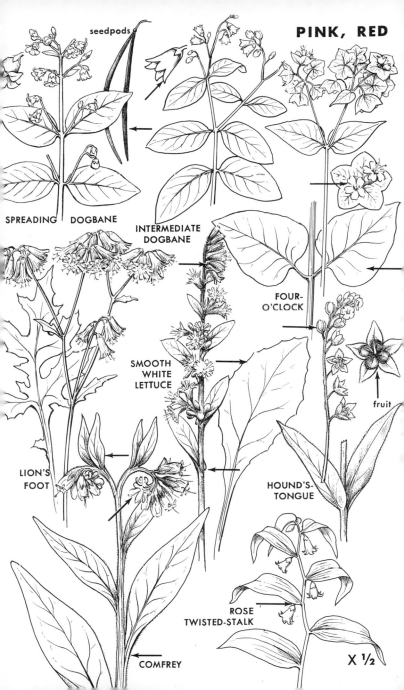

PINK, RED

seedpods

SPREADING DOGBANE

INTERMEDIATE DOGBANE

FOUR-O'CLOCK

SMOOTH WHITE LETTUCE

fruit

LION'S FOOT

HOUND'S-TONGUE

COMFREY

ROSE TWISTED-STALK

X ½

DOMED, UMBRELLALIKE CLUSTERS:
MILKWEEDS

MILKWEED FAMILY (Asclepiadaceae)

Note the unique flower structure (inset) long pointed seedpods, and thick milky juice of broken stems or leaves. See also other milkweeds, pp. 54, 72 (white), 208 (orange).

COMMON MILKWEED   *Asclepias syriaca*
A stout, *downy* plant. The domed, often somewhat drooping flower clusters are mostly in the leaf axils and vary in subtle shades of dusty rose, lavender, and dull brownish purple. The pointed gray-green seedpods can be told from those of our other milkweeds by their *warty* aspect. 3–5 ft. Roadsides, dry soil, fields. S. Canada south.   JUNE–AUG.

SULLIVANT'S MILKWEED   *Asclepias sullivantii*
(not shown)
Similar to Common Milkweed but *smooth*. Leaves blunt, oblong, sessile or indented at base. Pods slender, smooth. 2–5 ft. Moist ground, prairies. Minnesota to s. Ontario and south to Missouri, Illinois, Indiana, Ohio.   JUNE–JULY

BLUNT-LEAVED MILKWEED   *Asclepias amplexicaulis*
The *wavy leaves* with their deeply clasping bases are diagnostic. Flowers greenish stained with magenta-purple. Seedpods longer, more slender than in Common Milkweed; plant smooth. 2–3 ft. Dry soil, open places. Minnesota, Wisconsin, Michigan, Ohio, New York, Massachusetts south.   MAY–JULY

PURPLE MILKWEED   *Asclepias purpurascens*
Similar to Common Milkweed, but flowers *deep magenta-red;* leaves more pointed. Pods downy, but not warty. 2–3 ft. Woods, thickets. Minnesota, s. Ontario, s. New Hampshire south.   JUNE–JULY

SWAMP MILKWEED   *Asclepias incarnata*
Note the relatively *narrow lance-shaped leaves*. Smooth. The dull pink flowers are in relatively small umbels. 2–4 ft. Swamps, wet ground. Most of our area.   JUNE–AUG.

FOUR-LEAVED MILKWEED   *Asclepias quadrifolia*
The well-stalked leaves on midstem are in *whorls of 4;* upper leaves often paired. Flowers pink, lavender, or white. 1–2½ ft. Woods. Minnesota, s. Ontario, New Hampshire south.
MAY–JULY

RED MILKWEED (not shown)   *Asclepias rubra*
A purplish-red or orange-red coastal species. Flower clusters small, terminal. Leaves are round at base, taper to a long point. 2–4 ft. Swamps, bogs, pine barrens. Coastal plain from Long Island and New Jersey south.   JUNE–JULY

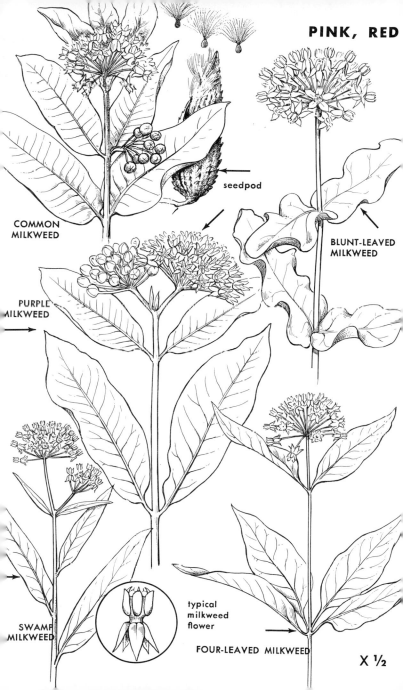

PINK, RED

COMMON MILKWEED

seedpod

BLUNT-LEAVED MILKWEED

PURPLE MILKWEED

SWAMP MILKWEED

typical milkweed flower

FOUR-LEAVED MILKWEED

X ½

DOMED CLUSTERS OR UMBELS

WILD ONION   *Allium stellatum*
LILY FAMILY   (Liliaceae)
Note the showy umbel of 6-point lavender flowers, grasslike
leaves, onion-reeking bulb. 1–2 ft. Rocky soil, prairies, shores.
Saskatchewan to Missouri; east to Ohio.   JULY–AUG.

FIELD GARLIC Alien   *Allium vineale*
LILY FAMILY   (Liliaceae)
Pink or white flowers mixed with bulblets; or, absent and re-
placed by bulblets with "tails." *Single* spathe below umbel.
Leaves *hollow*, ascend stem partway. 1–3 ft. Fields. Illinois,
Michigan, New York, Massachusetts south.   MAY–JULY

WILD GARLIC   *Allium canadense*
LILY FAMILY   (Liliaceae)
Similar to *A. vineale;* flowers usually fewer or absent. Spathe
at base of umbel *3-parted.* Leaves *not* hollow; flattened; mostly
near base. 8–24 in. Meadows, openings. Minnesota, Wisconsin, s. Ontario, s. Quebec south.   MAY–JULY

NODDING WILD ONION   *Allium cernuum*
LILY FAMILY   (Liliaceae)
Note the *crook* at the top of the stem, causing the pink or white
flower cluster to nod. 1–2 ft. Rocky soil, open woods, slopes.
Minnesota, Michigan, New York south.   JULY–AUG.

ORPINE, LIVE-FOREVER Alien   *Sedum telephium*
SEDUM FAMILY   (Crassulaceae)
Leaves fleshy, succulent, coarsely toothed; often with whitish
bloom. Stems often purplish. Flowers 5-pointed, pink-purple.
12–18 in. Roadsides, waste places. Local, Minnesota, e.
Canada to Indiana, Pennsylvania, New Jersey.   AUG.–SEPT.

ROSEROOT   *Sedum rosea*
SEDUM FAMILY   (Crassulaceae)
This *4-petaled* sedum may be yellowish (staminate) or purplish
(pistillate). Succulent leaves *overlap spirally.* Rocks. Arctic
south in mts. to Pennsylvania; on coast to Maine.
                                                     MAY–JUNE

VALERIAN Alien   *Valeriana officinalis*
VALERIAN FAMILY   (Valerianaceae)
Leaves deeply divided, *pinnate*, lower ones often toothed. Stem
stout, hairy below. Flowers tiny, in tight clusters, pale pink.
1–4 ft. A roadside escape. Minnesota to Quebec and south to
Ohio, Pennsylvania, New Jersey.   JUNE–JULY

PURPLE MEADOW-PARSNIP
                    Thaspium trifoliatum var. *atropurpureum*
PARSLEY FAMILY   (Umbelliferae)
Each spoke of the umbel ends in miniature umbel of tiny purple
florets. The typical form is yellow (see p. 162). Upper leaves
divided into *3 ovate, toothed leaflets*. Basal leaves long-stalked,
heart-shaped. 1–2½ ft. E. Pennsylvania and New Jersey
south, mainly in mts.; also mts. of s. Missouri. APRIL–JUNE

PINK, RED

WILD ONION

FIELD GARLIC

WILD GARLIC

NODDING WILD ONION

RPINE

ROSEROOT

VALERIAN

PURPLE MEADOW-PARSNIP

X ½

DOMED OR FLAT-TOPPED CLUSTERS

COMPOSITE OR DAISY FAMILY (Compositae)

SWEET JOE-PYE-WEED *Eupatorium purpureum*
Flowers dull, pale, pinkish purple, in a fuzzy, massive, some-what domed cluster. Stem usually *green*, often glaucous (with a slight whitish bloom); purplish or blackish at leaf joints. Leaves usually in whorls of 3 or 4; odor of vanilla when crushed. 2–6 ft. Thickets, woods. Minnesota to s. New Hampshire and south. JULY–SEPT.

SPOTTED JOE-PYE-WEED *Eupatorium maculatum*
Similar to *E. purpureum* but stem deep *purple* or purple-spotted, not glaucous. Flower clusters deeper in color, more flat-topped. Leaves in 4's and 5's. 2–7 ft. Wet thickets, meadows. Canada, northern states, and south in mts. JULY–SEPT.

HOLLOW JOE-PYE-WEED *Eupatorium fistulosum*
Similar to the first two species but leaves usually 6 (4–7), stem smooth, glaucous, tinged with purple but seldom spotted; *hollow or tubed* in cross section. Flower clusters domed. Wet thickets, meadows. 2–7 ft. Iowa, Illinois, Indiana, Ohio, New York, sw. Maine south. JULY–SEPT.

PURPLE BONESET *Eupatorium perfoliatum*
A color form (*purpureum*) of the familiar Boneset, which is usually white. See p. 46. Note stem piercing leaves.

JOE-PYE-WEED *Eupatorium dubium*
Similar to Spotted Joe-Pye-weed (purple-spotted stem) but leaves more ovate, *contracted abruptly* into petiole; *3 main veins* instead of 1. 2–5 ft. Swamps, shores. Mainly coastal plain, Nova Scotia, s. New Hampshire south. JULY–SEPT.

NEW YORK IRONWEED *Vernonia noveboracensis*
Ironweeds suggest Joe-Pye-weeds but have more open flower clusters, deeper in color (toward *violet*), and more slender, sessile, *alternate* leaves. Note the *hairlike tips* on the bracts of this species. 3–7 ft. Low thickets, streambanks. S. Ohio, se. New York, Massachusetts south. AUG.–OCT.

TALL IRONWEED (not shown) *Vernonia altissima*
A tall species; leaves *downy* on underside; bracts without long hairlike tips. 4–10 ft. Rich, wet soil. Missouri, Illinois, Indiana, s. Michigan, Ohio, New York south. AUG.–OCT.

WESTERN IRONWEED *Vernonia fasciculata*
Flower clusters smaller than in New York Ironweed, flatter, more tightly bunched. Bracts lack long hairlike tips. Leaves very numerous; *smooth* on both sides. 2–6 ft. Bottoms, prairies. Minnesota, Wisconsin to Ohio and south. JULY–SEPT.

SALT-MARSH FLEABANE *Pluchea purpurascens*
See p. 284.

YARROW Alien *Achillea millefolium*
Usually white but sometimes pink. See p. 44. JUNE–NOV.

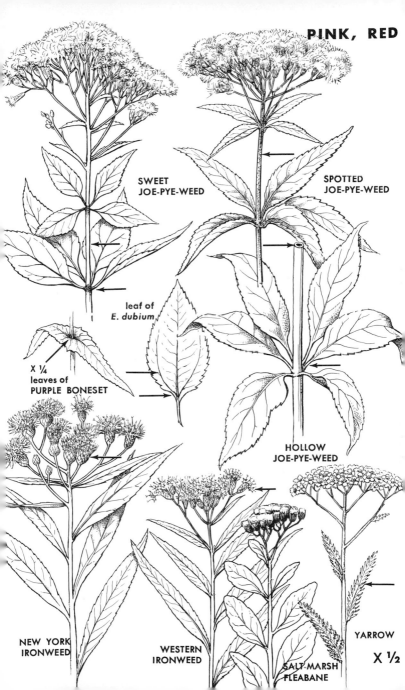

SWEET
JOE-PYE-WEED

SPOTTED
JOE-PYE-WEED

leaf of
E. dubium

X ¼
leaves of
PURPLE BONESET

HOLLOW
JOE-PYE-WEED

NEW YORK
IRONWEED

WESTERN
IRONWEED

SALT-MARSH
FLEABANE

YARROW

X ½

MOSTLY PRICKLY WEEDS:
TEASELS, BURDOCKS, ETC.

TEASEL Alien   *Dipsacus sylvestris*
TEASEL FAMILY   (Dipsacaceae)
Spines packed between the minute lavender florets create a pincushion effect (an egg-shaped pincushion). Stems also armed with prickles. Dried flower heads persist on dead stems throughout winter. Leaves paired, embrace stem. 2–6 ft. Roadsides, waste ground. Michigan, Ontario, and w. New England south. JULY–OCT.

TEASEL Alien   *Dipsacus laciniatus*
TEASEL FAMILY   (Dipsacaceae)
Similar to *D. sylvestris* but leaves *coarsely lobed*, their bases forming a *cup* around the stem and may hold rainwater. Waste ground. Local, Michigan to Massachusetts. JULY–AUG.

FIELD SCABIOUS Alien   *Knautia arvensis*
TEASEL FAMILY   (Dipsacaceae)
Related to Teasel but not prickly; instead of spines small hairs are interspersed among the 4-lobed florets of the rather flat pincushionlike heads. Florets lavender, asymmetrical, outer lobes longest, simulating rays. Leaves may be deeply lobed or not. 1–3 ft. Waste ground, roadsides. Local, se. Canada to New England, Pennsylvania. JUNE–AUG.

COMMON BURDOCK Alien   *Arctium minus*
COMPOSITE FAMILY   (Compositae)
The thistle-like burs, or flower heads, of this bushy plant are familiar. The hooked, bristly bracts form a roundish, *sessile or short-stalked bur* (½–¾ in. across) below the lavender florets. Lower leaves large, with hollow, unfurrowed stalks. 3–5 ft. Waste ground, roadsides. Most of our area. JULY–OCT.

GREAT BURDOCK Alien   *Arctium lappa*
COMPOSITE FAMILY   (Compositae)
Flower heads (burs) much larger than in *A. minus* (1–1½ in.) and on *long stalks*. Burs few, in flat-topped clusters. Lower leaves have *solid* stalks with a *groove* on upper surface. 4–9 ft. Roadsides, chiefly limy soil. E. Canada to Illinois, Michigan, Pennsylvania, New England. JULY–OCT.

WOOLLY BURDOCK Alien   *Arctium tomentosum*
COMPOSITE FAMILY   (Compositae)
Burs with long stalks. May be told from *A. lappa* by *webbing of fine hairs* on prickly bracts (inset). Leafstalks hollow. Waste ground. Local, e. Canada, ne. U.S. JULY–SEPT.

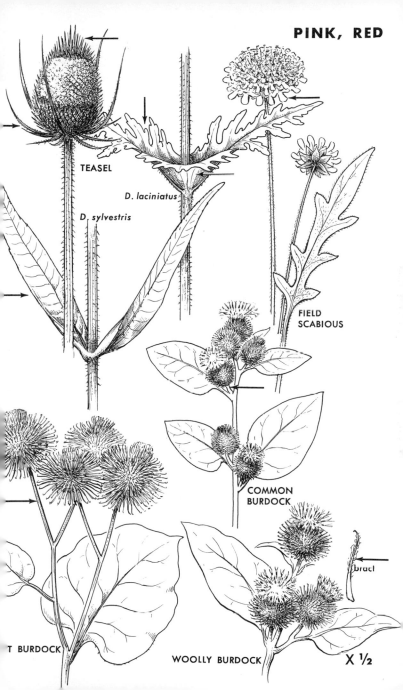

PINK, RED

TEASEL

D. laciniatus

D. sylvestris

FIELD SCABIOUS

COMMON BURDOCK

T BURDOCK

WOOLLY BURDOCK

bract

X ½

THISTLES
SPECIES WITH SPINES ON STEMS
(except Pasture Thistle, which has hairy stem)
<small>COMPOSITE OR DAISY FAMILY (Compositae)</small>

NODDING or MUSK THISTLE Alien *Carduus nutans*
Note the *strongly reflexed*, lanceolate, sepal-like purple bracts, the *nodding* reddish-purple flower head, and the interrupted prickly wings on the stem. Leaves very spiny. 1–3 ft. Fields, waste places. Local, Gulf of St. Lawrence south to Missouri, Maryland. JUNE–OCT.

WELTED THISTLE Alien *Carduus crispus*
Another species with spined wings running down the stem, but flowers *small* (¾ in.), erect, in small clusters. Much branched. Sepal-like bracts *narrow*, half spreading, woolly, green. 2–4 ft. Waste places. Local, Minnesota to Nova Scotia and south to Missouri, Ohio, Virginia. JUNE–SEPT.

MARSH THISTLE Alien in part *Cirsium palustre*
(not shown)
Similar to Welted Thistle (spiny-winged stem, small flowers) but note the *purplish* bracts, which are *appressed*, not spreading; also the *feathery* thistle down (hairs of thistledown not feathery in *Carduus crispus*). 2–6 ft. Wet woods, thickets, waste ground. Local, Maritime Provinces to Michigan, New York.
JULY–SEPT.

BULL THISTLE Alien *Cirsium vulgare*
Note the prickly wings on the stem and *rigid, yellow-tipped spines* on the flower bracts. Flower heads large, solitary or 2 or 3; reddish purple. Leaves pale or woolly beneath. 2–6 ft. Roadsides, fields. Most of area. JUNE–SEPT.

SCOTCH THISTLE Alien *Onopordum acanthium*
Note the *very heavy triangular spines* running down the winged stem. Plant whitish with cottony down. Flower head globular, pale purple, solitary; sepal-like bracts *cottony* at base and ending in *spreading yellow spines*. 2–4 ft. Roadsides, waste ground. Local, s. Canada to Michigan, Pennsylvania. JULY–SEPT.

PASTURE THISTLE *Cirsium pumilum*
Sometimes called Bull Thistle, a name more properly applied to *C. vulgare*. Our *largest-flowered* species (heads 2–3 in. across); very fragrant, light magenta or white. Note the *very hairy stems* (not winged as in *C. vulgare*). Leaves not pale beneath; spines very long. 1–3 ft. Dry soil, pastures. Ohio to s. Maine and south to Maryland, Delaware. JUNE–SEPT.

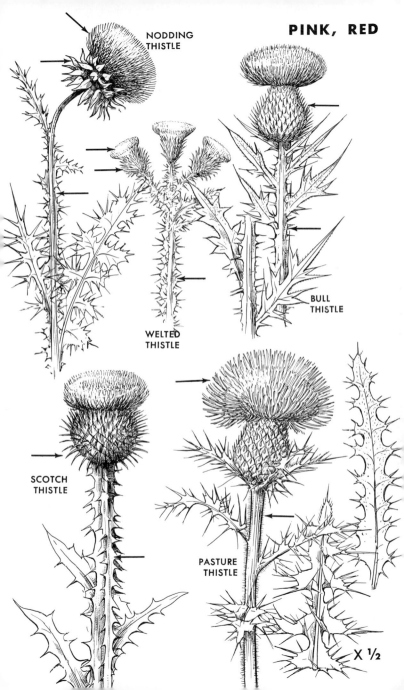

PINK, RED

NODDING THISTLE

WELTED THISTLE

BULL THISTLE

SCOTCH THISTLE

PASTURE THISTLE

X ½

THISTLES
SPECIES WITHOUT SPINES ON STEMS
COMPOSITE OR DAISY FAMILY (Compositae)
See also Pasture Thistle, p. 302.

FIELD THISTLE *Cirsium discolor*
The upper leaves *embrace* the flower head. Flowers purple, rarely white; sepal-like bracts end in long colorless bristles. Note *white wool* on undersurface of leaves. 3–9 ft. Compare Tall Thistle, below, and also Pasture Thistle, p. 302. Fields, open woods, prairies, waste ground. Manitoba, s. Quebec, sw. Maine and south. JULY–OCT.

CANADA THISTLE Alien *Cirsium arvense*
Actually a native of Europe, where it is known as Creeping Thistle. A hairless, much-branched plant springing from creeping roots; known by its *small, numerous,* often clustered, fragrant, pale lilac flower heads only ½–¾ in. across. Rarely white. Sepal-like bracts appressed, pointed, often purplish. Our commonest thistle. 1–5 ft. Roadsides, pastures, fields. Throughout. JULY–SEPT.

VIRGINIA THISTLE *Cirsium virginianum*
Best known by its narrow lanceolate leaves, which are *much reduced* on the upper part of the flowering stem. Leaves *white-felted* beneath. Flowers purplish, solitary, on a simple stalk or at ends of 2 or 3 slender branches. 1–4 ft. Bogs, wet pine barrens. Coastal plain, s. New Jersey south. AUG.–OCT.

SWAMP THISTLE *Cirsium muticum*
Flowering stem *hollow*, rising from a rosette of long-stalked, deeply incised leaves. Heads often clustered; rose-purple; rarely white. Bracts not tipped with spines but *sticky and cobwebby.* 2–10 ft. Swamps, wet woods, thickets. Most of our area.
JULY–SEPT.

TALL THISTLE *Cirsium altissimum*
Similar to *C. discolor* (above) in flower structure but most leaves lanceolate or long-ovate, tapered at each end and *not deeply lobed* or incised; whitish-woolly beneath as in *C. discolor*. 3–12 ft. Woods, thickets, banks. Minnesota, Wisconsin, Michigan, Ohio, s. New York, Massachusetts south. JULY–OCT.

PINK, RED

FIELD THISTLE

CANADA THISTLE

VIRGINIA THISTLE

SWAMP THISTLE

leaf
X ¼

TALL THISTLE

X ½

THISTLE-LIKE FLOWER HEADS:
STAR-THISTLES, KNAPWEEDS, ETC.

COMPOSITE OR DAISY FAMILY (Compositae)
Knapweeds lack spines; outer florets simulate rays.
Rose-purple; sometimes white.

CALTROPS, STAR-THISTLE Alien　　　*Centaurea calcitrapa*
Thistle-like, but with *long yellow spines* mainly on bracts of
flower head. Branches stiff, hairless. Leaves toothed; lower
ones with some spines. 1–2 ft. Roadsides, waste ground. Local,
s. Ontario, New York south.　　　　　　　　　　　JUNE–OCT.

BARBARA'S BUTTONS　　　　　*Marshallia grandiflora*
Note the lanceolate, *3-ribbed* leaves, mostly near base. Flower
heads long-stalked, solitary, superficially suggesting knapweeds
but receptacle *conic*, chaffy. Individual florets tubular, pink
with blue-purple anthers. 1–3 ft. Streamsides, clearings. Uplands, Pennsylvania south.　　　　　　　　　　　JUNE–JULY

SPOTTED KNAPWEED Alien　　　*Centaurea maculosa*
Much branched, wiry-stemmed. Leaves all *deeply cleft*. Flowers pink, purple, or white, bracts pale, ribbed, with a fringed
black triangular tip. A similar species, *C. diffusa*, with numerous
small white or rose flowers, has spine-tipped bracts (inset). 1–4
ft. Fields, roadsides. Most of area.　　　　　　　JUNE–AUG.

GREAT KNAPWEED Alien　　　　*Centaurea scabiosa*
Leaves deeply cut, suggesting *C. maculosa;* flower heads *much
larger* (2 in.), at tip of long, stiff, downy, grooved stalk, swollen
at summit. Flowers pink-purple. 1–2 ft. Fields, roadsides. S.
Ontario, Quebec to Iowa, Ohio.　　　　　　　　JULY–SEPT.

BLACK KNAPWEED, HARDHEADS Alien *Centaurea nigra*
Leaves lanceolate, not cleft; lower ones may be toothed. Note
dark, heavily fringed bracts that give a *blackish look* to globular
base of flower head. 2 forms: (1) without "rays," and (2) with
"rays." 1–3 ft. Fields, roadsides. S. Canada south to Ohio,
Maryland, Delaware.　　　　　　　　　　　　　JULY–SEPT.

TYROL KNAPWEED Alien　　　*Centaurea vochinensis*
Similar to *C. nigra* but always "rayed." The dark, fringed tips
of the bracts do not conceal the pale base and therefore give a
paler look to the receptacle. 1–3 ft. Fields, roadsides. Ontario
to Maine and south.　　　　　　　　　　　　　JUNE–SEPT.

BROWN KNAPWEED Alien　　　　*Centaurea jacea*
Note the very slender, untoothed upper leaves and jagged,
scale-like bracts that *lack long fringes* of other species. Lower
leaves long-stalked, often toothed. 1–3 ft. Roadsides, fields.
Quebec south to Iowa, Illinois, Ohio, Virginia.　JUNE–SEPT.

AMERICAN KNAPWEED　　　　*Centaurea americana*
Very large flower heads (2–3 in. across), usually solitary. Note
the *much-elongated*, bristle-tipped bracts. Stem swollen at summit. Leaves slender-oblong, untoothed. 1–4 ft. Prairies, fields.
Missouri south and southwest.　　　　　　　　　JUNE–AUG.

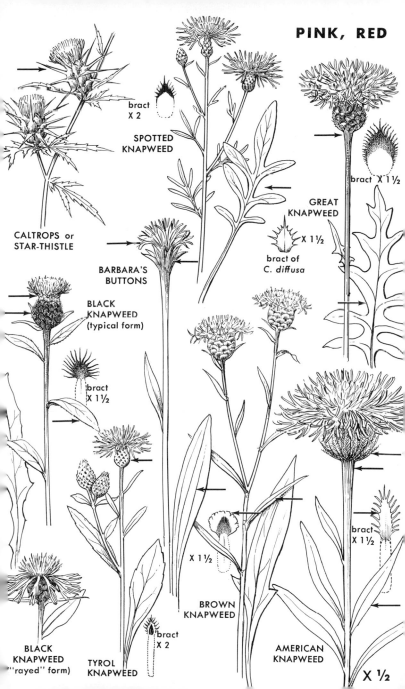

PINK, RED

CALTROPS or
STAR-THISTLE

SPOTTED
KNAPWEED

bract
X 2

GREAT
KNAPWEED

bract X 1½

bract of
C. diffusa

X 1½

BARBARA'S
BUTTONS

BLACK
KNAPWEED
(typical form)

bract
X 1½

BLACK
KNAPWEED
"rayed" form

TYROL
KNAPWEED

bract
X 2

X 1½

BROWN
KNAPWEED

AMERICAN
KNAPWEED

bract
X 1½

X ½

DAISYLIKE FLOWERS
Composite or Daisy Family (Compositae), except Field Scabious

PURPLE CONEFLOWER *Echinacea purpurea*
A large daisylike flower with *swept-back reddish-purple rays*. Lower leaves long-stalked, tapering, with *rough teeth*. 2–3 ft. Prairies, dry clearings. Iowa, Illinois, Michigan, Ohio, Virginia south. JUNE–OCT.

PALE PURPLE CONEFLOWER *Echinacea pallida*
Paler or more pinkish purple than *E. purpurea*. Lower leaves *lanceolate, parallel-veined, without teeth*. 2–4 ft. Prairies. Nebraska to Michigan and south. JUNE–JULY

NEW ENGLAND ASTER *Aster novae-angliae*
Usually violet, sometimes rose or magenta. See p. 356. **Note:** Other violet asters may tend toward purple; see violet-blue section, pp. 354–60. AUG.–OCT.

PINK TICKSEED *Coreopsis rosea*
Note the paired, linear, *grasslike leaves*. Rays 4 to 8, reflexed; pink, sometimes white. Our other *Coreopsis* are yellow (p. 188). 8–24 in. Wet sand, peat, shores. Coast, local. S. Nova Scotia, e. Massachusetts to e. Maryland. JULY–SEPT.

COMMON or PHILADELPHIA FLEABANE
Erigeron philadelphicus
Fleabanes have *very numerous* rays (up to 100–150 in this species). Slender, soft-hairy (sometimes smooth), with few to many pink or pale magenta flowers less than 1 in. across. Leaves clasp stem. 6–30 in. See also Daisy Fleabane (white), p. 94. Thickets, fields, open woods. Most of area. APRIL–JULY

ROBIN-PLANTAIN *Erigeron pulchellus*
Shorter and larger-flowered than Common Fleabane; very soft-hairy. Few-flowered (1–6); heads 1 to 1½ in. across, rays pale lilac or magenta to violet. Basal leaves well stalked, broad toward tip, bluntly toothed. Spreads by runners, often forming colonies. 6–16 in. Open woods, fields. Minnesota, s. Ontario, s. Quebec, s. Maine south. APRIL–JUNE

OYSTER-PLANT, SALSIFY Alien *Tragopogon porrifolius*
Note the *long grasslike leaves* and spiky, sepal-like *bracts that exceed the rays*. Flowers close by afternoon. Stems hollow. There is a similar yellow species, Yellow Goat's-beard (p. 110), with which it often hybridizes. 2–5 ft. Roadsides, fields. Ontario to Nova Scotia and south. MAY–JULY

FIELD SCABIOUS Alien *Knautia arvensis*
TEASEL FAMILY (Dipsacaceae)
Related to Teasel but lacks spines. Flower head rather flat, pincushionlike. Florets lavender, 4-lobed, asymmetrical; outer lobes longest, giving illusion of rays. Leaves lobed or not. 1–3 ft. Waste ground, roadsides. Local, se. Canada to New England, Pennsylvania. JUNE–AUG.

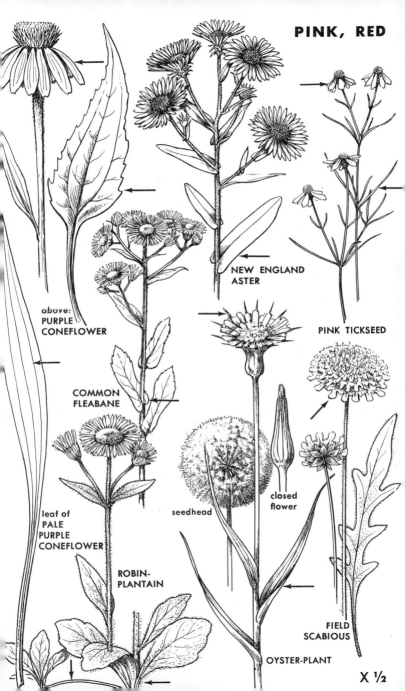

PINK, RED

NEW ENGLAND
ASTER

PINK TICKSEED

above:
PURPLE
CONEFLOWER

COMMON
FLEABANE

leaf of
PALE
PURPLE
CONEFLOWER

ROBIN-
PLANTAIN

seedhead

closed
flower

FIELD
SCABIOUS

OYSTER-PLANT

X ½

VARIOUS INCONSPICUOUS FLOWERS

COAST-BLITE   *Chenopodium rubrum*
GOOSEFOOT FAMILY   (Chenopodiaceae)
Chenopodiums (see also p. 378) have triangular, jagged leaves.
This one is fleshy, reddish. Flowers minute, with red, petal-like
sepals. 12–30 in. Salty soil. Coast south to New Jersey; local
inland.   JULY–OCT.

SEA-PURSLANE   *Sesuvium maritimum*
CARPETWEED FAMILY   (Aizoaceae)
Prostrate or reclining. Note *fleshy paddle-shaped leaves*. Flowers
in leaf axils, purplish within; petals absent. 2–12 in. Damp
sand. Coast, Long Island south.   JULY–SEPT.

WATER-PURSLANE   *Ludwigia palustris*
EVENING-PRIMROSE FAMILY   (Onagraceae)
Prostrate or floating, with reddish stems and paired, glossy,
red-veined leaves. Small 4-part flowers tucked in leaf axils.
Shallow water, shores. Most of area.   JUNE–SEPT.

KNOTWEEDS   *Polygonum*
BUCKWHEAT FAMILY   (Polygonaceae)
See p. 276. *P. prolificum* is shown here.

SLEEPY CATCHFLY   *Silene antirrhina*
PINK FAMILY   (Caryophyllaceae)
See p. 266.

SAND SPURREY Alien in part   *Spergularia rubra*
PINK FAMILY   (Caryophyllaceae)
Prostrate, with whorls of short linear leaves. Petals pink,
shorter than sepals. 2–6 in. Sandy soil. Most of area. A native
coastal species, *S. marina* (not shown), is pink or white, has
fleshy leaves.   JUNE–OCT.

SEA-LAVENDER   *Limonium nashii*
SEA-LAVENDER FAMILY   (Plumbaginaceae)
See p. 264.

WILLOW-HERBS   *Epilobium*
EVENING-PRIMROSE FAMILY   (Onagraceae)
See p. 270 for this (*E. strictum*) and other willow-herbs.

LOOSESTRIFES   *Lythrum*
LOOSESTRIFE FAMILY   (Lythraceae)
See p. 288 for 2 species shown here (*L. hyssopifolia* and *L.
lineare*) and for other loosestrifes.

SHEEP or COMMON SORREL   *Rumex acetosella*
BUCKWHEAT FAMILY   (Polygonaceae)
Reddish or greenish. See p. 380.

PINWEEDS   *Lechea*
ROCKROSE FAMILY   (Cistaceae)
Pinweeds (8 in our area) are insignificant, with numerous tiny
linear leaves and multitudes of minute flowers or seedpods.
Shown here are *L. minor* and *L. racemulosa*. Dry soil, sand.
Most of our area.   JULY–NOV.

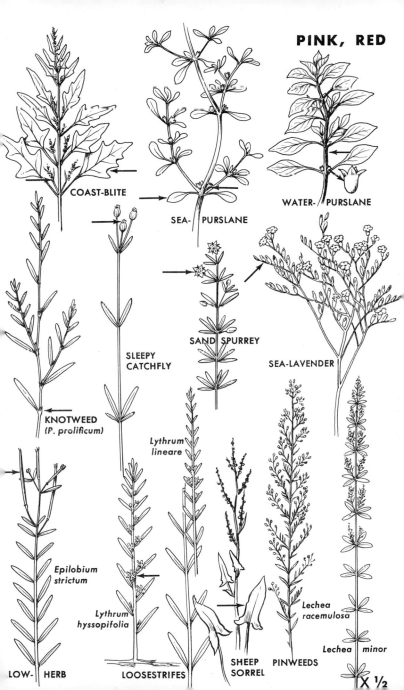

PINK, RED

COAST-BLITE

SEA- PURSLANE

WATER- PURSLANE

SLEEPY
CATCHFLY

SAND SPURREY

SEA-LAVENDER

KNOTWEED
(*P. prolificum*)

*Lythrum
lineare*

*Epilobium
strictum*

*Lythrum
hyssopifolia*

LOW- HERB

LOOSESTRIFES

SHEEP
SORREL

*Lechea
racemulosa*

PINWEEDS

Lechea minor

X ½

Violet to Blue
Flowers

We repeat the warning here that it is not always easy to separate some lavender or reddish-purple flowers (treated in the pink–red section, which starts on page 212) from some violet ones, shown here in the following pages. If in doubt, look in both places.

PETALS IN 3'S: IRISES, SPIDERWORTS

LARGER BLUE FLAG *Iris versicolor*
IRIS FAMILY (Iridaceae)
A graceful, sword-leaved plant similar to the garden iris; the showy, downcurved violet sepals are boldly veined. 2–3 ft. Marshes, wet meadows. Manitoba, s. Labrador south to Minnesota, Wisconsin, Ohio, Virginia. MAY–JULY

SLENDER BLUE FLAG *Iris prismatica*
IRIS FAMILY (Iridaceae)
Much more slender; leaves *almost grasslike.* 1–3 ft. Marshes near coast. Nova Scotia to Georgia. MAY–JULY

CRESTED DWARF IRIS *Iris cristata*
IRIS FAMILY (Iridaceae)
Note the *fluted yellow crest* on the downcurved sepals and the short leaves embracing the short stem. 3–8 in. Wet hills, woods. Indiana, s. Ohio, Maryland south. APRIL–MAY

DWARF or VERNAL IRIS *Iris verna*
IRIS FAMILY (Iridaceae)
Similar to *I. cristata* but *not crested;* leaves much more slender (up to 12 in.). 2–6 in. Sandy soil, coastal barrens, piedmont, mts. Pennsylvania, Maryland south. MARCH–MAY

VIRGINIA DAYFLOWER *Commelina virginica*
SPIDERWORT FAMILY (Commelinaceae)
Dayflowers have upper 2 petals larger than lower one, which supports curved stamens. Note heart-shaped spathe. In this species lower petal is *blue.* 1½–3 ft. Woods, thickets, Kansas, Illinois, s. Pennsylvania, s. New Jersey south. JULY–OCT.
SLENDER DAYFLOWER, *C. erecta* (not shown), is a native species with a very small *white* lower petal (like *C. communis*) but is *erect* like *C. virginica* and has similar leaves.

ASIATIC DAYFLOWER Alien *Commelina communis*
SPIDERWORT FAMILY (Commelinaceae)
This imported weed differs from the Virginia Dayflower by its *reclining* habit, small *white* lower petal, and wider leaves. Roadsides, waste places, edges. Wisconsin, Michigan, New York, Massachusetts south. JUNE–OCT.

SPIDERWORT *Tradescantia virginiana*
SPIDERWORT FAMILY (Commelinaceae)
Note the terminal cluster of violet flowers with *3 roundish,* symmetric petals, accented by golden stamens. Leaves long, irislike. Wood edges, thickets, roadsides; often cultivated. Minnesota, Wisconsin, New York, Maine south. APRIL–JULY
OHIO SPIDERWORT, *T. ohiensis* (not shown), midwestern, has *smooth* flower stalks and bracts (hairy in *C. virginiana*).
ZIGZAG SPIDERWORT, *T. subaspera* (not shown), W. Virginia to Missouri, has a more *zigzag* stem, much broader leaves. There are several other species, mostly in prairie states.

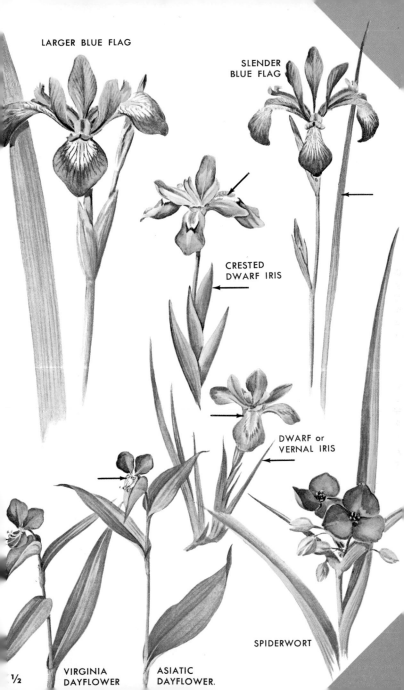

LARGER BLUE FLAG

SLENDER
BLUE FLAG

CRESTED
DWARF IRIS

DWARF or
VERNAL IRIS

SPIDERWORT

½

VIRGINIA
DAYFLOWER

ASIATIC
DAYFLOWER.

SHOWY SPIKES

CREEPING BELLFLOWER Alien *Campanula rapunculoides*
BLUEBELL FAMILY BLUEBELL SUBFAMILY (Campanuloideae)
The delicate 5-pointed bells hang mostly on 1 side of the
stiff stem; sepals thin, reflexed. Lower leaves heart-shaped.
1–3 ft. See other bellflowers, p. 340. Fields, roadsides. S.
Canada to central states.   JULY–SEPT.

GRAPE-HYACINTH Alien   *Muscari botryoides*
LILY FAMILY   (Liliaceae)
A tight, tapering cluster of small *ball-like* flowers, suggesting
tiny grapes. Leaves linear, with a *pale groove.* 4–10 in. Spread
from cultivation. Minnesota to New England and south to
Missouri, Virginia.   APRIL–MAY

WILD LUPINE   *Lupinus perennis*
PEA FAMILY   (Leguminosae)
Note the pealike flowers and *palmate* leaves (radiating into 7–9
segments). 1–2 ft. Dry soil, open woods, clearings. Minnesota,
s. Ontario, New York, s. Maine south. Garden lupines (not
shown), *Lupinus* — larger, blue-violet, pink, or white — are
roadside escapes in New England and mts.   APRIL–JULY

BLUE VERVAIN   *Verbena hastata*
VERVAIN FAMILY   (Verbenaceae)
Note the branching pencil-like spikes of small 5-petaled flowers
that bloom a few at a time, advancing toward the pointed tip.
Stem grooved, 4-sided. Lower leaves may be 3-lobed. See also
p. 286. Thickets, roadsides. Most of our area.   JULY–SEPT.

WILD HYACINTH   *Camassia scilloides*
LILY FAMILY   (Liliaceae)
Note the keeled linear leaves (5–15 in.) and pale blue *6-pointed*
stars on separate stalks. 1–2 ft. Meadows, open woods. Iowa,
s. Wisconsin, se. Michigan, s. Ontario, sw. Pennsylvania south,
mainly west of mts.   MAY–JUNE

VIPER'S BUGLOSS Alien   *Echium vulgare*
FORGET-ME-NOT FAMILY   (Boraginaceae)
A bristly plant. Note the short, curled flower branches, on
which 1 flower blooms at a time. Upper lip of flower exceeds
the lower; *long red stamens* project. 1–2½ ft. Roadsides, waste
places. Most of our area.   JUNE–SEPT.

GREAT LOBELIA   *Lobelia siphilitica*
BLUEBELL FAMILY LOBELIA SUBFAMILY   (Lobelioideae)
See discussion of lobelias, p. 342. This, the largest blue species,
is *striped with white* on 3 lower lobes and on belly of corolla.
1–3 ft. Swamps, wet ground. Manitoba to w. New England
and south.   AUG.–SEPT.

PICKERELWEED   *Pontederia cordata*
PICKERELWEED FAMILY   (Pontederiaceae)
The blue spires form beds in shallow water. Note the large
arrowhead-shaped leaves. 1–4 ft. Edges of ponds, streams.
Minnesota, s. Ontario, Nova Scotia south.   JUNE–OCT.

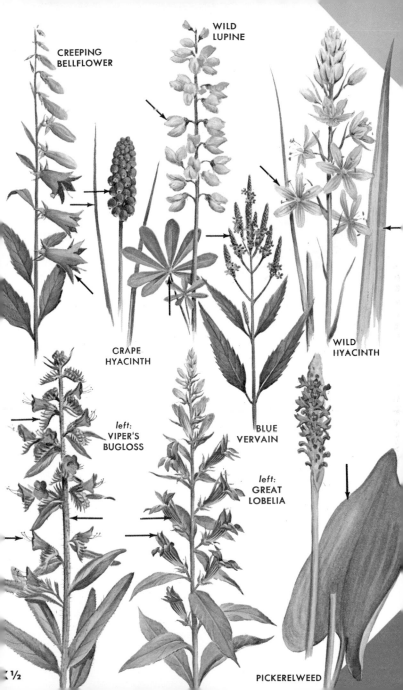

CREEPING
BELLFLOWER

WILD
LUPINE

GRAPE
HYACINTH

WILD
HYACINTH

left:
VIPER'S
BUGLOSS

BLUE
VERVAIN

left:
GREAT
LOBELIA

PICKERELWEED

× ½

SPURRED OR HOODED FLOWERS

BIRDFOOT VIOLET   *Viola pedata*
VIOLET FAMILY   (Violaceae)
Violets have 5 petals, the lowest often wider, heavily veined,
and extending back into a spur. This species has *finely segmented leaves* (9–15 points). One variety is *bicolored* (3 lower
petals paler); another is uniformly colored. 4–10 in. Dry
sandy fields, sunny rocks. Minnesota, Michigan, s. Ontario,
New York, Massachusetts south.   APRIL–JUNE

MARSH BLUE VIOLET   *Viola cucullata*
VIOLET FAMILY   (Violaceae)
In this violet the petals are *darker toward the throat;* lower petal
veined, *shorter.* Flower stems taller than leaves. 5–10 in. Wet
meadows, springs, bogs. Most of our area (in mts. southward).   APRIL–JUNE

COMMON BLUE VIOLET   *Viola papilionacea*
VIOLET FAMILY   (Violaceae)
Similar to *V. cucullata* but lateral petals also strongly veined;
lower petal *longer.* Leafstalks often longer than flower stalks,
sometimes downy. 3–8 in. Damp woods, meadows. N.
Dakota, s. Quebec, c. Maine south. See other blue violets with
heart-shaped leaves, pp. 328, 330.   MARCH–JUNE

BUTTERWORT   *Pinguicula vulgaris*
BLADDERWORT FAMILY   (Lentibulariaceae)
The solitary 5-lobed flower suggests a violet, but note the
basal rosette of *shiny, greasy leaves, with rolled-in edges.* 1–6 in.
Wet rocks, bogs. Across Canada and south to n. Minnesota,
n. Michigan, n. New York, n. Vermont.   JUNE–JULY

DWARF or SPRING LARKSPUR   *Delphinium tricorne*
BUTTERCUP FAMILY   (Ranunculaceae)
Note the 5- to 7-cleft, buttercuplike leaves and loose cluster
of spurred flowers (upper sepal extended to form an erect
spur). Blue or white. 12–30 in. Woods, slopes. Minnesota
to Pennsylvania and south in mts.   APRIL–MAY

TALL LARKSPUR   *Delphinium exaltatum*
BUTTERCUP FAMILY   (Ranunculaceae)
A taller, leafier species with numerous flowers; blooms later.
Leaves 3- to 5-lobed. 2–6 ft. Woods, slopes. Ohio, c. Pennsyl-
vania south. The GARDEN LARKSPUR, *D. ajacis* (not shown),
with finely cut leaves, frequently escapes. JULY–SEPT.

MONKSHOOD   *Aconitum uncinatum*
BUTTERCUP FAMILY   (Ranunculaceae)
The large upper sepal (covering 2 petals) is shaped *like a helmet.*
Leaves suggest a buttercup. 2–3 ft. Woods. S. Indiana, s.
Pennsylvania south in mts. An earlier species, *A. novebora-
cense* (not shown), is found locally in the Catskills, ne. Ohio,
and unglaciated Iowa and Wisconsin.   AUG.–OCT.

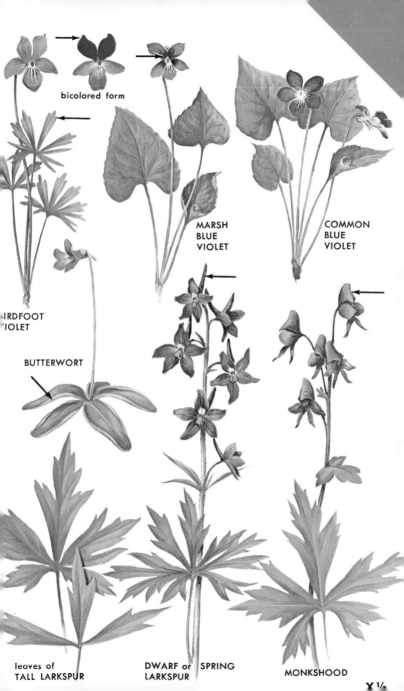

bicolored form

MARSH
BLUE
VIOLET

COMMON
BLUE
VIOLET

IRDFOOT
IOLET

BUTTERWORT

leaves of
TALL LARKSPUR

DWARF or SPRING
LARKSPUR

MONKSHOOD

X ½

ERECT, VASE-LIKE OR CLOSED TUBES
GENTIAN FAMILY (Gentianaceae)

SMALLER FRINGED GENTIAN   *Gentiana procera*
Similar to Fringed Gentian, but leaves *narrow*, 1-nerved.
Fringe shorter. 6–20 in. Wet prairies, bogs, wet sand. Interior,
Manitoba, Ontario south to Iowa, Indiana, Ohio.   JULY–OCT.

FRINGED GENTIAN   *Gentiana crinita*
Note the swirl of *4 delicately fringed petals* flaring out from
the deep corolla tube. Individual flowers on long stalks. 1–3
ft. Meadows, wet woods, banks. Manitoba to Ontario and
across n. U.S.; in mts. to Georgia.   SEPT.–NOV.

DOWNY GENTIAN   *Gentiana puberula*
Note the tight cluster of mostly stalkless, 5-pointed flowers
with no fringes. Stems minutely downy; leaves lanceolate.
8–20 in. Prairies, sandy soil. Minnesota, Wisconsin, Michigan, s. Ontario, w. New York south.   SEPT.–OCT.

PINE-BARREN GENTIAN   *Gentiana autumnalis*
Note the single (or 2 or 3) large 5-pointed flowers marked with
pale stripes and specklings; pointed pleats between the lobes.
Leaves *linear.* 8–18 in. Wet pine barrens, coastal bogs. S.
New Jersey; se. Virginia south.   AUG.–OCT.

SOAPWORT GENTIAN   *Gentiana saponaria*
Similar to Closed Gentian but paler (blue-violet or white);
flowers open slightly. When spread by hand, *petal tips are free*
of the fringed joining membrane (inset). Sepals *more erect* (not
reflexed). 1–2½ ft. Wet spots, swamps. Minnesota, Wisconsin, Indiana, New York south.   SEPT.–OCT.

CLOSED GENTIAN   *Gentiana andrewsii*
The deep blue petals stay *closed*, joined by and slightly exceeded by a fringed whitish membrane (inset). 1–2 ft. A very
similar species, *G. clausa* (not shown), has the petal tips free
of the joining membrane. Wet places, meadows. Manitoba,
s. Ontario, sw. Quebec, Vermont south.   AUG.–OCT.

NARROW-LEAVED GENTIAN   *Gentiana linearis*
The combination of *very slender leaves* and *rounded flower lobes*
separate this from the others. Blue to white. 6–24 in. Wet
meadows, bogs, wet woods. Lake Superior to Labrador
and south (mainly in mts.) to W. Virginia.   AUG.–SEPT.

STIFF GENTIAN   *Gentiana quinquefolia*
Note the *4-ridged stem* and the *tight clusters* of small, tubular
lilac flowers with 5 bristle-pointed lobes. Flowers often in
groups of 5. Leaves broadly ovate, clasping. 6–30 in. Rich
woods, wet fields, slopes. Minnesota, Michigan, Ontario, s.
Maine south, mainly in mts.   AUG.–OCT.

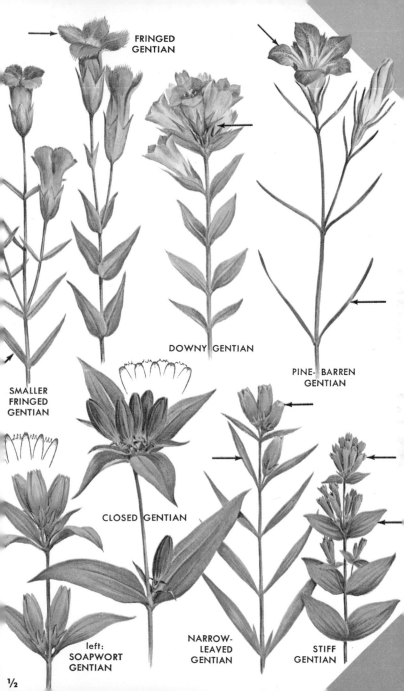

FRINGED
GENTIAN

DOWNY GENTIAN

PINE- BARREN
GENTIAN

SMALLER
FRINGED
GENTIAN

CLOSED GENTIAN

left:
SOAPWORT
GENTIAN

NARROW-
LEAVED
GENTIAN

STIFF
GENTIAN

½

5 PETALS: BELLS, PINWHEELS, ETC.

MERTENSIA, VIRGINIA COWSLIP   *Mertensia virginica*
FORGET-ME-NOT FAMILY   (Boraginaceae)
The nodding, trumpetlike flowers are pink in bud. Leaves oval, smooth, strongly veined; stem smooth, succulent. 1–2 ft. Bottomlands, river woods. E. Minnesota, s. Ontario, New York south.   MARCH–MAY

PERIWINKLE, MYRTLE   *Vinca minor*
DOGBANE FAMILY   (Apocynaceae)
Note the asymmetric petals that create a *pinwheel effect;* a star outlined in center. Leaves glossy, evergreen. A creeping ground cover, spreading from gardens.   MARCH–JUNE

BLUE PHLOX   *Phlox divaricata*
PHLOX FAMILY   (Polemoniaceae)
The pale violet flowers radiate from the tip of the stem. Petals wedge-shaped; stamens completely hidden. Stem hairy, sticky. 10–20 in. Rich open woods. Minnesota, Wisconsin, Michigan, Ontario, New York south.   APRIL–JUNE

MOSS PHLOX, MOSS-PINK   *Phlox subulata*
PHLOX FAMILY   (Polemoniaceae)
Note the creeping habit, *deeply notched petals,* and *needlelike leaves.* Pink, violet, white. 2–6 in. Rocky slopes, sandy soil. S. Michigan, s. Ontario, New York south (mainly in mts.) to N. Carolina; escaped elsewhere.   APRIL–MAY

JACOB'S-LADDER   *Polemonium van-bruntiae*
PHLOX FAMILY   (Polemoniaceae)
The loose clusters of blue-violet bells and the "ladder" of paired leaflets mark *Polemonium.* In this species the stamens *protrude;* leaflets more numerous (15–19). 1–3 ft. Wooded swamps, bogs, glades. Mainly mts. from New York, Vermont south to W. Virginia, Maryland.   JUNE–JULY

GREEK VALERIAN   *Polemonium reptans*
PHLOX FAMILY   (Polemoniaceae)
Similar but stem weaker, leaflets fewer (5–15); stamens *do not project* beyond flower. 8–15 in. Moist woods, bottoms. Minnesota to New York and south.   APRIL–JUNE

VIRGINIA WATERLEAF   *Hydrophyllum virginianum*
WATERLEAF FAMILY   (Hydrophyllaceae)
Flowers white or pale violet; suggest *Polemonium,* but note irregular *5- to 7-lobed leaves* (often marked as if stained with water). Plant smoothish. 1–3 ft. See also p. 54. Rich woods. Manitoba, Quebec, w. New England south.   MAY–AUG.

APPENDAGED WATERLEAF
     Hydrophyllum appendiculatum
WATERLEAF FAMILY   (Hydrophyllaceae)
Similar to preceding but hairier, leaves less deeply divided, *vaguely maple-like.* 1–2 ft. Rich woods. Minnesota, Ontario, New York south.   MAY–JUNE

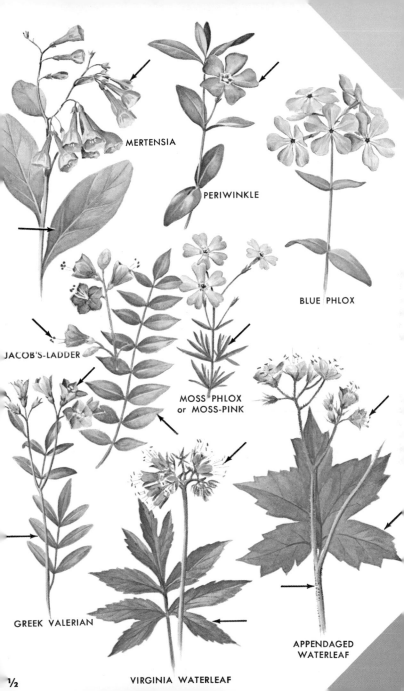

MERTENSIA

PERIWINKLE

BLUE PHLOX

JACOB'S-LADDER

MOSS PHLOX
or MOSS-PINK

GREEK VALERIAN

VIRGINIA WATERLEAF

APPENDAGED
WATERLEAF

½

MISCELLANEOUS VIOLET OR BLUE FLOWERS

NIGHTSHADE, BITTERSWEET Alien   *Solanum dulcamara*
TOMATO FAMILY   (Solanaceae)
Weak, vinelike. Note the 5 swept-back violet (sometimes white)'
petals and the protruding *yellow beak* formed by the anthers.
Leaves with *2 small lobes at base.* Fruit, drooping clusters of
egg-shaped berries; green turning to ruby-red. 2–8 ft. Moist
thickets. Throughout.   MAY–SEPT.

HORSE-NETTLE   *Solanum carolinense*
TOMATO FAMILY   (Solanaceae)
Flowers similar to Nightshade but larger, lobes wider; leaves
rough, *widely toothed;* stems *prickly.* Berries orange. 1–4 ft.
Sandy soil, fields, roadsides. Iowa, Illinois, Indiana, Ohio, s.
Ontario, New York, New England south.   MAY–OCT.

WATER-WILLOW   *Justicia americana*
ACANTHUS FAMILY   (Acanthaceae)
Note the slender, paired, willowlike leaves and the clusters of
bicolored flowers, pale violet or white with purple spots; lower
lip 3-lobed. 1–3 ft. Shallow water, wet shores. Wisconsin, s.
Ontario, Quebec, Vermont south.   JUNE–OCT.

CORN-SALAD Alien   *Valerianella olitoria*
VALERIAN FAMILY   (Valerianaceae)
A low forked plant with tiny pale blue flowers in small *flat,
leafy-bracted heads.* Leaves oblong, stalkless, opposite. 4–12 in.
Fields, waste places. Ontario, Maine south.   APRIL–JULY

RATTLESNAKE-MASTER   *Eryngium aquaticum*
PARSLEY FAMILY   (Umbelliferae)
Whitish, often with a bluish cast. See p. 44.

BLUE DOGBANE, WILLOW AMSONIA
DOGBANE FAMILY (Apocynaceae)   *Amsonia tabernaemontana*
The round cluster of *sky-blue stars* is distinctive. Leaves lanceo-
late, crowded, smooth. 1–3 ft. Woods, riverbanks. Missouri, s.
Illinois, se. Virginia south.   APRIL–MAY

BRANCHED BROOMRAPE Alien   *Orobanche ramosa*
BROOMRAPE FAMILY   (Orobanchaceae)
Flowers yellow and pale blue; leaves scale-like, stem branched.
Parasitic on tomato, tobacco, hemp, etc.   JULY–SEPT.

LESSER BROOMRAPE Alien   *Orobanche minor*
BROOMRAPE FAMILY   (Orobanchaceae)
Stem leafless but scaled, unbranched, yellow-brown, downy.
Flowers violet, in a *stout spike.* 4–18 in. Parasitic on roots of
clover. New Jersey to N. Carolina.   APRIL–JULY

MISTFLOWER   *Eupatorium coelestinum*
COMPOSITE FAMILY   (Compositae)
Note flat-topped clusters of fuzzy flowers. The *only bluish
Eupatorium.* Leaves paired, arrow-shaped. 1–3 ft. Thickets,
wood edges; often cultivated. Missouri, Illinois, Indiana,
Ohio, se. Pennsylvania, New Jersey south.   AUG.–OCT.

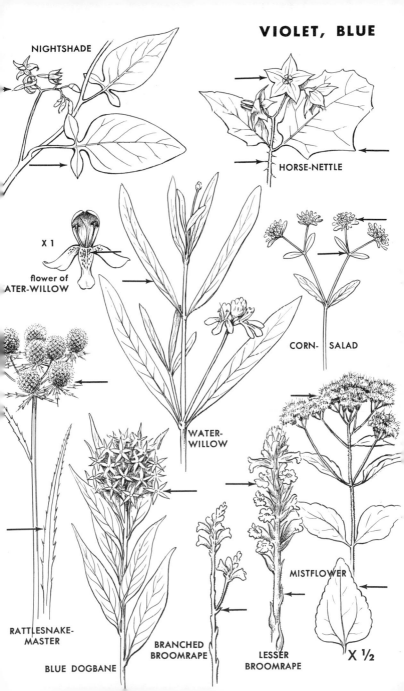

VIOLET, BLUE

NIGHTSHADE

HORSE-NETTLE

X 1

flower of
ATER-WILLOW

WATER-
WILLOW

CORN- SALAD

RATTLESNAKE-
MASTER

BLUE DOGBANE

BRANCHED
BROOMRAPE

LESSER
BROOMRAPE

MISTFLOWER

X ½

MISCELLANEOUS SIMPLE FLOWERS

 BLUE-EYED GRASSES   *Sisyrinchium*
Iris Family   (Iridaceae)
Stiff, grasslike plants. 6 petals, each tipped with a small point.
Fruit a small round pod. 9 species in our area; most are blue-
violet; 2 (*S. albidum* and *S. campestre*) are white.
1. **SPECIES WITH NO STEMS BRANCHED**
S. montanum has relatively wide leaves (⅛ in.), flat stems.
Flowers short-stalked, terminating stem and exceeded by a
pointed bract. 4–24 in. Meadows, shores. C. Canada to n.
Iowa, Great Lakes region; in mts. to w. Virginia. June–July
S. mucronatum has wiry stems and *very slender* leaves (1/12 in.
wide), *much shorter* than stems. 4–24 in. Fields, meadows.
Wisconsin to Maine and south.   May–June
2. **SPECIES WITH SOME STEMS BRANCHED**
S. angustifolium has flat stems and leaves (less than ¼ in.
wide). Flowers *long-stalked*. Meadows, shores. S. Canada
south.   May–July
S. atlanticum is more slender. Leaves *much shorter* than flower
stems. Meadows, marshes. S. Michigan, Ohio, New York,
New England south.   May–July

 MUD-PLANTAINS   *Heteranthera*
Pickerelweed Family   (Pontederiaceae)
Leaves floating; flowers emergent, 6-petaled, pale blue or white.
Ponds, wet mud. *H. reniformis* (Missouri to Connecticut and
south) has kidney-shaped leaves. *H. limosa* (Minnesota, s.
Illinois south) has lance-oval leaves, larger flowers. July–Sept.

 FLAX Alien   *Linum usitatissimum*
Flax Family   (Linaceae)
Delicate, slender. Flowers pale blue (½–¾ in.); 5 petals
slightly overlap. Leaves narrow, sharp, 3-veined, alternate.
9–20 in. Waste places, fields. Throughout.   June–Sept.

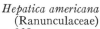 **ONE-FLOWERED CANCER-ROOT**   *Orobanche uniflora*
Broomrape Family   (Orobanchaceae)
White, pale lavender, or violet. See p. 232.

 ROUND-LOBED HEPATICA   *Hepatica americana*
Buttercup Family   (Ranunculaceae)
Flowers blue-lavender, pink, or white. See p. 238.

 VIOLET WOOD-SORREL   *Oxalis violacea*
Wood-Sorrel Family   (Oxalidaceae)
Purple-violet to rose-purple. See p. 238.

 PASQUEFLOWER   *Anemone patens*
Buttercup Family   (Ranunculaceae)
Pale blue-violet or white. See p. 22.

 CHEESES, COMMON MALLOW Alien   *Malva neglecta*
Mallow Family   (Malvaceae)
Pale blue-lavender, lilac-pink, or white. See p. 258.

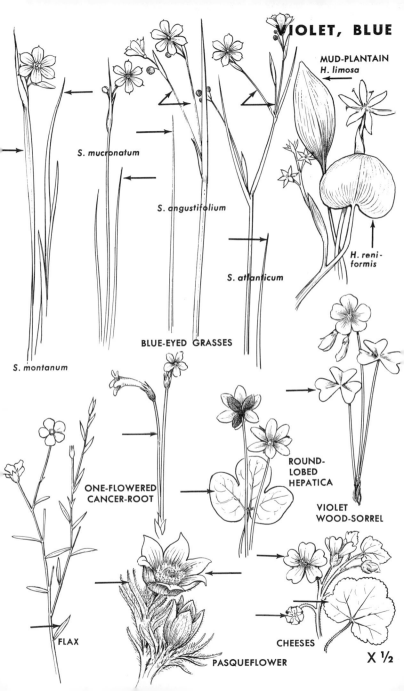

VIOLET, BLUE

MUD-PLANTAIN
H. limosa

S. mucronatum

S. angustifolium

S. atlanticum

S. montanum

H. reniformis

BLUE-EYED GRASSES

ROUND-
LOBED
HEPATICA

VIOLET
WOOD-SORREL

ONE-FLOWERED
CANCER-ROOT

FLAX

PASQUEFLOWER

CHEESES

X ½

5 PETALS AND A SPUR: VIOLETS
HEART-SHAPED LEAVES (except Field Pansy)
VIOLET FAMILY (Violaceae)

Low plants, suggesting tiny pansies; 5 petals, lowest heavily veined and extending back into a spur; lateral petals usually bearded. Hybrids frequent. See other violets on pp. 24 (white), 146 (yellow), 318, 330–32 (violet–blue), 366 (green).

1. **"STEMMED" VIOLETS** (leaves, flowers on same stalk)
LONG-SPURRED VIOLET   *Viola rostrata*
Note the *extremely long spur* and toothed stipules in leaf axils. Petals pale lavender, lower 3 with darker lines; *all petals beardless.* 4–8 in. Rich woods, limy soil. Wisconsin, sw. Quebec, Vermont south to Pennsylvania, n. New Jersey, Connecticut; in mts. to Georgia.   APRIL–JUNE
DOG VIOLET   *Viola conspersa*
Similar to *V. rostrata* but spur *shorter*, lateral petals bearded. 2–6 in. Meadows, low woods, streambanks. Minnesota, e. Canada, ne. U.S., and south in mts.   MAY–JULY
HOOKED-SPUR VIOLET (not shown)   *Viola adunca*
Similar to *V. conspersa* but lower, more spreading, *finely pubescent*, deeper in color. Dry rocky woods. Canada to Minnesota, Wisconsin, Michigan, New York, n. New England.
                                            MAY–JULY
FIELD PANSY Alien   *Viola kitaibelliana*
Whitish or pale blue. See p. 24.

2. **"STEMLESS" VIOLETS** (leaves, flowers on separate stalks)
GREAT-SPURRED VIOLET   *Viola selkirkii*
Note heavy spur with *enlarged rounded end.* Petals pale violet, *all beardless.* Leaves with *nearly closed notch,* upper side slightly hairy. 2–4 in. Cool wet woods, slopes. N. Canada south to Minnesota, Wisconsin, Michigan, Pennsylvania, n. and w. New England.   MAY–JULY
ALPINE MARSH VIOLET   *Viola palustris*
Similar to *V. selkirkii* but with a slighter spur and smoother leaves. Petals pale lilac or white, with dark lines. Note long underground *runners.* Wet soil; marshes. Subarctic south to Maritime Provinces, n. New England.   JUNE–AUG.
WOOLLY BLUE VIOLET   *Viola sororia*
Wide-leaved; *downy or woolly* throughout. Lateral petals bearded. (*V. septentrionalis* and *V. novae-angliae*, p. 330, are also downy but have lower petal bearded.) Woods, meadows. Minnesota, w. Quebec to New England; south in mts.
                                            MARCH–JUNE
SOUTHERN WOOD VIOLET   *Viola hirsutula*
Leaves *purplish below,* silvery-downy above; veins often purple. Flowers reddish-violet; lateral petals bearded with *clublike* hairs. Woods. S. New York, Connecticut.   APRIL–MAY

"STEMMED" VIOLETS

VIOLET, BLUE

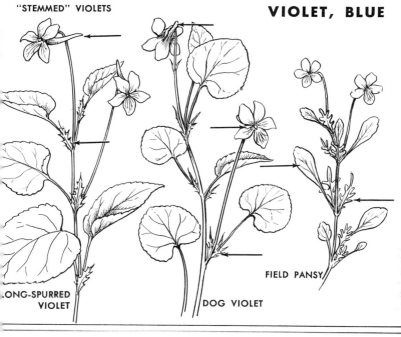

LONG-SPURRED VIOLET

DOG VIOLET

FIELD PANSY

"STEMLESS" VIOLETS

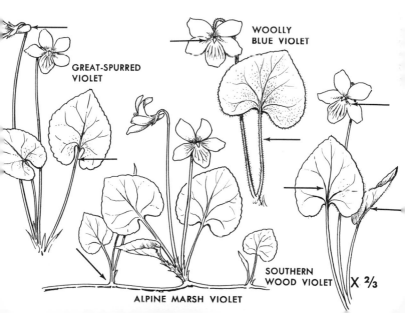

GREAT-SPURRED VIOLET

WOOLLY BLUE VIOLET

ALPINE MARSH VIOLET

SOUTHERN WOOD VIOLET

X ⅔

5 PETALS AND A SPUR: VIOLETS
HEART-SHAPED LEAVES
VIOLET FAMILY (Violaceae)
All blue violets on this page are "stemless," with flowers and leaves on separate stalks. See also p. 328.

COMMON BLUE VIOLET   *Viola papilionacea*
See also color plate, p. 318. Smooth; 2 lateral petals bearded, lower petal *longer*, unbearded; *all 3 lower petals* strongly veined. Flowers only slightly surmount leaves. 3–8 in. Damp woods, meadows. N. Dakota, s. Quebec, c. Maine south.

MARCH–JUNE

BROAD-LEAVED WOOD VIOLET   *Viola latiuscula*
Similar to *V. papilionacea* but grows in dry soil. Mature leaves wider, *purplish beneath*. Dry woods. New York, Vermont to mts. of nw. Pennsylvania, n. New Jersey.

APRIL–JUNE

MISSOURI VIOLET   *Viola missouriensis*
Similar to *V. papilionacea* but note the triangular leaf shape with outer margins often folded. Flowers paler blue, with a white center. Low woods, floodplains, creek banks. Iowa, Illinois, Indiana south.   APRIL–MAY

LE CONTE'S VIOLET   *Viola affinis*
Similar to *V. papilionacea* but *lowest petal also bearded*. Leaves *narrower*, with more tapering tips. Meadows, streambanks. Wisconsin to w. New England and south in mts.   APRIL–MAY

NORTHERN BLUE VIOLET   *Viola septentrionalis*
Similar to *V. papilionacea* but *downy* and *all 3* lower petals bearded at base. Leaves often *purplish* beneath. Open conifer woods. Canada south to Wisconsin, Michigan, New York, New England; in mts. to Virginia.   MAY–JUNE

NEW ENGLAND BLUE VIOLET   *Viola novae-angliae*
A *downy* northern violet with *3 bearded petals*, similar to *V. septentrionalis*, but leaves *narrower*, triangular, *not* purplish beneath. Petals darker, more *reddish violet*. Wet rocks, shores. Local, n. Minnesota, n. Wisconsin, n. Michigan, Ontario to n. Maine, New Brunswick.   MAY–JUNE

MARSH BLUE VIOLET   *Viola cucullata*
See also color plate, p. 318. Differs from *V. papilionacea* in having lower petal *shorter*. Lateral petals *darker toward throat;* beards *clavate* (like small clubs) not hairlike. Flower stalks longer than leafstalks. 5–10 in. Wet meadows, springs, bogs. Most of area (mts. southward).   APRIL–JUNE

NORTHERN BOG VIOLET   *Viola nephrophylla*
Similar to *V. cucullata* but more northern; *lowest petal also bearded*. Our bluest violet. Flowers do not much surmount leaves. Bogs, cool wet spots, shores. Canada south to Great Lakes, n. New York, w. and n. New England.   MAY–JULY

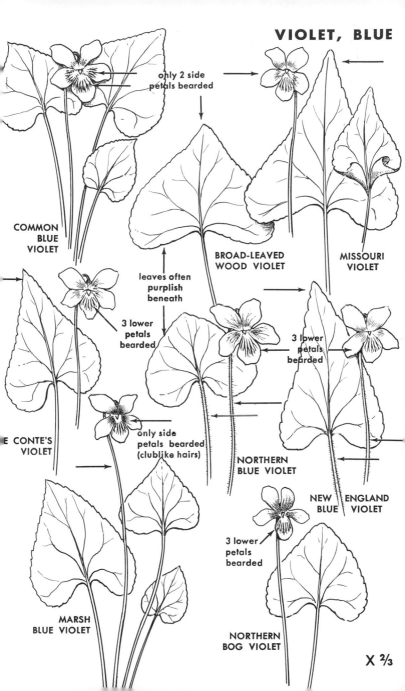

VIOLET, BLUE

only 2 side
petals bearded

COMMON
BLUE
VIOLET

BROAD-LEAVED
WOOD VIOLET

MISSOURI
VIOLET

leaves often
purplish
beneath

3 lower
petals
bearded

3 lower
petals
bearded

E CONTE'S
VIOLET

only side
petals bearded
(clublike hairs)

NORTHERN
BLUE VIOLET

NEW ENGLAND
BLUE VIOLET

3 lower
petals
bearded

MARSH
BLUE VIOLET

NORTHERN
BOG VIOLET

X ⅔

5 PETALS AND A SPUR: VIOLETS
LOBED OR ARROWHEAD LEAVES
Violet Family (Violaceae)

BIRDFOOT VIOLET   *Viola pedata*
See also color plate, p. 318. Leaves deeply segmented. A variety
is *bicolored* (upper 2 petals deep violet, 3 lower ones pale), another is uniformly colored. Upper petals flare backward; all
petals *beardless*. *Tips of orange stamens protrude conspicuously*
in center. 4–10 in. Sandy fields, slopes, sunny rocks. Minnesota, Michigan, s. Ontario, New York, Massachusetts south.
                                                  April–June
COAST VIOLET   *Viola brittoniana*
Leaves similar to *V. pedata*, but middle lobe often wider. A
form with broad uncleft leaves often grows with it. Flowers
deep reddish violet, with a conspicuous white throat, 3 lower
petals *densely bearded*. 4–8 in. Sandy or peaty soil. Coast
from s. Maine south; in south, also in mts.   April–June
PRAIRIE VIOLET   *Viola pedatifida*
Similar to *V. brittoniana* but not coastal. Flower paler; leaf
lobes *very narrow*. Prairies of Canada south to Oklahoma,
Missouri; eastward locally to n. Ohio.   April–June
EARLY BLUE or WOOD VIOLET   *Viola palmata*
Note *hairiness*. 2 side petals bearded. Woods, limestone ledges.
Minnesota, s. New Hampshire south.   April–May
THREE-LOBED VIOLET   *Viola triloba*
Hairy, similar to *V. palmata* but most leaves less deeply cut;
some 3-lobed, others heart-shaped suggesting *V. sororia* (p. 328).
All 3 lower petals bearded. Woods, limestone ledges. Illinois,
s. Indiana, Pennsylvania south.   April–May
STONE'S VIOLET (not shown)   *Viola stoneana*
Very similar to *V. triloba* (above) but comparatively *smooth*
and with longer leafstalks. Lowest petal *smooth*. Woods.
Pennsylvania, New Jersey south to Kentucky, Virginia.
                                                  April–June
ARROW-LEAVED VIOLET   *Viola sagittata*
Early leaves may be heart-shaped, later ones longer, arrowlike,
with jagged base; often purplish beneath. Open woods, prairies.
Minnesota to Massachusetts and south.   April–June
TRIANGLE-LEAVED VIOLET   *Viola emarginata*
Similar to *V. sagittata*, with narrowly triangular leaves that
usually lack the deeply jagged back-flaring basal points.
Petals often notched. Open woods, clearings. Missouri, Ohio,
New York, Massachusetts south.   March–May
NORTHERN DOWNY VIOLET   *Viola fimbriatula*
The narrowly arrow-shaped leaves are more ovate, less tri-
angular in contour than in preceding two; leaves are also *hairy*,
with much shorter leafstalks. Dry woods, clearings, fields.
Minnesota to Nova Scotia and south.   April–May

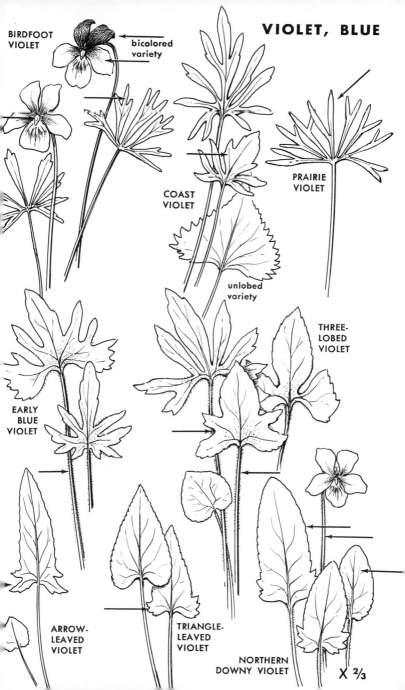

BIRDFOOT VIOLET

bicolored variety

VIOLET, BLUE

PRAIRIE VIOLET

COAST VIOLET

unlobed variety

THREE-LOBED VIOLET

EARLY BLUE VIOLET

ARROW-LEAVED VIOLET

TRIANGLE-LEAVED VIOLET

NORTHERN DOWNY VIOLET

X 2/3

5 PETALS; CURLED SPRAYS

TRUE FORGET-ME-NOT Alien   *Myosotis scorpioides*
FORGET-ME-NOT FAMILY   (Boraginaceae)
Flowers 5-petaled (¼ to ⅓ in.), *sky-blue, with yellow eye*, on 2 diverging branches (false racemes), which uncoil as flowers bloom. Stems lightly hairy, angled; leaves alternate, sessile, hairy. 6–24 in. Several other alien species in our area. Brooksides, wet places. Most of area.   MAY–OCT.

SMALLER FORGET-ME-NOT   *Myosotis laxa*
FORGET-ME-NOT FAMILY   (Boraginaceae)
Similar to True Forget-me-not but flowers smaller (⅛ in.) and paler; calyx lobes longer. Flowering branches usually with 1 or 2 leaves near base. 6–20 in. Shallow water, wet ground. Ontario to Newfoundland and south to n. Indiana, Ohio, Virginia, and in mts. to Georgia.   MAY–OCT.

MIAMI-MIST, SCORPIONWEED   *Phacelia purshii*
WATERLEAF FAMILY   (Hydrophyllaceae)
Note the *fringes* on the delicate blue petals. Leaves *pinnately cleft.* 6–20 in. Rich woods, fields. Wisconsin, Illinois, Indiana, Ohio, Pennsylvania south.   APRIL–JUNE

COMFREY Alien   *Symphytum officinale*
FORGET-ME-NOT FAMILY   (Boraginaceae)
White, cream, pink, purplish, or pale blue. See pp. 144, 292.

SMALL BUGLOSS Alien   *Lycopsis arvensis*
FORGET-ME-NOT FAMILY   (Boraginaceae)
A *bristly* plant with wavy, hairy leaves; flowers suggestive of large forget-me-nots but note the *kink* at base of the corolla. 8–18 in. Sandy soil, dry fields. Local, e. Canada to Nebraska, Ohio, Virginia; mainly in Northeast.   JUNE–SEPT.

SMALL-FLOWERED PHACELIA   *Phacelia dubia*
WATERLEAF FAMILY   (Hydrophyllaceae)
Similar to Miami-mist (above), but flowers smaller, petals *without fringes.* 5–12 in. Woods, clearings. E. Ohio, Pennsylvania, Delaware south.   APRIL–JUNE

WILD COMFREY   *Cynoglossum virginianum*
FORGET-ME-NOT FAMILY   (Boraginaceae)
In aspect somewhat like a forget-me-not, but large leaves *clasp* the hairy stem. Basal leaves stalked, forming a rosette. Fruits are small nutlets covered with spines. 1–2 ft. Open woods. Missouri, s. Illinois, Indiana, Ohio, Pennsylvania, New Jersey, sw. Connecticut south.   MAY–JUNE

SEA MERTENSIA, OYSTERLEAF   *Mertensia maritima*
FORGET-ME-NOT FAMILY   (Boraginaceae)
A seaside relative of Mertensia, *M. virginica* (p. 322), but prostrate, mat-forming, with *fleshy*, glaucous leaves *tasting of oysters.* Flowers pink, becoming blue. Beaches, rocks. Coast south to Massachusetts.   JUNE–SEPT.

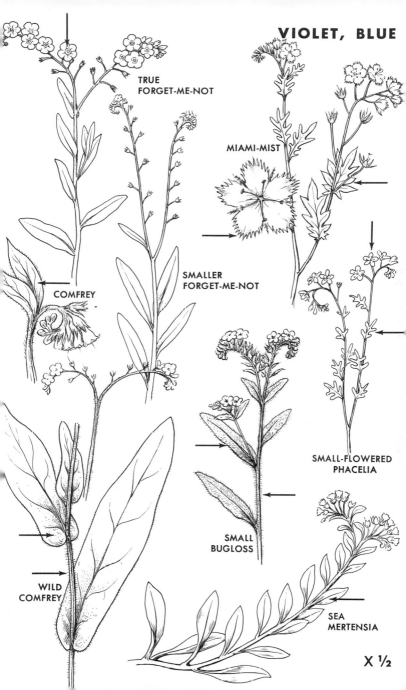

VIOLET, BLUE

TRUE
FORGET-ME-NOT

MIAMI-MIST

COMFREY

SMALLER
FORGET-ME-NOT

SMALL-FLOWERED
PHACELIA

WILD
COMFREY

SMALL
BUGLOSS

SEA
MERTENSIA

X ½

4 PETALS, SMALL FLOWERS

SPEEDWELLS   *Veronica*
Snapdragon Family   (Scrophulariaceae)
More than 20 species in our area; we show 10. Most are low,
creeping, less than 10 in., with small 4-petaled violet or blue
flowers with *2 stamens*. 3 petals are roundish; *lowest petal
smaller or narrower*. Distributed widely.   May–Sept.

1. **FLOWERS IN RACEMES**
   COMMON SPEEDWELL, *V. officinalis* (alien in part). Creep-
   ing, *hairy*. Leaves oval, toothed, narrow-based. Dry soil, fields.
   BIRD'S-EYE SPEEDWELL, *V. chamaedrys* (alien). Downy.
   Leaves ovate or heart-shaped, toothed, sessile. Roadsides.
   AMERICAN BROOKLIME, *V. americana*. Succulent, smooth.
   Leaves toothed, ovate or long-ovate, stalked. Brooks, swamps.
   WATER SPEEDWELL, *V. anagallis-aquatica* (alien in part).
   Similar to *V. americana* but leaves mostly stalkless, clasping,
   often toothless. Brooklets, ditches, shores.
   MARSH SPEEDWELL, *V. scutellata*. Note slender leaves,
   toothed or toothless. Swamps, wet places.
   LONG-LEAVED SPEEDWELL, *V. longifolia* (alien). Erect
   (to 3 ft.). Flowers violet, in a *long, tapering spikelike raceme*.
   Leaves *lanceolate*, toothed, stalked. Fields, roadsides.

2. **SINGLE FLOWERS IN LEAF AXILS**
   THYME-LEAVED SPEEDWELL, *V. serpyllifolia* (alien).
   Creeping. Leaves small, toothless, oval, short-stalked. Flowers
   pale blue with dark stripes. Grass, roadsides.
   CORN SPEEDWELL, *V. arvensis* (alien). Low (1–6 in.),
   hairy. Leaves oval, toothed; sepals *unequal*. Waste ground.
   FIELD SPEEDWELL, *V. agrestis* (alien). Similar to *V. arvensis*
   but lowest lobe of flower *white*, sepals *equal*. Roadsides, etc.
   SLENDER SPEEDWELL, *V. filiformis* (alien). Prostrate, with
   rather large blue flowers on threadlike stalks. Leaves small,
   roundish or kidney-shaped. An escape on lawns.

BLUETS   *Houstonia caerulea*
Bedstraw Family   (Rubiaceae)
Pale bluish to white, with a yellow eye. Stem leaves paired,
short, narrow. Often forms large colonies. 2–8 in. Grass,
fields. Wisconsin, Quebec, Nova Scotia south.   April–July

LARGE HOUSTONIA   *Houstonia purpurea*
Bedstraw Family   (Rubiaceae)
Leaves oval, paired, sessile, entire; 3-veined. Flowers in broad
terminal cluster; tubed, with 4 flaring lobes; pale violet to
whitish. 4–18 in. See also *H. longifolia*, p. 40. Sandy soil,
pine barrens, rocky slopes. Iowa, Illinois, s. Indiana, Ohio,
Pennsylvania, New Jersey south.   May–June

BLUE FIELD MADDER Alien   *Sherardia arvensis*
Bedstraw Family   (Rubiaceae)
A rough, prostrate, bedstrawlike plant, but flowers *bluish*.
Leaves in whorls of 4 to 6. 3–10 in. Fields.   May–Sept.

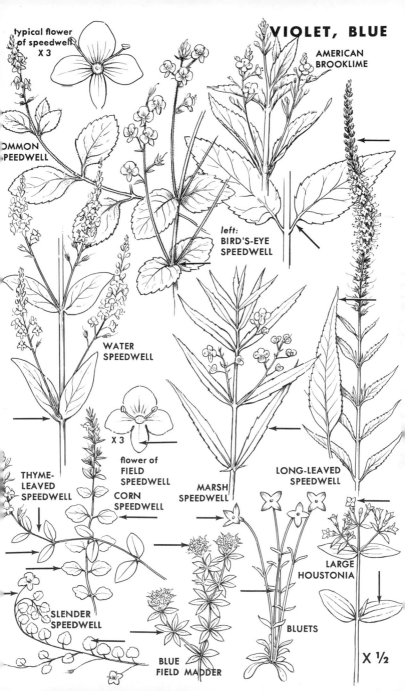

typical flower
of speedwell
X 3

VIOLET, BLUE

AMERICAN
BROOKLIME

COMMON
SPEEDWELL

left:
BIRD'S-EYE
SPEEDWELL

WATER
SPEEDWELL

X 3

flower of
FIELD
SPEEDWELL

CORN
SPEEDWELL

THYME-
LEAVED
SPEEDWELL

MARSH
SPEEDWELL

LONG-LEAVED
SPEEDWELL

SLENDER
SPEEDWELL

LARGE
HOUSTONIA

BLUE
FIELD MADDER

BLUETS

X ½

SHOWY BELL-LIKE OR TUBED FLOWERS

 PURPLE THORN-APPLE or JIMSONWEED Alien
TOMATO FAMILY (Solanaceae) *Datura stramonium* var. *tatula*
A coarse, erect, poisonous weed with pale violet, trumpet-shaped flowers 3 to 5 in. long; calyx tubular. Stem purplish. Note also the coarsely jagged leaves, spiny seedpods. There is also a white variety with a green stem (p. 12). 2–5 ft. Waste places. Local in n. U.S., commoner southward. JUNE–SEPT.

 PURPLE CLEMATIS *Clematis verticillaris*
BUTTERCUP FAMILY (Ranunculaceae)
The *4 showy mauve sepals*, downy inside and out, *do not expand fully* but remain as shown. Leaves in 3's. A rather scarce vine, climbing by tendrils. Rocky woods, slopes. Manitoba to e. Quebec and south to ne. Iowa, Wisconsin, Michigan, Ohio, W. Virginia, n. Maryland, Delaware. MAY–JUNE

 SMOOTH RUELLIA *Ruellia strepens*
ACANTHUS FAMILY (Acanthaceae)
From the leaf axils spring single lavender-blue trumpets with 5 flaring lobes. Each flower is on a stalk and is subtended by 2 small leaves. Plant essentially *smooth*. 1–3 ft. Rich woods, edges. S. Missouri, Illinois, Indiana, c. Ohio, s. Pennsylvania, c. New Jersey south. MAY–JULY

 HAIRY RUELLIA *Ruellia caroliniensis*
ACANTHUS FAMILY (Acanthaceae)
Similar to Smooth Ruellia but quite *hairy*. The flowers have *longer corolla tubes* and are *stalkless or near-stalkless* in the leaf axils. 1–2½ ft. Woods, clearings. Se. Ohio, W. Virginia, n. Maryland, s. New Jersey south. JUNE–SEPT.

 COMMON MORNING-GLORY Alien *Ipomoea purpurea*
MORNING-GLORY FAMILY (Convolvulaceae)
A twining vine; the garden morning-glory with broad *heart-shaped* leaves. Flowers purple, pink, blue, or white. Stems pubescent. Roadsides, etc. Widespread. JULY–OCT.

IVY-LEAVED MORNING-GLORY Alien *Ipomoea hederacea*
MORNING-GLORY FAMILY (Convolvulaceae)
Flowers violet-blue, white, or pink. See p. 12.

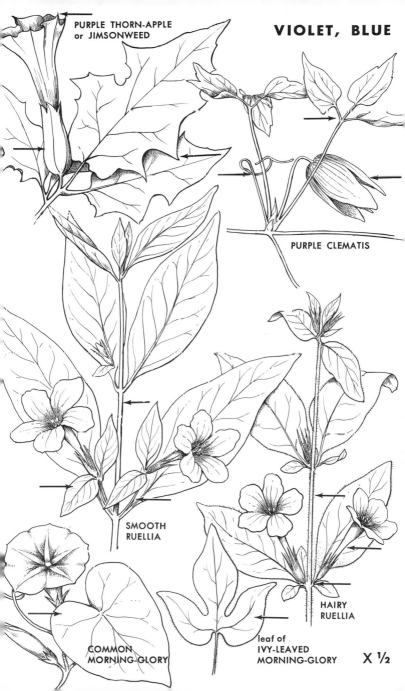

PURPLE THORN-APPLE
or JIMSONWEED

VIOLET, BLUE

PURPLE CLEMATIS

SMOOTH
RUELLIA

HAIRY
RUELLIA

COMMON
MORNING-GLORY

leaf of
IVY-LEAVED
MORNING-GLORY

X ½

BELL-LIKE FLOWERS, ETC.

BLUEBELL FAMILY (Campanulaceae)
BLUEBELL SUBFAMILY (Campanuloideae)
Note: Tall Bellflower and Venus' Looking-glass are not bell-like, but are related to the group.

HAREBELL   *Campanula rotundifolia*
Note the *wiry, hairlike stems, linear leaves*. Small *roundish basal leaves* wither early; usually absent. Bells violet-blue, nod from branch tips. 6–18 in. Meadows, grassy places, rocky slopes, alpine areas. N. Canada south to Missouri, Illinois, Indiana, Ohio, Pennsylvania, n. New Jersey.   JUNE–SEPT.

CREEPING BELLFLOWER Alien *Campanula rapunculoides*
The tapering 1-sided spikes of slender drooping bells (1 in. long) bloom from the bottom up. Flowers violet-blue, with a straight white style. Plant spreads by creeping runners. 1–3 ft. A garden escape. Roadsides, etc. S. Canada south to Missouri, Illinois, Ohio, W. Virginia, Maryland, Delaware.   JULY–SEPT.

CLUSTERED BELLFLOWER Alien   *Campanula glomerata*
The inch-long violet-blue bells are *erect and stalkless* in a *terminal cluster;* often 1 or 2 in upper leaf axils. Leaves *rounded at base.* 1–2 ft. A roadside escape. E. Canada to Minnesota, New England.   JUNE–JULY

TALL BELLFLOWER   *Campanula americana*
Does not have bells. The 5-lobed flowers are *flat*, pale blue, with a paler ring at the throat. Note the *long, curved and re-curved style.* 1½–6 ft. Rich soil, thickets, banks. Minnesota to s. Ontario, New York and south.   JUNE–AUG.

BEDSTRAW BELLFLOWER   *Campanula aparinoides*
Flowers small, *very pale blue or whitish.* Stems weak, reclining, with *short, rasping bristles* (suggesting some bedstraws). Leaves linear. 8–24 in. Damp meadows, wet spots. Minnesota to Maine and south.   JUNE–AUG.

MARSH BELLFLOWER   *Campanula uliginosa*
Similar to Bedstraw Bellflower but flowers bluer, stems stiffer, less spreading. Swamps, wet spots. Canada to Iowa, Illinois, Indiana, Ohio, e. Pennsylvania.   JUNE–AUG.

SOUTHERN HAREBELL   *Campanula divaricata*
A smooth, small-flowered species. Note the way the pale blue flowers dangle from *horizontal branchlets* in a compound panicle. Leaves toothed. 1–3 ft. Dry woods. Kentucky, W. Virginia, w. Maryland south.   JULY–SEPT.

VENUS' LOOKING-GLASS   *Specularia perfoliata*
Wandlike. Flowers violet-blue, with 5 spreading lobes, *not bell-like;* tucked *singly in axils* of *roundish, clasping* leaves. 6–30 in. *S. leptocarpa* (not shown) of prairie states has narrow leaves. Sterile fields, clearings. S. Minnesota, Wisconsin, Michigan, s. Ontario, New York, s. Maine south.   MAY–AUG.

VIOLET, BLUE

REBELL

CREEPING BELLFLOWER

CLUSTERED BELLFLOWER

TALL BELLFLOWER

BEDSTRAW BELLFLOWER

MARSH BELLFLOWER

SOUTHERN HAREBELL

VENUS' LOOKING-GLASS

X ½

LIPPED FLOWERS IN SPIKES: LOBELIAS
LEAVES ALTERNATE

BLUEBELL FAMILY (Campanulaceae)
LOBELIA SUBFAMILY (Lobelioideae)
Note the flower structure with 2 narrow lobes, or "ears,"
above, 3 wider lobes forming a lip below.

GREAT LOBELIA *Lobelia siphilitica*
See text and color plate, p. 316.

DOWNY LOBELIA *Lobelia puberula*
Finely downy. Flowers ½–¾ in. long, nearly size of those of
Great Lobelia; usually arranged along *1 side of stem;* lack dark
ribbing and inflated flower tube of Great Lobelia. Leaves
ovate, toothed. 1–3 ft. Open woods, clearings. Coastal plain.
Se. Pennsylvania, New Jersey south.   AUG.–OCT.

LONGLEAF LOBELIA *Lobelia elongata*
Flowers smaller than in above two species, deep blue. Note the
narrow sharp-toothed leaves. 2–4 ft. Wet places. Coast, Delaware south.   AUG.–OCT.

PALE-SPIKE LOBELIA *Lobelia spicata*
Flowers small, pale blue to white, in a spike (sometimes crowded)
on upper part of stem. Leaves nearly toothless, lance-shaped
or narrowly ovate. Meadows, fields, thickets. Most of our
area.   JUNE–AUG.

INDIAN-TOBACCO *Lobelia inflata*
The commonest lobelia. Flowers small, tucked singly into leaf
axils; not close together. Base of flower inflated, becoming a
swollen seedpod. Sepals long, reflexed. Leaves ovate, toothed;
stems hairy, sometimes branched. 6–30 in. Fields, roadsides,
gardens, open woods. Most of area.   JULY–OCT.

NUTTALL'S LOBELIA *Lobelia nuttallii*
Differs from Indian-tobacco in having very narrow linear stem
leaves; individual flowers stalked. Basal leaves spatulate or
oval. Flowers blue, with white center and 2 greenish spots at
base of lower lip. 8–30 in. Sandy soil. Kentucky, e. Pennsylvania, New Jersey, Long Island south.   JULY–OCT.

BROOK LOBELIA *Lobelia kalmii*
Similar to Nuttall's Lobelia but has a *wet* environment. Shorter
(4–16 in.) Upper leaves linear, basal leaves spatulate. Flowers
blue, with white center. Bogs, wet meadows, shores. Canada
south to Iowa, Illinois, Indiana, Ohio, Pennsylvania, n. New
Jersey.   JULY–SEPT.

WATER LOBELIA *Lobelia dortmanna*
Aquatic. The *thick, hollow, linear leaves* in a rosette at the base
of the plant are usually *submerged.* Flowers above water; pale
violet. 6–18 in. Pond margins. S. Canada south to Minnesota,
Wisconsin, n. Michigan, ne. Pennsylvania, n. New Jersey, Long
Island.   JULY–OCT.

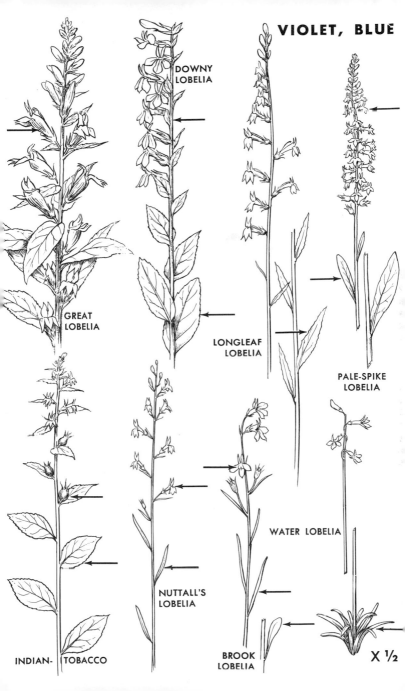

VIOLET, BLUE

DOWNY LOBELIA

GREAT LOBELIA

LONGLEAF LOBELIA

PALE-SPIKE LOBELIA

WATER LOBELIA

NUTTALL'S LOBELIA

INDIAN-TOBACCO

BROOK LOBELIA

X ½

LIPPED, TUBED FLOWERS

SNAPDRAGON FAMILY (Scrophulariaceae)

Flowers 2-lipped (2 lobes above, 3 below).

HAIRY BEARDTONGUE   *Penstemon hirsutus*
Beardtongues have a *tufted stamen* in the throat. The 17 species
in our area are often difficult to identify without recourse to
technical manuals. This species may be pink, lavender, or pale
violet. Note the *woolly stem* and the throat *nearly closed* by the
hairy tongue. 1–3 ft. Foxglove Beardtongue, *P. digitalis* (p. 58),
a *smooth* species, may be violet-tinged. Rocky woods, fields.
Wisconsin, s. Ontario, s. Quebec, Maine south.   JUNE–JULY

GRAY BEARDTONGUE   *Penstemon canescens*
Densely covered with *fine gray down*. Flowers pale violet (1–
1½ in.); throat more open than in *P. hirsutus*. 1–3 ft. Woods.
S. Indiana, Pennsylvania south; mainly in mts.   MAY–JUNE

LARGE-FLOWERED BEARDTONGUE

Penstemon grandiflorus
Note the plant's *pale, bluish, waxy look*. Flowers *very large*
(nearly 2 in.), pale violet or lavender-blue. Leaves roundish,
toothless, *clasping*. 2–4 ft. Prairies. East to Minnesota, Illinois,
sw. Missouri.   JUNE–AUG.

SQUARE-STEMMED MONKEY-FLOWER *Mimulus ringens*
The lobed violet lips suggest a face; mouth partly closed by a
2-ridged yellow palate. Flowers in pairs *on long stalks* in leaf
axils. Leaves *sessile*. Stem square-ridged. 1–3 ft. Swamps,
wet places, streamsides. Throughout.   JUNE–SEPT.

SHARP-WINGED MONKEY-FLOWER   *Mimulus alatus*
Similar to *M. ringens* but flowers *short-stalked*, leaves *well
stalked;* stem with thin "wings" along angles. Violet, pink, or
white. Swamps, wet places. S. Iowa, Illinois, s. Michigan, s.
Ontario, New York, Connecticut south.   JUNE–SEPT.

BLUE-EYED MARY   *Collinsia verna*
Note the *bicolored* flowers (upper lobes white, lower bright blue).
Middle lobe of lower lip *folded* lengthwise and concealed. 6–24
in. Rich woods, slopes. S. Wisconsin and e. Iowa east to w.
New York and south to Arkansas, Kentucky, w. Virginia.
                                                       APRIL–JUNE

KENILWORTH-IVY Alien   *Cymbalaria muralis*
Low, trailing. Note the short *spur* and roundish, ivy-shaped,
shallowly-lobed leaves. Flowers mauve, with white and yellow
lip. Stone walls, roadsides. A local garden escape.   MAY–OCT.

BLUE or OLD-FIELD TOADFLAX   *Linaria canadensis*
Superficially suggests a small lobelia (see p. 342) but note the
slender spurs. Leaves linear, shining. Flowers pale violet, with
a 2-humped white palate. Dry sandy or acid soil. Throughout.
                                                       APRIL–SEPT.

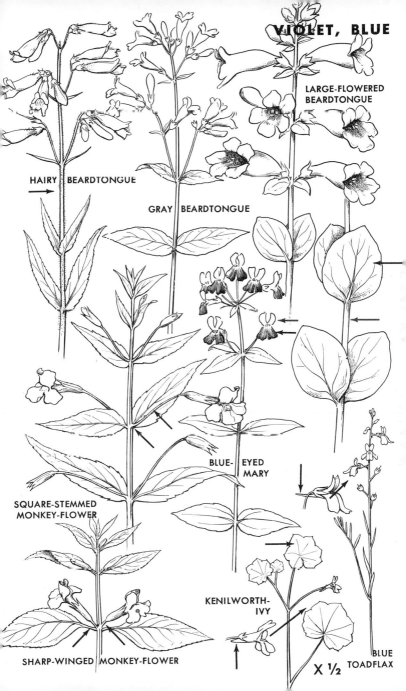

VIOLET, BLUE

LARGE-FLOWERED
BEARDTONGUE

HAIRY BEARDTONGUE

GRAY BEARDTONGUE

BLUE-EYED
MARY

SQUARE-STEMMED
MONKEY-FLOWER

KENILWORTH-
IVY

SHARP-WINGED MONKEY-FLOWER

X ½

BLUE
TOADFLAX

LIPPED, HOODED FLOWERS: SKULLCAPS
SQUARE STEMS; PAIRED LEAVES

Mint Family (Labiatae)
Flowers violet or blue (rarely pink or white).

MAD-DOG SKULLCAP *Scutellaria lateriflora*
Easily recognized because the flowers are in slender *1-sided racemes* in the *leaf axils*. 1–3 ft. Rich thickets, meadows, wet woods. Most of our area. June–Sept.

COMMON or MARSH SKULLCAP *Scutellaria epilobiifolia*
This and the next two species have *single flowers in the leaf axils*. Leaves short-stalked or stalkless, slightly toothed; longer than in the next two species. 1–3 ft. Shores, wet meadows, swampy thickets. Canada south to Missouri, Illinois, Indiana, Ohio, s. Pennsylvania, Delaware. June–Sept.

VEINED SKULLCAP *Scutellaria nervosa*
Flowers *single in leaf axils* as in Common Skullcap, but leaves shorter, wider. 6–24 in. Damp woods, thickets. S. Illinois, s. Indiana, s. Ontario, e. Pennsylvania south. May–July

SMALLER SKULLCAP *Scutellaria parvula*
Similar to Veined Skullcap but much smaller. Leaves with 2 or 3 scallops; most veins run lengthwise. 3–12 in. Limy soils. Minnesota, sw. Quebec, Maine south. May–July

SHOWY SKULLCAP *Scutellaria serrata*
Smooth. Flowers in a *terminal raceme*. Leaves large, ovate, toothed, *tapering abruptly into long stalks*. 8–24 in. Woods, banks. Appalachians; se. New York south. May–June

HAIRY SKULLCAP *Scutellaria elliptica*
Leaves similar in shape to those of Showy Skullcap, but *hairy*, broadly *scalloped*. Flowers in *branching racemes* near summit. 1–3 ft. Dry woods, thickets. Missouri, s. Ohio, Pennsylvania, n. New Jersey, se. New York south. May–July

DOWNY SKULLCAP *Scutellaria incana*
Hoary with minute whitish hairs. The inflorescence branches into several or *many racemes* of flowers. Leaves ovate, longer than those of Hairy Skullcap. 1–3½ ft. Dry woods, clearings. Iowa east to sw. New York, n. New Jersey, and south.
June–Sept.

HEART-LEAVED SKULLCAP *Scutellaria ovata*
The well-stalked, *heart-shaped* leaves are typical of this softly hairy species. Flowers blue, with whitish lower lip; in branched racemes at summit. 1–3 ft. Limy soils, woods, riverbanks. Minnesota, Wisconsin, Illinois, Indiana, Ohio, West Virginia, Maryland south. May–July

HYSSOP SKULLCAP *Scutellaria integrifolia*
Note the slender *untoothed* leaves. 6–30 in. Wood edges, clearings. Missouri, s. Ohio, s. Pennsylvania, se. New York, Connecticut south. May–July

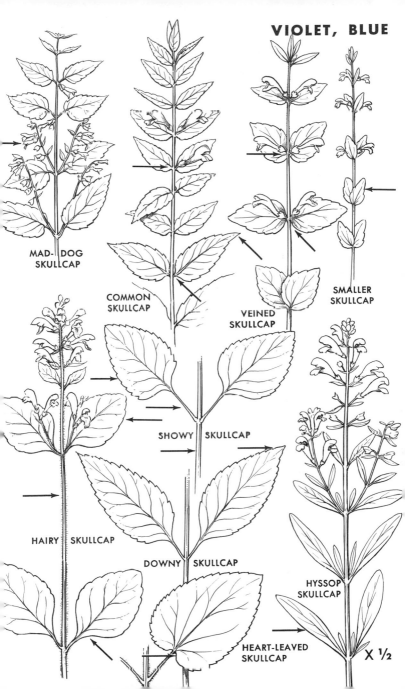

VIOLET, BLUE

MAD-DOG
SKULLCAP

COMMON
SKULLCAP

VEINED
SKULLCAP

SMALLER
SKULLCAP

SHOWY SKULLCAP

HAIRY SKULLCAP

DOWNY SKULLCAP

HYSSOP
SKULLCAP

HEART-LEAVED
SKULLCAP

X ½

SQUARE STEMS; PAIRED LEAVES: MINTS
FLOWERS IN UPPER LEAF AXILS
MINT FAMILY (Labiatae)

BLUE GIANT HYSSOP   *Agastache foeniculum*
Flowers violet-blue, in axils of bracts, forming an interrupted spike. *2 pairs of protruding stamens*, 1 pair curving upward, the other downward, *crossing*. Leaves with *odor of anise;* white-downy beneath. 2–4 ft. Thickets, prairies, dry ground. Prairie states; locally eastward.   JUNE–SEPT.

SPEARMINT Alien   *Mentha spicata*
Resembles Peppermint (p. 350) but leaves sessile, or nearly so; odor characteristic. Flowers pale violet or pink; stamens protruding. 10–20 in. Wet places. Throughout.   JUNE–OCT.

WILD MINT   *Mentha arvensis*
Note the strong mint odor. Downy or hairy. Flowers in leaf axils; pale violet, lavender, or white; tiny, bell-shaped. 6–24 in. Damp soil, shores. Canada, n. U.S.   JULY–SEPT.

WATER MINT Alien   *Mentha aquatica*
Similar to Spearmint, Peppermint, but flower head wider; leaves *round-ovate*, often purplish. Flowers pale lavender. 18–30 in. Wet places. Nova Scotia to Delaware.   AUG.–OCT.

BLUECURLS   *Trichostema dichotomum*
The *deeply curled, blue-stalked stamens* are distinctive (see inset). Flowers with 4 lobes above, a longer lobe below. Plant sticky, leaves toothless. 4–30 in. Dry open woods, clearings. Michigan to s. Maine and south. *T. setaceum* (not shown), more southerly, has narrow, single-nerved leaves.   AUG.–OCT.

AMERICAN PENNYROYAL   *Hedeoma pulegioides*
Very aromatic. Soft-hairy. Flowers pale violet or bluish in tufts in leaf axils. Calyx with 3 short teeth above, 2 long curved teeth below. 6–18 in. Dry fields. Minnesota to s. Quebec, Nova Scotia, and south.   JULY–SEPT.

HYSSOP Alien   *Hyssopus officinalis*
Note the narrow, stalkless, toothless leaves. Flowers pale violet or purple, erect, clustered in upper leaf axils, often forming spike; stamens protrude. 1–2 ft. Dry soil, roadsides. Minnesota, Ontario, s. New England south.   JULY–OCT.

FALSE PENNYROYAL   *Isanthus brachiatus*
Clammy. Leaves sessile, toothless, linear-veined. Flowers few, small, bluish; on stalks in leaf axils. 6–20 in. Dry soil. Minnesota, s. Quebec, Nova Scotia south.   JULY–SEPT.

GILL-OVER-THE-GROUND, GROUND-IVY
Alien   *Glechoma hederacea*
A creeping, ivy-like plant with scalloped roundish or kidney-shaped leaves; often purplish. Flowers violet, in whorls in leaf axils. Roadsides, lawns, shady spots. Se. Canada south locally to Missouri, Virginia.   APRIL–JULY

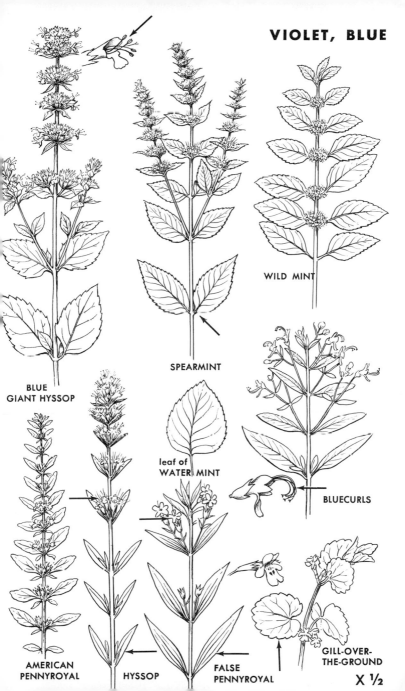

VIOLET, BLUE

WILD MINT

SPEARMINT

BLUE
GIANT HYSSOP

leaf of
WATER MINT

BLUECURLS

AMERICAN
PENNYROYAL

HYSSOP

FALSE
PENNYROYAL

GILL-OVER-
THE-GROUND

X ½

DOWNY WOOD-MINT *Blephilia ciliata*
Flowers blue-purple; in whorls separated by a row of fringed, colored bracts. Stem leaves almost sessile, narrowed at base, whitish-downy beneath. 1–3 ft. Dry woods, thickets. Wisconsin to Vermont and south. June–Aug.

HAIRY WOOD-MINT (not shown) *Blephilia hirsuta*
Similar to Downy Wood-mint, but *hairy*. Leaves *long-stalked*. Moist shade. Minnesota, Quebec, and south. May–Sept.

HEAL-ALL, SELFHEAL Alien *Prunella vulgaris*
Low or creeping, with ovate, slightly toothed or toothless leaves. Flowers violet, hooded, lower lip fringed; crowded among bracts in a square or oblong head. 3–12 in. Roadsides, lawns, waste ground. Throughout. May–Sept.

BUGLE Alien *Ajuga reptans*
Low, creeping by leafy runners. Leaves hairless; often bronze or purplish, especially beneath. Flowers powder-blue, with short upper lip; in leafy spike (uppermost leaves shorter than flowers). 4–8 in. Fields, roadsides. Wisconsin to Gulf of St. Lawrence; south to Ohio, Pennsylvania. May–July

ERECT BUGLE Alien (not shown) *Ajuga genevensis*
Similar to *A. reptans*, but lacking runners; stem much more downy. 4–8 in. Fields, roadsides. Ontario south to Illinois, Ohio, Pennsylvania. May–July

LYRE-LEAVED SAGE *Salvia lyrata*
Leaves mostly in basal rosette, *irregularly cleft*. Flowers blue or violet (about 1 in.) in interrupted spike. Sandy woods, clearings. Missouri, Illinois, Indiana, Ohio, Pennsylvania, se. New York, sw. Connecticut south. April–June

EUROPEAN HORSEMINT Alien *Mentha longifolia*
Similar to Spearmint (p. 348) with sessile or near-sessile leaves, but coarser and hoarier; *hairy;* leaves longer, white-woolly beneath; odor less pungent. 1–2½ ft. Roadsides, thickets. Indiana to Massachusetts; south to Missouri, Virginia.
July–Sept.

PEPPERMINT Alien *Mentha piperita*
Smooth, branching; stems purplish. Note the fragrance and *hot taste* of chewed leaves. Flowers in a short *or interrupted spike*, pale violet or pink-purple. 1½–3 ft. Shores, wet meadows, roadsides. Throughout. July–Sept.

CATNIP Alien *Nepeta cataria*
Note the stalked, jagged, arrow-shaped leaves; whitish beneath. Flowers crowded; pale violet or white, purple-dotted. 6–24 in. Waste places. Throughout. June–Sept.

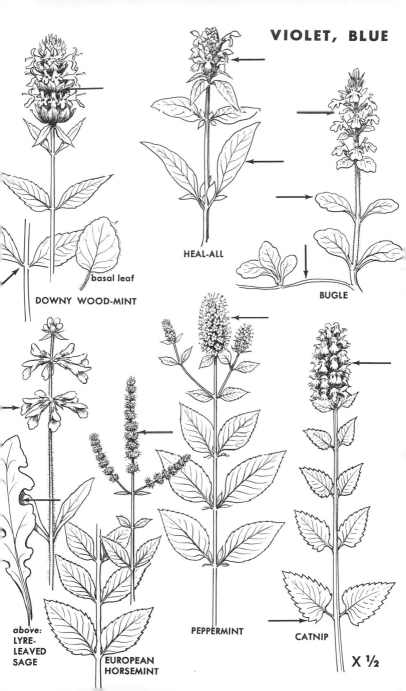

VIOLET, BLUE

HEAL-ALL

basal leaf

DOWNY WOOD-MINT

BUGLE

above:
LYRE-
LEAVED
SAGE

EUROPEAN
HORSEMINT

PEPPERMINT

CATNIP

X ½

PEALIKE FLOWERS

PEA FAMILY (Leguminosae)
See also pink and lavender species on p. 252.

1. LEAVES PINNATE (leaflets in opposing rows)

COW or TUFTED VETCH Alien   *Vicia cracca*
Finely downy. Flowers many, blue-violet, on long-stalked *1-sided* spikes. Leaves with 8 to 12 pairs of leaflets and terminating in a tendril. 2–3 ft. Fields, thickets. S. Canada south to Illinois, Michigan, Virginia.   MAY–AUG.
HAIRY VETCH Alien (not shown)   *Vicia villosa*
Hairier than *V. cracca;* 6 to 8 pairs of leaflets. Flowers usually *bicolored* (blue and white). Fields.   MAY–OCT.
PURPLE VETCH (not shown)   *Vicia americana*
Similar to *V. cracca* but *smooth.* See p. 252.
LEADPLANT   *Amorpha canescens*
Note the *white hairiness* of the numerous leaflets. Flowers in dense violet spike. 20–40 in. Prairies. Saskatchewan to Michigan; south to Arkansas, Illinois, Indiana.   JUNE–AUG.
BEACH PEA   *Lathyrus japonicus*
Pink-lavender to violet. See p. 252.

2. LEAFLETS CLOVERLIKE, IN 3's (or 5's)

SILVERLEAF SCURF-PEA   *Psoralea argophylla*
Note the *silky white hairs* that cover the 3 to 5 leaflets. Flowers dark blue. 1–2 ft. Prairie states.   JUNE–AUG.
SAMPSON'S SNAKEROOT   *Psoralea psoralioides*
Leaflets in 3's; long (2–3 in.) and narrow. Flowers blue-purple, in slender spikes above leaves. 1–3 ft. Prairies, open woods. Kansas to Virginia and south.   MAY–JULY
SAINFOIN   *Psoralea onobrychis*
Smooth, similar to *P. psoralioides* but note wider leaflets. Flowers blue, in a spike that does not usually rise above the leaves. 3–5 ft. Prairies, open woods. Iowa to Ohio and south to Missouri, Kentucky, w. Virginia.   JUNE–JULY
ALFALFA, LUCERNE Alien   *Medicago sativa*
Low, often prostrate; leaves cloverlike. Flowers ¼ to ½ in. long, blue to violet, in short spikes; stalks shorter than calyx tube. Seedpods twist spirally. 1–1½ ft. Fields. Cultivated, but often a roadside escape.   MAY–OCT.
BLUE FALSE INDIGO   *Baptisia australis*
Large cloverlike leaves (to 3 in.); leaflets wider toward tips. Flowers large (1 in.), dark blue or violet, in erect racemes. 3–5 ft. Woods, thickets. S. Indiana, W. Virginia, Pennsylvania south. Introduced northward.   MAY–JUNE
BUTTERFLY PEA   *Clitoria mariana*
Low, smooth, twining by tendrils. Flowers *very large* (nearly 2 in.), pale blue, suggesting garden Sweet Pea. Leaflets in 3's (1–2 in.). 1–3 ft. Dry soil. Iowa, s. Illinois, s. Indiana, s. Ohio, s. New York south.   JUNE–AUG.

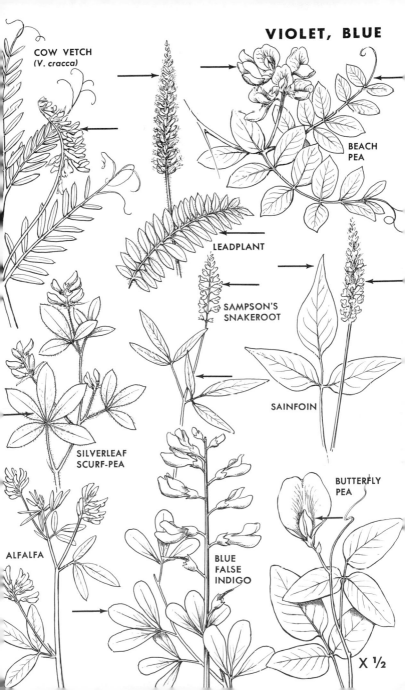

VIOLET, BLUE

COW VETCH
(V. cracca)

BEACH
PEA

LEADPLANT

SAMPSON'S
SNAKEROOT

SAINFOIN

SILVERLEAF
SCURF-PEA

BUTTERFLY
PEA

ALFALFA

BLUE
FALSE
INDIGO

X ½

ASTERS
ARROWHEAD- OR HEART-SHAPED LEAVES
Composite or Daisy Family (Compositae)

LARGE-LEAVED ASTER *Aster macrophyllus*
Basal leaves *very large* (4–8 in. wide); heart-shaped, rough; often with a broad basal notch. Upper leaves small, ovate, sessile. Stems purplish. Rays violet (or white); disk becomes reddish; floral bracts downy, with broad tips; flowering branches *sticky* with minute glands. 1–5 ft. Woods, clearings. Minnesota to maritime Canada and south to Illinois, Indiana, Ohio, Maryland; in mts. to N. Carolina. Aug.–Sept.

HEART-LEAVED ASTER *Aster cordifolius*
Leaves sharp-toothed, broadly heart-shaped, often deeply notched at base; most leafstalks slender. Stem smooth, much branched. Flower heads small (⅝ in.), in dense clusters; rays pale blue-violet or white; disk turns red early; floral bracts smooth, narrow, blunt. Variable. 1–4 ft. Open woods, clearings. S. Canada, n. U.S., and south in mts. Aug.–Oct.

ARROW-LEAVED ASTER *Aster sagittifolius*
The *narrow, toothed, arrowhead-shaped leaves* are on *flat, winged stalks*. Stem smooth. Rays pale blue, lavender, or white; floral bracts very narrow, smooth. 2–5 ft. Dry open woods, clearings. N. Dakota east to Vermont and south. Aug.–Oct.

LOWRIE'S ASTER *Aster lowrieanus*
Variable, leaves often heart-shaped; most typically with flat, winged petioles. Note the *greasy feel* of the smooth leaves. Flowers pale blue or white; in open panicles or erect racemes. Woodlands. S. Michigan, sw. Ontario to Connecticut and south in mts. Sept.–Oct.

SHORT'S ASTER *Aster shortii*
Leaves toothless (or few-toothed), *narrowly heart-shaped*, on wiry stalks. Stem smooth. Flower panicle leafy-bracted. Rays pale blue-violet, pinkish, or white; floral bracts finely pubescent. 2–4 ft. Wood edges, slopes. E. Iowa, Wisconsin to w. Pennsylvania. Aug.–Oct.

WAVY-LEAVED ASTER *Aster undulatus*
Note the pale hoary look and extraordinary winged leafstalks, which dilate into *lobes clasping the stem*. Leaves rough; wavy-edged or slightly toothed. Rays pale blue-violet; bracts downy. 1–3 ft. Dry woods, clearings. Minnesota, s. Ontario, New England, Nova Scotia south. Aug.–Nov.

AZURE ASTER *Aster azureus*
Leaves rough, mostly toothless; lower ones long-arrowhead-shaped, *narrowing* into long stalks; basal leaves may be slightly indented at base. Rays bright blue or violet, floral bracts smooth; flowering branches with many tiny leafy bracts. 1–4 ft. Wood edges, fields, prairies. Minnesota east to s. Ontario, w. New York, and south. Aug.–Oct.

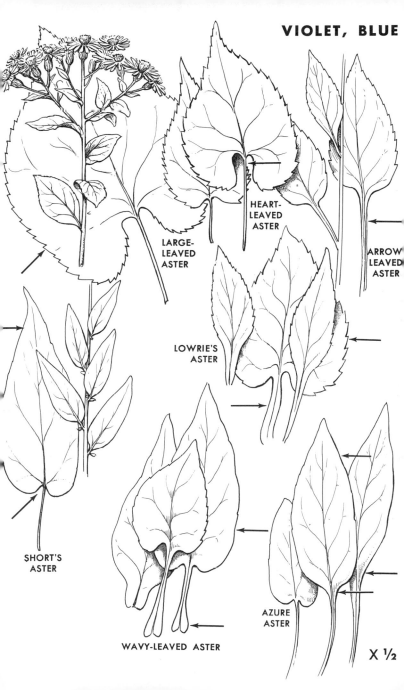

VIOLET, BLUE

LARGE-LEAVED ASTER

HEART-LEAVED ASTER

ARROW LEAVED ASTER

LOWRIE'S ASTER

SHORT'S ASTER

WAVY-LEAVED ASTER

AZURE ASTER

X ½

ASTERS
LEAVES CLASPING STEM

Composite or Daisy Family (Compositae)

1. LEAVES MOSTLY TOOTHLESS

NEW ENGLAND ASTER *Aster novae-angliae*
Our most showy wild aster, *deeper violet* than the others; rarely rose-colored. Leaves *lanceolate, crowded*, toothless, basal lobes clasping *hairy* stem. Rays *numerous* (45–100). Floral bracts sticky. 3–7 ft. Thickets, meadows, wet spots; often cultivated. Saskatchewan, Quebec, Maine south (mostly in uplands).
Aug.–Oct.

SMOOTH ASTER *Aster laevis*
Smooth, with a pale glaucous bloom. Leaves mostly toothless, thick, stiffish, clasping (lower leaves may have a few teeth and a winged stalk). 1–3 ft. Dry soil, wood edges. Saskatchewan to Maine and south. Aug.–Oct.

LATE PURPLE ASTER *Aster patens*
Lobes of relatively *short*, ovate-oblong, toothless leaves nearly encircle *hairy* stem. Flowers mostly single at ends of slender branchlets; rays 15 to 25, deep blue-violet, rarely pink. Floral bracts sticky, rough; tips spreading. 1–3 ft. Dry open woods, clearings. Minnesota to Maine and south. Aug.–Oct.

CROOKED-STEMMED ASTER *Aster prenanthoides*
Note the smooth *zigzag* stem and the clasping leaves, *narrowed and toothless below the middle*. Rays pale violet; floral bracts narrow, translucent. 1–3 ft. Wood edges, banks, wet thickets. Minnesota to w. Massachusetts; south to Iowa, Kentucky, Virginia, Delaware. Aug.–Oct.

2. LEAVES MOSTLY TOOTHED

PURPLE-STEMMED ASTER *Aster puniceus*
Note *bristly purplish stems* in combination with rough, usually toothed leaves that clasp stem. Variable (may occasionally be toothless or have a smooth green stem!). Rays light violet or violet-blue. 2–7 ft. Swamps, wet thickets. Manitoba, Ontario, Newfoundland south to Ohio and through mt. states to Georgia.
Aug.–Nov.

NEW YORK ASTER *Aster novae-belgii*
Deep violet, similar in color to New England Aster (above) but stem nearly *smooth* or only slightly downy. Leaves *narrowly lanceolate*, toothed (or not), smooth, not deeply clasping. Floral bracts reflexed. 1–4 ft. Meadows, shores, wet spots. Mainly along seaboard; Newfoundland south. July–Oct.

3. HEART-SHAPED LEAVES

WAVY-LEAVED ASTER (not shown) *Aster undulatus*
See text and illustration, p. 354.

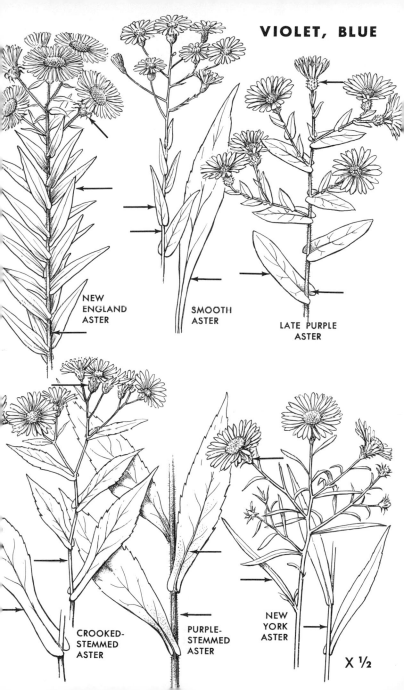

VIOLET, BLUE

NEW
ENGLAND
ASTER

SMOOTH
ASTER

LATE PURPLE
ASTER

CROOKED-
STEMMED
ASTER

PURPLE-
STEMMED
ASTER

NEW
YORK
ASTER

X ½

ASTERS
LEAVES SESSILE, NOT STRONGLY CLASPING
COMPOSITE OR DAISY FAMILY (Compositae)

SHOWY ASTER *Aster spectabilis*
A showy, rather short coastal species; bright violet-purple. Note the *long-stalked, lanceolate,* usually toothless *basal leaves.* 6–24 in. Sandy soil, pine barrens near coast. E. Massachusetts to Maryland. AUG.–OCT.

EASTERN SILVERY ASTER *Aster concolor*
Slender, *wandlike,* smooth; leaves *silky;* flowers in a *narrow raceme.* Rays lilac or blue. Leaves *numerous, oblong, ascending;* sessile, only slightly clasping. 1–2 ft. Sandy soil, pine barrens. Massachusetts south. SEPT.–OCT.

AROMATIC ASTER *Aster oblongifolius*
Low, stiff, bushy, with *hairy or sticky stems;* rough, rigid, toothless leaves. Rays rich violet; floral bracts *sticky, reflexed.* 1–2 ft. Dry open ground, prairies, limestone banks. Minnesota east to Pennsylvania and south. SEPT.–OCT.

WESTERN SILVERY ASTER *Aster sericeus*
Leaves *silvery silky;* similar to *A. concolor* (above) but note different range. Inflorescence more branching; flowers larger, floral bracts spreading. 1–2 ft. Dry open places. Minnesota to Missouri, Illinois. AUG.–SEPT.

WILLOW ASTER *Aster praealtus*
Under a hand glass note the *network (reticulation)* of *small veins* on the underside of the slightly toothed leaves. Flowers small, violet, rarely white. 2–5 ft. Meadows, prairies, thickets. Manitoba to Massachusetts and south to Missouri, Kentucky, W. Virginia, Maryland. AUG.–OCT.

ROUGH-LEAVED ASTER *Aster radula*
Leaves *toothed,* rough, *wrinkled and veiny;* sessile. Stem smooth. Rays pale violet; flower bracts slightly recurved. 1–3 ft. Swamps, wet woods. E. Canada south to Pennsylvania, Virginia (mts.), Delaware. JULY–SEPT.

PRAIRIE ASTER *Aster turbinellus*
Smooth, with lanceolate leaves tapering at each end. Flower heads in open panicles; solitary at tips of branchlets, which have *many small bractlets.* Rays violet; involucre top-shaped. Dry prairies, open woods. Nebraska to Illinois and south. SEPT.–OCT.

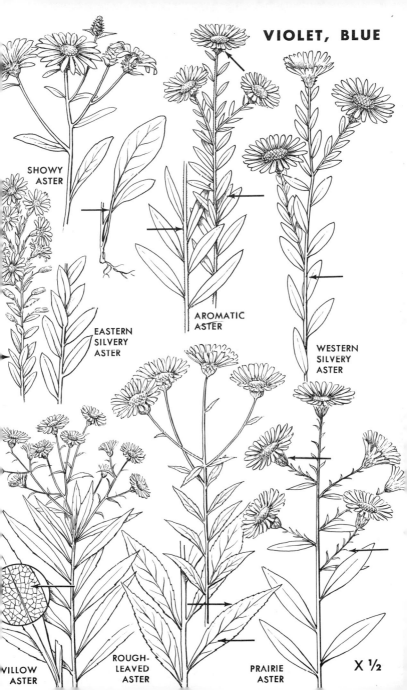

VIOLET, BLUE

SHOWY
ASTER

EASTERN
SILVERY
ASTER

AROMATIC
ASTER

WESTERN
SILVERY
ASTER

WILLOW
ASTER

ROUGH-
LEAVED
ASTER

PRAIRIE
ASTER

X ½

ASTERS
LEAVES LINEAR
COMPOSITE OR DAISY FAMILY (Compositae)

BUSHY ASTER *Aster dumosus*
Smoothish, bushy, broadly branched. Flowering branches with *many tiny bractlike leaves*. Main leaves linear, narrow, spreading, or reflexed. Flowers small; rays pale blue-lavender to white. 1–3 ft. Sandy soil. Mainly coastal from Massachusetts south; local in Great Lakes area. AUG.–OCT.

SOUTHERN ASTER *Aster hemisphericus*
A smooth southern species with thick, hard, linear leaves; midrib prominent beneath. Flowers deep violet, on stalks in leaf axils; pappus tawny or reddish. Sandy soil, open woods, prairies. S. U.S. north to Missouri, N. Carolina. AUG.–OCT.

BOG ASTER *Aster nemoralis*
Flower heads large (1–1½ in.), *solitary* or several on slender stalks. Rays light violet-purple; floral bracts very narrow, purple-tinged. Leaves *very numerous*, narrow, tapering at both ends, sessile, toothless. *Spreads by runners.* 6–24 in. Acid bogs, peat. Hudson Bay, Newfoundland south to n. Michigan, n. New York, New Jersey. AUG.–SEPT.

STIFF ASTER *Aster linariifolius*
Note the numerous, *rigid, 1-nerved, needlelike leaves.* Stems stiff, in tussocks; flower heads in small cluster or solitary. Rays light blue-violet. 6–20 in. Dry rocky soil, ledges. Minnesota to New Brunswick and south. SEPT.–OCT.

RUSH ASTER *Aster junciformis*
Stem very slender, smooth; leaves *grasslike, rough-margined.* Rays violet to white; floral bracts *bristly, spreading.* 1–3 ft. Bogs, swamps. Canada south to Iowa, Wisconsin, n. Indiana, Ohio, n. Pennsylvania, n. New Jersey. JUNE–SEPT.

PERENNIAL SALT-MARSH ASTER *Aster tenuifolius*
Leaves *extremely slender, fleshy.* Flower heads ½ *to 1 in. across;* pale lilac or white. Pappus *tawny.* 1–2 ft. Salt marshes. Coast, N. Hampshire south. AUG.–OCT.

ANNUAL SALT-MARSH ASTER *Aster subulatus*
Similar to *A. tenuifolius* but *rays very short,* hardly exceeding the *white* pappus. 6–30 in. Salt marshes. Coast, New Brunswick, s. Maine south; very local inland. JULY–OCT.

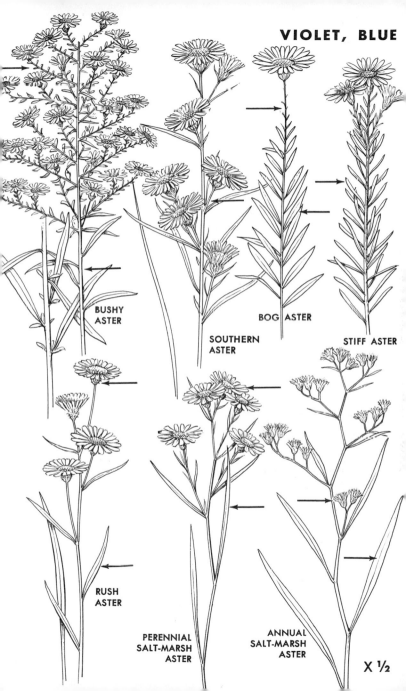

VIOLET, BLUE

BUSHY
ASTER

SOUTHERN
ASTER

BOG ASTER

STIFF ASTER

RUSH
ASTER

PERENNIAL
SALT-MARSH
ASTER

ANNUAL
SALT-MARSH
ASTER

X ½

ASTERLIKE FLOWERS
Composite or Daisy Family (Compositae)

BLUE LETTUCES *Lactuca*
Plants of the genus *Lactuca* are tall and leafy, with loose panicles
of many small flowers that may be blue, yellow (often drying
to blue), or white. Much variation; critical identification often
highly technical. Of the blue species we show 3: (1) *L. floridana*
has a loose panicle of many small (½ in.) flowers; sometimes
white. Pappus (hairs or bristles that replace calyx) *white*.
Leaves usually deeply lobed, dandelionlike. There is an unlobed variety (*villosa*). 3–7 ft. Moist thickets, woods. Minnesota, Illinois, Indiana, s. New York, se. Massachusetts south.
(2) *L. biennis* is often taller (to 15 ft.), very leafy, with a narrower, more crowded inflorescence. Pappus *brown*. Damp
thickets. S. Canada south to Iowa, N. Carolina. (3) *L. pulchella*, more western, is pale or glaucous, with showy flowers
that are larger and fewer than in above two. Leaves more
narrowly lobed or unlobed. Prairies, riverbanks. W. U.S. east
to Michigan, Missouri. July–Oct.

NEW YORK IRONWEED *Vernonia noveboracensis*
Ironweeds are rayless composites on the indeterminate borderline between red-purple and violet-blue. Therefore we are re-
peating them in both the pink–red and the violet–blue sections.
See p. 298 for text of this species and *V. altissima*.

BACHELOR'S-BUTTON, CORNFLOWER *Centaurea cyanus*
Alien
Usually *deep bright blue*, but also may be pink or white. As in
the closely related knapweeds (*Centaurea*), which have flower
heads of similar form, the marginal florets are larger and simulate rays. The grooved stem and linear leaves are cottony.
1–2 ft. Roadsides; a garden escape. July–Sept.

ROBIN-PLANTAIN *Erigeron pulchellus*
One of the fleabanes (*Erigeron*). Very soft-hairy. Flower heads
few (1–1½ in.) Rays numerous, pale violet to pale lilac or
magenta. Disk large. Basal leaves well stalked, broad toward
tip, bluntly toothed. Spreads by runners, often forms colonies.
6–16 in. Open woods, fields. Minnesota, s. Ontario, s. Quebec,
s. Maine south. See also other fleabanes, pp. 88, 94 (white),
p. 308 (pink). April–June

CHICORY Alien *Cichorium intybus*
Clear-blue *stalkless flowers* (1½ in.) hug the *rigid, nearly naked
stem*. Rays blue (often white, rarely pink), square-tipped, and
fringed; closed by noon. Basal leaves dandelionlike. To 4 ft.
Roadsides, waste places. Widespread. June–Oct.

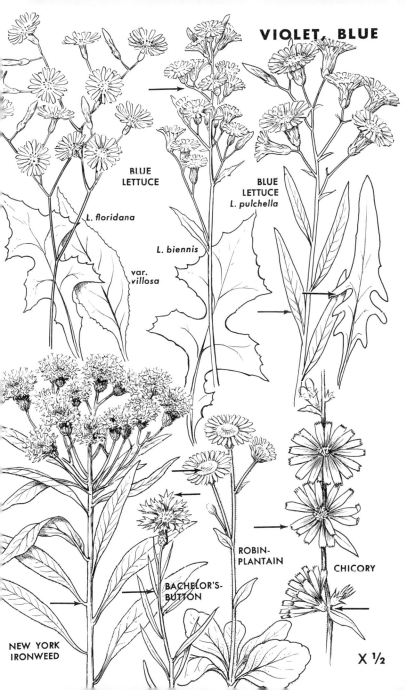

VIOLET, BLUE

BLUE
LETTUCE

L. floridana

var.
villosa

L. biennis

BLUE
LETTUCE
L. pulchella

NEW YORK
IRONWEED

BACHELOR'S-
BUTTON

ROBIN-
PLANTAIN

CHICORY

X ½

Green and
Brown Flowers

Some flowers, such as Jack-in-the-pulpit, may be either green or brown — or both. We have tried to separate green flowers (which start on the next page) from brown flowers (which start on page 388). However, there is some repetition — Blue Cohosh, Jack-in-the-pulpit, Skunk Cabbage, Early Meadow-rue, Feverwort — and also some unavoidable overlap (pages 380 and 384).

MISCELLANEOUS GREEN FLOWERS

GREEN VIOLET   *Hybanthus concolor*
VIOLET FAMILY   (Violaceae)
Hardly recognizable as a violet except for the *clublike pistil*,
distinctive of the family. Flowers small, green, drooping singly
from the leaf axils. Plant coarse and somewhat downy. 1–3 ft.
Rich woods, bottomlands. Wisconsin, Michigan, s. Ontario,
New York, Connecticut south.   APRIL–JUNE

TOADSHADE, SESSILE TRILLIUM   *Trillium sessile*
LILY FAMILY   (Liliaceae)
Maroon or yellowish green. Trilliums have leaves, petals, and
sepals in whorls of 3. This species has *sessile* (stalkless) flowers
with *erect petals* and *erect or slightly spreading sepals*. 4–12 in.
Prairie Trillium (p. 240; Iowa to Ohio and south) is similar but
leaves *with petioles* and sepals *recurved* or drooping. Woods.
Missouri, Illinois, Indiana, Ohio, w. New York, Pennsylvania
south.   APRIL–JUNE

GINSENG   *Panax quinquefolius*
GINSENG FAMILY   (Araliaceae)
Terminating a low stem are 3 long-stalked leaves, each divided
horse-chestnut-like into 5 toothed leaflets. Flowers in a small
rounded cluster on a slender stalk in the leaf axil; pale yellow-
green, often with odor of Lily-of-the-valley. Berries red. 8–16
in. See Dwarf Ginseng (white), p. 52. Rich woods. Minnesota
to Quebec and south.   JULY–AUG.

BEGGAR-TICKS, STICKTIGHT   *Bidens frondosa*
COMPOSITE FAMILY   (Compositae)
Dull yellow or greenish. See p. 168.

CROSS-LEAVED or MARSH MILKWORT *Polygala cruciata*
MILKWORT FAMILY   (Polygalaceae)
White, purplish, or greenish. See p. 244.

BLUE COHOSH   *Caulophyllum thalictroides*
BARBERRY FAMILY   (Berberidaceae)
The clusters of 6-pointed flowers, yellow-green to brown, are
replaced later by deep blue berries. Shape and arrangement of
leaflets suggest meadow-rue. Young plants may have a waxy
whitish bloom. 1–3 ft. Rich woods. S. Canada south to
Missouri, Tennessee; in mts. to S. Carolina.   APRIL–JUNE

WHORLED MILKWORT   *Polygala verticillata*
MILKWORT FAMILY   (Polygalaceae)
Whitish, pinkish, purplish-tinged, or greenish. See p. 244.

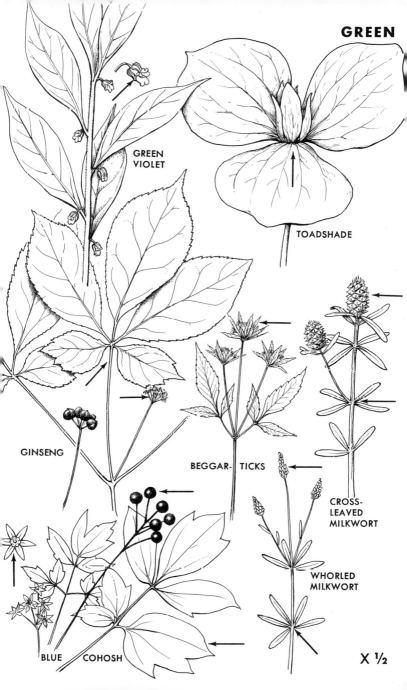

GREEN

GREEN
VIOLET

TOADSHADE

GINSENG

BEGGAR-TICKS

CROSS-
LEAVED
MILKWORT

WHORLED
MILKWORT

BLUE COHOSH

X ½

HOODED FLORAL LEAF (SPATHE)*
ENFOLDING CLUBLIKE SPADIX
ARUM FAMILY (Araceae)
*Note: Spathe is lacking in Sweetflag

JACK-IN-THE-PULPIT *Arisaema*
The flaplike spathe is green or purplish brown, often striped, and curves gracefully over the club-shaped spadix (the "Jack" or preacher in his canopied pulpit). Flowers tiny, at base of spadix; staminate and pistillate flowers often on separate plants. Leaves 1 or 2, long-stalked, 3-parted. Fruit a cluster of scarlet berries. 1–3 ft. There are variations, which some authorities consider as varieties of a single species (*A. triphyllum*); others recognize 3 species: (1) WOODLAND JACK-IN-THE-PULPIT, *A. atrorubens*. Woods and swamps, most of our area. Usually 2 leaves (each with 3 parts), gray-green beneath. (2) SWAMP OR SMALL JACK-IN-THE-PULPIT, *A. triphyllum* (not shown). Wet soil of coastal plain and Piedmont from s. New England south. Usually smaller, with a single 3-part leaf, bright green beneath. Spathe sometimes black inside. (3) INDIAN-TURNIP OR NORTHERN JACK-IN-THE-PULPIT, *A. stewardsonii* (not shown). Swamps, bogs; e. Canada and south in Appalachians. Tube of spathe corrugated with white ridges.
APRIL–JUNE

SKUNK CABBAGE *Symplocarpus foetidus*
The sheathing, shell-like spathe, mottled and varying from green to purple-brown, envelops the heavy rounded spadix, on which are borne flowers containing both stamens and pistils. The broad leaves, which appear after the flowers, are at first coiled, later become very large and have a *foetid odor* when crushed. 1–3 ft. Wet soil in woods and in open swamps. S. Canada, n. U.S., and south in mts. FEB.–APRIL

SWEETFLAG, CALAMUS *Acorus calamus*
The *tapering, fingerlike, yellow-green spadix* juts at an angle from the side of the 2-edged stem. There is *no spathe*. The bladelike stem that bears the spathe resembles the rigid irislike leaves. 1–4 ft. Streambanks and pond edges, shores, swamps. Most of our area. MAY–AUG.

ARROW ARUM, TUCKAHOE *Peltandra virginica*
The slender spadix is almost concealed by the *long* (4–7 in.) *erect, pointed spathe*. Leaves large, *arrow-shaped*. Fruit a cluster of green berries. 12–18 in. Swamps, wet spots. S. Ontario, sw. Quebec, New England south. MAY–JULY

GREEN DRAGON, DRAGON ARUM *Arisaema dracontium*
In this species the 4- to 8-in. spadix *far exceeds* the narrow pointed spathe. Leaf divided into 5 to 15 pointed segments. 1–4 ft. Rich woods, streambanks. Local, Wisconsin, Michigan, s. Ontario, sw. Quebec, Vermont south. MAY–JUNE

GREEN

JACK-IN-THE-PULPIT
(A. atrorubens)

SKUNK CABBAGE

SWEETFLAG

ARROW ARUM

GREEN DRAGON

X ½

6-PART FLOWERS; LENGTHWISE LEAF VEINS

Lily Family (Liliaceae)

FALSE HELLEBORE, INDIAN POKE   *Veratrum viride*
The large, clasping, *heavily ribbed* leaves are conspicuous in early spring. Flowers star-shaped, in large clusters (8–20 in.), yellow-green at first, dull green later. 2–8 ft. Wet woods, swamps. Minnesota, Ontario, Quebec, New Brunswick south to Maryland; in uplands to Georgia.   May–July

CLINTONIA, CORN-LILY   *Clintonia borealis*
Yellow or yellowish green. See text and color plate, p. 102.

YELLOW MANDARIN   *Disporum lanuginosum*
The yellow-green flowers dangle singly or in pairs from tip of the stem; petals flare outward. Leaves alternate on forking stems. Plant densely downy. Fruit a red berry. See bellworts, p. 102. 18–30 in. Woods. S. Ontario, w. New York south, mainly in Appalachians.   May–June

TWISTED-STALK, WHITE MANDARIN
    Streptopus amplexifolius
A single greenish flower with recurved petals dangles beneath each leaf. Note the *kink* in the flower stalk. Fruit a red berry. 1–3 ft. Woods, thickets. Iowa, Illinois, s. Michigan, s. Ontario, New York, Connecticut south.   May–June

FLY-POISON   *Amianthium muscaetoxicum*
Flowers whitish, becoming greenish with age. See p. 64.

GREAT SOLOMON'S-SEAL   *Polygonatum canaliculatum*
Similar to *P. biflorum* (below) but taller and coarser. Intermediates occur. Flowers usually in larger clusters (2–10) and leaves with 3 or more strong veins each side of midrib. Usually over 4 ft. (2–8 ft.). Rich woods, riverbanks, thickets. S. Manitoba to c. New England and south.   May–June

SOLOMON'S-SEAL   *Polygonatum biflorum*
Paired yellow-green flowers dangle from axils of the alternate, sessile leaves. Berries blue-black. 1–3 ft. See also False Solomon's-seal, p. 66. Woods, thickets. Iowa, Illinois, Michigan, s. Ontario, New York, Connecticut south.   May–June

HAIRY SOLOMON'S-SEAL   *Polygonatum pubescens*
(not shown)
Similar to *P. biflorum* but with hairs along veins beneath. Woods. S. Canada, n. U.S.; in mts. to S. Carolina. May–June

GREENBRIER, CATBRIER   *Smilax rotundifolia*
Greenbriers are green-stemmed, often evergreen vines climbing by tendrils. Most are thorny. For 7 woody species see *A Field Guide to Trees and Shrubs* by George A. Petrides. Shown here is *S. rotundifolia*, woody, stout, thorny, with leathery leaves. Berries blue-black. Woods, thickets. Great Lakes area, s. Ontario, New England, Nova Scotia south.   April–June

CARRION-FLOWER   *Smilax herbacea*
Unlike *S. rotundifolia*, not woody; lacks prickles. Flowers smell of carrion. Thickets, woods. Most of area.   May–June

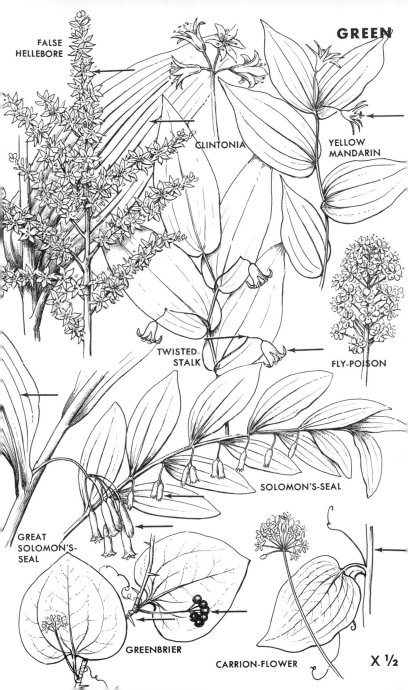

FALSE
HELLEBORE

CLINTONIA

GREEN

YELLOW
MANDARIN

FLY-POISON

TWISTED-
STALK

SOLOMON'S-SEAL

GREAT
SOLOMON'S-
SEAL

GREENBRIER

CARRION-FLOWER

X ½

ORCHID FAMILY (Orchidaceae)

RAGGED FRINGED ORCHIS   *Habenaria lacera*
Creamy to yellowish green. The *deeply fringed* 3-part lip distinguishes this from other greenish orchids. 8–32 in. Swamps, marshes, bogs, glades, thickets. Manitoba to Newfoundland and south.   JULY–AUG.

LONG-BRACTED ORCHIS   *Habenaria viridis* var. *bracteata*
Note the *long, leafy flower bracts*. Flowers green, with a long *forked lip* and *short rounded spur*. 6–20 in. Woods, thickets, meadows. S. Canada, Minnesota, Great Lakes area to New England; south in mts. to S. Carolina.   JUNE–AUG.

NORTHERN GREEN ORCHIS   *Habenaria hyperborea*
Tall, leafy. Flowers green or yellow-green in a dense spikelike raceme. Petals and lip narrow, spur *short*, incurved. 8–30 in. Bogs, woods, thickets. Canada south to Minnesota, Great Lakes states, New England.   MAY–JULY

PALE GREEN ORCHIS, SOUTHERN REIN-ORCHIS
                               Habenaria flava
Leafy-bracted. Note the roundish petals and broad lip, usually with a small tooth on each side. 6–24 in. Wet woods, swales, shores. E. Missouri, s. Illinois, s. Indiana, Kentucky, Maryland south; also s. Nova Scotia.   JULY–SEPT.

WHORLED POGONIA   *Isotria verticillata*
Greenish-yellow, with *3 long madder-purple sepals;* see p. 118. See also Small Whorled Pogonia, *I. medeoloides*, p. 118.

HOOKER'S ORCHIS   *Habenaria hookeri*
Two roundish leaves suggest Round-leaved Orchis, *H. orbiculata* (p. 16), but flowers yellowish green not greenish white, and have a more tapering spur. Note lack of bracts on stem, present in *H. orbiculata*. 7–16 in. Woods. Ontario, Quebec, Nova Scotia to n. Iowa, Great Lakes states, New Jersey. MAY–AUG.

GREEN ADDER'S-MOUTH   *Malaxis unifolia*
Note the *single, oval, pointed leaf* embracing the stem and the tiny green flowers with their *threadlike lateral petals*. 4–12 in. See also White Adder's-mouth, *M. brachypoda*, p. 18. Woods, swamps, bogs. Most of our area.   JUNE–AUG.

BOG TWAYBLADE   *Liparis loeselii*
The *2 well-keeled basal leaves* suggest Trout-lily. Raceme few-flowered. Note *flaring threadlike petals*. 2–8 in. Bogs, swamps, wet meadows, shores. S. Canada south to e. Missouri, Great Lakes states, Pennsylvania, New Jersey, Maryland; in mts. to Alabama.   JUNE–JULY

HELLEBORINE Alien   *Epipactis helleborine*
Leafy; strongly veined leaves clasp stem. Flowers greenish, tinged purple. Lip heart-shaped, *forming a sac*, pointed tip *turned under*. 1–3 ft. Woods, ravines, thickets. Se. Canada, ne U.S.; locally to Missouri, D.C.   JULY–SEPT.

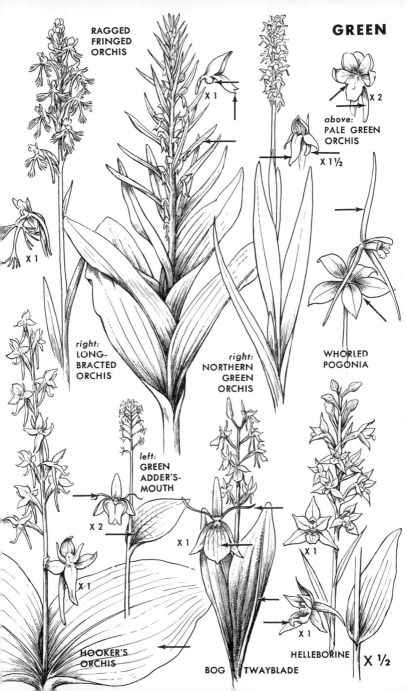

RAGGED FRINGED ORCHIS

GREEN

X 1

above:
PALE GREEN ORCHIS

X 2

X 1½

right:
LONG-BRACTED ORCHIS

right:
NORTHERN GREEN ORCHIS

WHORLED POGONIA

X 1

left:
GREEN ADDER'S-MOUTH

X 2

X 1

X 1

X 1

X 1

HOOKER'S ORCHIS

BOG TWAYBLADE

HELLEBORINE

X ½

WORMWOODS and MUGWORTS *Artemisia*
COMPOSITE FAMILY (Compositae)
Weedy plants with long clusters of tiny yellow-green flower heads without rays. 17 species in our area; we show 6.
TALL WORMWOOD, *A. caudata. Stringy, forked leaves*, nodding flowers. 2–5 ft. Sand. Coast from s. Maine south; inland from s. Canada to Missouri, Great Lakes states. JULY–OCT.
MUGWORT, *A. vulgaris* (alien). Deeply cut leaves, silvery-downy beneath. Flower heads erect; aromatic. 2–4 ft. Waste ground. Se. Canada, ne. U.S.; locally west. JULY–AUG.
ABSINTHE WORMWOOD, *A. absinthium* (alien). Similar to *A. vulgaris* but much more aromatic; flower heads larger, drooping; leaves white, silky on both sides, segments blunt. 1–3 ft. Waste ground. S. Canada, ne. U.S. JULY–SEPT.
ANNUAL WORMWOOD, *A. annua* (alien). Finely cut fern-like leaves. 1–3 ft. Waste ground. Most of area. AUG.–OCT.
BIENNIAL WORMWOOD, *A. biennis* (alien). *Linear forked leaves intersperse liberally* among flower clusters, which hug stem. 1–3 ft. Waste ground. S. Canada, n. U.S. AUG.–OCT.
WESTERN MUGWORT or WHITE SAGE. *A. ludoviciana* var. *gnaphalodes.* Lanceolate leaves with *white felt beneath.* Variable; may have a few teeth. 1½–3 ft. Prairies. Michigan west and south. Adventive to eastern seaboard. JULY–SEPT.

COMMON RAGWEED *Ambrosia artemisiifolia*
COMPOSITE FAMILY (Compositae)
Note the dissected, artemisia-like leaves and interrupted racemes of tiny nodding green flower heads carrying the yellow pollen that causes hay fever. 1–5 ft. GREAT RAGWEED, *A. trifida* (leaf shown), which grows to 15 ft., has pointed 3-lobed leaves. Roadsides, fields. Throughout. AUG.–OCT.

SPURGES *Euphorbia*
SPURGE FAMILY (Euphorbiaceae)
Of the 37 euphorbias in our area, at least 12 have greenish umbels of the type illustrated here; we show 3. The pair of yellow-green "petals" are really bracts supporting the small, curious flowers. Juice of plant milky.
CYPRESS SPURGE, *E. cyparissias* (alien). Numerous *needle-like pale green leaves.* Bracts may turn red. 6–12 in. Roadsides, cemeteries, vacant lots. Throughout. APRIL–AUG.
LEAFY SPURGE, *E. esula* (alien). Broader, *oblanceolate leaves.* 8–24 in. Dry soil, roadsides. S. Canada south to Iowa, Illinois, Indiana, Pennsylvania. MAY–SEPT.
SUN SPURGE, *E. helioscopia* (alien). *Finely toothed oval leaves.* 4–12 in. Waste ground, dry soil. S. Canada south locally to Illinois, Ohio, Maryland. JULY–SEPT.

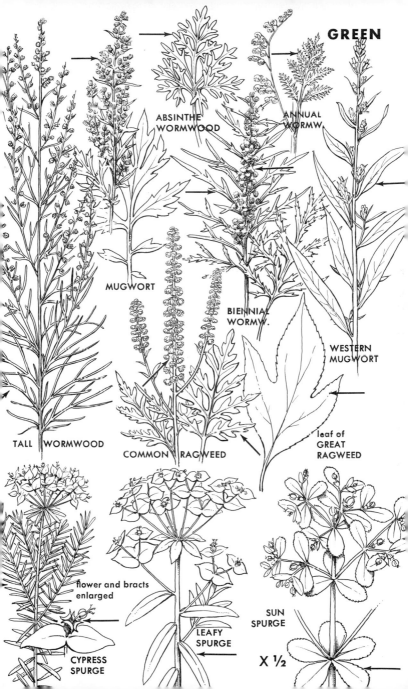

GREEN

ABSINTHE WORMWOOD

ANNUAL WORMW.

MUGWORT

BIENNIAL WORMW.

WESTERN MUGWORT

TALL WORMWOOD

COMMON RAGWEED

leaf of GREAT RAGWEED

flower and bracts enlarged

CYPRESS SPURGE

LEAFY SPURGE

SUN SPURGE

X ½

SLENDER TERMINAL CLUSTERS

ALUMROOT *Heuchera americana*
SAXIFRAGE FAMILY (Saxifragaceae)
A slender, woodland plant suggesting Miterwort (p. 68), but flowers bell-shaped, drooping from short branching stems. Petals green or red-tinged; stamens tipped with orange anthers. Leaves slightly maple-shaped. Quite variable. 2–3 ft. *H. richardsonii*, grows in prairies, dry woods, from Michigan to Minnesota, south and west. Petals greener, flower stalks and petioles shaggy, with whitish hairs. 6 other species of *Heuchera* in southern parts of our area. Dry woods, shady rocks. Michigan, s. Ontario to Connecticut and south. APRIL–JUNE

NAKED MITERWORT *Mitella nuda*
SAXIFRAGE FAMILY (Saxifragaceae)
Similar to *M. diphylla* (p. 68), but smaller, usually lacking stem leaves; basal leaves more rounded. Flowers greener, fringes more threadlike. 3–8 in. Woods, bogs. N. Canada to Minnesota, Michigan, n. Ohio, Pennsylvania. MAY–AUG.

SWAMP SAXIFRAGE *Saxifraga pensylvanica*
SAXIFRAGE FAMILY (Saxifragaceae)
Whitish, greenish, yellowish, or purplish. See p. 68.

DITCH STONECROP *Penthorum sedoides*
SAXIFRAGE FAMILY (Saxifragaceae)
Placed by some botanists in Sedum Family, but leaves not succulent. Flowers yellow-green, on 2 or 3 diverging branches at end of an erect stalk. Leaves lanceolate, finely toothed. 1–3 ft. Wet spots, riverbanks. Minnesota, Wisconsin, Michigan, s. Ontario, New England south. JULY–SEPT.

EARLY MEADOW-RUE *Thalictrum dioicum*
BUTTERCUP FAMILY (Ranunculaceae)
Whitish or greenish to purplish brown. See pp. 72, 390.

ROADSIDE PEPPERGRASS Alien *Lepidium ruderale*
MUSTARD FAMILY (Cruciferae)
Similar to white peppergrasses (p. 82) but flowers *green*. Leaves *linear*. Odor strong. 6–12 in. Waste ground, roadsides. Michigan to Newfoundland and south. JUNE–AUG.

HORSEWEED *Erigeron canadensis*
COMPOSITE FAMILY (Compositae)
Flower heads green, with insignificant white rays. See p. 88.

FIGWORT *Scrophularia lanceolata*
SNAPDRAGON FAMILY (Scrophulariaceae)
Note the curious shiny flowers, green outside, brown within. Besides 4 normal stamens there is 1 wide sterile stamen. Leafstalks flow into stem. 3–8 ft. A similar species, *S. marilandica* (not shown), of similar range, blooms later (July–Oct.), has the broad rudimentary stamen *deep purple* (yellow in *lanceolata*). Wood edges, thickets. Most of area. MAY–JULY

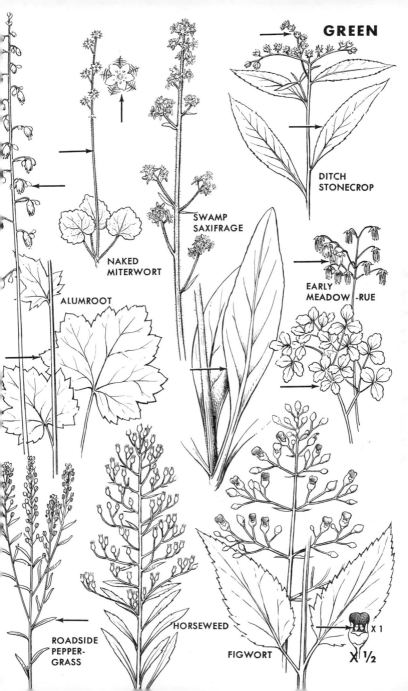

GREEN

DITCH
STONECROP

SWAMP
SAXIFRAGE

NAKED
MITERWORT

EARLY
MEADOW-RUE

ALUMROOT

HORSEWEED

ROADSIDE
PEPPER-
GRASS

FIGWORT

X 1

X ½

CLUSTERS, TERMINAL AND IN UPPER AXILS

MAPLE-LEAVED GOOSEFOOT, SOWBANE
GOOSEFOOT FAMILY (Chenopodiaceae) *Chenopodium hybridum*
Similar to Lamb's-quarters (below) but leaves brighter green, *more maple-like*, with fewer teeth. Flowers in open, interrupted clusters. 9–24 in. Woods, clearings. S. Canada south to Missouri, Kentucky, Virginia (mts.), Delaware.   JULY–OCT.

LAMB'S-QUARTERS, PIGWEED Alien *Chenopodium album*
GOOSEFOOT FAMILY   (Chenopodiaceae)
A branching weed; stems often mealy, red-streaked. Leaves diamond-shaped, broadly toothed, often mealy white beneath. Flowers small, greenish, may turn reddish. Variable. 1–3 ft. Roadsides, fields, waste ground. Throughout.   JUNE–OCT.

STRAWBERRY-BLITE   *Chenopodium capitatum*
GOOSEFOOT FAMILY   (Chenopodiaceae)
Note the irregular *triangular* leaves and *tight round clusters* of tiny flowers, which in fruit become bright red, *berrylike*. 6–24 in. Woods, clearings. Canada, n. U.S.   JUNE–AUG.

MEXICAN-TEA Alien   *Chenopodium ambrosioides*
GOOSEFOOT FAMILY   (Chenopodiaceae)
Similar to Lamb's-quarters, but note wavy-toothed leaves. Aromatic. Flower spikes dense, leafy. 2–4 ft. Waste ground. Wisconsin, s. Ontario, New England south   AUG.–NOV.

ORACHE   *Atriplex patula*
GOOSEFOOT FAMILY   (Chenopodiaceae)
Atriplex, 7 or 8 species in our area, are small weedy plants (see technical manuals). This, the most widespread, is mealy, often reddish; leaves triangular, with lower teeth pointing outward; flowers in interrupted spikes in axils. 9–24 in. Saline or alkaline soil, waste ground. Throughout.   JUNE–NOV.

JERUSALEM-OAK Alien   *Chenopodium botrys*
GOOSEFOOT FAMILY   (Chenopodiaceae)
Similar to Lamb's-quarters but sticky; odor of turpentine. Note oaklike lobes of leaves. 8–24 in. Waste places, roadsides. S. Canada to Missouri, Kentucky, Virginia.   JULY–OCT.

GREEN AMARANTH Alien   *Amaranthus retroflexus*
AMARANTH FAMILY   (Amaranthaceae)
Downy, gray-green. Note the well-stalked, pointed-oval leaves and dense spikes of chaffy greenish flowers mixed with long, bristle-like bracts. 6–24 in. Roadsides, fields, waste ground. S. Canada, New England south.   AUG.–OCT.

GREEN AMARANTH Alien   *Amaranthus hybridus*
AMARANTH FAMILY   (Amaranthaceae)
Similar to *A. retroflexus* (above) but taller, smoother, darker, with more slender bending flower spikes; green or red. 2–6 ft. For other, less noticeable members of genus see technical manuals. Waste ground, roadsides. Most of area.   AUG.–OCT.

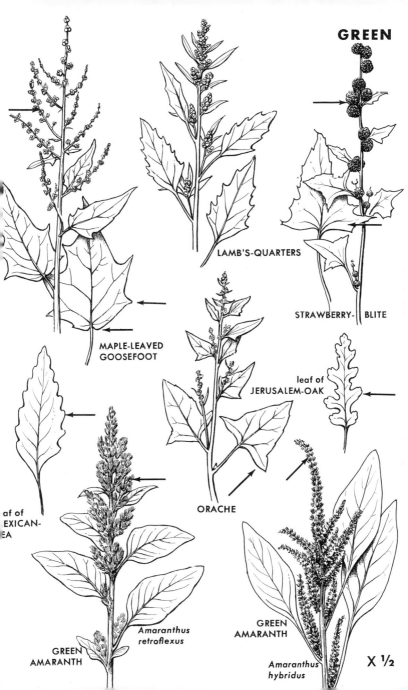

GREEN

LAMB'S-QUARTERS

STRAWBERRY- BLITE

MAPLE-LEAVED
GOOSEFOOT

leaf of
JERUSALEM-OAK

af of
EXICAN-
EA

ORACHE

GREEN
AMARANTH

*Amaranthus
retroflexus*

GREEN
AMARANTH

*Amaranthus
hybridus*

X ½

SLENDER CLUSTERS, TERMINAL & IN AXILS
BUCKWHEAT FAMILY (Polygonaceae)

SHEEP or COMMON SORREL Alien   *Rumex acetosella*
Note the small, *arrow-shaped* leaves with spreading lobes.
Leaves *acrid* to taste. Flower heads minute, interrupted, green,
often turning brown-red. 4–12 in. Thin fields, roadsides, acid
soils. Throughout.   JUNE–OCT.

GARDEN SORREL Alien   *Rumex acetosa*
Larger than Sheep Sorrel; upper leaves *clasp stem;* flower spikes
larger, more compact. 6–24 in. Fields, roadsides. Canada
south to n. Pennsylvania, n. and w. New England. JUNE–SEPT.

COMMON SMARTWEED, WATER-PEPPER
                              Polygonum hydropiper
Most smartweeds are pink (pp. 274–76) but may be tinged with
green. This one has greenish, *nodding clusters. Sheath bristles
lacking* or nearly so. Leaves extremely *peppery* to taste. Stems
reddish. Damp soil, shores. Most of area.   JUNE–NOV.

CLIMBING FALSE BUCKWHEAT   *Polygonum scandens*
A climbing vine with *arrowhead-shaped* leaves, reddish stems,
and racemes of whitish, pink, or greenish smartweedlike flowers
or winged fruits in leaf axils. Low woods, thickets, shores.
Most of our area.   AUG.–NOV.

BLACK BINDWEED Alien   *Polygonum convolvulus*
(not shown)
Similar to *P. scandens* (above) but flowers and fruits *nearly
sessile* in leaf axils, *not* in slender racemes.   JULY–SEPT.

SEABEACH DOCK   *Rumex pallidus*
Of 20 species of *Rumex*, or dock, in our area we show 7. Most
have coarse leaves and dense heads of small greenish flowers or
winged brownish seeds. This species has *narrow whitened leaves*.
Seeds nearly as long as seed wings. 1–2 ft. Coastal marshes,
beaches. Long Island north.   JUNE–SEPT.

WATER DOCK   *Rumex orbiculatus*
A *very large* water-loving species with long-stalked leathery
leaves that may be 2 ft. long. Large heart-shaped fruits. 3–7
ft. Swamps, shores. S. Canada, south to Iowa, Illinois, Indiana,
Ohio, Pennsylvania, New Jersey.   JUNE–SEPT.

PATIENCE DOCK Alien   *Rumex patientia*
Suggests a large Curled Dock but blooms earlier. Spikes
thicker; leaves not very wavy. Basal leaves broad-based. 2–6
ft. Waste ground, roadsides. Local, n. U.S.   MAY–JUNE

BROAD or BITTER DOCK Alien   *Rumex obtusifolius*
Sturdy; *broad basal leaves* rounded or *heart-shaped* at base.
Seed wings with *prominent teeth*. 1–4 ft. Fields, waste ground,
roadsides. Throughout.   JUNE–SEPT.

CURLED DOCK Alien   *Rumex crispus*
Note the *wavy leaf margins*. Seed wings heart-shaped. 1–4 ft.
Fields, waste ground. Throughout.   JUNE–SEPT.

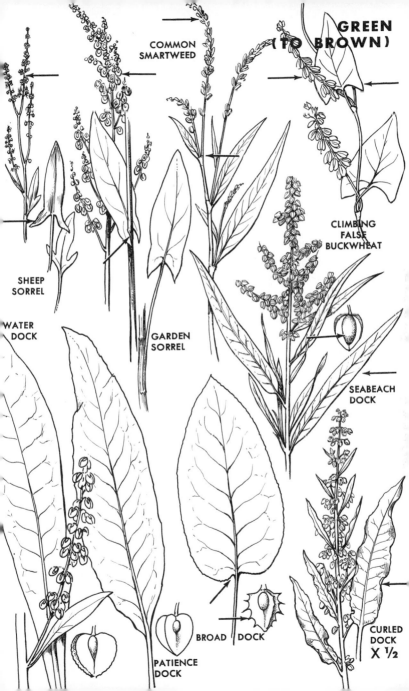

GREEN (TO BROWN)

COMMON SMARTWEED

SHEEP SORREL

WATER DOCK

GARDEN SORREL

CLIMBING FALSE BUCKWHEAT

SEABEACH DOCK

BROAD DOCK

PATIENCE DOCK

CURLED DOCK X ½

SLENDER CLUSTERS IN LEAF AXILS
PAIRED, TOOTHED LEAVES
NETTLE FAMILY (Urticaceae)

STINGING NETTLE Alien   *Urtica dioica*
Do not touch. A weed densely covered with *coarse, stinging hairs*.
Note the well-stalked, coarsely toothed, heart-shaped leaves.
The tiny greenish flowers are on slender, interrupted clusters in
the leaf axils; staminate and pistillate flowers often on separate
plants. Stem hollow, 4-angled. 2–4 ft. Roadsides, waste
ground, light soils. Most of our area.   JUNE–SEPT.

SLENDER NETTLE   *Urtica gracilis*
Similar to Stinging Nettle (above) but much more sparingly
beset with stinging hairs. Leaves narrower, often less heart-
shaped at base. 2–3 ft. Damp soil, thickets. Across Canada
and south to Minnesota, c. New York, n. and w. New England;
in mts. to W. Virginia.   JULY–SEPT.

FALSE NETTLE, BOG-HEMP   *Boehmeria cylindrica*
Nettle-like but devoid of stinging hairs. Leaves usually more
ovate; 3 main nerves from base. Flower clusters more compact.
16–40 in. Shady places, moist ground. Minnesota, s. Ontario,
s. Quebec, Maine south.   JULY–OCT.

CLEARWEED   *Pilea pumila*
Nettle-like in appearance but shorter in stature and devoid of
stinging hairs. Leaves short, with relatively few teeth. Flower
clusters short, curved, and drooping. Stem smooth and translucent. 4–20 in. Often colonial. Moist, shady places. Most of
our area.   JULY–OCT.

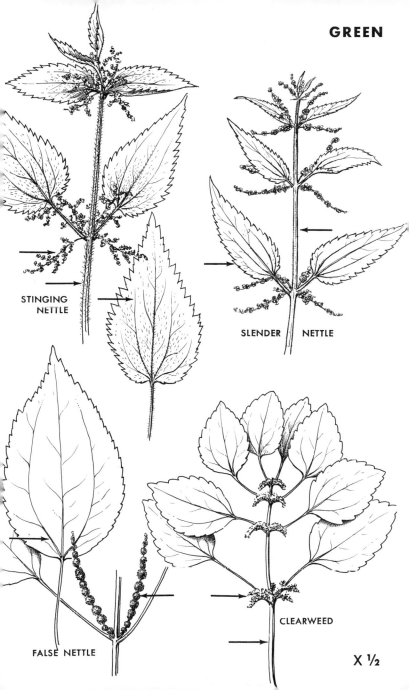

GREEN

STINGING
NETTLE

SLENDER NETTLE

FALSE NETTLE

CLEARWEED

X ½

FLOWERS MOSTLY IN LEAF AXILS

CLOTBUR, COCKLEBUR *Xanthium chinense*
COMPOSITE FAMILY (Compositae)
See also burdocks (p. 300), often called clotburs. Clotburs have
staminate flowers in short racemes above; the pistillate flowers
are enclosed in an ovoid greenish, yellowish, or brownish bur
covered with hooked spines. *Xanthium* is a variable group;
whereas Gray recognizes 15 species in our area, Britton and
Brown allows only 2, lumping all except the Spiny Clotbur,
X. spinosum (below), in a single plastic species, *X. strumarium.*
Leaves of the one shown here are somewhat maple-shaped,
bristly, often with reddish petioles. 1–6 ft. Roadsides, waste
places, cultivation. Most of area. AUG.–OCT.

BEACH CLOTBUR, SEA-BURDOCK *Xanthium echinatum*
COMPOSITE FAMILY (Compositae)
Similar to *X. chinense* but *stems mottled with purple.* Leaves
slightly lobed or unlobed. 6–24 in. Beaches, dunes, salt-marsh
margins. Coast, Nova Scotia to Virginia. AUG.–OCT.

BUR-REEDS *Sparganium*
BUR-REED FAMILY (Sparganiaceae)
Bur-reeds (10 in our area) are marsh or water plants, usually
erect, sometimes floating, with linear irislike leaves and pistillate
flowers that form *burlike balls.* The staminate flowers form
smaller and separate balls. The one shown here is *S. americanum.*
1–6 ft. Marshes, shallow water, borders of ponds, rivers.
Throughout. MAY–AUG.

SPINY CLOTBUR Alien *Xanthium spinosum*
COMPOSITE FAMILY (Compositae)
The shiny leaves, tapered at both ends, have 3 to 5 lobes and
are *downy white* beneath and dark above, conspicuously veined
with white. Note the *3 long orange spines* in each leaf axil.
Flower heads small, covered with hooked spines. 6–24 in.
Waste places. Local throughout our area. JULY–SEPT.

FEVERWORT, TINKER'S-WEED *Triosteum perfoliatum*
HONEYSUCKLE FAMILY (Caprifoliaceae)
Leaves paired, with flaring margins along the petioles, meeting
and *surrounding the stem* (perfoliate). Flowers green to dull
purple-brown; bell-shaped, with *5 long sepals.* Fruit orange,
hairy, containing 3 nutlets. 2–4 ft. Woods, thickets. Minnesota, Wisconsin, Michigan, Massachusetts south. MAY–JULY

THREE-SEEDED MERCURY *Acalypha virginica*
SPURGE FAMILY (Euphorbiaceae)
Note the *lobed bracts* in the leaf axils which subtend the tiny
petal-less flowers. 8–24 in. Dry woods, fields. Iowa, Indiana
to Massachusetts and south. AUG.–OCT.

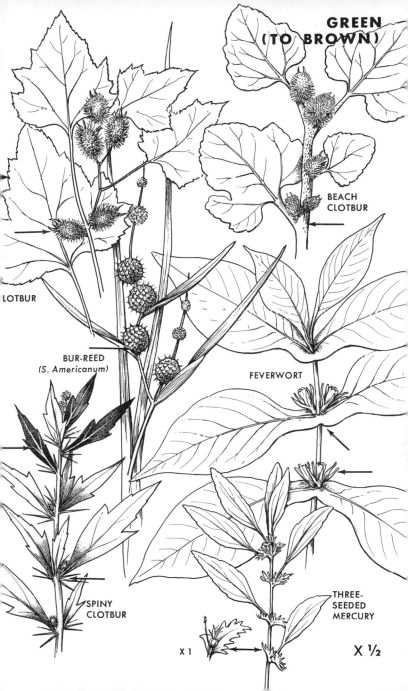

GREEN (TO BROWN)

BEACH CLOTBUR

LOTBUR

BUR-REED
(S. Americanum)

FEVERWORT

SPINY CLOTBUR

THREE-SEEDED MERCURY

X 1

X ½

TINY FLOWERS IN LEAF AXILS

TUMBLEWEED   *Amaranthus graecizans*
AMARANTH FAMILY   (Amaranthaceae)
White-stemmed, with pale, spatulate leaves. Flowers crowded
in leaf axils, each with 3 sharp bracts. Withered plant tumbled
by wind. 6–20 in. Waste ground. Throughout.   JUNE–SEPT.

ERECT KNOTWEED   *Polygonum erectum*
BUCKWHEAT FAMILY   (Polygonaceae)
Knotweeds have papery sheaths at the leaf joints. This species
has oval leaves and greenish sepals with yellowish or whitish
margins. Stem erect. 4–36 in. Waste ground. Wisconsin, sw.
Quebec, New England south.   AUG.–OCT.

PROSTRATE KNOTWEED Alien   *Polygonum aviculare*
BUCKWHEAT FAMILY   (Polygonaceae)
Reclining or prostrate; leaves blue-green; flowers pale greenish
with pink tips. Torn silvery sheaths at joints. Roadsides,
gardens, waste ground. Throughout.   JUNE–NOV.

KNAWEL Alien   *Scleranthus annuus*
PINK FAMILY   (Caryophyllaceae)
Tiny, wiry, bushy, often prostrate, with pointed, linear, opposite leaves. No petals; sepals green, bordered with white. 1–4
in. Waste ground. Most of area.   MARCH–OCT.

MANY-FRUITED FALSE LOOSESTRIFE
EVENING-PRIMROSE FAMILY (Onagraceae) *Ludwigia polycarpa*
Flowers sessile; petals rudimentary, or none. Leaves lanceolate.
Seed capsule and stems 4-sided. 6–30 in. Wet spots. Minne-
sota, Great Lakes area, New England and south.   JULY–SEPT.

SEA-BLITE   *Suaeda maritima*
GOOSEFOOT FAMILY   (Chenopodiaceae)
Tiny, often prostrate. Leaves pointed, fleshy, with whitish
bloom. Flowers tiny, buttonlike, tucked singly in axils. 3–12
in. Salt marshes, beaches. Quebec to Virginia.   JULY–OCT.

GLASSWORTS   *Salicornia*
GOOSEFOOT FAMILY   (Chenopodiaceae)
Succulent, jointed, cylindrical plants that may turn red in fall.
Leaves reduced to fleshy sheaths. Flowers minute, sunk into
joints; stamens visible. 4 species.   AUG.–OCT.
DWARF GLASSWORT, *S. bigelovii*. Erect, branching; joints
wider than long. 2–12 in. Salt marshes. Maine south.
SLENDER GLASSWORT, *S. europaea*. Erect or sprawling;
more slender; joints *longer* than wide. 2–16 in. Coast, Nova
Scotia south; local in Michigan, Wisconsin, Illinois.
RED GLASSWORT, *S. rubra* (not shown). An *inland* species
of alkaline soil from Manitoba, w. Minnesota west.
WOODY GLASSWORT, *S. virginica*. *Creeping woody stems*,
from which ascend unbranched or sparingly branched stalks
4 to 12 in. tall. Salt marshes. S. New Hampshire south.

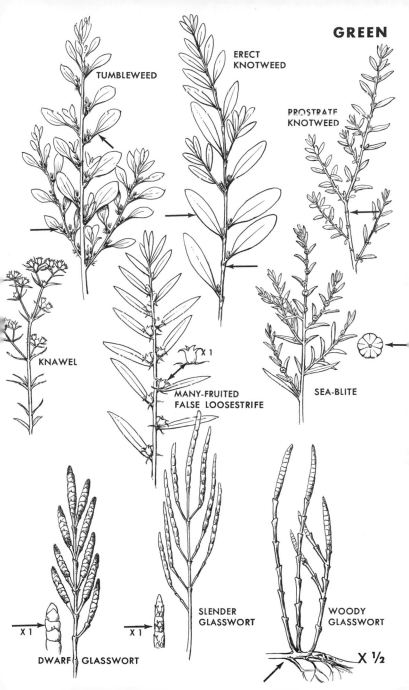

GREEN

TUMBLEWEED

ERECT KNOTWEED

PROSTRATE KNOTWEED

KNAWEL

MANY-FRUITED FALSE LOOSESTRIFE

X 1

SEA-BLITE

DWARF GLASSWORT

X 1

X 1

SLENDER GLASSWORT

WOODY GLASSWORT

X ½

MISCELLANEOUS BROWN FLOWERS

COMMON CATTAIL   *Typha latifolia*
CATTAIL FAMILY   (Typhaceae)
Cattails are tall marsh plants growing in dense stands. Leaves erect, bladelike; stems stiff, with a sausagelike brown head of minute, tightly packed, pistillate flowers. Above is a slender "tail" of paler staminate flowers, which disappears later. In this widespread, broad-leaved species the staminate "tail" touches the pistillate part. 3–9 ft. Fresh marshes, shallows. Throughout.   MAY–JULY

NARROW-LEAVED CATTAIL   *Typha angustifolia*
CATTAIL FAMILY   (Typhaceae)
Similar to Common Cattail, but *narrower*. Staminate flowers *separated by a gap* from pistillate flowers. 2–5 ft. Fresh and brackish marshes. Most of area, especially seaboard. *T. glauca* (not shown), of similar range, is taller (6–10 ft.). *T. domingensis* (not shown), coast from Delaware south, is 7 to 12 ft., with 10 or more *flat leaves*, not convex on back.   MAY–JULY

JACK-IN-THE-PULPIT   *Arisaema atrorubens*
ARUM FAMILY   (Araceae)
Green or purplish brown, often striped. See p. 368.

SKUNK CABBAGE   *Symplocarpus foetidus*
ARUM FAMILY   (Araceae)
Green to purple-brown, or mottled. See p. 368.

VIRGINIA SNAKEROOT   *Aristolochia serpentaria*
BIRTHWORT FAMILY   (Aristolochiaceae)
Note the longish, heart-shaped leaves. Flowers dull green or purple-brown, similar to those of Dutchman's-pipe (below) but smaller and rising from slender, crooked stems near the base. 8–20 in. Woods. Missouri, s. Illinois, Indiana, Ohio, s. New York, sw. Connecticut south.   MAY–JULY

DUTCHMAN'S-PIPE   *Aristolochia durior*
BIRTHWORT FAMILY   (Aristolochiaceae)
See also p. 240. A climbing vine grown as an ornamental on porches, arbors. Leaves large, heart-shaped. Flower pipelike, terminated by 3 short purple-brown lobes. Vine may reach length of 30 ft. Woods, streambanks. Sw. Pennsylvania, south in mts. to Georgia. *A. tomentosa* (not shown), a similar, *downy* species, is found from Missouri, Indiana south.   MAY–JUNE

WILD GINGER   *Asarum canadense*
BIRTHWORT FAMILY   (Aristolochiaceae)
The single curious cup-shaped flower with 3 red-brown calyx lobes is at ground level in the crotch between 2 leafstalks. Leaves large, heart-shaped, with hairy stalks. 6–12 in. 3 or 4 similar species of *Asarum* enter our area in Kentucky, W. Virginia, and Virginia. Rich woods. Minnesota to the Gaspé and south to Arkansas, N. Carolina.   APRIL–MAY

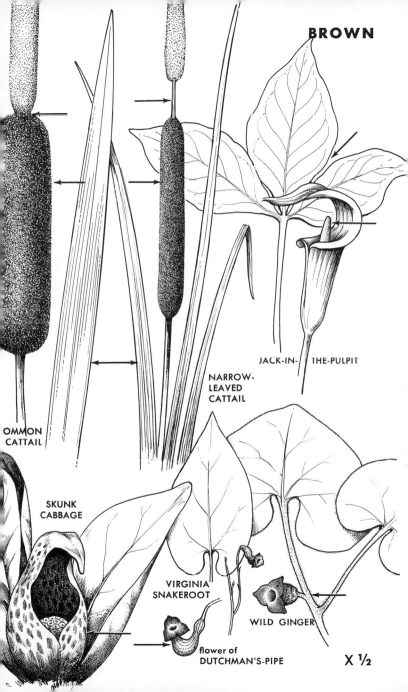

BROWN

JACK-IN- THE-PULPIT

NARROW-
LEAVED
CATTAIL

OMMON
CATTAIL

SKUNK
CABBAGE

VIRGINIA
SNAKEROOT

WILD GINGER

flower of
DUTCHMAN'S-PIPE

X ½

MISCELLANEOUS BROWN FLOWERS

 GROUNDNUT $Apios\ americana$
PEA FAMILY (Leguminosae)
A small vine climbing over bushes. Note the short thick cluster of velvety, pealike flowers in leaf axils; *maroon or chocolate;* very fragrant. Leaves divided into 5 to 7 broad, sharp-pointed leaflets. Thickets. Minnesota, through Great Lakes area to New Brunswick and south. JULY–SEPT.

 BLACK SWALLOWWORT Alien $Cynanchum\ nigrum$
MILKWEED FAMILY (Asclepiadaceae)
A climbing vine, 3 to 6 ft. long, with paired, pointed leaves and clusters of small 5-petaled purple-brown flowers in leaf axils. In fruit, may be recognized as related to milkweeds by slender floss-filled pods. Roadsides, fields. A local escape in ne. U.S.; Ohio to New England. JUNE–SEPT.

 BLUE COHOSH $Caulophyllum\ thalictroides$
BARBERRY FAMILY (Berberidaceae)
The 6-pointed flowers (greenish yellow or yellow-green to brown) are replaced later by clusters of deep blue berries. The leaves, divided into 7 to 9 leaflets, suggest meadow-rue. Young plants may have a waxy whitish bloom. 1–3 ft. Rich woods. S. Canada south to Missouri, Tennessee; in mts. to S. Carolina. APRIL–JUNE

EARLY MEADOW-RUE $Thalictrum\ dioicum$
BUTTERCUP FAMILY (Ranunculaceae)
This early-blooming meadow-rue has distinctive drooping flowers and foliage. The 4 to 5 sepals vary from greenish white to purplish brown; the drooping stamens are terra-cotta or orange-tinted. Leaves divided into roundish blunt-lobed leaflets, as shown. 1–2 ft. Woods, ravines. Minnesota, s. Ontario, sw. Quebec, Maine south. APRIL–MAY

PURPLE MEADOW-RUE $Thalictrum\ dasycarpum$
(not shown) BUTTERCUP FAMILY (Ranunculaceae)
More robust and later than *T. dioicum.* Stem purple, sometimes with whitish bloom. Flowers whitish, often tinged purplish or brown. Leaves finely downy beneath. 2–6 ft. Swamps, wet thickets. Midwestern; Alberta to Ontario, south to Missouri, Illinois, Indiana, Ohio. MAY–JULY

 FEVERWORT, TINKER'S-WEED $Triosteum\ perfoliatum$
HONEYSUCKLE FAMILY (Caprifoliaceae)
Leaves paired; petioles with flaring margins or wings that meet and surround stem (perfoliate). Flowers green or yellowish to dull purple-brown, bell-shaped, embraced by 5 long sepals. Fruit orange, hairy, with 3 nutlets. 2–4 ft. Woods, thickets. Minnesota, Wisconsin, Michigan, Massachusetts south.
MAY–JULY
A similar species, WILD COFFEE, *T. aurantiacum* (not shown), has its opposing leaves tapering to bases.

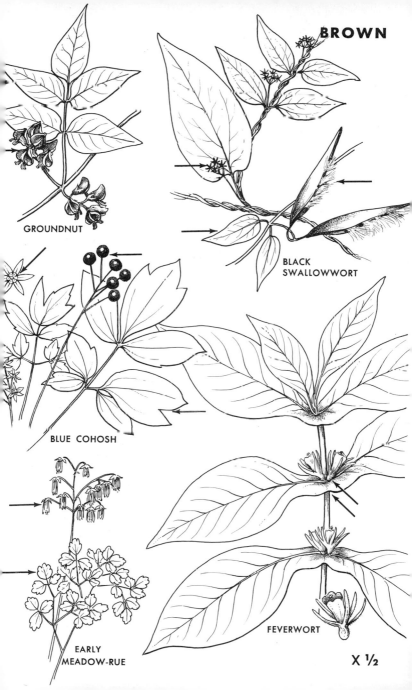

BROWN

GROUNDNUT

BLACK
SWALLOWWORT

BLUE COHOSH

EARLY
MEADOW-RUE

FEVERWORT

X ½

NO GREEN PIGMENT; NAKED OR SCALED STEMS: PARASITIC AND SAPROPHYTIC PLANTS

SPOTTED CORALROOT   *Corallorhiza maculata*
ORCHID FAMILY   (Orchidaceae)
Coralroots lack green pigment and bear their flowers on a leafless stalk. This is the largest species. Flowers tawny yellow, deepening to dull purple or purple-brown; lower lip white-spotted with purple-red. 8–20 in. See other coralroots on p. 242. Woods; a saprophyte, living on decaying leaves. Canada, n. U.S.; in mts. to N. Carolina.   JULY–AUG.

SQUAWROOT   *Conopholis americana*
BROOMRAPE FAMILY   (Orobanchaceae)
Note the fleshy, scaly, tawny or yellow-brown stalk, suggestive of the cone of a white pine. This is surmounted by a spike of lipped and hooded yellowish to light brown flowers. 3–8 in. Parasitic on roots of trees, especially oaks. Wisconsin, Michigan, New England, Nova Scotia south.   MAY–JUNE

BEECHDROPS   *Epifagus virginiana*
BROOMRAPE FAMILY   (Orobanchaceae)
Yellowish, reddish, or brown. Scale-like leaves and lack of green pigment are typical of this family. The *branching habit* distinguishes this species from all others except Branched Broomrape, *Orobanche ramosa* (p. 324; an alien parasitic on tomato, tobacco, hemp, etc.). 6–24 in. Parasitic; under beech trees. Ontario, Gulf of St. Lawrence south.   AUG.–OCT.

PINESAP   *Monotropa hypopithys*
WINTERGREEN FAMILY   (Pyrolaceae)
Similar to Indian-pipe, p. 20, but with *several* nodding flowers (not 1). These are tan, dull yellow, or reddish (not white). Seedpod erect. 4–14 in. Woods, leaf mold. Throughout our area.   JUNE–OCT.

SWEET PINESAP, PYGMY-PIPES   *Monotropsis odorata*
(not shown)   WINTERGREEN FAMILY   (Pyrolaceae)
See illustration on p. 232. Smaller, scarcer, more southern than Pinesap; often hidden by fallen leaves. At first much recurved. Light rose to purple-brown. Very fragrant; odor of violets. 2–4 in. Pine woods. W. Virginia, Maryland south.
      MARCH–APRIL

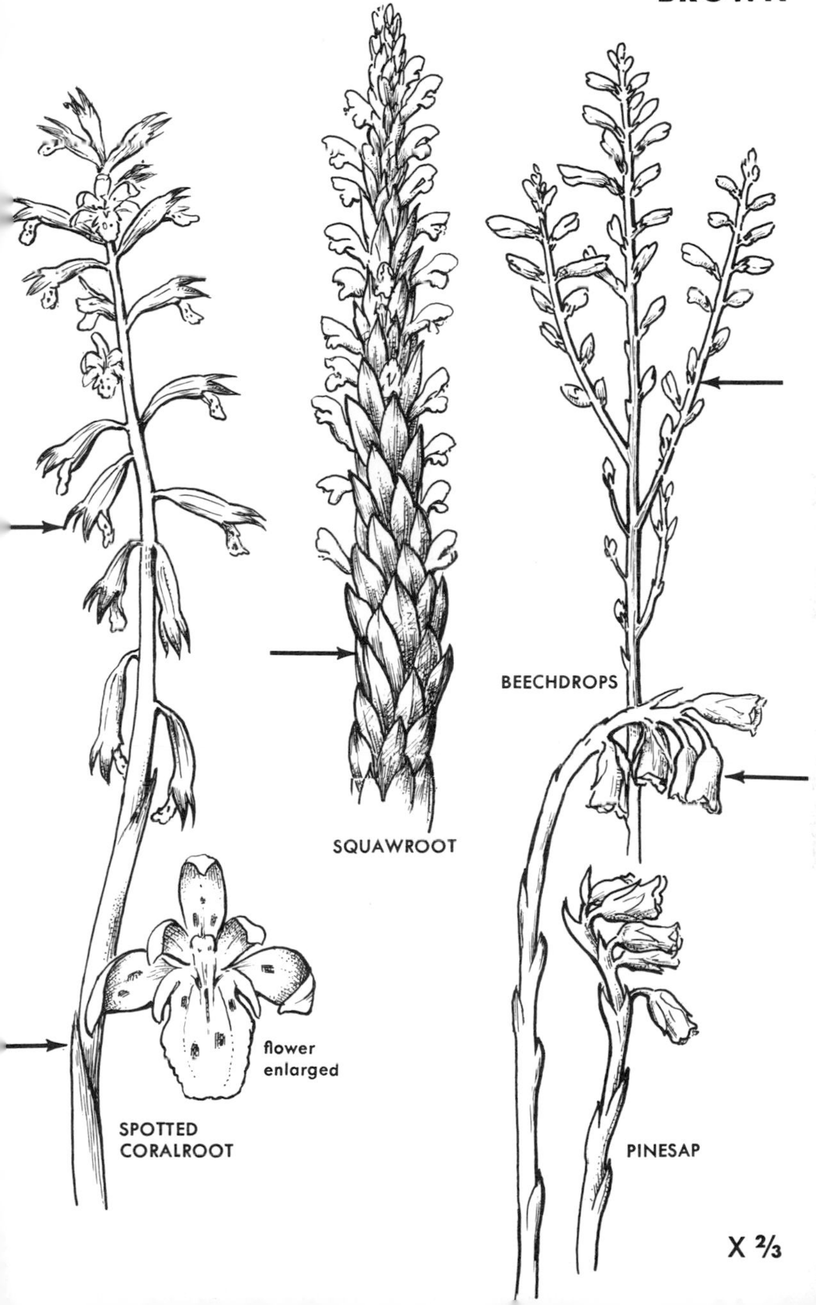

BROWN

SQUAWROOT

BEECHDROPS

flower
enlarged

SPOTTED
CORALROOT

PINESAP

X ⅔

Index

An italicized number indicates that the species is not illustrated.

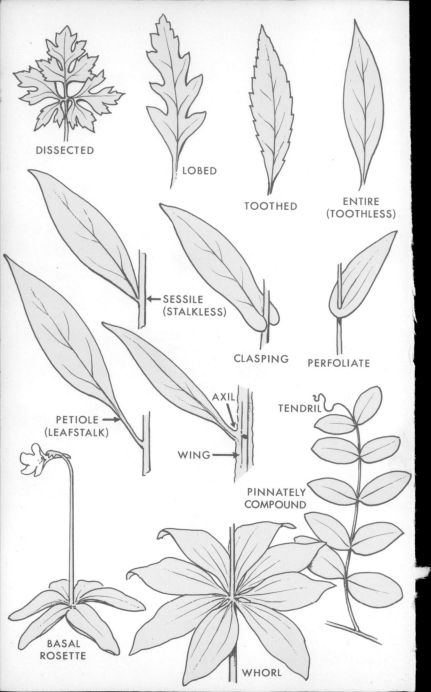

DISSECTED

LOBED

TOOTHED

ENTIRE
(TOOTHLESS)

SESSILE
(STALKLESS)

CLASPING

PERFOLIATE

PETIOLE
(LEAFSTALK)

AXIL

TENDRIL

WING

PINNATELY
COMPOUND

BASAL
ROSETTE

WHORL